LONGMAN LINGUISTICS LIBRARY
Title no 20

PROBLEMS IN FRENCH SYNTAX
TRANSFORMATIONAL-GENERATIVE STUDIES

LONGMAN LINGUISTICS LIBRARY

General Editors
R. H. Robins, University of London
G. N. Leech, University of Lancaster

Problems in French Syntax
Transformational-Generative Studies

Nicolas Ruwet
translated by
Sheila M. Robins

LONGMAN

LONGMAN GROUP LIMITED LONDON
Associated companies, branches and representatives throughout the world

Originally published in French under the title
Théorie Syntaxique et Syntaxe du Français
© Editions du Seuil 1972
This English translation © Longman Group Ltd 1976

This English translation first published 1976
ISBN 0 582 55058 0

Printed in Hong Kong by
Sheck Wah Tong Printing Press

for Roman and Krystyna Jakobson

Preface

This is a collection of the principal articles that I have written over the past few years on the generative grammar of French. Some of these articles have appeared in French, some in English, and the longest (Chapter 5) had not been published before. They have all been considerably revised and expanded. They deal with closely related problems: syntax of the verb, relationship between syntax and lexicon, between syntax and semantics, justification and limitations of the transformational model.[1]

Two ideas are of central importance in this book. The first, one of general methodology, is that it is always necessary to make a distinction between a description that 'works' and a description that is truly explanatory. The transformational model is very powerful, and certain recent innovations – the introduction of a highly structured lexicon into the grammar, lexical redundancy rules, various kinds of rules of semantic interpretation, and 'global' constraints on derivations – have increased its power still further. So, whenever one is dealing with any particular syntactic problem, it is usually possible from the start to think of a number of different descriptions which all, at least at first sight, enable us to account for the facts. It is not, then, very interesting to put forward a description and leave it at that. Rather, we must

[1] I have omitted from this collection my article 'A propos des prépositions de lieu en français' (*Mélanges Fohalle*, Ch. Hyart, ed, Gembloux: Duculot, 1969) which was written from a slightly different point of view. I have also omitted two texts which circulated in mimeograph, that now seem to me outdated: 'Adverbs. A note on the question: Where do they all come from?' (MIT, 1968), and 'Le Principe cyclique et le principe non-cyclique dans la syntaxe transformationnelle du français' (Vincennes, 1969).

consider systematically the various possible solutions, and try to decide firstly whether these solutions are not simply equivalent notational variants, and then, if that is not the case, which solution is empirically the most significant. This approach always leads to extending the field of the description to include other facts, which are sometimes at first sight very different from those previously considered. Each chapter of this book is organized so as to present several solutions to a given problem and then to attempt to decide in favour of one of them, which will not necessarily be the same type in every case.

The second guiding idea concerns the general form of a generative grammar and in particular the status of the level of deep structure. This level was first introduced to resolve a number of syntactical problems that the phrase structure model could not deal with. Recently, the growing interest that generative linguists have been taking in semantic questions has led some of them to doubt the validity of an autonomous level of deep structure, distinct both from surface structure and from semantic representation. This book is concerned to show that it is necessary to preserve this level, for syntactical as well as semantic reasons, and endeavours to define certain of its properties more precisely.

A few remarks on the terminology used. In my *Introduction à la grammaire générative*, I systematically introduced French symbols (P, SN, SV, etc). I now think it preferable to standardize the abbreviations and to return to the English terms. I shall therefore use the following symbols: S (sentence), NP (noun phrase), VP (verb phrase), AP (adjective phrase) and PP (prepositional phrase); I shall also designate adjectives simply as A and prepositions as P. I shall occasionally use the symbol *-pé* (or simply *-é*) to designate the past participle affix.

The references in brackets refer to the bibliography at the end of the book.

I can never adequately thank all those who in various ways have made it possible for this study to be undertaken. To Noam Chomsky and Morris Halle I owe almost everything, as does anyone working in generative grammar; their influence is to be felt in every page of this book. I am also indebted to them, and to Roman Jakobson, for having been able to spend a year, in 1967–8, as Postdoctoral Research Fellow, in the Department of Linguistics at MIT, where I really learned this method of working. I also wish to thank all my linguist friends in France and in the United States for their advice, their criticism and their encouragement, and in particular Ed Klima, Haj Ross, Yuki Kuroda, David Perlmutter, François Dell, Ray Jackendoff, Mike Helke, Maurice

Gross, Jean-Claude Chevalier, Jean Stéfanini, Dick Carter and Jean-Paul Boons. I owe a special debt to Jacques Mehler, who showed me the importance of the psycholinguistic approach in dealing with problems that appeared at first to be purely linguistic: his influence is apparent in Chapter 6 of this book. I have learned much from my contacts with Joe Emonds, whose imagination and talent for finding solutions beyond the beaten track are especially stimulating. What I owe to Richie Kayne is incalculable: his rigour in our numerous discussions over the course of four years has forced me to push my analyses ever further; in this book he will find many arguments, possibly distorted, that he was the first to suggest. Finally, I should like to thank my informants for their patience and collaboration, especially Jacqueline Benoît, and my students, among them Roland Dachelet, Marie-Louise Moreau, Mitsou Ronat, Anne Hertz, Henk van Riemsdijk, and Hans Georg Obenauer.

To Émile Benveniste, cut off from us by a cruel illness, I must say how decisive his writings and his lectures at the Collège de France were for me. I hope that a complete recovery will soon restore him to linguistics, where he is still so much needed.

In dedicating this book to Roman and Krystyna Jakobson, I am fulfilling a promise. I hope they will take it as a token of respect, affection and loyalty.

Finally I would like to express my gratitude to the publishing houses who have kindly given me permission to reproduce here texts of which they published the first versions: the Librairie Larousse (Paris), Mouton (The Hague), North Holland (Amsterdam), Reidel (Dordrecht, Holland), and Éditrice Lint (Trieste).

Paris   NR
February 1972

Translator's note

Names of transformations appear in small capital letters (PASSIVE, SUBJECT-RAISING, etc). Where possible I have tried to find English equivalents for the French terms, but I have left EN-AVANT in French in preference to attempting to reproduce the punning nature of this term ('*en*-forward' and 'on ahead').

At the author's request I have given English versions of the French sentence examples. Where it seemed necessary, I have given a literal, rather than a stylistic, equivalent of the French construction so as to illustrate the grammatical point more precisely. It was not always possible to reproduce sentences that are unacceptable in French (the examples marked with an asterisk) by sentences that are unacceptable in English in a similar way (to invent the 'right' form of being 'wrong' was a forlorn hope), but I have always attempted an English version of the deviant variants of grammatical sentences when new vocabulary was introduced in these variants.

SMR

Contents

Acknowledgements

We are indebted to the following for permission to reproduce copyright material:

Massachusetts Institute of Technology for an extract from page ii of a PhD dissertation *Root and Structure-Preserving Transformations* by J. E. Emonds, 1970, and the Société Encyclopédique Universelle for an extract by Jean Dubois *et al*, 1966, from the *Dictionnaire du Français contemporain*.

ERRATUM, page 5

The printer regrets the accidental omission of example [6]. Shown below is the diagram that should have appeared at the foot of page 5.

[6]

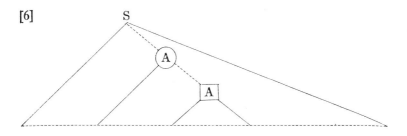

acceptable to all generative linguists working at the present time. I shall here follow very closely the formulation given by Chomsky (1971; see also Chomsky, 1972 and Lakoff, 1971).

The grammar of any given language can be conceived of as a system of rules which relates a semantic representation and a phonetic representation of the sentences of that language. These two representations are given in principle[1] in terms of two universal systems independent of any particular language: a system of phonetic representation, in the style of that proposed by Chomsky and Halle (1968), and a system of semantic representation, the nature of which, as we all recognize, is still largely unknown. The grammar specifies, moreover, an infinite set of well-formed surface structures, which are converted into phonetic representations by a system of phonological rules.[2] The grammar also contains a set of transformational rules, each of which converts a phrase-marker into another phrase-marker. These transformational rules are subject to various constraints, some universal and others applying to particular grammars. A grammar thus conceived generates an infinite set K of derivations, *ie* of finite sequences of phrase-markers, such that each of these sequences $P_1, \ldots, P_n$, satisfies the following conditions:

[A] i: P_n is a surface structure
     ii: each P_i is formed by the application of a transformation to P_{i-1}, in conformity with the conditions on the transformations
     iii: there is no P_0 such that $P_0, P_1, \ldots, P_n$ meets conditions (i) and (ii).

The phrase-marker P_1 is called the *K-initial* phrase-marker, and the members of K are called the *syntactic structures* generated by the grammar.

Further, the grammar contains a lexicon, an unordered set of lexical entries, each one specifying the syntactic, semantic and phonological properties of a lexical item. Each lexical entry incorporates a set of transformations which insert the lexical item in question into the phrase-markers, according to the following condition:

[B] a lexical transformation associated with the lexical item I maps a phrase-marker P containing a substructure Q into another phrase-marker P′ formed by replacing Q by I in P.

The standard theory, and all the theories proposed since, can be assumed to envisage this general framework in one way or another. Thus standard theory adds the following condition to conditions [A] and [B]:

Chapter 1

Some recent developments in generative theory*

1

My *Introduction à la grammaire générative* (IGG), which appear
1967 but which was finished at the end of 1966, gave a fairly ade-
picture of the state of generative grammar towards 1965. Since
generative grammar has developed so greatly, and practical and the
cal researches have so multiplied – though no new overall study
parable to those of Katz-Postal (1964) and Chomsky (1965) has
appeared – that another volume on the same scale as the first wou
needed to give any idea of it. In this short chapter, I shall not be a
do more than draw attention to certain trends in research which se
me personally to be particularly important from the point of vi
general theory.

What impresses one immediately in considering current resear
that the unity of theory which characterized Chomskyan linguists f
six years ago has disappeared, at least on the surface. All sorts of
gences have arisen, often leading to somewhat bitter controversy.
however, possible that these divergences are less clear-cut than the
of their discussion would lead us to believe, and it is not always
when confronted with an innovation which seems to be radically dive
from the 'standard' theory (this is how Chomsky now describe
theory set out in Chomsky, 1965), to distinguish between what is
new and empirically significant, and what is simply a change in ter
ology. So above all it is important to give a general outline which wou

---

* Revised version of the French original of a text which appeared as an app
  to the English translation of the *Introduction à la grammaire génér*
  Amsterdam: North Holland (1973).

[C] Given $(P_1, \ldots, P_n)$ in K, there is an i such that for $j < i$, the transformation used to form P_{j+1} from P_j is lexical, and for $j \geqslant i$, the transformation used to form P_{j+1} from P_j is non-lexical.

In other words, in the standard theory, all the transformations that insert lexical items in phrase-markers are ordered 'before' the syntactic transformations proper. In the standard theory, a grammar contains, as well as a lexicon, transformational rules and phonological rules, a system of rules of semantic interpretation, and a system of context-free phrase structure (categorial) rules, with a fixed terminal element Δ (these phrase structure rules generate the K-*initial* phrase-markers (P_1)).[3] The substructure Q mentioned in condition [B] is in this theory always limited to the element Δ. The standard theory thus defines a *post-lexical structure* (the P_i of condition [C]), which is traditionally called the *deep structure* of the sentence. This deep structure contains all the lexical items of the sentence. In addition, the configurations of the K-initial phrase-marker P_1 define the grammatical relations and functions; these configurations are preserved in the deep structure. The standard theory assumes that the semantic interpretation is determined from the intrinsic semantic content of the lexical items and by the way in which they are interrelated (in terms of grammatical relations) at the deep structure level. In other words, the deep structure determines the semantic interpretation of a sentence – to the exclusion of the derived structures, and especially of the surface structure; this amounts to saying that transformations do not alter meaning.

2

Before dealing with various modifications that have been proposed for the standard theory, which essentially concern the relations between syntax and semantics, I should like to say a few words about the studies that have been undertaken with the purpose of establishing what conditions or constraints transformations are subject to. We know that the chief weakness of the transformational model lies in its enormous descriptive power. It is therefore of basic importance to succeed in reducing this descriptive power, on the one hand by limiting the type of operation that transformations can employ, and on the other hand, by formulating severe constraints on their conditions of application. In these two areas, Chomsky (1965) had made some suggestions which have been followed up and developed (although we are still far from having obtained completely satisfactory results).

Among the various conditions on the application of transformations, first there are those that govern the order of their application. The cyclic principle, formulated by Chomsky (1965), and demonstrated notably by Rosenbaum (1967), has had fresh justification.[4] On the other hand, it does seem that not all transformations apply cyclically. As well as cyclic transformations, the existence of post-cyclic transformations (or, alternatively, last cyclic rules) seems to be justified: these transformations cannot be applied until the last cycle has been reached; they then apply to the derived structure, sometimes once, sometimes repeatedly.[5] On the other hand, the existence of pre-cyclic transformations (applying to the underlying structure before the cyclic transformations), or of 'anywhere rules' which can apply at any time once their structure index is satisfied (*cf* Ross, 1970b), is not yet empirically well justified. But there is still considerable uncertainty as to the exact order in which some quite common rules should be applied, and we may possibly have to give up the principle of the extrinsic ordering of rules (*cf* IGG, and Chomsky, 1965). Perhaps the order of transformations is in large measure determined by properties internal to these rules, rules of one type applying automatically before or after those of another type. (See below the discussion of Emonds' theory, 1970.) At all events, at the stage that research has reached at present, these considerations are still very speculative, and there is a lot of work still to be done in this area.

Apart from constraints on the order of transformations, and those proposed by Chomsky (1965) on deletion and substitution transformations, the most interesting research has been concerned with the constraints that should be applied to movement transformations. Following Emonds' terminology (1970), two types of constraint can be recognized: the first specifies certain configurations *out of which* an element cannot be moved (even if in other respects these configurations satisfy the structure index of a movement transformation); the second specifies certain configurations *into which* an element cannot be moved. In other words, those of the first type are constraints on the structure index of a transformation, those of the second type are constraints on the structural change that it effects.

2.1

The first type of constraint has been studied by Ross in particular (1967), and he has proposed several of them. One example is the Coordinate Structure Constraint, by which a transformation cannot move any element embedded in a coordinate structure. So, whereas by the WH-

FRONTING rule,[6] [1*b*] and [2*b*] can be generated respectively from underlying structures such as [1*a*] or [2*a*]:[7]

[1] *a:* Pierre croit que Paul pense que Jean a rencontré *quelqu'un*
    Peter believes that Paul thinks that John met *someone*
  b: *qui* Pierre croit-il que Paul pense que Jean a rencontré?
    who does Peter believe that Paul thinks that John met?

[2] *a:* le garçon [$_S$ Pierre a donné un livre *à ce garçon*] ...
    the boy [$_S$ Peter gave a book *to that boy*] ...
  b: le garçon *à qui* Pierre a donné un livre ...
    the boy *to whom* Peter gave a book ...

it is impossible to obtain sentences such as [3*b*] and [4*b*] from well-formed underlying structures such as [3*a*] and [4*a*] by the operation of the same rule:

[3] *a:* Pierre a rencontré Paul et *quelqu'un* d'autre
    Peter met Paul and *someone* else
  b: *qui Pierre a-t-il rencontré Paul et d'autre?
    *who did Peter meet Paul and else?

[4] *a:* le garçon [$_S$ Pierre a parlé *à ce garçon* et à cette fille] ...
    the boy [$_S$ Peter spoke *to that boy* and to that girl] ...
  b: *le garçon *à qui* Pierre a parlé et à cette fille ...
    *the boy *to whom* Peter spoke and to that girl ...

In fact, before Ross, Chomsky had proposed a much more general and abstract universal principle, of which the Coordinate Structure Constraint is only one particular case; this is the A-over-A principle (see Chomsky, 1964, 1968, 1973). This principle states that 'if a transformation applies to a structure of the form:

[5] [S ... [A ...]A ...]S

for any category A, then it must be so interpreted as to apply to the *maximal* phrase of the type A' (Chomsky, 1968, 43). In other words, if a transformation has to move a constituent of category A, and a configuration like that represented in [6] is involved:

where a constituent of type A is embedded in (dominated by) another constituent of type A, only the maximal constituent of type A (circled in [6]) can be moved, to the exclusion of any constituent of type A embedded in it (for example the one boxed in [6]).

Let us return to examples [1–4]; the WH-FRONTING rule is of approximately the following form:

$$[7] \quad X - Y - \begin{Bmatrix} NP \\ PP \end{Bmatrix} - Z$$

$$1 \qquad 2 \qquad 3 \qquad 4 \rightarrow 1 - 3 + 2 - \emptyset - 4$$

(in other terms, it moves a noun phrase or a prepositional phrase to the left of a string of any length). Now in [1a] and [2a], the phrases which comply with the structure index of this rule (*quelqu'un* and *à ce garçon* respectively) also comply with the A-over-A principle, inasmuch as the only possible analysis of the underlying strings is respectively [8] and [9]:

[8] $\underline{\emptyset}$ — $\underline{\text{Pierre croit que Paul pense que Jean a rencontré --}}$
     1   2

     $\underline{\text{quelqu'un}}$ — $\underline{\emptyset}$
     3   4

     ($\underline{\emptyset}$ — $\underline{\text{Peter believes that Paul thinks that John met}}$ —
     1   2

     $\underline{\text{someone}}$ — $\underline{\emptyset}$)
     3   4

[9] $\underline{\text{le garçon}}$ — $\underline{\text{Pierre a donné un livre}}$ — $\underline{\text{à ce garçon}}$ — $\underline{\emptyset}$
     1   2   3   4

     ($\underline{\text{the boy}}$ — $\underline{\text{Peter gave a book}}$ — $\underline{\text{to that boy}}$ — $\underline{\emptyset}$)
     1   2   3   4

The movable phrase is maximal in the sense that it is not embedded in another phrase of the same category. The case is different for [3a] and [4a], which can both be analysed in two different ways in terms of rule [7]; thus, for example, [3a] can be analysed either as in [10a] or as in [10b]:

[10] *a:* $\underline{\emptyset}$ — $\underline{\text{Pierre a rencontré}}$ — $\underline{\text{Paul et quelqu'un d'autre}}$ — $\underline{\emptyset}$
      1   2   3   4

     $\underline{\emptyset}$ — $\underline{\text{Peter met}}$ — $\underline{\text{Paul and someone else}}$ — $\underline{\emptyset}$
      1   2   3   4

b: Ø — Pierre a rencontré Paul et — quelqu'un — d'autre

1   2   3   4

Ø — Peter met Paul and — someone — else

1   2   3   4

Here, the maximal analysis is that of [10*a*]; in [10*b*], *quelqu'un* is not maximal, being embedded in a phrase of the same category (NP), which is *Paul et quelqu'un d'autre*. The application of WH-FRONTING is therefore blocked.

If the A-over-A principle proved to be valid, it would be decidedly preferable to constraints such as Ross's, which would then only be particular cases of it. But it was in fact the existence of counter-examples to the A-over-A principle that led Ross to undertake his work. In the present state of affairs, it is still difficult to decide who is right. In fact it is not certain that all the counter-examples to A-over-A given by Ross are true counter-examples, insofar as many of them depend on particular syntactic analyses which are not the only possible ones (for a discussion see Chomsky, 1968, Chapter 2, and also Chomsky, 1973). Note that R. S. Kayne (1969) has shown that some apparently very strange facts of French syntax can be explained quite naturally in terms of the A-over-A principle, but not in terms of any of the constraints proposed by Ross (*cf* Chapter 6).

2.2

Emonds (1970) has in essence proposed limiting possible transformations to two formally distinct types,[8] which he calls, respectively, 'root transformations' and 'structure-preserving transformations'. Some examples will illustrate what is involved. It has often been proposed that the sentences of examples (*a*) below should be derived transformationally from underlying structures similar to the surface structures of the corresponding (*b*) examples:

[11] *a:* Pierre semble être bien malade
        Peter seems to be very ill
     b: il semble que Pierre est bien malade
        it seems that Peter is very ill

[12] *a:* le pays qu'a visité Pierre est très passionnant
        the country that Peter visited is very fascinating
     b: le pays que Pierre a visité est très passionnant
        (as for *a*)

[13] *a:* est-il parti?
      has he gone?
    b: il est parti
      he has gone

[14] *a:* 'Pierre,' je crois, 'arrivera trop tard'
      'Peter,' I believe, 'will arrive too late'
    b: je crois que Pierre arrivera trop tard
      I believe that Peter will arrive too late

[11*a*] is derived from [11*b*] by the (subject) RAISING rule (*cf* Rosen-baum, 1967, Kiparsky and Kiparsky, 1970, Gross, 1968, and Chapter 2 of this book) which converts a subordinate clause subject into a main clause subject; [12*a*] is derived from [12*b*] by STYLISTIC INVERSION (*cf* Kayne, 1969, 1972) which permutes the subject NP and the verb; [13*a*] is derived from [13*b*] by a rule which permutes a clitic subject and the conjugated element of the verb (*cf* Kayne, 1969, 1972); lastly, [14*a*] is derived from [14*b*] by the QUOTE PREPOSING rule which preposes all or part of a quotation before the main clause (*cf* Emonds, 1970).

At even a cursory examination, the transformations which account for [11*a*–12*a*] bring about results which differ greatly from those which account for [13*a*–14*a*]. Roughly speaking, the derived structures of [11*a*] and [12*a*] resemble deep structures, as opposed to those of [13*a*] and [14*a*]. For example, the SUBJECT-RAISING rule produces, in [11*a*], a string NP – AUX – V – ... which corresponds to the kind of strings generated by the base rules S→NP – VP and VP→AUX – V – ... Similarly, the STYLISTIC INVERSION rule produces, in [12*a*], a string V – NP that corresponds to the kind of strings generated by the rule VP→V NP. On the other hand, the transformations that account for [13*a*] and [14*a*] produce strings that there are good reasons for not genera-ting directly in other cases by means of the phrase structure rules of the base. In other words, there are transformations which in a sense preserve the base structure, and others which upset this structure more or less completely. From observations of this kind, Emonds was led to formulate the following hypothesis:

A phrase node[9] X in a tree T can be moved, copied, or inserted into a new position in T, according to the structural change of a trans-formation whose structural description T satisfies, only if at least one of two conditions is satisfied: (i) In its new position in T, X is immedi-ately dominated by the highest S ...[10] (A transformation having such an effect is a 'root transformation'); (ii) The new position of X is a position in which a phrase structure rule, motivated independently of the transformation in question, can generate the category X. (A transformation having such an effect is a 'structure-preserving transformation'). (Emonds, 1970, ii)

These very strong constraints make some empirically significant predictions. Firstly, they predict that a 'structure-preserving transformation' is blocked whenever the derived structure that results from it contains a subconfiguration not generatable by the base rules. Thus, we might expect that [15a], or [15b], could be generated, by STYLISTIC INVERSION, from [15c] (cf [12]); but [15a–b] contain a string V – NP – NP which is not generated by the phrase structure rules of French; as Emonds' constraints predict, [15a–b] are ungrammatical:

[15] a: *la ville où rencontrera Pierre cet homme est très provinciale
     b: *la ville où rencontrera cet homme Pierre est très provinciale
     c: la ville où Pierre rencontrera cet homme est très provinciale
       the town where Peter will meet this man is very provincial

Another example of a 'structure-preserving transformation' in French is the INDEFINITE NP EXTRAPOSITION rule (cf Kayne, 1969, Picabia, 1970) which generates [16a] from [16b] but which cannot generate [17a] from [17b]:

[16] a: il est venu quelqu'un hier
       there came someone yesterday
     b: quelqu'un est venu hier
       someone came yesterday

[17] a: *il a rencontré $\begin{cases} \text{Paul quelqu'un} \\ \text{quelqu'un Paul} \end{cases}$
     b: quelqu'un a rencontré Paul
       someone met Paul

Here again, Emonds' constraints explain why, when [18a] is possible (INDEFINITE NP EXTRAPOSITION being applied after PASSIVE), [19a], which one could apparently expect to be generated from sentence [19b], which is superficially very close to [18b], is ungrammatical:

[18] a: il a été contenté beaucoup de monde
       there were many people contented
     b: beaucoup de monde a été contenté
       many people were contented

[19] *a:* *il a été content beaucoup de monde
      b: beaucoup de monde a été content
      many people were content

The reason for this is that *contenté* in [18] is the past participle of a verb, and the string V NP is generatable by the base rules, whereas *content* in [19] is an adjective, and there is no independent reason to have a base rule such as VP→*être* AP NP . . . (where AP = adjective phrase).

In the second place, Emonds' constraints predict that the 'root transformations' are only allowed in main clauses, whereas the 'structure-preserving transformations' are not subject to this limitation; these predictions are confirmed by the following examples:

[20] *a:* le fait que Pierre te semble être très malade est inquiétant
      the fact that Peter seems to you to be very ill is disturbing
      b: pourquoi crois-tu que Pierre me semble être très malade?
      why do you think that Peter seems to me to be very ill?

[21] *a:* je voudrais savoir où est allé Pierre
      I would like to know where Peter has gone
      b: l'endroit où est allé Pierre est très mal famé
      the place where Peter has gone has a very bad reputation

[22] *a:* je me demande où il est parti
      I wonder where he has gone
      b: *je me demande où est-il parti

[23] *a:* je ne sais pas s'il est parti
      I do not know if he has gone
      b: *je ne sais pas si est-il parti

[24] *a:* Paul s'imagine que je crois que Pierre arrivera trop tard
      Paul fancies that I think that Peter will arrive too late
      b: *Paul s'imagine que Pierre, je crois, arrivera trop tard
      *Paul fancies that Peter, I think, will arrive too late

[25] *a:* le fait que je crois que Pierre arrivera trop tard ne t'intéresse
          apparemment pas
      the fact that I think that Peter will arrive too late apparently does
          not interest you
      b: *le fait que Pierre, je crois, arrivera trop tard ne t'intéresse ap-
          paremment pas
      *the fact that Peter, I think, will arrive too late apparently does
          not interest you

2.3

Emonds' constraints, like the A–over–A principle and the other constraints on the extraction and insertion of elements out of or into subordinate structures recently proposed by Chomsky (1973), are attended by problems. For example, Kayne (1972) has shown that Emonds' constraints are not sufficient to account for the limitations on STYLISTIC INVERSION, contrary to what our simplified examples might indicate. The interest and the difficulties of this kind of constraint, which is at the same time very general and very specific, arise from the fact that they correspond to very strong hypotheses on the form of grammars, and that consequently they are easily falsifiable. There can be no doubt that before they can be considered adequate they must undergo important modifications. But, whatever their inadequacies may be, they still represent a step in the right direction, that is towards specifying and limiting the form of possible grammars.

It is a different matter with other types of constraint which have also recently been proposed, and which have the opposite tendency of increasing the power of the linguistic theory. For example one might cite the surface structure constraints or 'output conditions' which have been studied mainly by D. M. Perlmutter (1969, 1971; see also Ross, 1967, 1972). Perlmutter has shown in particular that it is impossible to account in purely transformational terms for the permitted or prohibited sequences and combinations of clitic pronouns in Spanish and French. He therefore proposed to allow the transformations that place the clitic pronouns in the preverbal position to apply freely, and to add to them a mechanism that, operating as a filter on surface structures, enumerates the sequences and combinations of clitics that are permitted. In other words, in this case the transformations will generate well-formed surface structures as well as ungrammatical surface structures, and the latter have to be 'filtered out' by the surface structure constraint. It is at once apparent that a grammar that allows surface structure constraints as well as phrase structure rules and transformations, has its descriptive power vastly increased. In a multitude of cases where difficulties in generating the correct surface structures by transformations are encountered, it is easy enough to invent surface structure constraints to resolve the problem, but these constraints at best only describe the observed facts correctly. It is quite possible that, for reasons of observational or descriptive adequacy, one might be obliged to make use of output conditions in certain cases, but the theoretical interest of such additions to the grammar is slender as long as the conditions in which they can be used are not strictly specified and limited.[11]

Several linguists, prominent among whom is George Lakoff, have recently proposed enriching the grammar by mechanisms that increase its descriptive power still further. Following on some suggestions by McCawley (1968a), Lakoff (1969, 1971) proposed to reinterpret the notion of rule of grammar in terms of conditions on derivations. The phrase structure rules are interpreted as well-formedness conditions on trees and the transformations as 'local' derivational constraints. A transformation is a local derivational constraint in the sense that it specifies certain conditions that two *adjacent* phrase markers in a derivation must satisfy for this derivation to be well-formed (it can be seen that the notion of well-formedness is extended here to derivations, not confined to surface structures only). In addition to these local constraints, Lakoff proposes to introduce 'global derivational constraints', which specify conditions on *non-adjacent* phrase markers. An abstract example of global derivational constraint is the following:

[26] Let there be, in a derivation D, a phrase marker P_i and a phrase marker P_j, such that $j \geqslant i + 1$; if P_i can be analysed as $[_S \ldots A^1 \ldots A^2 \ldots]_S$ and P_j as $[_S \ldots A^2 \ldots A^1 \ldots]_S$, the derivation D is ill-formed.

In other words, if A^2 appears on the right of A^1 at some stage of the derivation, and if subsequently, at any stage of the derivation, following the operation of one or more transformations, A^2 is found on the left of A^1, then the derivation D is ill-formed.

In this particular case, it is clear that this global derivational constraint is the equivalent of a constraint on movement transformations, and it is not difficult to show that all Ross's constraints, for example, can be interpreted as global derivational constraints. In other cases, however, it is possible to formulate, in terms of global derivational constraints, conditions that it would be impossible to formulate as constraints on the application of particular transformations; this is the case in particular with surface structure constraints, and the constraints proposed by Lakoff for dealing with the facts of pronominalization (1968b) and with certain facts relating to quantifiers (Lakoff, 1969, 1971). Lakoff seems to envisage the introduction of the notion of global constraints as a significant generalization and simplification, but this idea is misleading. It must, in fact, be recognized that the general admission of global constraints considerably increases the descriptive power of the grammar: a grammar that has this power would seem to be capable of describing almost anything.[12] Chomsky (1972) remarked that to say that a grammar must contain global derivational constraints amounts to the truism that a grammar must contain rules. A theory which did not attempt to specify further the form of the rules would be of little interest. Let us repeat once more that although it may prove to be necessary for reasons of descriptive adequacy to use such powerful mechanisms, unless one's primary objective is the severe restriction of their use, such enrichments have little theoretical interest.

Another example of facts which it would be tempting to deal with in terms of a global derivational constraint is to be found in the agreement of the past participle with a preposed object pronoun in French. Consider the following facts:

[27] Pierre a $\left\{ \begin{array}{l} \text{écrit} \\ \text{*écrite} \end{array} \right\}$ cette lettre

Peter has written that letter

[28] Pierre l'a $\left\{ \begin{array}{l} \text{*écrit} \\ \text{écrite} \end{array} \right.$

Peter has written it

[29] la lettre que Pierre a $\left\{ \begin{array}{l} \text{*écrit} \\ \text{écrite} \end{array} \right\}$ n'est jamais arrivée à destination

the letter that Peter wrote never reached its destination

[30] la lettre que Paul a $\left\{ \begin{array}{l} \text{dit} \\ \text{*dite} \end{array} \right\}$ que Pierre a $\left\{ \begin{array}{l} \text{*écrit} \\ \text{écrite} \end{array} \right\}$ n'est jamais

arrivée à destination

the letter that Paul said that Peter wrote never reached its destination

The facts of [27] show that the agreement between the past participle of a transitive verb and its object cannot be introduced at the stage when the object is still in the post-verbal position. The agreement must follow the transformations (CLITIC PLACING in [28], WH-FRONTING in [29–30]) that moved the objects into the preverbal position. Moreover, the facts of [30] show that the pronoun can be indefinitely far removed from the verb of which it was the object in deep structure; they also show that it is only the past participle of the verb of which the pronoun was originally the object which can agree (cf the contrast dit/*dite as opposed to *écrit/écrite). A global constraint, citing both the stage of the derivation when the pronoun is still in the object position, and the stage when it is moved into the preverbal position, would enable us to account for these facts.

But, even leaving out of account the doubtful nature of the facts of agreement of the past participle in modern French, such a constraint amounts
only to a formulation of the observed facts; it cannot be said to explain
them. In fact, Fauconnier (1971) has proposed another way of dealing
with these facts, which dispenses with global constraints while having
greater explanatory power and representing only an innocuous extension of the standard model.

2.4

In any case, even if we retain only specific constraints like those of Emonds
or the A–over–A principle (supposing that these constraints are indeed
well-founded and universal), the question arises: Why are there these
constraints? One answer, which would seem to be Chomsky's (1968,
1972), is that these universal constraints, these invariables of human
language, are the manifestations of certain innate linguistic capacities and
limitations, manifestations of man's innate 'language faculty'.

   Nevertheless, there is another possible answer. With the object, both
of explaining the reason for these various constraints and also of meeting
the difficulties involved in working them out, various linguists and
psycholinguists (cf Klima, 1970, Bever, 1970, Bever and Langendoen, 1971, and Chapter 6 of this book) have recently proposed a somewhat different conception, which consists essentially in redefining the
relations between competence and performance. Up to now, generative
linguists have proceeded from the assumption that the phenomena of
the utterance and reception of speech gave a distorted picture of internal
linguistic competence, whereas the speaker's intuitions (in matters of
grammaticality, ambiguity, etc) gave a more direct idea of it. The problems encountered in formulating constraints on grammars, on the one
hand, and, on the other hand, the untrustworthiness of intuitions, the
divergences of judgment (even that of linguists, cf the discussion in
Kimball, 1970) when it comes to fairly subtle points, have led to a revision
of this point of view. Not only can intuitions be of various types – whence
the necessity for a phenomenology of linguistic intuitions – but, after all,
the exercise of linguistic intuition is itself also a type of behaviour, on a
level with the utterance and reception of speech, and it can be subject to
distortion resulting from constraints on behaviour. From this it is de-
duced, firstly, that the data on which the linguist works are all behavioural
data, but of various types – utterances, reception, memory, judgments and
predictions about structures. Then follows the hypothesis that the constraints shown in the intuitions of native speakers do not necessarily

reflect innate linguistic limitations, but that they may result from the interaction of these limitations with certain 'strategies' governing learning, perception, etc, strategies whose field of application goes beyond the domain of language. The concrete proposals that have been made in this direction are rather vague as yet, but they seem to me to be very promising. It must be borne in mind that if such general 'strategies' can be precisely formulated, we may perhaps succeed at the same time in defining much more rigorously the role and form of grammar in the strict sense of the term, and we may perhaps be able to eliminate some constraints from the grammar which are either much too particular or much too powerful.

3

If there is one point on which everybody is now agreed, in the matter of the relations between syntax and semantics, it is that the model proposed by Katz, Fodor and Postal, and adopted by Chomsky (1965) (though with some reservations, *cf* Chomsky, 1965, note 9, Chapter 3), is inadequate and must be revised. After this purely negative agreement, opinion is divided. It would be impossible for me to review here all the problems posed by the relations between syntax and semantics and all the proposals made for dealing with them. I shall confine myself to the two main tendencies which are at present dominant: on the one hand, the theory of *generative semantics*, represented by the work of Lakoff, Ross, McCawley, Postal, Bach, etc, and on the other hand, the *interpretative theory* or the *extended standard theory*, illustrated by the recent work of Chomsky (1971, 1972), and that of Jackendoff (1969a, 1969b, 1971a), Dougherty (1969, 1970b), etc. Original work that does not fit in exactly with either of these theories includes that of Gruber (1965, 1967) on the theory of the lexicon, that of Fillmore (1968, etc) on 'case grammar', and various studies by Kuroda.

3.1

It is not necessary to look far to realize that the assertion that only deep structures determine meaning is inadequate – if by that we understand the type of deep structure familiar in the work of Chomsky (1965), Klima (1964a, 1964b), Katz-Postal (1964), Rosenbaum (1967), etc. Here are some representative examples. Linguists working within the framework of the standard theory have proposed deriving all the examples of [31], all those of [32], etc, from the same deep structure.[13] But it is quite

easy to see that these sentences, although they are clearly related, do not
have a paraphrase relationship:

[31] a: une seule flèche n'a pas atteint la cible
      only one arrow did not hit the target
      b: pas une seule flèche n'a atteint la cible
      not a single arrow hit the target
      c: la cible n'a pas été atteinte par une seule flèche
      the target was not hit by a single arrow

[32] a: chaque candidat démocrate espère que chaque candidat démo-
      crate sera élu
      each Democratic candidate hopes that each Democratic candidate
      will be elected
      b: chaque candidat démocrate espère être élu
      each Democratic candidate hopes to be elected

[33] a: peu de sonnets de Mallarmé sont limpides et peu de sonnets de
      Mallarmé sont irréguliers
      few of Mallarmé's sonnets are clear and few of Mallarmé's sonnets
      are irregular
      b: peu de sonnets de Mallarmé sont (à la fois) limpides et irréguliers
      few of Mallarmé's sonnets are (both) clear and irregular

[34] a: c'est Pierre qui a frappé Paul
      it was Peter who hit Paul
      b: c'est Paul que Pierre a frappé
      it was Paul whom Peter hit

[35] a: je ne connais que les églises de Rome
      I only know the churches in Rome
      b: de Rome, je ne connais que les églises
      in Rome, I only know the churches

[36] a: même Pierre boit du gin avant le petit déjeuner
      even Peter drinks gin before breakfast
      b: Pierre boit même du gin avant le petit déjeuner
      Peter even drinks gin before breakfast
      c: Pierre boit du gin même avant le petit déjeuner
      Peter drinks gin even before breakfast

[37] a: le jardin grouille de vermine
      the garden swarms with vermin
      b: la vermine grouille dans le jardin
      vermin swarms in the garden

The three sentences of [31] are clearly different in terms of truth-values: [31a] implies that all the arrows except one hit the target; [31b] implies that no arrow hit the target; and [31c] is ambiguous, but its two possible readings are not on the same level: the more natural is synonymous with [31b], but it is also possible to understand [31c] as meaning that the target was not hit by one arrow but by several. The sentences of [32] also differ in their truth-values: the truth of [32a] necessarily entails that of [32b], but not vice versa. The same applies in the case of [33a] and [33b].

Examples [34–36] pose different problems: the various related sentences here differ in terms of 'focus' and 'presupposition'(cf Chomsky, 1971). For example, sentences [34a] and [34b] both mean that Peter hit Paul, but [34a] presupposes that someone hit Paul, and supplies the new information that it was Peter who hit him (*Peter* is the 'focus' of the sentence); [34b], in contrast, presupposes that Peter hit someone, and supplies the information that it was Paul who was hit (*Paul* is the 'focus'). The difference is seen clearly if we think of the questions to which these two sentences would be natural answers: [34a] is a natural answer to [38a], but not to [38b], and for [34b] it is the other way round:

[38] *a:* qui a frappé Paul?
          who hit Paul?
      b: qui Pierre a-t-il frappé?
          who did Peter hit?

[35] sets a similar problem, though slightly more complicated; again the difference becomes clear in terms of natural answers to questions: [35a] is a natural answer to [39a], for example, but not to [39b], and for [35b] it is the other way round:

[39] *a:* quelles églises connaissez-vous?
          what churches do you know?
      b: que connaissez-vous de Rome?
          what do you know in Rome?

In [36], the three sentences all say that Peter drinks gin before breakfast, but each also suggests something different: [36a] presupposes that other people than Peter drink gin before breakfast, and suggests that it is unexpected that this should be the case with Peter too; [36b] presupposes that Peter drinks before breakfast, and suggests that it is unexpected that it should be gin that he drinks under the circumstances; lastly, [36c] presupposes that Peter drinks gin, and suggests that it is unexpected that

he should drink it before breakfast. To conclude, the non-synonymy of
the two sentences of [37] may not be apparent at first sight, but it is real:
in fact, [37*b*] could be true if the vermin is concentrated only in one part
of the garden, whereas [37*a*] suggests that the whole garden is full of
vermin (*cf* Chomsky, 1972).

3.2

Two attitudes are possible towards facts of this sort. Either one can
adopt the analysis that attributes the same deep structure to sentences
which are related but semantically different; in this case one has to abandon the principle that transformations do not change meaning, and turn
to rules of semantic interpretation which operate on a different level from
that of deep structure. Or else one retains the principle that transformations do not change meaning, and then one has to modify the analysis,
and to propose different deep structures for related sentences.

Linguists like Postal, Lakoff, Ross, etc, have adopted the second course.
Systematic maintenance of the principle that transformations do not
modify meaning has had considerable consequences: it led to the construction of very complex and very abstract deep structures (that is to say
very remote and very different from the corresponding surface structures)
and at the same time to the introduction of new transformations with
formal properties often very different from those of the transformations
familiar in the standard theory. Here is one example: we have just seen
that if we keep to the idea that [33*b*] is derived from [33*a*] by the CON-
JUNCTION REDUCTION transformation, this transformation modifies
the meaning; on the other hand, it is clear, if we consider [31–33], that
the differences of meaning noticed are connected with the presence of
quantifiers (*une seule, chaque, peu*) in these sentences. It is possible to keep
both the CONJUNCTION REDUCTION transformation and the principle
that transformations do not alter meaning, providing that it is admitted,
following Lakoff (1968, 1971), that the deep structures of [33*a*] and of
[33*b*] are, respectively, [40*a*] and [40*b*], which show the same differences
of meaning as [33*a*] and [33*b*]:

[40] *a:* les sonnets de Mallarmé [$_S$ les sonnets de Mallarmé sont lim-
              pides]$_S$ sont peu et les sonnets de Mallarmé [$_S$ les sonnets de
              Mallarmé sont irréguliers]$_S$ sont peu
         Mallarmé's sonnets [$_S$ Mallarmé's sonnets are clear]$_S$ are few and
         Mallarmé's sonnets [$_S$ Mallarmé's sonnets are irregular]$_S$ are
         few

b: les sonnets de Mallarmé [s les sonnets de Mallarmé sont limpides
et les sonnets de Mallarmé sont irréguliers]s sont peu
Mallarmé's sonnets [s Mallarmé's sonnets are clear and Mallarmé's sonnets are irregular]s are few

This analysis, then, amounts to treating the quantifiers, which in surface structure are determiners of NPs, as predicates of main clauses, whereas the main clauses in surface structure are treated as relative clauses to the subjects of the main clauses in deep structure. [33a] is then obtained by applying to [40a] the new transformation of QUANTIFIER LOWERING, which has the effect of substituting the quantifier for the determiner of the subject of the relative clause, and deleting all the rest of the main clause; [33b] is obtained by applying CONJUNCTION REDUCTION in the relative clause of [40b] followed by QUANTIFIER LOWERING. We see that the QUANTIFIER LOWERING rule is distinct from traditional transformations in that it converts a subordinate clause into a main clause, and that it introduces morphological material from the main clause into the subordinate clause – a type of operation that does not seem to be permitted in traditional transformations.[14]

Other considerations, relating to selectional restrictions and the semantic role of grammatical relations, have also contributed to the setting up of more complex and more abstract deep structures. Take sentences such as:

[41] *a:* Adèle a cuit $\begin{cases} \text{le ragoût} \\ \text{*ce rocher} \end{cases}$

Adèle cooked $\begin{cases} \text{the stew} \\ \text{*this rock} \end{cases}$

b: $\begin{rcases} \text{le ragoût} \\ \text{*ce rocher} \end{rcases}$ cuit

$\begin{rcases} \text{the stew} \\ \text{*this rock} \end{rcases}$ is cooking

[42] *a:* $\begin{rcases} \text{Pierre} \\ \text{*ce rocher} \end{rcases}$ méprise $\begin{cases} \text{l'argent} \\ \text{les femmes} \\ \text{les idées de Paul} \end{cases}$

$\begin{rcases} \text{Peter} \\ \text{*this rock} \end{rcases}$ despises $\begin{cases} \text{money} \\ \text{women} \\ \text{Paul's ideas} \end{cases}$

b: l'argent ⎫
      les femmes ⎬ degoûte(nt) { Pierre
      les idées de Paul ⎭   *ce rocher

      money ⎫
      women ⎬ disgust(s) { Peter
      Paul's ideas ⎭   *this rock

If it is agreed, as in the standard theory, that on the one hand the grammatical relations of deep structure determine the semantic interpretation,
and on the other hand that identical selectional restrictions in different
constructions must be formulated only once in the grammar, it might be
supposed that the deep structures of these sentences are rather different
from their surface structures. For example it is clear that the semantic
relation between the verb and the subject is not the same in [41a] and
[41b], or in [42a] and [42b]; on the other hand, the semantic relation
between the object and the verb in [41a] resembles that between the
subject and the verb in [41b], and the subject and the object seem to have
converse relations with the verb in [42a] and [42b]. These facts have led
various linguists to propose that [41a] should be derived from a complex
construction, similar to that underlying [43] (*cf* Lakoff, 1970c, McCawley,
1968c), and to suggest that [42b] has an underlying structure in which the
selectional restrictions are distributed as in [42a] (*cf* [44]), a transformational rule, called PSYCH-MOVEMENT (*cf* Postal, 1971) then permuting
the subject and the object:

[43] Adèle a fait cuire le ragoût
      Adèle caused the stew to cook

[44] Pierre — dégouter — l'argent
      Peter — disgust — money

   In this way deep structures that were more complex than the corresponding surface structures were being set up (from examples [40] and [43]
it can be seen that deep structures containing embedded clauses are
postulated as underlying sentences that are simple in surface structure,
and these are only very elementary examples, in fact) and the transformational component was being extended to include a whole series of new
transformations; at the same time a radical simplification of deep structure was being introduced. Similarities of behaviour between verbs and
auxiliaries (*cf* Ross, 1970a), between verbs and adjectives (*cf* Lakoff,
1970c), verbs and nouns (*cf* Bach, 1968), and verbs and prepositions, and
doubt as to the validity of different categories of adverbs (*cf* Lakoff

1968a, 1970c), led to the idea that these differences of category were superficial, and that the list of categories in deep structure was much more restricted; one thus ended up with a phrase structure component reduced to a few rules, assumed to be universal, introducing only a few categories, namely S, NP and V.

The consequence of all this was that deep structures began to look more and more like semantic or logical representations – the phrase structure component becoming a variant of predicate calculus, where the Ss are propositions, the Vs are predicates, and the NPs are arguments – and that the function that in the standard theory was assigned to rules of semantic interpretation (on which, however, the standard theory was not very explicit) became more and more circumscribed. From this it was a short step to questioning (*cf* McCawley, 1968b, 1968c) whether there did exist an autonomous level of deep structure, distinct both from the semantic representation and the surface structure, and it was proposed to simplify the form of grammars in the following way: the phrase structure rules directly generate semantic representations (hence the name *generative semantics* that was given to this theory), the P_1 of [A] above then being a semantic representation set out in the form of a tree, and these semantic representations are converted into surface structures by derivations subject to local constraints (transformations) and to global constraints; this theory does not require an intermediate level of deep structure. The relationship between syntactic structure and phonetic structure is essentially the same as in the standard theory.

The abandoning of condition [C] above, which specified that the lexical insertion transformations are all ordered before the syntactic transformations proper, plays a particularly crucial part in this reformulation. In generative semantics, the substructure Q of condition [B], for which a lexical transformation substitutes a lexical item I, is no longer a fixed terminal symbol Δ, but a phrase structure configuration, which may be quite complex, dominating a string of terminal elements representing minimal semantic entities. Let us turn once more to McCawley's famous example (1968c): sentences [45a and b] (*cf* also [41], [43]) would both have as their underlying structure [46], in which the terms in capitals represent semantic primitives (presumed to be universal): [15]

[45] *a:* Pierre a tué Paul
         Peter killed Paul
     b: Pierre a fait mourir Paul
         Peter caused Paul to die

[46] PIERRE CAUSE [ₛPAUL MOURIR]
    PETER CAUSE [ₛ PAUL DIE]

This underlying structure may or may not be subject to an optional syntactic transformation, PREDICATE RAISING, which attaches the subordinate predicate (DIE) to the right of the main verb (CAUSE), producing the intermediate structure [47]:

[47] PIERRE — CAUSE + MOURIR — PAUL
    PETER — CAUSE + DIE — PAUL

If this operation has taken place, the lexical insertion rule then substitutes the lexical item (*ie* here the morphophonological form) *kill* for this configuration CAUSE + DIE, and we obtain [45*a*]; if PREDICATE RAISING has not operated, the lexical items *cause* and *die* will be substituted, respectively, for CAUSE and for DIE in [46], and, after other transformations, we get [45*b*]. Other similar analyses have recently been proposed (*cf* Lakoff, 1970a, 1971), which all crucially involve syntactic transformations ordered before lexical insertions. The most detailed and ambitious of these analyses is the one proposed by Paul Postal (1970a) for the verb *remind* (in one of its possible readings). Postal proposes deriving [48] from the semantic structure [49*a*], by the successive application of SUBJECT RAISING (*cf* [11]), PSYCH-MOVEMENT (*cf* [42], [44]), PREDICATE RAISING, and *remind*-formation (lexical insertion):

[48] Larry reminds me of Winston Churchill

[49] *a:* I — perceive — [ₛ Larry — is similar to — Winston Churchill]ₛ
         →SUBJECT-RAISING→
     b: I — perceive — Larry — [ₛ be similar to — Winston Churchill]ₛ
         →PSYCH-MOVEMENT
     c: Larry — perceive — me — [ₛ be similar to — Winston Churchill]ₛ
         →PREDICATE RAISING→
     d: Larry — perceive + similar — me — Winston Churchill
         →*remind*-formation and other rules→[48]

3.3

Like the introduction of global derivational constraints, the abandonment of condition [C] and of the level of deep structure has the result of considerably increasing the descriptive power of grammars, by minimally constraining their form. Let us repeat that it might happen that, for empirical reasons, one might be forced to abandon this condition, and Postal (1970a) tries at length to provide empirical arguments in favour of his analysis. The whole question is whether there are not other possible alternatives which would account for the same facts while constraining the form of the grammar much more.

Firstly, let it be said that there is no agreement on the validity of particular analyses of the kind that we have just described. Dougherty (1970b) has proposed an analysis of coordination that eliminates the CONJUNCTION REDUCTION rule from the derivation of sentences like [33*b*] and which, at the same time, modifies the semantic problem of the relation between [33*a*] and [33*b*]. Hall-Partee (1970) and Jackendoff (1971b) have shown that the analysis of quantifiers proposed by Lakoff was not without its difficulties. Postal's analysis of *remind* has already been the subject of important criticisms (see especially Kimball, 1970, and Ronat, 1972), which question the correctness of some of the facts on which it is based and show that there are important generalizations which it fails to formulate. Various linguists (Fodor, 1970, and Chapter 4 of this book) have shown that the analysis of factitive transitive verbs of the type of *cuire* (*cf* [41]) or of *tuer* (*cf* [45]) entails all sorts of difficulties, both semantic and syntactic. Several of the transformations which play a crucial part in these analyses have little or no other independent syntactic justification: this is the case with PREDICATE RAISING which (*cf* Chomsky, 1972) has no other *raison d'être* than to make possible the analysis proposed by McCawley; it is also to a large extent the case with PSYCH-MOVEMENT: the facts cited by Postal (1971) to justify this rule can be handled just as well in another theoretical framework (*cf* Jackendoff, 1969b) and there are other facts for which it makes a satisfactory description impossible (*cf* Chapter 5 of this book).

On the whole, in the matter of lexical insertion, the proposals of those who support generative semantics often seem to be rather unsystematic: a particular analysis of one or two lexical items is proposed, but the general question of the lexicon is not dealt with,[16] and important traditional problems, like those of homonymy, metaphor, the relations between the 'basic meanings' and the 'derived meanings' of words, etc, are avoided (*cf* Chapter 5). On the other hand, generative semantics rests on a fundamental assumption, which is never explicitly discussed, concerning the possibility of constructing a universal semantic structure, independent of particular languages; this is the old problem of (philosophical) universals, of which philosophical discussions have taught us to be wary. Jackendoff (1972, 14) remarks that 'it is not even clear that one can construct a formal object which corresponds to the intuitive notion "semantic interpretation of a sentence", because of the infinite divisibility of many

semantic properties and the (perhaps undecidable) problem of choosing
what information is part of the [semantic, N.R.] reading [of a lexical item,
N.R.] and what information merely follows from the reading.' Chomsky
(1969, 80) remarks also that it is perhaps not possible to 'distinguish
sharply between the contribution of grammar to the determination of
meaning, and the contribution of so-called "pragmatic considerations",
questions of fact and belief and context of utterance' (see also, in connection with Postal's analysis of *remind*, Bar-Hillel, 1971).

It must be admitted that certain areas of ambiguity or vagueness in the
standard theory, as formulated by Katz-Postal (1964) and Chomsky
(1965), have contributed to the direction taken by generative semantics.
Take for example the idea that the grammatical relations in deep structure determine a fundamental aspect of the semantic interpretation of
sentences. Although Chomsky (1965) gives a method for defining relations such as subject-predicate, verb-object, etc, he is not very explicit as
to the role that these relations play in semantic interpretation. Since,
moreover, the purely combinatory conception of the semantic projection
rules in Katz and Fodor (1963) could not account for differences as clear
as those found (in the relation between the subject and the verb for example) between sentences such as [41*a–b*] or [42*a–b*], the step leading to
analyses such as those proposed by Postal and McCawley (or those of
another kind proposed by Fillmore, 1968) was easily taken. But everything depends on the way in which the role of the semantic component
of the grammar is conceived. If the rules of semantic interpretation are
complex and diversified, if they do not amount to a projection of grammatical relations, other analyses become possible (*cf* Jackendoff, 1969b,
1971a; Anderson, 1971). Let us then consider the simple and complex
factitive constructions:

[50] *a:* Alice cuit le ragoût (*cf* [41*a*])
        Alice cooks the stew
      b: Alice fait cuire le ragoût
        Alice causes the stew to cook

One of the semantic difficulties of the analysis proposed by Lakoff and
McCawley lies in the fact that these related constructions are not generally
synonymous, *cf:*

[51] *a:* Alice a fait remonter Humpty Dumpty sur son mur mais elle ne
        l'a pas fait remonter elle-même sur son mur
        Alice made Humpty Dumpty get back on his wall but she did not
        herself make him get back on his wall

b: Alice a fait remonter Humpty Dumpty sur son mur mais elle ne
l'a pas remonté elle-même sur son mur
Alice made Humpty Dumpty get back on his wall but she did not
herself put him back on his wall

[52] *a:* Graham Hill a fait caler le moteur de la Ferrari de Jacky Ickx
Graham Hill caused the engine of Jacky Ickx's Ferrari to stall
b: Graham Hill a calé le moteur de la Ferrari de Jacky Ickx
Graham Hill stalled the engine of Jacky Ickx's Ferrari

[51*a*] is contradictory, but [51*b*] is not; in fact, for Alice to *remonter*
Humpty Dumpty on his wall, she would have to have a direct physical
effect on him, for example by putting her arms round him to lift him onto
the wall; whereas she can *faire remonter* him simply by persuasion, without herself taking direct action. The case of [52] is more subtle: [52*b*]
implies that Graham Hill is at the wheel of Ickx's Ferrari, whereas [52*a*]
implies nothing of the sort: Graham Hill could, for example, have caused
the engine of the Ferrari to stall while he himself was driving a Lotus that
obstructed Ickx at a bend. Moreover, the simple and the complex transitives do not generally show the same selectional restrictions, *cf:*

[53] *a:* Delphine a fait entrer la voiture dans le garage
Delphine got the car into the garage
b: Delphine a entré la voiture dans le garage
Delphine put the car into the garage

[54] *a:* Delphine a fait entrer les invités au salon
Delphine showed the guests into the drawing-room
b: *Delphine a entré les invités au salon
? Delphine put the guests into the drawing-room

All these facts, and many others, begin to be comprehensible if we agree,
(i) that the deep structures of [41*a–b*] and of constructions of the same
type are, in the main, the same as their surface structures, and, (ii) if we
define a semantic notion of 'agent' derivatively from the notion of deep
subject; in other words, in certain conditions (depending on the semantic
content of the subject, of the verb, etc), a deep subject, and only a deep
subject, can be interpreted semantically as an agent. Given that, in deep
structure, a simple transitive construction such as [41*a*] or [53*b*] has only
one subject, whereas a complex factitive construction has two, the subject
of the main clause and that of the subordinate, we can thus account for
the differences noted; for example, in the second coordinate of [51*b*],

Humpty Dumpty, the deep object, cannot be an agent – whereas he can
be in the first coordinate; again, [53a and b] are equally possible, because
a car can be conceived of both as the passive object of an action and as
endowed with autonomous activity; in contrast, [54b] is impossible because, in principle, when one has guests in one's house, one treats them
as free and autonomous individuals. All this has been rather briefly
summarized; for more details, see Chapter 4.

These remarks do not remove the difficulties which gave rise to the proposals of Lakoff and McCawley, namely the relationship of constructions
such as [41a–b]. But certain possibilities offered by the standard theory
have not yet been considered. In the framework of Chomsky's first
theory, that of *Syntactic Structures*, the only way of connecting related
sentences of this kind was in fact to derive them transformationally from
the same underlying structure. But as soon as the grammar contains a
lexicon organized along the lines of Chomsky (1965), there are other
possibilities.

In fact, the standard theory admits the necessity of having recourse to
lexical redundancy rules, which extract all the redundant features from
the lexical entries, *ie* all the features which can be predicted by more or
less general rules from other features appearing in the same entries. Such
rules have been familiar in phonology since the early work of Halle and
that of Jakobson still earlier. They are equally necessary in morphology.
A good example is that of grammatical gender in French. It is well known
that in French the grammatical gender of nouns is to a large extent
arbitrary, and not predictable by general rules. The fact that *fauteuil*
(armchair) or *fromage* (cheese) are masculine, *armoire* (cupboard) or *tarte*
(tart) feminine, will have to be marked in the lexical entry of these nouns.
If we use the feature [±MASCULINE] for this, the lexical entries for
fauteuil and *fromage* will contain the feature [+MASC] among others, and
the entries for *armoire* and *tarte* will contain the feature [−MASC]. It is
well known, however, that, for a whole series of cases, grammatical gender
is predictable. The best known case is that of human nouns: normally, all
nouns designating human beings of the male sex are grammatically
masculine, and all those designating human beings of the female sex are
grammatically feminine. This regularity can be expressed by a redundancy rule appearing as an appendix to the lexicon. Let us designate the
semantic feature differentiating beings according to sex by [±MALE].
Instead of having the two features [+MASC, +MALE] in the entry for
garçon (boy), for example, or the two features [−MASC, −MALE] in the
entry for *fille* (girl), it will be sufficient to have, respectively, the features

[+MALE] and [−MALE]. A redundancy rule such as [55] will then provide a means of accounting for the regularity which relates sex and grammatical gender in human nouns:

[55] [+N], [+HUMAN], [α MALE]→[α MASC]
  (where α is a variable on + and −)

There is nothing to prevent us extending the use of the same type of mechanism to syntax (and, if need be, to semantics). To return to the constructions which concern us, [41a–b], transitive and intransitive constructions thus related could both be generated directly in the base. A verb such as *cuire* will be specified in the lexicon as having only the features, for example, of an intransitive verb, say:

[56] *cuire:* [+V], [+ —— #], [+[+F] ——], . . .

(where [+F] covers the set of syntactico-semantic features which are involved in the selectional restrictions of *cuire*). Next, a fairly general redundancy rule will specify that verbs such as *cuire* can also appear in a transitive frame, with the same selectional restrictions on the object as those that they impose on the subject in an intransitive frame. This rule might have the following form:

[57] [+V], [+ —— #], [+[+F] ——], . . . →
  [+V], [+ —— NP], [+ —— [+F]], . . .

(for more details of this rule, see Chapters 3 and 4).

Redundancy rules such as [55] and [57] make it possible to dispense with a large number of features in the lexicon, in the same way as transformations. But, unlike transformations, they operate '*en bloc*' (they are non-ordered) in the lexicon, before the lexical insertion rules.

This method, then, consists of making a more extensive and more systematic use of lexical features. It is the 'lexicalist' hypothesis – as opposed to the 'transformationalist' hypothesis – proposed by Chomsky in his article on nominalizations in English (1970). It can also be used to account for the similarities of distribution and selection described earlier between members of different syntactic categories (nouns and verbs, verbs and adjectives, etc). For example, instead of reducing verbs and adjectives to a single category, or of deriving nominalizations from sentences (*cf* Lees, 1960), nouns, verbs and adjectives can be introduced as such in the base, but with a system of classificatory features (nouns and verbs will have a common feature, and so will verbs and adjectives, etc), and the regularities in question will be formulated in terms of these features. Various studies, as yet unpublished for the most part, are being undertaken from this point of view and seem to be promising (*cf* Bresnan, 1970, 1971, 1972, Selkirk, 1970, etc).

As soon as there is the possibility of recourse to different mechanisms – in this case, transformations or lexical redundancy rules – to deal with the same facts, the problem of justifying the analyses becomes much more acute. Thus, on the basis of a systematic comparison of two types of nominalization in English, 'gerundive nominals' (*cf* [58]) and 'derived nominals' (*cf* [59]), Chomsky (1970) tried to establish certain general criteria for preferring one analysis over the other:

[58] John's refusing the offer

[59] John's refusal of the offer

We see that these constructions differ from several points of view: the productivity of the process, the general nature of the relation between the nominals and the corresponding sentences, and the internal structure of the phrases. Thus, the process by which the 'gerundives' are derived is very productive, the way in which they are related to sentences is very regular, and they have an internal sentence structure. These are exactly the characteristics that would be predicted by an analysis deriving the 'gerundives' transformationally from underlying sentences. On the other hand, the process forming the 'derived nominals' is not very productive (some verbs have no corresponding nouns and vice versa); the relationship between sentences and derived nominals is erratic (from the semantic point of view, for example, the related verbs and nouns diverge in all sorts of odd ways); and lastly, the 'derived nominals' have the internal structure of noun phrases. All this would be predicted by an analysis introducing the 'derived nominals' directly in the base, while dealing in the lexicon with the regularities of their relationship to sentences (by means of redundancy rules), as well as with the peculiarities that differentiate them. Other considerations must be taken into account: for example, normally a transformation can apply to a structure that has already been transformationally derived, whereas, by definition, a redundancy rule establishes a connection between two deep structures generated separately in the base. Thus we should expect to find 'gerundives' with structures derived by transformation, and, further, we should expect the corresponding structures to be impossible for the 'derived nominals'. Now let us look at the following examples, with Chomsky (1970):

[60] *a:* John is eager to please
       b: John's being eager to please
       c: John's eagerness to please

[61] *a:* John is easy to please
       b: John's being easy to please
       c: *John's easiness to please

[62] *a:* John gave a book to Mary
       b: John's giving a book to Mary
       c: John's gift of a book to Mary

[63] *a:* John gave Mary a book
       b: John's giving Mary a book
       c: *John's gift (of) Mary (of) a book

We can make the following observation: [60*a*] and [62*a*] show their elements (subject-predicate, subject – verb – direct object – indirect object) on the surface in the same order and with the same relations as in deep structure; the 'gerundives' [60*b*] and [62*b*] as well as the corresponding 'derived nominals' [60*c*] and [62*c*] are grammatical. On the other hand, it is generally agreed that [61*a*] is derived from *it is easy to please John* by the OBJECT RAISING rule (*cf* Chomsky, 1964); similarly, [63*a*] would be derived from [62*a*] by the DATIVE MOVEMENT rule (see especially Emonds, 1972b). Now, though the corresponding 'gerundives' [61*b*] and [63*b*] are quite grammatical, the corresponding 'derived nominals' [61*c*] and [63*c*] are excluded. These facts conform exactly with the predictions of a theory deriving the 'gerundives' by transformation from underlying sentences and, on the other hand, generating the 'derived nominals' directly in the base. (I have simplified somewhat: certain facts, particularly those relating to the existence of passive 'derived nominals' – *the city's destruction by the enemy*, etc – pose special problems, which are dealt with by Chomsky, 1970.)

3.4

In the lexicalist hypothesis, condition [C] and the level of deep structure are thus preserved, and even take on greater importance than before. Let us now return to the problem raised in section 3.1, by sentences arising from identical deep structures but differing semantically. In most cases, for the advocates of the lexicalist hypothesis, the syntactically justified deep structures, for [31] for example, are those that were first suggested (*cf* note 13). The lexicalist hypothesis thus comes into line with the abandonment of the idea that only deep structures determine meaning. At first sight it might be thought that this is too high a price to pay, the Katz-Postal hypothesis being very strong and therefore very interesting. Nonetheless it must be realized that the renunciation of this idea does not necessarily entail abandoning the hope of describing the relationships between syntax and semantics in a systematic way.

It will be remembered that Katz–Fodor's first idea (1963) was that each syntactic rule should be associated with a semantic rule showing its effect on the interpretation. There were thus two types of projection rules, those associated with the phrase structure rules and those associated with the transformational rules. The hypothesis that transformations preserve meaning enabled this second type of rule to be dispensed with. Moreover, this hypothesis also involved associating the interpretation rules, not directly with the syntactic rules, but with generated structures (in the event, with the deep structures only).

The hypothesis now held by Chomsky, Jackendoff, etc, in the framework of the 'extended standard theory' is that the relationship between syntax and semantics can still be sufficiently constrained by associating the interpretation rules, not with any rule or any stage of the derivation, but only with two levels, on the one hand that of deep structure, and on the other hand that of surface structure.[17] Moreover, the deep structures on the one hand, and the surface structures on the other hand, would determine different and quite specific aspects of the semantic interpretation. An illustration will show what is involved (here I am mainly following Jackendoff, 1969a, 1969b). Let us look again at example [31], which I repeat here for convenience, and let us also consider examples [64] and [65]:

[31] *a:* une seule flèche n'a pas atteint la cible
          only one arrow did not hit the target
       b: pas une seule flèche n'a atteint la cible
          not a single arrow hit the target
       c: la cible n'a pas été atteinte par une seule flèche
          the target was not hit by a single arrow

[64] *a:* un seul manifestant n'a pas été arrêté par la police
          only one demonstrator was not arrested by the police
       b: pas un seul manifestant n'a été arrêté par la police
          not a single demonstrator was arrested by the police
       c: la police n'a pas arrêté un seul manifestant
          the police did not arrest a single demonstrator

[65] *a:* un seul sonnet de Mallarmé n'est pas facile à comprendre
        only one sonnet by Mallarmé is not easy to understand
   b: pas un seul sonnet de Mallarmé n'est facile à comprendre
        not a single sonnet by Mallarmé is easy to understand
   c: il n'est pas facile de comprendre un seul sonnet de Mallarmé
        it is not easy to understand a single sonnet by Mallarmé

Let us first consider [31] alone. If we hold that all these sentences are derived from the same deep structure, we might try to get over the difficulty by associating one or more semantic rules with each of the transformations involved in their derivation: the transformation attaching the negative elements to the auxiliary in [31*a*], that associating *pas* with the subject NP in [31*b*],[18] PASSIVE, and the rule that attaches the negative elements to the auxiliary in [31*c*].

But now look at [64]. [64*a*] means that all the demonstrators except one were arrested by the police; [64*b*] means that no demonstrator was arrested, and [64*c*] is ambiguous, with a dominant reading like that of [64*b*] and another meaning that the police arrested more than one demonstrator.

There is a clear parallelism between [31] and [64],[19] but, looking only at the sentences which have or have not undergone the PASSIVE rule, we see that the active sentences of [31] have parallel interpretations with the passive sentences of [64], and vice versa. In these conditions it seems difficult to associate a constant rule of semantic interpretation with the PASSIVE, since this rule has opposite effects in [31] to those that it has in [64].

Things become even more complicated if we look at [65]. It has been generally agreed (*cf* Chomsky, 1964) that sentences of the type of [65*a–b*] are derived from a deep structure close to [65*c*], by a rule that converts a subordinate clause object into a main clause subject (*cf* example [61] above; see also Kayne, 1969, and Bresnan, 1971). Now, the interpretations of [65*a–c*] again show a striking parallelism with those of [31] and [64]: [65*a*] says that there is only one of Mallarmé's sonnets which is not easy to understand; [65*b*] says that none of Mallarmé's sonnets is easy to understand; and [65*c*] is ambiguous, with the same hierarchy of readings as in [31] and [64]. If we still maintained the idea of associating semantic rules with transformations, we should find ourselves associating very similar interpretative rules with the PASSIVE rule and with the OBJECT RAISING rule, and at the same time complicating these rules as a result of other factors.

Let us look more closely at our examples. We have already noticed that the presence of quantifiers (*une seule flèche*, *un seul manifestant*, etc) helps to disturb the semantic interpretation. Similarly, the complications that negation causes in the interpretation of sentences are well known. Now, all the (*a*) examples have something in common, as do all the (*b*) examples and all the (*c*) examples: namely, that in surface structure, the linear order of the quantifier and the negative is the same in each case: in the (*a*) examples, the quantifier (*un(e) seul(e)*) precedes the negative (*pas*), and in the (*b*) and (*c*) examples, it is the other way round. So there seems to be a regularity there: the semantic interpretation, insofar as it depends on the quantifiers and the negatives, is connected with their order in surface structure, whatever their positions in deep structure may be, and whatever the transformations involved in the derivation. On this basis, Chomsky (1971) formed the hypothesis that, at least so far as the role of negation and the quantifiers is concerned, surface structures, and only surface structures, determine the semantic interpretation; in other words, it is possible to determine the scope of negatives or quantifiers in terms of their position in surface structure (for more details, see Jackendoff, 1969a, 1969b).

On the other hand, there are fundamental aspects of semantic interpretation that still seem to be connected with deep structure: *une seule flèche* in [31], *la police* in [64], are 'agents' of the action expressed by the verb; this aspect of the interpretation remains constant, whatever the position of these elements may be in surface structure, and can be given by interpretation rules which (*cf* above) associate the semantic function of agent with the syntactic function of deep subject. Similar observations about the role of deep objects, etc, could be made.

We thus arrive at a more diversified conception of the relations between syntax and semantics. Some aspects of the semantic representation are determined by the deep structure, some by the surface structure, others by both. A basic aspect of the semantic representation concerns what might be called the 'functional structure of a semantic reading' (*cf* Jackendoff, 1969b); in particular it involves the idea that verbs can be represented semantically as functions; this functional structure brings into play semantic notions such as those of 'agent' and 'patient' of an action, 'location' of a process, 'direction', etc. This part of the semantic representation seems to be determined by the grammatical relations of deep structure; for some interesting suggestions about the interconnection of this functional structure and the grammatical relations, see especially the work of Gruber (1965, 1967) and Jackendoff (1969b) on 'thematic relations' (*cf* Chapter 5).

Nevertheless, other aspects seem to bear no relation to this functional structure, and it is in connection with these aspects that the question of the role of surface structure in semantic interpretation arises. One of these aspects concerns the phenomena of coreferentiality (pronouns, etc) of which I have said nothing here; coreferentiality poses very complicated problems, but it seems that both deep structure and surface structure play a part in it (cf Chomsky, 1971, 1972, Jackendoff, 1969b, Dougherty, 1969, and, for a 'generative semantic' view, Grinder and Postal, 1971). Yet another aspect concerns the facts relating to the distinction between 'focus' and 'presupposition' (cf examples [34–36] above), which seem to be determined by surface structure (cf Chomsky, 1971, Akmajian, 1970, and for the point of view of generative semantics, Lakoff, 1970c). Still other aspects concern the phenomena of 'scope' of negation, quantifiers and certain adverbs; we have just seen that these are also determined by surface structures. Lastly, there is a whole series of aspects connected with the internal structure of NPs: the specific or non-specific character of an NP, the facts relating to generic NPs, the phenomena of 'referential opacity', etc. These facts, which have often been discussed by philosophers (Carnap, Russell, Quine, etc) pose very complicated problems, and it seems that surface structure plays a part in them also (for a recent study of some of these problems, see Jackendoff, 1971a).

3.5 Conclusion

In this rapid survey, I have not been able to do full justice to all the work which has been undertaken and which is still going on. For example, I have said almost nothing about the developments in generative grammar outside the United States, especially in Europe where, in various countries (Great Britain, the Netherlands, France, Germany, Scandinavia, etc), very interesting research has begun.[20] No doubt also I have insisted too much on the opposition between generative semantics and the extended standard theory. In many respects, as I pointed out at the beginning, some of the divergences are purely terminological. The rules of semantic interpretation of surface structures, for example, can often be reformulated as global derivational constraints (cf Lakoff, passim). The most important subject of disagreement, I believe, is still that of the status of deep structure and lexical insertion. On these points, the extended standard theory seems to me decidedly preferable to the theory of generative semantics (see Chapters 4 and 5). Undoubtedly the most striking thing – and the various discussions between advocates of different viewpoints have made a great contribution here – is the level of

sophistication and subtlety that the argument has reached. This has
enabled many concrete examples to be discussed in an illuminating way,
examples which one could not even have dreamed of dealing with in the
framework of traditional grammars, or even in the framework of transformational grammar only a few years ago. At all events, in spite of all the
disagreements, there is still an underlying unity in methods of presenting
arguments and justifying them, among all linguists schooled in generative
grammar of Chomskyan inspiration; this is clearly seen if their work is
compared with that of linguists who still have a different approach, even
those who are primarily concerned with formalization.

Notes

1 I say 'in principle' because, as far as a universal system of semantic representation is concerned, there are serious doubts as to the possibility of constructing such a system; cf some remarks on this subject below, section 3.3.
2 Some recent studies (cf Bierwisch, 1968, Bresnan, 1971) have to a certain
  extent called into question the idea that only the syntactic information
  contained in surface structure is necessary for the phonetic interpretation of
  sentences, but I shall not discuss this here.
3 It will be recalled (cf note 6, Chapter 6, of IGG) that, in the standard theory,
  as opposed to Chomsky's first theory (1957), it is the base component
  which is assigned the role of accounting for the recursive aspects of the
  grammar, by the introduction of recursive symbols (S, but also in some
  versions NP, VP, etc; see especially Dougherty, 1970b).
4 Cf especially Postal, 1970b, Kayne, 1969, Dougherty, 1970b, Bresnan, 1971,
  etc.
5 See especially Ross (1967), and also Kayne (1969), where it is shown that
  the rule placing the clitic pronouns in preverbal position in French is post-
  cyclic.
6 Cf especially Klima, 1964b.
7 Generally speaking, the examples are presented here in a very simplified
  form; a number of technical details are omitted, and the deep structures are
  given in a rather rough form, showing only the elements relevant to the
  discussion.
8 Emonds also considers a less important third type of movement rule, the
  minor movement rules, which do not affect the phrase nodes (see note 9).
9 Emonds divides the syntactic nodes into phrase nodes (= S, NP, VP, AP, PP)
  and nonphrase nodes (N, V, etc); only the first are affected by the constraints in question.
10 This represents a simplification; the facts are rather more complex, but they
  can be reduced to an underlying regularity.
11 Emonds (1970) proposed interpreting the surface structure constraints on
  clitic pronouns within the general framework of his constraints on movement transformations.
12 Lakoff even more recently proposed introducing 'transderivational' constraints into the grammar, which block a derivation if, at some point, it
  interferes with another derivation (cf Lakoff, 1970b, and, for a different view
  of similar facts, Chapter 6 of this book).

13 Following Klima (1964a), the sentences of [31] would all be derived from something like [I]:

[I] NEG — [$_{NP}$ une seule flèche] — [$_{AUX}$ Pres — Perfect] — [$_{VP}$ atteindre la cible]

According to Rosenbaum (1967), [32b] is derived essentially from the same deep structure as [32a] by the rule deleting a subordinate clause subject if identical with the NP of a main clause (EQUI–NP DELETION, cf also Postal, 1970b). [33b] would be derived from [33a] by the CONJUNCTION REDUC-TION rule (cf Gleitman, 1969). [34a and b] would be derived by 'extraction' (cf Gross, 1968) from something like [II]:

[II] c'est Δ que Pierre a frappé Paul
     it is Δ that Peter hit Paul

[35b] could be derived from [35a] by the ADVERBIAL PREPOSING rule which derives [IV] from [III]:

[III] j'ai rencontré Pierre à Paris
      I met Peter in Paris

[IV] à Paris, j'ai rencontré Pierre
     in Paris, I met Peter

Kuroda (1969) suggested deriving sentences of the type of [36] from an underlying structure like [V], by various 'attachment' transformations:

[V] même – Pierre boit du gin avant le petit déjeuner
    even – Peter drinks gin before breakfast

Fillmore (1968) suggested deriving [37a and b] from the same underlying structure (see Anderson's criticism, 1971).

14 Chomsky (1965, 145–6) even suggested a universal constraint that 'no morphological material . . . can be introduced into a configuration dominated by S once the cycle of transformational rules has already completed its application to this configuration'. For other possible applications of this constraint, see Kayne (1969), Dougherty (1970b), Bresnan (1970). Chomsky has recently reformulated this constraint in other terms (see Chomsky, 1973).

15 This represents a simplification. McCawley would in fact derive [45a–b] from an underlying structure such as:

[I] PIERRE CAUSE — PAUL DEVIENT — PAUL EST NON-VIVANT
    PETER CAUSE — PAUL BECOMES — PAUL IS NOT ALIVE

by means of several applications of PREDICATE RAISING (the representation [I] is again very simplified; in particular, it does not take account of verbal tenses).

16 For more extensive research on the lexicon, see Gruber (1965, 1967), and, from a different viewpoint, the work carried out under the direction of Maurice Gross at the Laboratoire d'Automatique documentaire et linguis-tique of the CNRS (cf Gross, 1969).

17 Perhaps it is necessary to bring in another, intermediate, level also, that Postal proposed to call 'shallow structure'; it is defined as the level at which all the cyclic transformations have operated and the operation of post-cyclic rules begins.

18 It might be thought that, in [31b], *pas* is associated with the NP from the deep structure onward, but the fact that this *pas* is never found associated

with an NP other than the subject (*cf *je n'ai rencontré pas une seule personne,
la cible n'a été frappée par pas une flèche, etc) can be explained by the transformational derivation outlined.

19 In reality the facts are more complex. [31c] seems to me also to have a reading
    synonymous with [31a]; an equivalent reading seems to me impossible in
    the case of [64c]; this is perhaps connected with the direct object status of
    un seul manifestant in [64c], as opposed to the prepositional phrase status of
    par une seule flèche in [31c]. [65] also shows some subtle differences in com-
    parison with [31] and [64]: [65a] could, I think, be ambiguous. I shall not
    take these complications into account here.

20 For an overall picture of generative linguistics in Europe, see Kiefer and
    Ruwet, eds (1973).

Chapter 2

The syntax of the pronoun *en* and the 'subject-raising' transformation*

1

In this chapter I should like to demonstrate at least two things in connection with a very specialized and apparently very limited problem. Firstly, only systematic reference to data arising from the intuition of native speakers – to their judgment as to whether or not such and such a sequence of words is a well-formed French sentence – can reveal certain strange and interesting facts which must be accounted for by an adequate grammar of French, but which could only with difficulty be discovered by research limited to the study of a finite corpus. Secondly, whereas a grammar of the distributional type, for example, which confines itself to classifying linguistic elements into various categories and describing the permitted sequences, can at most only say what are the observed facts, a grammar with more powerful and abstract procedures, such as transformational rules, can not only describe the facts, but, in a sense, explain them. Indeed, the apparently very strange facts that will be discussed here follow naturally from the hypothesis that the linguistic competence of native speakers of a language can only be described by a grammar which includes at least a level of surface structure and a level of deep structure, the two levels being related by ordered transformations.

2

The preverbal (clitic) pronouns of French have already been closely studied by transformationalists (*cf* Gross, 1968; Kayne, 1969, forth-

* Revised and expanded version of an article which appeared in *Langue française* (Paris, Larousse) 6 (1970), 70–83, under the title 'Notes sur la syntaxe du pronom *en* et d'autres sujets apparentés.'

coming). These studies have shown that the preverbal pronouns are noun phrases in the deep structure, occupying the 'normal' positions of noun phrases (subject, direct object, indirect object, etc), and that their preverbal position must be reached by one or more transformations which, in effect, move them from their original position and attach them to the left of the main verb. Thus, the deep structure of [1] would be something like [2], which strongly resembles [3]:

[1] Pierre le lui donnera
     Peter will give it to him

[2] Pierre donnera le à lui

[3] Pierre donnera le livre à Paul
     Peter will give the book to Paul

These rules are also applicable to the preverbal pronoun *en*, which corresponds to the preposition *de* followed by a noun phrase reduced to a pronoun, *cf* [4]:

[4] *a:* j'en parle
        I am speaking of it
     b: je parle de cela
        I am speaking of that

One of the peculiarities of *en*, which distinguishes it from the other clitic pronouns, is that the sequence *de NP* which corresponds to it in the deep structure may be found either to the right of the verb, as in [4] or [5], or to the left as in [6] (in this case, *en* corresponds to a noun phrase complement of the subject):

[5] *a:* Noam a écrit la préface de ce livre
        Noam has written the preface of this book
     b: Noam en a écrit la préface
        Noam has written the preface of it

[6] *a:* la préface de ce livre est trop flatteuse
        the preface of this book is too flattering
     b: la préface en est trop flatteuse
        the preface of it is too flattering

I shall deal here with certain peculiarities of the distribution of *en* when, as in [6], it has its origin in a complement of the subject. Let us recall firstly (*cf* Gross, 1968, 25) that there are a certain number of restrictions on the possibility of having *en* in this case. These restrictions arise,

sometimes from the nature of the element of which the *de NP* source of *en*
is the complement (*cf* [7] as compared with [8]):

[7] *a:* plusieurs de ces livres sont exécrables
         several of these books are appalling
     b: *plusieurs en sont exécrables

[8] *a:* j'ai lu plusieurs de ces livres
         I have read several of these books
     b: j'en ai lu plusieurs
         I have read several of them

sometimes from the nature of the verb to which *en* is attached (*cf* [9–10]):

[9] *a:* la cheminée de l'usine est penchée
         the factory chimney is leaning
     b: la cheminée en est penchée

[10] *a:* la cheminée de l'usine fume
         the factory chimney smokes
     b: ? la cheminée en fume

If *en* has its origin in a complement situated on the right of the verb,
there are not the same limitations. The conditions in which *en* arising
from the subject is unacceptable are not clear, and no doubt there are
variations between one informant and another. In general, *en* is always
acceptable when the verb is *être*.

3

I shall not concern myself here with these restrictions, which are of an
obscure nature, but with another class of facts. There is a whole series of
verbs, apparently very different from each other, if only from the semantic point of view – but which all have a complement in the infinitive (which
may or may not be preceded by a preposition) in the surface structure,
and which show the following peculiarity: if the subject of these verbs
includes a noun phrase complement of the form *de NP*, and if we replace
this complement by *en*, the resulting sentences are ungrammatical if *en*
precedes the verb in question, but they are grammatical if, as it were, *en*
'jumps over' the main verb and is attached to the infinitival complement.
As these verbs are very varied, I must give a fairly long list of examples:

[11] *a:* l'auteur de ce livre va devenir célèbre
         the author of this book is going to become famous
     b: *l'auteur en va devenir célèbre
     c: l'auteur va en devenir célèbre

[12] *a:* la solution de ce problème vient d'être trouvée
      the solution of this problem has just been found
      b: *la solution en vient d'être trouvée
      c: la solution vient d'en être trouvée

[13] *a:* la porte de la cathédrale semble être fermée
      the door of the cathedral seems to be shut
      b: *la porte en semble être fermée
      c: la porte semble en être fermée

[14] *a:* la solution de ce problème $\begin{Bmatrix} \text{doit} \\ \text{peut} \end{Bmatrix}$ être simple

      the solution of this problem $\begin{Bmatrix} \text{must} \\ \text{may} \end{Bmatrix}$ be simple

      b: *la solution en $\begin{Bmatrix} \text{doit} \\ \text{peut} \end{Bmatrix}$ être simple

      c: la solution $\begin{Bmatrix} \text{doit} \\ \text{peut} \end{Bmatrix}$ en être simple

[15] *a:* l'auteur de ce livre commence à être célèbre
      the author of this book is beginning to be famous
      b: *l'auteur en commence à être célèbre
      c: l'auteur commence à en être célèbre

[16] *a:* la solution de ce problème mérite d'être publiée
      the solution of this problem deserves to be published
      b: *la solution en mérite d'être publiée
      c: la solution mérite d'en être publiée

[17] *a:* l'auteur de ce livre mérite d'être célèbre
      the author of this book deserves to be famous
      b: *l'auteur en mérite d'être célèbre
      c: l'auteur mérite d'en être célèbre

[18] *a:* les conditions du traité menacent d'être dures
      the conditions of the treaty threaten to be severe
      b: *les conditions en menacent d'être dures
      c: les conditions menacent d'en être dures

[19] *a:* la lecture de ce livre promet d'être passionnante
      reading this book promises to be fascinating
      b: *la lecture en promet d'être passionnante
      c: la lecture promet d'en être passionnante

[20] *a:* les circonstances de la rencontre risquent d'être désagréables
   the circumstances of the meeting risk being unpleasant
 b: *les circonstances en risquent d'être désagréables
 c: les circonstances risquent d'en être désagréables

[21] *a:* l'histoire de la révolution exige d'être écrite
   the history of the revolution needs to be written
 b: *l'histoire en exige d'être écrite
 c: l'histoire exige d'en être écrite

[22] *a:* la solution de ce problème est susceptible d'être révisée
   the solution of this problem is liable to be revised
 b: *la solution en est susceptible d'être révisée
 c: la solution est susceptible d'en être révisée

I have presented all the (*b*) examples as ungrammatical and all the (*c*) examples as grammatical. In reality the facts are more complex, and the distinction must be understood as relative: on the whole, the (c) examples are better than the (*b*) examples, and this is the central fact which must be explained. But the (*c*) examples are sometimes doubtful. This is perhaps the case with [17*c*], and if we compare [17*c*] with [16*c*], we might perhaps be led to make certain distinctions according to the nature [$\pm$ANIMATE] (or [$\pm$ HUMAN]) of the head noun of the subject NP.

Moreover, certain (*b*) examples (especially [11*b*], [14*b*]) are acceptable to certain informants. But here archaisms are involved. It is known that the distribution of clitic pronouns was different in earlier periods in the history of the French language. In the seventeenth century sentences such as [11*b*] or [14*b*] were acceptable, in the same way as [23*b*–24*b*], which are not admissible today:

[23] *a:* Pierre $\begin{Bmatrix} \text{peut} \\ \text{doit} \end{Bmatrix}$ faire ce travail

  Peter $\begin{Bmatrix} \text{can} \\ \text{must} \end{Bmatrix}$ do this work

 b: *Pierre le $\begin{Bmatrix} \text{peut} \\ \text{doit} \end{Bmatrix}$ faire

 c: Pierre $\begin{Bmatrix} \text{peut} \\ \text{doit} \end{Bmatrix}$ le faire

  Peter $\begin{Bmatrix} \text{can} \\ \text{must} \end{Bmatrix}$ do it

[24] *a:* Pierre veut tuer cet homme
      Peter wants to kill this man
    b: *Pierre le veut tuer
    c: Pierre veut le tuer
      Peter wants to kill him

We shall not be concerned here with the reasons for these diachronic differences. Finally, we must note, to avoid all confusion, that sentences containing *en* are often ambiguous, because of the diversity of the possible sources of *en* (noun phrase complement, indirect object with *de*, different types of adverbials). Thus [25a] is ambiguous, where *en* may correspond to a complement of the subject, as in [25b], or to a causal adverbial, as in [25c]:

[25] *a:* l'auteur en est devenu célèbre
    b: l'auteur de ce livre est devenu célèbre
      the author of this book has become famous
    c: l'auteur est devenu célèbre $\begin{cases} \text{à cause de cela} \\ \text{de ce fait} \end{cases}$
      the author has become famous $\begin{cases} \text{because of this} \\ \text{for this reason} \end{cases}$

Also, a sentence such as [16b] may be grammatical if it is interpreted as referring to something like [26] rather than to [16a]:

[26] de ce fait, la solution mérite d'être publiée
    for this reason, the solution deserves to be published

I shall return later to certain implications of these observations relating to the possible ambiguity of *en* (*cf* [44] and section 10).

Whatever may be the case with these additional complexities, what view must the linguist take of facts such as those of [11–22]? He could confine himself to stating them, as I have done up to now, in as much detail as possible. Let us recognize that even this represents a considerable advance on traditional grammars, which, if I am not mistaken, have never mentioned these facts (they are not referred to by either Sandfeld or Martinon (1927), although they made many interesting observations on preverbal pronouns). This is probably not just a matter of chance: it is a question of the actual type of facts which emerge only if one's aim is to formulate explicit rules accounting for the intuitions of the native speaker, and to consult these intuitions systematically while varying certain data (here, the place of the pronoun *en*). There is a risk that this type of fact will go unnoticed if we confine ourselves to observing a corpus.

In any case, if we merely note the facts, we go no further than the level of observational adequacy (*cf* Chomsky, 1965). We must also describe them in a simple and systematic way; and especially try to explain this strange distribution of *en*. There must be a systematic principle at work behind these facts. Only when we have revealed this principle can we claim to have given an account of the competence of native speakers of French.

4

I said earlier that a transformational grammar accounts for the distribution of clitic pronouns by means of rules which move them from their original position of noun phrase (or prepositional phrase, in the case of *en* and *y*), and attach them to the left of the main verb in the same simple sentence. In the most usual case of pronouns having their origin in the base to the right of the verb, the rule will be in the following form (*cf* Kayne, 1969, forthcoming):

[27] CLITIC-PLACING:

$$X - V - Y - PRO - Z$$

1	2	3	4	5
⇒ 1	4+2	3	Ø	5

Notice that from this point of view the 'auxiliaries' *être* and *avoir* behave like main verbs, *cf:*

[28] *a:* Pierre a rencontré Paul
     Peter met Paul
   b: Pierre l'a rencontré
     Peter met him
   c: *Pierre a le rencontré

[29] *a:* Pierre a trouvé la solution de ce problème
     Peter has found the solution of this problem
   b: Pierre en a trouvé la solution
   c: *Pierre a en trouvé la solution

[30] *a:* Pierre est venu de Paris
     Peter has come from Paris
   b: Pierre en est venu
     Peter has come from there
   c: *Pierre est en venu

In the case of *en* having its origin in a complement of the subject, we shall have a rule which moves a prepositional pro-phrase from left to right. Let us call this rule the EN-AVANT rule:[1]

[31] EN-AVANT:

$$X - \left[_{NP} \quad Y - \left[\begin{matrix} PP \\ PRO \end{matrix}\right]\right] - Z - V - W$$

1	2	3	4	5	6
⇒ 1	2	∅	4	3+5	6

PRO, then, here stands for the prepositional pro-phrase of which the phonological form is *en*. For the reasons for treating *en*, and likewise *y*, as prepositional pro-phrases, see Kayne (1969, forthcoming). At first sight, if we consider the sentences of [6], for example, it seems incorrect to talk about a movement rule: *en* apparently stays in the same place as the *de NP* to which it corresponds, and we can only talk of substitution of *en* for *de NP*. Nevertheless, we have only to consider the facts of [32] to see that *en* must have been moved:

[32] *a:* la solution de ce problème n'a pas été publiée
           the solution of this problem has not been published
      b: *la solution en n'a pas été publiée
      c: la solution n'en a pas été publiée

Moreover, Kayne (1969, forthcoming) has a certain number of arguments according to which the preverbal pronouns must be attached to the verb, in such a way that they are dominated by the node V. This is incompatible with a simple substitution of *en* for *de NP*, without movement.

We might envisage accounting for the facts of [11–22] by means of a constraint on the application of this EN-AVANT rule. The constraint would run somewhat as follows: 'in certain conditions, *en* jumps over the main verb and is attached to the subordinate verb'. The trouble is that it is very difficult to formulate these conditions at all precisely. Obviously, it is not sufficient to say that *en* jumps over the main verb if this verb is accompanied by an infinitive complement, as the following examples show:

[33] *a:* l'auteur de ce livre a oublié d'être à l'heure
              (pour signer le service de presse)
           the author of this book has forgotten to be on time
              (to sign the press copies)
      b: ?l'auteur en a oublié d'être à l'heure
      c: *l'auteur a oublié d'en être à l'heure

[34]   *a:* le chef de la révolte a daigné être magnanime
           the leader of the rebellion condescended to be magnanimous
       b: ?le chef en a daigné être magnanime
       c: *le chef a daigné en être magnanime

Examples [33*b*], [34*b*], are not very good, because of constraints arising
from the nature of the verb (*cf* [9–10]); but it is clear that examples
[33*c*], [34*c*] are altogether excluded. Notice that [33–34] preclude us from
formulating the constraint on EN-AVANT by saying that it is the presence
of certain subordinate verbs, especially *être*, which 'attracts' *en*.

Certain examples might suggest that the condition depends on the
nature, animate or inanimate, of the head noun of the subject of which *en*
is the complement, *cf* [35–36] as against [18–19]:

[35]   *a:* le chef de cette bande a menacé les révoltés d'être impitoyable
           the leader of this band threatened the rebels that he would be
               merciless
       b: ?le chef en a menacé les révoltés d'être impitoyable
       c: *le chef a menacé les révoltés d'en être impitoyable

[36]   *a:* le chef de la police a promis d'être magnanime
           the chief of police promised to be magnanimous
       b: ?le chef en a promis d'être magnanime
       c: *le chef a promis d'en être magnanime

(I shall return to these examples later, *cf* section 11.)

But if this distinction seems to play a part, which is in any case not
clear, examples such as [15] and [17] are enough to show that it is in-
sufficient. Consider also the following sentences:

[37]   le chef doit en être courageux
       the leader of it must be brave

[38]   l'auteur semble en être stupide
       the author of it seems to be stupid

[39]   l'auteur risque d'en rester inconnu[2]
       the author of it risks remaining unknown

Thus, if we wish to account for the facts by means of conditions on the
application of EN-AVANT, these conditions will have to be very complex:
they will have to include a list of the verbs (*aller, sembler, menacer*, etc)
which allow *en* to pass over them, and in addition, for certain of these
verbs (*menacer, promettre*, etc) restrictions connected with the nature

(animate/non-animate) of their subject, plus perhaps still more restrictions. But even supposing it possible to formulate these conditions, we
should still only have stated the facts, not explained them. Moreover,
certain other facts show that things are even more complicated, *cf:*

[40] *a:* les conditions du traité semblent commencer à être susceptibles
        d'être adoucies
        the conditions of the treaty seem to be starting to be likely to be
        eased
      b: *les conditions en semblent commencer à être susceptibles d'être
        adoucies
      c: *les conditions semblent en commencer à être susceptibles d'être
        adoucies
      d: *les conditions semblent commencer à en être susceptibles d'être
        adoucies
      e: les conditions semblent commencer à être susceptibles d'en être
        adoucies

[41] *a:* la solution du problème risque de devoir être révisée
        the solution of the problem risks having to be revised
      b: *la solution en risque de devoir être révisée
      c: *la solution risque d'en devoir être révisée
      d: la solution risque de devoir en être révisée

These examples show that, if verbs of the class which allow *en* to pass
over them are embedded one below the other, *en* must pass over them
all, however many there are; apparently, *en* must be able to jump over an
indefinite number of these verbs, and the condition on EN-AVANT must
be able to control whether or not the embedded verbs belong to this
class. A condition of this sort is rather strange, and even if it could be
formulated, once again it would amount only to repeating the observed
facts, without giving any explanation of them.

In view of the following facts:

[42] *a:* l'auteur de ce livre semble être intelligent
        the author of this book seems to be intelligent
      b: l'auteur semble en être intelligent
        the author of it seems to be intelligent

[43] *a:* Pierre semble avoir donné ce livre à Paul
        Peter seems to have given this book to Paul
      b: Pierre semble le lui avoir donné
        Peter seems to have given it to him

we could say that *en* 'is placed in the same position as other preverbal pronouns'. But this solution (supposing that it could be precisely formulated) breaks down in view of a sentence such as [44b]:

[44] *a:* la solution de ce problème a failli être publiée de ce fait
  the solution of this problem missed being published for this
  reason
b: la solution en a failli en être publiée

In fact, in [44b], it is the *en* on the left of *a failli* which is interpreted as corresponding to *de ce fait*, and the *en* which is attached to *être publiée* which is interpreted as corresponding to the complement of the subject. The two *en*'s have apparently crossed over. It will be seen later that with the solution I propose, [44b] poses no problem; on the contrary, it helps to confirm the validity of that solution (see below, section 10).

5

There is in fact a simple way of accounting for the distribution of *en* without introducing special constraints on the EN-AVANT rule. But for this two things are necessary. First, it must be admitted that the deep structure of sentences [11–22] is more abstract than one might think; in particular it is quite different from the surface structures [11a–22a]. Secondly, it will be necessary to bring in several ordered transformations to generate [11c–22c]. This might appear to be a complication, but we shall see that other facts, apparently not connected with the distribution of *en*, will be clarified at the same time.

To understand what I am aiming at, we must first make a detour. Consider the following pairs of sentences:

[45] *a:* Justine a giflé le marquis
  Justine slapped the Marquis
b: le marquis a été giflé par Justine
  the Marquis was slapped by Justine

[46] *a:* il est difficile de corrompre la concierge
  it is difficult to bribe the concierge
b: la concierge est difficile à corrompre
  the concierge is difficult to bribe

[47] *a:* il semble que Jean-François n'a rien compris à la démonstration
  it seems that Jean-François did not understand the demonstration
    at all

b: Jean-François semble n'avoir rien compris à la démonstration
Jean-François seems not to have understood the demonstration
at all

The transformationalists (see Chomsky, 1957, 1964; Rosenbaum,
1967) have proposed to generate the (*b*) sentences, not directly, by phrase
structure rules, but indirectly, by deriving them from (structures underlying) the corresponding (*a*) sentences, by means of various transformations (for example PASSIVE in the case of [45*b*]). These sentences then
have this in common, that an NP which, in surface structure, appears as
the subject of the verb, is not the subject of this verb in the deep structure.
Thus, in [45], *le marquis* is the object of the verb *gifler* in deep structure; in
[46], *la concierge* is the object of the subordinate verb *corrompre* and finally
becomes the subject of the main verb; in [47], *Jean-François* is first the
subject of the subordinate clause and becomes the subject of the
main clause.

It is important to note that this type of transformational derivation is
not justified solely by semantic arguments – that there is a relationship
of paraphrase between examples (*a*) and (*b*) in each case; furthermore we
know that sentences connected by such a relationship as this are not
always in the relationship of paraphrase (*cf* Chapter 1). The identity of
selectional restrictions in examples (*a*) and (*b*) would not be a sufficient
argument to justify this derivation, either (but see below, section 7).
The important point is that there are also syntactic arguments in favour
of this transformational analysis. Here is one, inspired by an argument
suggested for English by Chomsky, 1970.

Normally, in French, a common noun cannot appear in the position
of noun phrase unless preceded by a determiner; *cf* [48–51]:

[48] $\left.\begin{matrix} \text{la} \\ *\emptyset \end{matrix}\right\}$ justice est inflexible

justice is inflexible

[49] $\left.\begin{matrix} \text{le} \\ *\emptyset \end{matrix}\right\}$ tort tue

error kills

[50] Pierre a mangé $\left\{\begin{matrix} \text{cette} \\ *\emptyset \end{matrix}\right\}$ pomme

Peter ate that apple

[51] Ernestine se consacre à $\left\{\begin{matrix} \text{l'} \\ *\emptyset \end{matrix}\right\}$ assistance aux filles
publiques repenties

Ernestine devotes herself to helping reformed prostitutes

Nevertheless, there are a certain number of exceptions to this rule. Among these exceptions we find a series of expressions, of a somewhat idiomatic character, which contain a transitive verb, of general semantic content, followed by a 'direct object' reduced to a noun without article *cf: faire plaisir* (to give pleasure, to please), *faire peur* (to frighten), *avoir soif* (to be thirsty), *avoir honte* (to be ashamed), *prendre garde* (to take care), *perdre courage* (to lose heart), *donner soif* (to make (someone) thirsty), etc. Mostly, these expressions are fixed, in the sense that they cannot be subjected to various transformational processes, *cf:*

[52] *a:* Jules a repris haleine
        Julius got his breath back
      b: *haleine a été reprise par Jules

[53] *a:* Justine a crié grâce
        Justine cried for mercy
      b: *grâce semble avoir été criée par Justine

[54] *a:* il est facile de prendre froid dans ce pays
        it is easy to catch cold in this region
      b: *froid est facile à prendre dans ce pays

Nevertheless, for certain of these expressions there are corresponding passive sentences, *cf:*

[55] *a:* le roi a rendu justice sous un chêne
        the king dispensed justice beneath an oak tree
      b: justice a été rendue par le roi sous un chêne
        justice was dispensed by the king beneath an oak tree

[56] *a:* on a prêté assistance aux personnes sans abri
        people gave help to the homeless
      b: assistance a été prêtée aux personnes sans abri
        help was given to the homeless

[57] *a:* tout le monde a donné tort à Gilles de Rais
        everyone attributed blame to Gilles de Rais
      b: tort a été donné par tout le monde à Gilles de Rais
        blame was attributed by everyone to Gilles de Rais

Some of these sentences may appear clumsy, or may belong to a peculiar style. The important thing is that they are possible, whereas [52b–54b] are totally excluded. This difference must be accounted for.
As examples [48–51] show, nouns such as *justice, tort, assistance*, etc,

cannot appear without a determiner except in sentences of the type [55–57], *ie* in active sentences, as the object of certain specific verbs, and in passive sentences, as the subject of these same verbs. However unusual in character these exceptions may be, there is clearly a regularity there which can be expressed by a grammar deriving passive sentences, by transformation, from corresponding active sentences. On the other hand, a grammar which did not establish a connection between active and passive sentences would be obliged to treat as separate facts the existence of sentences [55*a*–57*a*] on one side, and that of sentences [55*b*–57*b*] on the other; such a grammar would be incapable of expressing the fact that, if for example [55*b*] is possible, while [48] is not, it is, in a sense, for the same reason that [55*a*] is possible; in other words, this grammar would be incapable of formulating a certain generalization on French grammar. Facts of this sort, then, provide a purely syntactic argument in favour of the existence of the passive transformation in French.

Similar facts are perceptible in constructions analogous to those of [46] and [47], *cf:*

[58] *a:* il est difficile de rendre justice
it is difficult to dispense justice
b: justice est difficile à rendre
justice is difficult to dispense

[59] *a:* il semble que tort a été donné à la police
it seems that blame was laid on the police
b: tort semble avoir été donné à la police
blame seems to have been laid on the police

Sentences such as [58*b*], [59*b*] are easily explained if we derive them, respectively, from structures underlying [58*a*], [59*a*]. Let us consider [59], which brings in one of the verbs that interest us (*cf* [13] above). Let us assume that the underlying structure of sentences whose main verb is *sembler*, whether in [47*a* or *b*], or [59*a* or *b*], is of the following form:

[60] [$_s$ Δ sembler [$_s$NP VP]]

where Δ represents a 'dummy' subject. We introduce the following optional transformation:

[61] SUBJECT-RAISING (optional):

$$\Delta \;-\; \text{sembler} \;-\; [_s\text{NP} - \text{X}] \;-\; \text{Y}$$

1	2	3	4	5
⇒ 3	2	Ø	4	5

To generate [47*b*], we start from the deep structure [62], and rule [61] will convert this into [47*b*]:

[62] [$_S$ Δ semble [$_{S2}$ [$_{NP}$ Jean-François] $_{VP}$[n'avoir rien compris à la démonstration]]]

If rule [61] has not been applied to [62], a late rule will insert *il* in place of the dummy subject Δ, and other rules (insertion of *que*, etc) will finally account for sentence [47*a*]. Notice that I have simplified things; in particular I have not taken into account the precise way in which the verbal tenses should be shown. This point is not of importance for what directly concerns us here. Further, term 2 of the structure index of [61] should not mention *sembler*, but a class of verbs which includes also *paraître* (to appear), *s'avérer* (to profess (oneself to be . . .)), *se révéler*, (to be revealed), etc (see Gross, 1968).

In the case of [59], we shall have the following derivation. Starting from the deep structure [63*a*], we apply the passive transformation in the subordinate clause, which gives [63*b*]; then, the application of SUBJECT-RAISING gives [63*c*], which is identical with [59*b*]. If SUBJECT-RAISING were not applied, we should have [64].

[63] *a:* Δ semble [$_S$ Δ avoir donné tort à la police]
     b: Δ semble [$_S$ tort avoir été donné à la police]
     c: tort semble avoir été donné à la police

[64] il semble que tort a été donné à la police

6

We are now in a position to explain the problem posed by the distribution of *en*. Let us return to example [13], which I reproduce here:

[13] *a:* la porte de la cathédrale semble être fermée
     b: *la porte en semble être fermée
     c: la porte semble en être fermée

If, as for [47] and [59], we admit that the underlying structure of [13*a*] is [65], we shall derive [13*a*] by applying SUBJECT-RAISING to [65]; if we do not apply this rule, we get [66]:

[65] [$_S$ Δ semble [$_S$[$_{NP}$ la porte de la cathédrale] [$_{VP}$ être fermée]]]

[66] il semble que la porte de la cathédrale est fermée

Further, the deep structure of [13c], which differs from [13a] only by the presence of a pronoun instead of the NP *la cathédrale*, will be [67]:

[67] [$_S$ Δ semble [$_S$[$_{NP}$ la porte de PRO] [$_{VP}$ être fermée]]]

Notice that, if we do not apply the SUBJECT-RAISING rule, the EN-AVANT rule applies normally in the subordinate clause, without being subject to a special condition, which gives the grammatical sentence [68]:

[68] il semble que la porte en est fermée

We see, then, that it is sufficient to order the EN-AVANT rule *before* the SUBJECT-RAISING rule in order automatically to obtain the correct sentence [13c] and eliminate the ungrammatical sentence [13b]. In fact, starting from [67], we shall first obtain (by EN-AVANT) structure [69]:

[69] [$_S$ Δ semble [$_S$[$_{NP}$ la porte] [$_{VP}$ en être fermée]]]

Then SUBJECT-RAISING will convert [69] into [13c]. The crucial point here is the fact that, with the application of SUBJECT-RAISING, the NP subject of the subordinate clause (term 3 of the structure index of [61]) is reduced to *la porte*, because of the previous application of EN-AVANT, which detached *de* PRO from the NP subject and attached it to the VP (ultimately to the verb).

My hypothesis, then, is that the two transformations, EN-AVANT and SUBJECT-RAISING – which in any case are each necessary in their own right to account for [9b] or [47b], for example – are applied in the order:

(1) EN-AVANT
(2) SUBJECT-RAISING

Moreover – and this is a crucial point – I think that this type of derivation which, as we have just seen, allows the generation of [13c] and the exclusion of [13b], must also enable us to account for the other examples of [11–22]. In other words, I claim that the SUBJECT-RAISING rule intervenes in their derivation, which amounts to saying that the subjects of these sentences in surface structure are not their subjects in deep structure.

For example, I will say that the underlying structure of [18a], instead of being very like its surface structure, is the following:

[70] Δ menace [$_S$ les conditions du traité être dures]

It is the application of SUBJECT-RAISING that will account for [18a]. The absence of [18b] and the grammaticality of [18c] would then be described in exactly the same way as the absence of [13*b*] and the existence of [13*c*].

Yet, at first sight, examples of the type of [18] – and, in fact, all the examples of [11–22] except [13] – pose a problem that [13] did not pose. In fact, what made the derivation of [13] by means of the SUBJECT-RAIS-ING rule immediately plausible was the existence alongside [13*a*] of a well-formed sentence such as [66]. As we have seen, in the case of *sembler*, *paraître*, *se révéler*, etc, the SUBJECT-RAISING rule is optional; whether or not it is applied, the result is always grammatical, and we always have a well-formed surface structure. But it is not the same for the other cases in [11–22], since in relation to [14], [16] or [18] for example, we have none of the following sentences:

[71] *il $\left\{\begin{array}{l}\text{peut}\\ \text{doit}\end{array}\right\}$ que la solution de ce problème soit simple

[72] *il mérite que la solution de ce problème soit publiée

[73] *il menace que les conditions du traité soient dures

We must say, then, that the SUBJECT-RAISING rule is obligatory for all the verbs of the type of [11–22], with the exception of *sembler*, *paraître* and some others. In other words, we should have to mark all these verbs, in the lexicon, with a *rule feature* [+ SUBJECT-RAISING]. This sort of mechanism is provided for by generative theory, and Lakoff (1970c) has constructed a complete formalization to deal with it. One may be obliged to resort to it in a whole series of cases. It is nonetheless the case that we have here a very powerful mechanism, which should in principle be regarded as very costly. One should only have recourse to it as a last extreme, if there are no other means of proceeding, or if one really has other good reasons for doing so. In the case with which we are dealing, this solution seems, at first sight, even more awkward because it appears that all we have done is to move the difficulty from one place to another: instead of saying that the verbs *pouvoir*, *devoir*, *menacer*, *commencer*, etc, are exceptions to the EN-AVANT rule, we have marked them as excep-tional in relation to the SUBJECT-RAISING rule (exceptional in the sense that they require the obligatory application of a normally optional rule).

We therefore have to justify the proposed analysis of sentences [11–22] by other arguments. The question is to determine whether or not this analysis enables us to explain other peculiarities of the syntax of the verbs *pouvoir*, *devoir*, *commencer*, etc. If it can be shown that, by setting up deep structures of the type of [70] and bringing in the SUBJECT-RAISING transformation, we can explain certain facts, which are in principle different from the distributional peculiarities of *en* and independent of them, that analysis will be justified, and the cost of resorting to 'rule features' will be offset.

Let us note in passing that, if sentences [71–73] are ungrammatical, we nevertheless find French sentences which differ only slightly from them, such as:

[74] il faut que la solution de ce problème soit simple

[75] il se peut que la solution de ce problème soit simple

Moreover, I have the intuitive impression that the ungrammaticalness of sentences such as [71–73] is accidental. It seems unlikely that the structure of French would be greatly upset if such sentences became acceptable. The absence of such sentences is more suggestive of accidental 'gaps' than of a deep regularity (*cf* the peculiarities of 'neutral' verbs treated in Chapter 3). If these are really accidental gaps, the treatment that we propose, which results in marking the verbs *menacer*, etc, in the lexicon as exceptional, would be appropriate. But, of course, these intuitions cannot by themselves be sufficient to justify this treatment. Other arguments are necessary.

7

Let us point out, first of all, that, quite independently of the question raised in French by the distribution of *en*, certain linguists (Garcia, 1967; Perlmutter, 1970, 1971) have proposed a derivation similar to the one that we have just put forward, for the English equivalents of some of our verbs, namely for aspectuals such as *begin*, etc (*cf* [15]). I will not give a detailed account of the arguments advanced, but most of them are valid also for French. Thus, a verb like *commencer* does not impose selectional restrictions on its surface subject. Most verbs do not accept any subject without discrimination:

[76] *a:* la foule s'est attroupée
        the crowd gathered
      b: les badauds se sont attroupés
        the idlers gathered
      c: *l'archevêque s'est attroupé
        *the Archbishop gathered

[77] *a:* l'archevêque aime la musique pop
        the Archbishop likes pop music
      b: *mon couteau de cuisine aime la musique pop
        *my kitchen knife likes pop music

Verbs must be classified according to whether or not they require a collective (or plural) subject, like *s'attrouper*, a human subject, like *aimer*, etc. But a verb like *commencer* can have any subject at all; or more precisely, the constraints on the surface subject of *commencer* are in fact determined by the nature of the verb that forms the complement of *commencer*, *cf*:

[78] *a:* la foule a commencé à s'attrouper
        the crowd began to gather
      b: les badauds ont commencé à s'attrouper
        the idlers began to gather
      c: *l'archevêque a commencé à s'attrouper
        *the Archbishop began to gather

[79] *a:* l'archevêque commence à aimer la musique pop
        the Archbishop is beginning to like pop music
      b: *mon couteau de cuisine commence à aimer la musique pop
        *my kitchen knife is beginning to like pop music

[80] mon couteau de cuisine commence à rouiller
      my kitchen knife is beginning to rust

This is exactly what is predicted if the deep structure of sentences with *commencer* is as we have assumed, say:

[81] $[_{S1} \Delta$ commencer $[_{S2} \ldots]]$

The impossibility of having [78c] or [79b] is explained by exactly the same reasons that exclude [76c] or [77b] – *ie* by the selectional constraints between subject and verb within S_2 – and the fact that any noun phrase can be the subject of *commencer* would be explained by the absence of constraint on the operation of SUBJECT-RAISING.

The same remarks apply in general to the other verbs of [11–22] and to related verbs, *cf* for example:

[82]   la foule ⎫   ⎧ menace(nt) ⎫
         les badauds ⎬ ⎨   ⎬ de s'attrouper
        *l'archevêque ⎭   ⎩ risque(nt) ⎭

              the crowd ⎫
               the idlers ⎬ threaten(s) to gather
          *the Archbishop ⎭

                              ⎧ the crowd   ⎫
        there is a risk that ⎨ the idlers   ⎬ will gather
                              ⎩ *the Archbishop ⎭

[83]   l'archevêque⎱ continue à aimer la musique pop
    *mon couteau de cuisine⎰

    the Archbishop⎱ continues to like pop music
    *my kitchen knife⎰

[84] *a:*   cette décision⎱ concerne Paul
        *la soeur de Pierre⎰

    this decision⎱ concerns Paul
    *Peter's sister⎰

b: cette décision ⎧semble   ⎫
     *la soeur de Pierre ⎨risque de ⎬ concerner Paul
                          ⎪commence à ⎪
                          ⎩pourrait   ⎭

    this decision   ⎧seems to   ⎫
    *Peter's sister ⎨is liable to ⎬ concern Paul
                     ⎪begins to   ⎪
                     ⎩could   ⎭

A particularly striking case of the same phenomenon is presented by the verb *barder*, in its popular intransitive use; normally, this verb admits only the pronoun *ça* as its subject, *cf:*

[85] *a:* ça barde drôlement entre Octave et Gudule
        there's a devil of a row going on between Octave and Gudule
    b: *il barde entre Justine et le marquis
        *it rages between Justine and the Marquis
    c: *Staline barde avec Trotsky
        *Stalin is raging with Trotsky
    d: *la situation barde vachement
        *the situation is raging furiously

We find exactly the same restrictions on the surface subject of *commencer*, *menacer*, *risquer*, etc, if these verbs have *barder* as complement, *cf:*

[86] *a:* ça a commencé à barder vers deux heures du matin
        things began to get stormy about two o'clock in the morning
    b: ça menace de barder ferme du côté de la Palestine
        serious trouble threatens from Palestine
    c: *il a commencé à barder du côté de chez Swann
        *it began to rage down Swann's way

    d: *les néo-fascistes commencent à barder avec la police
      *the neo-Fascists are beginning to rage with the Police
    e: *la situation menace de barder en Irlande du Nord
      *the situation threatens to rage in Northern Ireland

These facts, too, can without difficulty be submitted to an analysis
which starts from deep structures such as [70] and derives the surface
structure from them by SUBJECT-RAISING. To account for [85] and [86]
at the same time, it will be enough to mark *barder* in the lexicon as being
able to take as subject only the pronoun *ça*. The same reasoning could be
applied to sentences in which the 'impersonal' subject *il* appears. The
meteorological verbs *neiger, pleuvoir*, etc, permit only *il* as subject. Again,
we find sentences such as:

[87] $\left.\begin{array}{l} \text{il} \\ \text{*Dieu} \end{array}\right\}$ a commencé à neiger

    $\left.\begin{array}{l} \text{it} \\ \text{*God} \end{array}\right\}$ began to snow

[88] $\left.\begin{array}{l} \text{il} \\ \text{*le temps} \end{array}\right\}$ menace de pleuvoir

    $\left.\begin{array}{l} \text{it} \\ \text{*the weather} \end{array}\right\}$ threatens to rain

Sentences such as those of [89] would be treated in the same way:

[89] il $\left\{\begin{array}{l} \text{commence à} \\ \text{risque de} \end{array}\right\}$ y avoir trop de monde ici

    there $\left\{\begin{array}{l} \text{begin to be} \\ \text{risk being} \end{array}\right\}$ too many people here

Let us note in passing that these sentences, in which *il* has undergone
SUBJECT-RAISING, show that the expression *il y a* is not so fixed as some
have maintained.[3]

7.1

In principle, grammatical theory, in its present state, would enable the
facts of selection that we have been discussing to be treated in another
way. We know that the grammar of French, like that of English, must
contain another transformation, called *equivalent noun phrase deletion*
(more simply EQUI; see Rosenbaum, 1967, Gross, 1968, Postal, 1970b);

this rule deletes a subordinate subject if it is coreferential with an NP of the main clause. It generates [90a] from the underlying structure [90b]:[4]

[90] *a:* Pierre veut partir
       Peter wants to leave
      b: Pierre$_i$ veut [$_S$ PRO$_i$ partir]

This transformation is necessary to account for the following paradigm:

$$[91] \quad a: \text{je veux} \begin{cases} \text{que} \begin{cases} \text{tu} \\ \text{il} \\ \text{*je} \end{cases} \text{parte(s)} \\ \text{partir} \end{cases}$$

$$b: \text{tu veux} \begin{cases} \text{que} \begin{cases} \text{*tu} \\ \text{il} \\ \text{je} \end{cases} \text{parte(s)} \\ \text{partir} \end{cases}$$

$$c: \text{Pierre}_i \text{ veut} \begin{cases} \text{que} \begin{cases} \text{tu} \\ \text{je} \\ \text{*il}_i \end{cases} \text{parte(s)} \\ \text{partir} \end{cases}$$

With a main verb such as *vouloir*, it is impossible to have a subject in the subordinate clause coreferential with the main subject; in every case, in place of this gap in the paradigm, we find a complement in the infinitive, and the sense of the sentence in question corresponds to that of the impossible sentence.

The EQUI transformation enables us to account for sentences such as:

[92] Pierre veut être présenté à Paul par Marie
      Peter wants to be introduced to Paul by Mary

Such sentences pose no problem if we start from the deep structure [93a]. We first apply PASSIVE in the subordinate clause, which gives [93b], and then EQUI converts [93b] into [92]:

[93] *a:* Pierre$_i$ veut [$_S$ Marie présenter PRO$_i$ à Paul]
      b: Pierre$_i$ veut [$_S$ PRO$_i$ être présenté à Paul par Marie]

Certain verbs require, not only the obligatory application of EQUI if the subordinate subject is coreferential with an NP of the main clause, but also the obligatory coreferentiality of the subordinate subject and a main NP; this is the case for verbs of motion, such as *partir*, or for verbs like *oser*, *cf:*

[94] *a:* Pierre est parti travailler
       Peter has left to work
    b: *Pierre est parti que Paul travaille
       *Peter has left for Paul to work

[95] *a:* le marquis n'a pas osé frapper Justine
       the Marquis did not dare to strike Justine
    b: *le marquis n'a pas osé que le jeune page frappe Justine
       *the Marquis did not dare that the young page strike Justine

It is apparently necessary, therefore, to impose a constraint on these verbs, requiring the coreferentiality of the subordinate subject and the main subject, which makes the application of EQUI obligatory.

Once the existence of this constraint is admitted, we can consider extending it to verbs such as *menacer*, *commencer*, *pouvoir*, etc. Let us look again at the examples of [86]. *Barder* being marked in the lexicon as permitting only one subject, *ça*, only underlying structures such as [96] would satisfy this constraint, and that would explain the facts of selection noted earlier:

[96] *a:* [$_{NP}$ ça] commence à [$_S$ [$_{NP}$ ça] barder]
    b: [$_{NP}$ ça] menace de [$_S$ [$_{NP}$ ça] barder]

The two analyses, the one applying EQUI, and the one applying SUBJECT-RAISING, would thus be equally adequate at the observational level. However – independently of the arguments which are to follow – certain facts of selection incline us to favour the analysis using SUBJECT-RAISING. We have seen that, in general, verbs impose selectional restrictions on their subjects or their objects. Verbs such as *commencer*, *pouvoir*, etc, are exceptional in this respect. Now, in general, verbs which permit or require the EQUI transformation on their complement, also impose restrictions on their subject, restrictions which are independent of the nature of the subordinate verb, *cf:*

[97] l'archevêque ⎱ estime que ⎰ la foule s'est dispersée trop tôt
      *ce camembert ⎰   ⎱ Paul n'a rien compris
                                   la solution du problème est fausse

      the Archbishop ⎱ considers that ⎰ the crowd broke up too soon
      *this Camembert ⎰   ⎱ Paul understood nothing
                                          the solution of the problem is
                                            wrong

Estimer, like *croire*, *vouloir*, etc, requires a human subject. This means that, in general, in a sentence with an embedded substantival clause that has undergone EQUI, the class of possible subjects will be the intersection of the class of possible subjects of the main verb and of the class of possible subjects of the subordinate verb, *cf* [98], where the subject must be at the same time [−SEMANTICALLY SINGULAR] and [+HUMAN]:

[98] la foule
      les badauds
      *l'archevêque   estime(nt) s'être dispersé(e)(s) trop tôt
      *ce camembert

      the crowd
      the idlers   consider(s) it has (they have) (he has) been
      *the Archbishop   dispersed too soon
      *this Camembert

In the case of verbs such as *partir* or *oser*, the coreferentiality constraint, to which they are subject, obviously prevents us from determining independently which selectional restrictions are due to the main verb and which are due to the subordinate verb. It is clear, nevertheless, that *partir* or *oser* impose their own restrictions on their subjects, [5]*cf*:

[99]   Pierre
        le train   est parti pour Paris
        *ce camembert

        Peter
        the train   left for Paris
        *this Camembert

[100]   Pierre
        *le train   a osé une plaisanterie risquée
        *ce camembert

        Peter
        *the train   ventured a risky joke
        *this Camembert

In a general way, then, the analysis of a construction in terms of EQUI tends to predict that the selectional restrictions on the subject are a function both of the selectional restrictions imposed by the main verb and of the restrictions imposed by the subordinate verb. An analysis in terms of SUBJECT-RAISING, on the other hand, predicts that the selectional restrictions are a function solely of the subordinate verb. Even if both analyses enable us to describe the facts of selection noted in the preceding section, the analysis in terms of SUBJECT-RAISING has a greater explanatory power. The analysis by EQUI would predict that it is a chance occurrence if *partir* or *oser* impose their own restrictions while *commencer* or *menacer* do not.

One more point. It is not certain that recourse to the joint action of the coreferentiality constraint and of the EQUI transformation is the best way of accounting for the behaviour of *partir* or *oser*. The syntactic arguments which justify the introduction of EQUI into the grammar are essentially those that we have briefly recalled (*cf* [91–93]). EQUI enables us to regularize certain paradigms, by excluding sentences such as **je veux que je parte*, at the same time establishing a connection between these impossible forms and sentences such as *je veux partir*. Moreover, EQUI must be applied to structures that have already undergone transformations, such as the PASSIVE. But these arguments are inoperative for verbs like *partir* or *oser*. The absence of sentences such as [94*b*], [95*b*], removes the problem posed by the irregular paradigm [91]. Moreover, it is impossible to embed transformationally derived structures under *partir* or *oser*, *cf*, in contrast with [92], the impossibility of:

[101] *Pierre part être frappé par Paul

[102] *Pierre ose être présenté à Paul par Marie

Partir and *oser*, then, require not only that the subordinate subject should be coreferential with the main subject, but further that it should be a deep subject, and not a derived one (for other examples, see Chapter 3, section 5).

In these conditions, we may ask whether it would not be better to generate sentences such as [94*a*–95*a*] directly in the base, by means of the rule VP→V VP. Moreover, as we have already seen, *sembler*, *commencer*, *pouvoir*, *menacer*, etc, are not subject to the constraint referred to above. *Cf* [59–63], [12], [16], [22], etc.[6]

8

Let us turn to another type of argument. It is in fact the same as the one that we developed in section 5 on the subject of *sembler*. Parallel to sentences [55–59], the following grammatical sentences are found:

[103] hommage va être rendu au Prix Nobel de la Paix
       tribute will be paid to the Nobel Peace Prize

[104] monts et merveilles viennent d'être promis par le premier ministre
wonders have just been promised by the Prime Minister

[105] assistance doit être portée aux gauchistes en péril
help must be sent to the Left in danger

[106] tort ne peut pas ne pas être donné aux affameurs du peuple
blame cannot escape being laid on those who starve the people

[107] hommage commence à être rendu aux obscurs précurseurs de la
pataphysique
tribute is beginning to be paid to the obscure forerunners of 'pata-
physics'†

[108] justice ne mérite pas d'être rendue dans ces conditions
justice does not deserve to be done under these conditions

[109] tort risque (menace) d'être donné à l'opposition de Sa Majesté
blame risks being (threatens to be) laid on His/Her Majesty's
Opposition

[110] assistance doit commencer à être portée aux nécrophiles repentis
help must begin to be given to reformed necrophiliacs

[111] justice commence à risquer de ne jamais être rendue
justice begins to risk never being done

It is clear that, if the deep subject of all these verbs was identical with
their surface subject, it would be difficult to explain how these sentences
are possible – while, of course, sentences such as [112–114] are entirely
excluded; if we generate these sentences from a deep structure of the
type of [70], and with obligatory application of SUBJECT-RAISING,
there is no problem; [103–111] will be generated in the same way as [55*b*–
59*b*], and [112–114] will be excluded for the same reasons that [48–54]
are excluded:

[112] *tort doit tuer
*error must kill

[113] *haleine commence à être reprise par Jules
*breath begins to be got back by Julius

[114] *soif risque d'être donné à Nicolas par cette conférence
*thirst risks being caused to Nicolas by this lecture

† 'La pataphysique' – Alfred Jarry's science of 'solutions imaginaires'; *cf*
Jarry, *Gestes et Opinions du Docteur Faustroll, Pataphysicien, roman néo-
scientifique* (Éditions Fasquelle, Paris, 1911). [*Translator's note*]

9

Another argument in favour of the analysis by SUBJECT-RAISING is provided by certain facts relating to the distribution of the interrogative element *quel*. *Quel* is normally a determiner, *cf*:

[115]   *a:* quelle femme porte encore des corsets aujourd'hui?
           what woman still wears corsets nowadays?
      b: quels films de Fritz Lang as-tu vus plus de trois fois?
           what films of Fritz Lang's have you seen more than three times?
      c: à quelle décision Pierre s'est-il arrêté?
           to what decision did Peter come?

Nevertheless *quel* can appear alone, as an NP, if it is the subject of a predicative sentence with *être*, of which the predicate is an NP, *cf*:

[116]   *a:* quel est le meilleur livre de James Joyce?
           what is James Joyce's best book?
      b: quelle est la couleur favorite de Picasso?
           what is Picasso's favourite colour?
      c: *quel est venu hier?
      d: *quelle porte des minijupes?
      e: *quel est furieux?
      f: *quel as-tu rencontré hier?
      g: *à quel penses-tu?

But this very strict and very strange rule admits exceptions. *Quel* can be the subject of a sentence of which the main verb is *aller*, *venir de*, *sembler*, *pouvoir*, *devoir*, etc, if the infinitive complement consists of the verb *être* followed by an NP predicate:

[117]   *a:* quelle va $\begin{cases} \text{être l'issue de cette guerre?} \\ \text{*porter des minijupes?} \end{cases}$

        what is going to $\begin{cases} \text{be the result of this war?} \\ \text{*wear miniskirts?} \end{cases}$

      b: quel semble $\begin{cases} \text{être le meilleur livre de James Joyce?} \\ \text{*être venu hier?} \end{cases}$

        what seems $\begin{cases} \text{to be James Joyce's best book?} \\ \text{*to have come yesterday?} \end{cases}$

      c: quelle pourrait bien $\begin{cases} \text{être la bonne solution?} \\ \text{*faire taire ce bavard?} \end{cases}$

what might well $\begin{cases} \text{be the right solution?} \\ \text{*silence this chatterer?} \end{cases}$

d: quel risque d' $\begin{cases} \text{être le résultat de ces élections?} \\ \text{*arriver demain?} \end{cases}$

what is liable $\begin{cases} \text{to be the outcome} \\ \quad \text{of these elections?} \\ \text{*to arrive (happen)} \\ \quad \text{tomorrow?} \end{cases}$

These facts, which would be very difficult to explain otherwise, are the automatic consequence of analysis by SUBJECT-RAISING.[7] The restriction on the distribution of *quel* as NP will be formulated uniquely in terms of the context/ —— *être* NP, and the SUBJECT-RAISING transformation will convert the deep structure [118], for example, into [117*b*]:

[118] Δ semble $[_S[_{NP}$ quel] être le meilleur livre de James Joyce]

10

In this section, I shall look at some fairly complex sentences; it will be seen that the proposed analysis provides a very simple way of deriving them.

For the sake of convenience, let us repeat the examples of [41] above, which we shall consider first:

[41]   *a*: la solution du problème risque de devoir être révisée
       b: *la solution en risque de devoir être révisée
       c: *la solution risque d'en devoir être révisée
       d: la solution risque de devoir en être révisée

For [41*a*] we will assume the following deep structure:

[119] $[_{S_0} \Delta$ risque $[_{S_1} \Delta$ devoir $[_{S_2} \Delta$ réviser la solution du problème]]]

We then apply successively to [119]: (i) PASSIVE in S_2, giving [120*a*]; (ii) SUBJECT-RAISING in S_1, giving [120*b*]; (iii) SUBJECT-RAISING in S_0, giving [41*a*]:

[120]   *a*: $[_{S_0} \Delta$ risque $[_{S_1} \Delta$ devoir $[_{S_2}$ la solution du problème être révisée]]]
       b: $[_{S_0} \Delta$ risque $[_{S_1}$ la solution du problème devoir être révisée]]

Let us turn to [41*d*]. This time the underlying structure will be [121]:

[121] $[_{S_0} \Delta$ risque $[_{S_1} \Delta$ devoir $[_{S_2} \Delta$ réviser la solution de PRO]]]

We shall then have the following transformations – i: PASSIVE in S_2, giving [122a]; ii: EN-AVANT in S_2, giving [122b];[8] iii: SUBJECT-RAIS-ING in S_1, giving [122c];[9] iv: SUBJECT-RAISING in S_0, giving [41d]. As the EN-AVANT rule can only operate in S_2, [41b] and [41c] cannot be generated.

[122] a: $[_{S_0} \Delta$ risque $[_{S_1} \Delta$ devoir $[_{S_2}$ la solution de PRO être révisée]]]
        b: $[_{S_0} \Delta$ risque $[_{S_1} \Delta$ devoir $[_{S_2}$ la solution en être révisée]]]
        c: $[_{S_0} \Delta$ risque $[_{S_1}$ la solution devoir en être révisée]]

Now taking sentences [123] and [124]:

[123] Pierre risque de devoir en réviser la solution

[124] Pierre risque de vouloir en réviser la solution

The deep structure of [123] will be [125]:

[125] $[_{S_0} \Delta$ risque $[_{S_1} \Delta$ devoir $[_{S_2}$ Pierre réviser la solution de PRO]]]

To this structure we then apply successively – i: CLITIC-PLACING in S_2,[10] giving [126a]; ii: SUBJECT-RAISING in S_1, giving [126b]; iii: SUBJECT-RAISING in S_0, giving [123].

[126] a: $[_{S_0} \Delta$ risque $[_{S_1} \Delta$ devoir $[_{S_2}$ Pierre en réviser la solution]]]
        b: $[_{S_0} \Delta$ risque $[_{S_1}$ Pierre devoir en réviser la solution]]

The deep structure of [124] will be [127]:

[127] $[_{S_0} \Delta$ risque $[_{S_1}$ Pierre$_i$ vouloir $[_{S_2}$ PRO$_i$ réviser la solution de PRO]]]

We shall have the successive transformations – i: CLITIC-PLACING in S_2, giving [128a]; ii: EQUI in S_1, giving [128b]; iii: SUBJECT-RAISING in S_0, giving [124].

[128] a: $[_{S_0} \Delta$ risque $[_{S_1}$ Pierre$_i$ vouloir $[_{S_2}$ PRO$_i$ en réviser la solution]]]
        b: $[_{S_0} \Delta$ risque $[_{S_1}$ Pierre vouloir en réviser la solution]]

Finally, let us consider the sentences of [44], given again here:

[44] a: la solution de ce problème a failli être publiée de ce fait
       b: la solution en a failli en être publiée

The underlying structures of [44a] and [44b] will be, respectively, [129] and [130]:

[129] $[_{S_0} \Delta$ avoir failli $[_{S_1} \Delta$ publier la solution de ce problème] de ce fait]

[130] $[_{S_0} \Delta$ avoir failli $[_{S_1} \Delta$ publier la solution de PRO] de PRO]

[129] will undergo the successive transformations – i: PASSIVE in S_1, giving [131]; ii: SUBJECT-RAISING in S_0, giving [44a].

[131] $[_{S_0}$ Δ avoir failli $[_{S_1}$ la solution de ce problème être publiée] de ce fait]

As for [130], it will undergo successively – i: PASSIVE in S_1, giving [132a]; ii: EN-AVANT in S_1, giving [132b]; iii: SUBJECT-RAISING in S_0, giving [132c]; iv: CLITIC-PLACING in S_0, giving [44b].

[132] a: $[_{S_0}$ Δ avoir failli $[_{S_1}$ la solution de PRO être publiée] de PRO]
        b: $[_{S_0}$ Δ avoir failli $[_{S_1}$ la solution en être publiée] de PRO]
        c: $[_{S_0}$ la solution avoir failli en être publiée de PRO]

Thus the 'cross-over' of the two *en*'s in [44b] is explained quite naturally. Each of them is attached to the left of the main verb of the simple sentence to which it belongs, in conformity with the general principle governing the placing of clitic pronouns.

11

It must be admitted that it would be an excessive simplification to claim that all the verbs of [11–22] enter only into deep structures of the type of [70]. If this theory seems to be correct at least for the verbs of [11–14], it needs to be amended for verbs such as *menacer* or *promettre*, more particularly. But this amendment will itself give us a better understanding of a number of interesting facts about the syntax and the semantics of these verbs and at the same time will make the proposed analysis more convincing. Let us take the case of *menacer*. This verb appears, in surface structure, in two types of syntactic 'frames' (see Gross, 1968, 1969), represented respectively by [133] and [134] ([18] also is an example of the second frame):

[133] le marquis a menacé Justine de la fouetter
         the Marquis threatened Justine that he would whip her

[134] a: la maison menace de s'écrouler
          the house threatens to collapse
        b: l'enquête menace d'être longue
          the enquiry threatens to be lengthy
        c: la situation menace d'empirer
          the situation threatens to deteriorate

THE SYNTAX OF THE PRONOUN 'EN'

At first sight, the second frame seems to be only a variant of the first, without a direct object, and the formula of the syntactic frame in which *menacer* enters could be [137], taking into account [135–136]:

[135] le marquis a menacé Justine
       the Marquis threatened Justine

[136] la $\left\{\begin{array}{l}\text{pluie}\\\text{guerre}\end{array}\right\}$ menace

       $\left.\begin{array}{l}\text{rain}\\\text{war}\end{array}\right\}$ threatens

[137] NP V (NP) (*de* VP)

But the position is more complex. Let us note firstly that, in the case of [133], there is no reason to postulate a deep structure much different from the surface structure (with one reservation, to which I shall return shortly). In fact, first of all, the NP object has all the characteristics of a deep object: possibility of becoming the subject of a passive sentence (*cf* [138*a*]), and of being pronominalized as *le* or *la* (*cf* [138*b*]). It can also be absent (*cf* [138*c*]):

[138] *a:* Justine a été menacée par le marquis d'être fouettée[11]
           Justine was threatened by the Marquis with being whipped
       b: le marquis l'a menacée de la fouetter
           the Marquis threatened her that he would whip her
       c: le marquis a menacé de la fouetter
           the Marquis threatened to whip her

Further, the sequence *de VP* displays the properties of a prepositional phrase: it can be pronominalized by means of *en* (cf [139*a*]), relativized as *dont* (*cf* [139*b*]), made interrogative as *de quoi* (*cf* [139*c*]), and cleft (*cf* [139*d*]):

[139] *a:* le marquis en a menacé Justine
           the Marquis threatened Justine with it
       b: ce dont le marquis a menacé Justine, c'est de la fouetter
           what the Marquis threatened Justine with was whipping her
       c: de quoi le marquis a-t-il menacé Justine?
           with what did the Marquis threaten Justine?
       d: c'est de la fouetter que le marquis a menacé Justine
           it was with whipping her that the Marquis threatened Justine

Moreover, it is possible to have a noun phrase in place of the VP on the right of *de*, *cf:*

[140] *a:* le marquis a menacé Justine de mort
      the Marquis threatened Justine with death
    b: le marquis a menacé Justine de son fouet[12]
      the Marquis threatened Justine with his whip

This fact might lead us to think that at some stage the VP of [137] must be dominated by NP.

Again, the grammaticality of sentences such as [138*a*] indicates that it would be incorrect to confine ourselves simply to [137] as the deep syntactic frame of [133]. As we saw earlier (*cf* section 7.1, especially the discussion of example [92],) this sentence indicates that *menacer* takes as complement a sentence, of which the subject obligatorily undergoes the EQUI rule. The deep structure of [133] would then be [141]:

[141] $[_{NP}$ le marquis$_i$] $[_V$ a menacé $][_{NP}$ Justine$_j$] $[_{PP}$ $[_P$ de] $[_{NP}$ $[_S$ PRO$_i$
     fouetter PRO$_j$]]]]

This deep structure is certainly very different from that proposed in [70] above. But, in fact, apart from the arguments given earlier in favour of [70], we shall see that there are several reasons for thinking that constructions of the type of [134] are very different from the type [133]. One of the ways of describing this difference is to set up two distinct deep structures: one – of the type of [141] (with or without a direct object present) – will be used for sentences like [133]; the other, of the type of [70], will be used for cases like [134].

Let us note, firstly, that while it is possible to omit the object in [133], (*cf* [138*c*]), it is impossible to introduce one in [134]. All the following sentences are ungrammatical:

[142] *a:* *la maison menace le propriétaire de s'écrouler
      *the house threatens the owner with collapsing
    b: *l'enquête menace les détectives d'être longue
      *the enquiry threatens the detectives with being lengthy
    c: *la situation menace le doyen d'empirer
      *the situation threatens the Dean with deteriorating

Secondly, contrary to what happens in [139–140], there is no reason to postulate an NP or a PP underlying the *de VP* of [134]. All the tests which succeed for [133] fail here:

[143] *a:* *la maison en menace (de s'écrouler)
    b: *ce dont la maison menace, c'est de s'écrouler

c: *de quoi menace la maison?

d: *c'est de s'écrouler que la maison menace

Lastly, some at least of the sentences having the form NP *menacer de* VP (without a direct object) are ambiguous. This ambiguity is obvious, for example, in [144] which can be approximately paraphrased either by [145*a*] or by [145*b*]:

[144] le Liechtenstein menace d'envahir Monaco
      Liechtenstein threatens to invade Monaco

[145] *a:* le Liechtenstein menace Monaco de l'envahir
          Liechtenstein threatens Monaco with invasion
      b: le Liechtenstein risque d'envahir Monaco
          Liechtenstein risks (looks like) invading Monaco

Another example is found in [146], which can be approximately paraphrased by [147*a*] or by [147*b*]:

[146] les gauchistes menacent de faire un scandale
      the Left threaten to cause a scandal

[147] *a:* les gauchistes menacent les autorités de faire un scandale
          the Left threaten the authorities with causing a scandal
      b: les gauchistes risquent de faire un scandale
          the Left risk causing a scandal

Notice that the verb *promettre*, which could have a very similar analysis to the one we have made of *menacer*, shows the same occurrences of ambiguity; *cf* [148] which can be approximately paraphrased by [149*a* or *b*]:

[148] ce jeune garçon promet de devenir un grand artiste
      this young lad promises to become a great artist

[149] *a:* ce jeune garçon a promis à ses parents de devenir un grand artiste
          this young lad has promised his parents to become a great artist
      b: ce jeune garçon a des chances de devenir un grand artiste
          this young lad has the potentiality of becoming a great artist

All these facts are clarified if we agree that *menacer* enters into two different deep structures. There will therefore be two verbs *menacer* in the lexicon, which will be marked respectively by features [150] and [151]:

[150] *menacer*$_1$: $\begin{cases} [+\text{———} (\text{NP}) (de \text{ NP}) \text{ (where the last NP can dominate} \\ \text{S)} \\ [+[+\text{ANIMATE}] \text{———}] \\ [+\text{———} [+\text{ANIMATE}]] \end{cases}$

$$[151] \quad menacer_2: \begin{cases} [+ \; \Delta \text{ —— } S] \\ [+ \text{OBLIGATORY SUBJECT-RAISING}] \end{cases}$$

Menacer$_1$ appears in [133]. The features of [150] enable us to account for the distributional, transformational and selectional characteristics that we have pointed out. *Menacer*$_2$ appears in [134], and obligatorily undergoes the SUBJECT-RAISING rule. The selectional constraints on *menacer*$_1$, the absence of a direct object in [151] and the absence of any selectional restrictions imposed by *menacer*$_2$, explain both the ungrammaticalness of [142] and the ambiguity of [144] and [146] (in [144] names of countries can be treated as animates). Finally, let us observe that there is a clear difference in meaning between *menacer*$_1$ and *menacer*$_2$: the first implies that the subject 'expresses a threat' (*menace*),[13] which is obviously not the case for *menacer*$_2$.

Let us return once more to the distributional peculiarities of *en*. We have seen that the deep structure into which *menacer*$_2$ enters and the order (1) EN-AVANT, (2) SUBJECT-RAISING allow us to explain the facts of [18], etc. But, on the other hand, we noticed the different behaviour of *en* in [35–36]. I repeat [35] here:

[35] *a:* le chef de cette bande a menacé les révoltés d'être impitoyable
       the leader of this band threatened the rebels that he would be
       merciless
   b: ?le chef en a menacé les révoltés d'être impitoyable
   c: *le chef a menacé les révoltés d'en être impitoyable

We are now in a position to account for these differences, which have no direct connection with the distinction animate/inanimate. The sentences of [35] in fact have the same type of deep structure as [133], either [152a or b] (corresponding respectively to [35a and b]):

[152] *a:* [$_{NP}$ le chef de cette bande]$_i$ a menacé les révoltés de [$_S$ PRO$_i$ être impitoyable]
   b: [le chef de PRO]$_i$ a menacé les révoltés de [$_S$ PRO$_i$ être impitoyable]

It is the application of EQUI that converts [152a] into [35a]. The application of the same rule and that of EN-AVANT to [152b] gives [35b]. The important point is that, as the *de* PRO phrase corresponding to *en* is in the subject of the main clause from the start, it is impossible for it to jump over the main verb, *menacer*, and be attached to the subordinate verb. Hence the ungrammaticalness of [35c]. If [35b] is not perfect either, this fact is due to the special constraints on EN-AVANT, relating to the nature of the verb to which *en* is attached, which we pointed out in section 2.

11.1

The analysis that we have just suggested leaves several problems unsolved. The first concerns the status of *de* in sentences of the type [134]. We have seen that there was no reason to introduce this *de* into the deep structure. The question is to decide how it is introduced. The same problem arises for the *de* of *risquer de*, *venir de*, etc, and for the *à* of *commencer à*, etc. In fact it is more general and does not concern only the verbs which interest us here, *cf* the paradigm:

[153] *a:* travailler ici est impossible
    to work here is impossible
  b: il est impossible de travailler ici
    it is impossible to work here
  c: *il en est impossible

The formalization of generative theory in its present state is rich enough to allow the introduction of these 'prepositions', by marking the verbs as having special features (*menacer$_2$* will be marked [+DE], *commencer* [+A], etc) and 'spelling out' these features as morphemes by late rules. But this procedure remains *ad hoc* and explains nothing. In particular, it cannot be a matter of chance that *de* appears in the surface structure of *menacer$_2$* as in that of *menacer$_1$*. This type of problem, which is very general, (for numerous examples, see Gross, 1968, 1969) has so far resisted every attempt at systematization, and I shall not discuss it further here.

A second problem concerns the existence beside [134] of sentences such as [136]:

[136] la $\begin{Bmatrix} \text{pluie} \\ \text{guerre} \end{Bmatrix}$ menace

  $\begin{Bmatrix} \text{rain} \\ \text{war} \end{Bmatrix}$ threatens

These sentences are very close in meaning to sentences of the type [134], such as:

[154] *a:* il menace de pleuvoir
    it threatens to rain
  b: la guerre menace d'éclater
    war threatens to break out

It might be useful to unify these phenomena by proposing for sentences [134], not the deep structure [70], but structure [155]:

[155] NP *menacer*

where the subject NP could dominate an S. (If it does not dominate S, it would be subject to rather severe selectional restrictions). Structures of the type [70] would be derived from it by the EXTRAPOSITION rule, which is necessary in other respects (see Gross, 1968), and the SUBJECT-RAISING rule would be applied afterwards. That I did not suggest this deep structure from the start was because there are other verbs for which the deep structure [70] is justified; this is the case for *sembler*, *risquer*, etc (for *sembler*, see Gross, 1968). In fact, these verbs never appear as intransitive verbs with an NP subject, *cf*:

[156] *a:* *la folie de Pierre semble
  b: il semble que Pierre est fou
   it seems that Peter is mad

[157] *a:* *la pluie risque
  b: il risque de pleuvoir
   there is a risk of rain

On the other hand, a verb like *commencer* behaves like *menacer*$_2$ from this point of view, *cf*:

[158] le concert⎱ a commencé
   la guerre⎰

  the concert⎱ has begun
   the war ⎰

We could, then, account for these differences between the verbs of [11–22] by giving them different deep structures and marking them differently in the lexicon. *Risquer*, for example, would have the features [159] (which are those that we first attributed to *menacer*$_2$, *cf* [151]), and *menacer*$_2$ or *commencer* would have the features [160]:

[159]: *risquer:* [+ Δ —— S]
     [+ OBLIGATORY SUBJECT-RAISING]

[160] *menacer*$_2$ ⎱ . [+ NP —— #]
  commencer ⎰ ᐧ [+ OBLIGATORY EXTRAPOSITION][14]
      [+ OBLIGATORY SUBJECT-RAISING]

However, these facts would still need a more searching analysis, as would the question whether other verbs of [11–22], apart from *menacer* and *promettre*, need a double analysis in terms of EQUI and SUBJECT-RAISING (see Perlmutter, 1970, 1971; Newmeyer, 1969, 1970).

This double analysis, again, raises one more problem. By distinguishing two verbs *menacer* in the lexicon, we have been able to explain a certain number of facts, but at the same time we have given up the unity of *menacer*. To suggest the two lexical entries [150] and [151] (or [160]), amounts to saying that *menacer*₁ and *menacer*₂ are two homonyms, which, intuitively, seems unsatisfactory. There is clearly a connection of meaning between these two verbs. Later on (*cf* Chapter 3) we shall see cases where it is possible to account for a relationship between lexically distinct verbs in terms of lexical redundancy rules. But these rules apply to fairly large classes of verbs. Clearly, such a rule applying only to *menacer*₁ and *menacer*₂ would be no more economical than directly setting up two distinct lexical entries. The solution of this problem therefore requires a more searching analysis of all the verbs of class [11–22].

Let us note, however, that the proposed analysis of *menacer* enables us to make an important advance towards a correct semantic interpretation both of *menacer*₁ and *menacer*₂, at the same time suggesting a connection between them. According to Chomsky (1965), the only grammatical relations which contribute to semantic interpretation are the grammatical relations defined in deep structure. Now, if we look once again at the two deep structures attributed to *menacer*, we see that, in one case (*menacer*₁), the deep structure defines three grammatical relations in which the verb participates: subject-verb, verb-direct object, and verb-'complement'. If we use the theory of 'thematic functions' stated by Gruber (1965, 1967) and Jackendoff (1969b) (see Chapter 5 below), it seems quite natural to interpret, in [133], the subject *le marquis* as 'agent' of the threat (*menace*), the object *Justine* as 'patient' or 'goal' of this threat, and the complement (*le marquis*) *fouetter* (*Justine*) as 'theme' of the threat. On the other hand, the configuration of deep structure in which *menacer*₂ belongs (whether we analyse it as in [151] or as in [160]), defines only one grammatical relation, and it seems quite natural to identify this relation with the one linking the verb to the 'complement' in the case of *menacer*₁. In other words, in [134a] for example, *la maison . . . s'écrouler* would be interpreted as the 'theme' of the threat, and it would be meaningless to talk of an 'agent' or a 'patient'. In the same way, in [136] *la pluie* or *la guerre* would be interpreted as 'themes' of the threat. This seems intuitively fairly satisfactory. But much remains to be done before these remarks can be precisely formulated and integrated into a unified semantic theory.

12

By way of conclusion, I should like to return to the question of the descriptive and explanatory validity of the transformational model, mentioned in section 1.

The transformational model is descriptively adequate in the sense that it has enabled us to describe, by means of some fairly simple rules, a collection of very varied facts: the distribution of *en*, the distribution of *quel* as subject, the existence of idiomatic expressions of the type of [55–59], [103–111], various selectional restrictions, the syntactic differences between [138–139] and [142–143], the ambiguity of [144], [146], etc. It has, therefore, enabled us to give a reasonably unified view of a collection of facts which undeniably form part of the linguistic competence of native speakers of French.

The model has an explanatory value in the following sense. The idea that, in order adequately to describe natural languages, linguistic theory must provide certain specific concepts, and that the grammars of these languages must have a determined form – containing, especially, a level of deep structure and a level of surface structure, linked by transformational rules of a certain form, linearly ordered, etc – was developed from observations (mainly on English, *cf* Chomsky, 1957) which had nothing to do with the facts that have been concerning us. What is important is that, once the general theory has these concepts at its disposal, the facts relating to the distribution of *en*, for example, strange as they may seem at first sight, are exactly the sort of facts that we would expect to find if this theory is correct. In a sense, the theory predicts and explains them.

Notes

1 From now on in this text, for reasons of exposition, I shall always refer to *de* PRO rather than to $\left\{{PP \atop PRO}\right\}$, but it should be understood that, as Kayne has shown, the rules which account for clitics only move pure pronouns, in this instance prepositional pro-phrases.

2 [39] is, of course, ambiguous, as *en* can correspond either to a complement of the subject, or to a complement of *inconnu*, as in *l'auteur risque de rester inconnu du public* (the author risks remaining unknown to the public); only the first reading concerns me here.

3 A few words on the underlying structure of sentences such as [87]–[89]. At first sight one might think that sentences such as *il pleut* or *il y a du monde ici* have in their deep structure an NP subject which is a third person pronoun,

lui or *celui* (see Gross, 1968), and that it is this pronoun which is moved by SUBJECT-RAISING and becomes *il* by the rule which positions subject clitics (see Kayne, 1972). But there are arguments against the presence of such an NP in deep structure. When an NP appears in subject position in deep structure, we usually find signs of this when there is a pronoun in question, *cf* for example:

[I] *a:* je regarde Pierre travailler
     I am watching Peter work
  b: je le regarde travailler
     I am watching him work

If an NP pronoun were present in the deep structure of *il pleut*, etc, one would expect sentences such as [IIa] to be grammatical; but this is not the case, and on the contrary, we have [IIb]:

[II] *a:* *je le regarde pleuvoir
   b: je regarde pleuvoir
     I am watching it rain

These facts suggest that *pleuvoir, y avoir*, etc, are introduced in deep structure with a dummy subject Δ, which is converted into *il* by a late rule. The deep structure of [87] would then be [III], and it is this dummy subject which would undergo the SUBJECT-RAISING rule.

[III] $[_{NP}\Delta]$ commence $[_S[_{NP}\Delta]$ neiger]

If we consider the paradigm:

[IV] *a:* que Pierre arrive en retard est probable
     that Peter will arrive late is probable
  b: il est probable que Pierre arrivera en retard
     it is probable that Peter will arrive late
  c: je (*le) crois probable que Pierre arrivera en retard
     I think it probable that Peter will arrive late

the same reasoning leads us to think that the EXTRAPOSITION rule, which accounts for the relationship between [IVa] and [IVb], should be formulated as in [V] and not as in [VI]:

[V] EXTRAPOSITION: $[_{NP}$ S$]$ — VP
         1   2 $\Rightarrow \emptyset$ — 2+1
[VI] EXTRAPOSITION: $[_{NP}$ celui — S$]$ — VP
         1   2   3 $\Rightarrow$ 1 — $\emptyset$ — 3+2

4 As in the formulation of SUBJECT-RAISING, I am leaving aside several points: the question of the origin of the *que* when EQUI has not been applied, the verbal tenses, the subjunctive. For the arguments in favour of the idea that the subject of the subordinate clause, coreferential with an NP in the main clause, must be a pronoun at the time when EQUI is applied, see Postal, 1970b, and Jackendoff, 1969b.

5 Broadly speaking, *partir* and *oser* require animate subjects, although the content of the notion of animate is not exactly the same in both cases.

6 Nevertheless there are verbs, subject to the obligatory application of EQUI, which do not require that the deleted subordinate subject should be a deep subject (*cf* below [138a]).

7 I must add that not all the verbs of [11–22] behave in exactly the same way. Some native speakers find [117d] unacceptable, likewise [1]:

[1] quel mérite d'être le meilleur ami de Paul?

8 On the justification for the order [I] PASSIVE, [II] EN-AVANT, see Kayne, 1969. This order provides an explanation, in particular, of the following paradigm:

[I]   *a:* Pierre a lu plusieurs de ces livres
            Peter has read several of these books
      b: plusieurs de ces livres ont été lus par Pierre
            several of these books have been read by Peter

[II] *a:* Pierre en a lu plusieurs
            Peter has read several of them
      b: *plusieurs en ont été lus par Pierre (*cf* [7–8] above).

9 In the formulation that I give here, I grant that the node S_2 (and afterwards the node S_1) is eliminated ('pruned') in consequence of the operation of SUBJECT-RAISING. This decision does not involve any empirical consequence for the facts that concern us.

10 In fact, as Kayne (1969, forthcoming) has shown, CLITIC-PLACING is a post-cyclic rule. This fact entails no consequences here.

11 Maurice Gross (1969) has pointed out that, when the main clause of which *menacer* is the verb, is put into the passive, the subordinate verb must also be put into the passive, *cf*:

[I] *Justine a été menacée par le marquis de la fouetter

The real generalization, though, seems to be as follows: (i) the subject (deleted by EQUI) of the subordinate clause is obligatorily coreferential with the surface subject of the main clause; (ii) if the main clause is in the passive, the subordinate subject cannot be semantically an agent. In short, the following sentences are grammatical:

[II] Justine a été menacée (par le marquis) $\begin{cases} \text{de subir les pires} \\ \text{tortures} \\ \text{de recevoir des coups} \\ \text{de bâton} \\ \text{de se faire fouetter} \end{cases}$

Justine was threatened (by the Marquis) $\begin{cases} \text{with suffering} \\ \text{terrible tortures} \\ \text{with being beaten} \\ \text{with getting} \\ \text{whipped} \end{cases}$

Another strange characteristic of *menacer* is that the direct object cannot undergo a movement transformation (question-forming, relativization, cleft-formation, but not clitic placing, *cf* [138*b*]) if it is coreferential with an NP of the embedded statement complement, different from the deleted subject of that complement, *cf*:

[III] *qui le marquis a-t-il menacé de le fouetter?

[IV] *la pauvre fille que le marquis a menacée de
       la fouetter s'est évanouie de peur

[V] *c'est Justine que le marquis a menacée de la fouetter

Sentences [VI–VIII] are grammatical, but they correspond to a deep structure of the type of [IX], with no direct object of *menacer*:

[VI] qui le marquis a-t-il menacé de fouetter?
      who did the Marquis threaten to whip?

[VII] la pauvre fille que le marquis a menacé de fouetter s'est évanouie de
       peur
       the poor girl that the Marquis threatened to whip fainted with fear

[VIII] c'est Justine que le marquis a menacé de fouetter
        it was Justine that the Marquis threatened to whip

 [IX] le marquis$_i$ a menacé de [$_s$ PRO$_i$ fouetter NP]

Notice that *menacer*, while it imposes a constraint of identity between its
subject and the subject of the subordinate clause (deleted by EQUI), imposes
no syntactic constraint of identity between its object and an NP of the
subordinate clause. It is only necessary that, from the semantic viewpoint
(or simply from the viewpoint of general knowledge of the world), there
should be reason to think that the referent of the NP object of *menacer* 'has
an interest' in the 'theme' of the threat (*menace*) expressed (see section 11.1),
cf:

 [X] Ney a menacé Napoléon de refuser la Légion d'Honneur
      Ney threatened Napoleon with refusing the Légion d'Honneur

[XI] le producteur a menacé Fritz Lang de couper la dernière scène du
      Tombeau hindou
      the producer threatened Fritz Lang with cutting the last scene of *Le
      Tombeau hindou*

[XII] le marquis a menacé Justine de faire subir les derniers outrages à
       Juliette
       the Marquis threatened Justine with outraging Juliette

It is not clear whether these sentences can undergo movement transformations, *cf*:

[XIII] ?c'est Napoléon que Ney a menacé de refuser la Légion d'Honneur
        ?it was Napoleon that Ney threatened with refusing the Légion
        d'Honneur

[XIV] ?Justine, que le marquis a menacée de faire subir les derniers outrages à
       Juliette, en est morte de peur
       ?Justine, whom the Marquis threatened with outraging Juliette,
       thereupon died of fright

The facts of [III–V] could be treated by means of a global derivational
constraint (*cf* Lakoff, 1969, 1971) stating that a derivation containing stages
[xv*a* and xv*b*] is badly formed:

[XV] *a:* X — Y — *menacer* — NP$_i$ — Z — NP$_j$ — W
      b: X — NP$_i$ — Y — *menacer* — Z — NP$_j$ — W

(where NP$_i$ is coreferential with NP$_j$).
   But it is evident that such a constraint would have no explanatory value.
Moreover, it would not account for the doubtful character of [XIII–XIV].
12 [140*b*] is ambiguous: *de son fouet* can be understood, either as practically
synonymous with *de la fouetter* in [133], or as an instrumental; *cf* the possibility of interrogativizing with *comment*:

[1] comment le marquis a-t-il menacé Justine? $\left\{\begin{array}{l} \text{— de son fouet} \\ \text{— *de la faire} \\ \quad \text{fouetter} \\ \text{— *de mort} \end{array}\right.$

how did the Marquis threaten Justine?
$\left\{\begin{array}{l} \text{— with his whip} \\ \text{— *with having} \\ \qquad \text{her whipped} \\ \text{— *with death} \end{array}\right.$

This instrumental, while clearly distinct from the complement in *de* VP or *de* NP which concerns us here, is nevertheless incompatible with this complement in the same sentence. Moreover, *menacer* has a somewhat different meaning according to which of these two types of complements one has: in the one case (that of [133]; see below in the text), a threat is expressed verbally; in the other (that of the instrumental) the verb *menacer* excludes the idea of verbal expression.

13 But not always. See note 12.
14 In fact, this feature is not necessary; given our statement of SUBJECT-RAISING, if EXTRAPOSITION does not apply, the derivation will 'block'.

Chapter 3

Neutral and middle pronominal constructions*

1

Among the verbs which, in French, appear in pronominal constructions of the form NP — *se* — V — X, a large number also appear in transitive constructions of the form NP — V — NP — X. If we consider the relationships between these two types of construction solely from the point of view of selectional restrictions, we observe that, in a certain number of cases, the verb shows, in the pronominal construction, selectional restrictions with its subject which are the same as those that it has with its subject in the transitive construction (in general, the set of possible subjects then represents a subset of the set of possible objects);[1] this is the case with the 'true reflexives' (or with the reciprocals), as in:

[1] *a:* Juliette⎫ se lave
     *la sincérité⎭

     Juliet⎫ is washing herself (itself)
   *sincerity⎭

  b: Juliette⎫   ⎧Émile
            ⎪les enfants
    *la sincérité⎭ lave ⎨sa nouvelle voiture
                 ⎩ de sport

* Originally a communication to the Colloque sur la Formalisation en Phonologie, Syntaxe et Sémantique (IRIA, Rocquencourt, 27–29 April, 1970), this text appeared, under the title 'Les constructions pronominales en français. Restrictions de sélection, transformations et règles de redondance', in *Le Français moderne* (Paris, d'Artrey, April 1972); it also appears in the Proceedings of the conference (*The Formal Analysis of Natural Languages*, 1973, The Hague, Mouton) edited by Maurice Gross, Morris Halle and Marcel-Paul Schützenberger. This is a revised version.

Juliet⎫
*sincerity⎭ is washing ⎰Émile
                       ⎱the children
                       ⎱her (its) new sports-car

[2] a: Fritz⎫ s'admire[2]
       *ce sapin⎭

            Fritz⎫ admires himself (itself)
     *this fir-tree⎭

    b: Fritz⎫ admire ⎰Raoul
       *ce sapin⎭   ⎱le courage
                          ⎱la voiture de sport de
                              Marlène

            Fritz⎫ admires ⎰Raoul
     *this fir-tree⎭   ⎱courage
                            ⎱Marlene's sports-car

[3] a: Gary et Marilyn⎫
                les chrétiens⎬ s'aiment (les uns les autres)
          *le miel et les cendres⎭
              *les théorèmes⎭

        Gary and Marilyn⎫
              Christians⎬ love one another
         *honey and ashes⎭
            *theorems⎭

    b: Gary et Marilyn⎫   ⎰Paul et Virginie
                les chrétiens⎬ aiment ⎱la musique
          *le miel et les cendres⎭   ⎱les pommes de terre
              *les théorèmes⎭   au lard

        Gary and Marilyn⎫   ⎰Paul and Virginia
              Christians⎬ love   ⎱music
         *honey and ashes⎭   ⎱potatoes done
            *theorems⎭   with bacon

In a large number of other cases, which are those that will interest us
here, the verb in the pronominal construction shows selectional restrictions with its subject which are identical, not with those that exist between the verb and the subject of the transitive construction, but with
those that exist between the verb and the object, cf:

[4] *a:* le chef a réuni {
les soldats
l'équipe
*Pierre
}

the leader assembled {
the soldiers
the team
*Peter
}

b: les soldats se sont
l'équipe s'est
*Pierre s'est
} réuni(e)(s)

the soldiers
the team
*Peter
} assembled

[5] *a:* les policiers ont dispersé {
*le taureau
la foule
les étudiants
}

the police dispersed {
*the bull
the crowd
the students
}

b: *le taureau s'est
la foule s'est
les étudiants se sont
} dispersé(e)(s)

* the bull
the crowd
the students
} dispersed

[6] *a:* le vent a dissipé {
le brouillard
les nuages
*mon couteau de poche
}

the wind dispelled {
the fog
the clouds
*my pocket-knife
}

b: le brouillard s'est
les nuages se sont
*mon couteau de poche s'est
} dissipé(s)

the fog
the clouds
*my pocket-knife
} lifted

[7] *a:* le vent a aggloméré la neige contre les murs de la maison
        the wind piled up the snow against the walls of the house
     b: la neige s'est agglomérée contre les murs de la maison
        the snow piled up against the walls of the house

[8] *a:* la NASA va espacer $\begin{cases} \text{*le programme spatial} \\ \text{les vols vers la lune} \end{cases}$

        NASA is going to space out $\begin{cases} \text{*the space programme} \\ \text{flights to the moon} \end{cases}$

     b: $\left.\begin{array}{l} \text{*le programme spatial va} \\ \text{les vols vers la lune vont} \end{array}\right\}$ s'espacer

        $\left.\begin{array}{l} \text{*the space programme is} \\ \text{flights to the moon are} \end{array}\right\}$ going to become less frequent

[9] *a:* Pierre a brisé $\begin{cases} \text{la glace} \\ \text{*l'eau} \end{cases}$

        Peter broke $\begin{cases} \text{the ice} \\ \text{*the water} \end{cases}$

     b: $\left.\begin{array}{l} \text{la glace} \\ \text{*l'eau} \end{array}\right\}$ s'est brisée

        $\left.\begin{array}{l} \text{the ice} \\ \text{*the water} \end{array}\right\}$ broke

[10] *a:* Ernestine a lavé ce veston en dix minutes
         Ernestine washed this jacket in ten minutes
      b: ce veston se lave en dix minutes
         this jacket can be washed in ten minutes

[11] *a:* nous avons mangé le caviar avec de la vodka
         we ate the caviare with vodka
      b: le caviar se mange avec de la vodka
         caviare is eaten with vodka

[12] *a:* mon libraire m'a vendu ce livre
         my bookseller sold me this book
      b: ce livre s'est bien vendu
         this book sold well

It is clearly necessary to account for the systematic nature of the correspondence between the selectional restrictions in the two types of construction illustrated by examples (*a*) and (*b*). But, within the framework of transformational theory (*cf* Chomsky, 1965, 1970), several solutions are *a priori* possible.

One solution would be to assume that only the transitive constructions (examples (*a*)) are generated directly in the base, and that the pronominal constructions are derived from them transformationally. More precisely, we would agree that the subject NPs of the pronominal constructions are generated in the object position in transitive sentences with a 'dummy' subject, and the surface structures of examples (*b*) would be reached by means of one or more transformations which would have the effect of moving the object NP into the subject position and inserting the *se* (the first of these operations strongly resembling one of the two rules which operate in the PASSIVE – the NP-PREPOSING of Chomsky, 1970); we should then have something like:

[13] $\Delta - V - NP - X$
    $1 \quad 2 \quad 3 \quad 4 \Rightarrow 3 - se + 2 - \emptyset - 4$

This solution was suggested by Gross (1968) for some of these examples. Gross calls this rule the MIDDLE-SE ('SE-MOYEN') transformation.

Another solution would be to introduce the two constructions corresponding to examples (*a*) and (*b*) directly in the base, by a rule such as:

[14] $VP \rightarrow (se) \ldots V (NP) \ldots$

The pronominal verbs would then be subcategorized, in the lexicon, in terms of the feature $[+ se \ldots \underline{\quad}]$; or, alternatively, they would have the feature $[+ REFLEXIVE]$, which would be ultimately 'spelled out' as *se*. (In this case, *se* would not be introduced by rule [14]). I shall not take any stand here on the question of which of these two possibilities should be chosen; that choice is not relevant to the problem which concerns us. What counts in this case, whether we choose to introduce *se* directly in the base, as in [14], or to spell it out at a later stage as the realization of a feature $[+ REFLEXIVE]$, is that the selectional regularities should be described by means of lexical redundancy rules (*cf* Chomsky, 1965, Chapter 4, § 2). For example, it is clear that in order to account for the choice of objects in [4*a*–7*a*], verbs such as *réunir, disperser, dissiper, rassembler, agglomérer*, etc, must be marked in their lexical entry with the feature $[+ \underline{\quad} [- SEMANTICALLY SINGULAR]]$ (*cf* Dougherty, 1970b). In order to account for the choice of subjects in [4*b*–7*b*], it would be sufficient to propose a redundancy rule such as:

[15] $[+ V], [+ \underline{\quad} [- SEM SING] X] \rightarrow [+ V],$
    $[+ [- SEM SING] se \underline{\quad} X]$

The verbs *réunir*, *disperser* etc, would then be marked individually in the lexicon as appearing only in contexts [+ —— NP], [+ —— [−SEM SING]], and it would be rule [15] which would account for the possibility that they have of appearing also in the pronominal frame.[3]

We see that the two solutions, one 'transformational' (resort to rule [13]) and the other 'lexical' (resort to rules [14] and [15]), equally enable us to formulate the selectional regularities common to examples (*a*) and (*b*) above in one statement. *A priori*, there is no reason to choose one rather than the other, and there would be no justification for assuming *a priori* that one of the two is simpler than the other. Moreover, there is nothing to indicate that we must adopt the same solution for all the verbs of examples [4–12]. It is therefore a question of finding empirical arguments which will enable us to decide.

In fact, my principal aim in this chapter will be to try to show that the pronominal constructions of examples [4–12] can be divided into two main groups, of which one must be treated in transformational terms, and the other in terms of lexical redundancy rules.

2

In the first place, we must also envisage the possibility that some of our examples (*b*), if not all, may be generated from the transformational rule or rules which account for the 'true reflexives' (for a transformational treatment of the reflexives and the reciprocals in French, see Kayne, 1969, forthcoming). It has been generally agreed (*cf* Lees and Klima, 1963, Postal, 1964) that the condition of application for these rules depends on the possibility of having the same NPs in subject position and in object position in transitive sentences. The possibility of [16] is linked with paradigm [17] (where the subscript indices show that the two NPs are coreferential).[4]

[16] Juliette se lave
        Juliet is washing herself

[17] *a:* Juliette lave Justine
        b: Justine lave Juliette
        c: *Juliette$_i$ lave Juliette$_i$

        a: Juliet is washing Justine
        b: Justine is washing Juliet
        c: *Juliet$_i$ is washing Juliet$_i$

We see straight away why it is impossible to treat some of our examples as true reflexives. If we consider, for example, [8] and [10], we cannot see what correct transitive sentences we could construct which would have as subjects the subjects of examples (*b*), *cf:*

[18] *les vols vers la lune vont espacer les opérations du coeur
　　*flights to the moon are going to space out heart operations

[19] *ce veston a lavé une jolie cravate
　　*this jacket washed a pretty tie

But the position is much less clear for a certain number of other examples, in particular those which involve animate noun phrases. If we consider paradigm [20], it seems at first sight that we have exactly the same situation as in [16–17]:

[20] *a:* les manifestants se sont dispersés
　　　　the demonstrators dispersed
　　b: les policiers ont dispersé les manifestants
　　　　the police dispersed the demonstrators
　　c: les manifestants ont dispersé les policiers
　　　　the demonstrators dispersed the police
　　d: *les manifestants$_i$ ont dispersé les manifestants$_i$
　　　　*the demonstrators$_i$ dispersed the demonstrators$_i$

Apart from semantic considerations, there are other arguments against ranking our examples with true reflexives (or with reciprocals). In the case of the true reflexives, in fact, there are a certain number of syntactical environments where, the rules which introduce *se* not having been able to operate, we find the non-clitic reflexive pronoun *lui-même* (where *-même* is generally optional) instead of *se*, in the same positions as a normal NP. In this way, beside [21] we find [22–23] (the rules which position the clitics are blocked by the restrictive constructions in *ne . . . que*):

[21] *a:* Pierre la regarde
　　　　Peter is looking at her
　　b: Pierre ne regarde qu'elle
　　　　Peter is looking only at her

[22] *a:* Pierre se regarde (dans le miroir)
　　　　Peter is looking at himself (in the mirror)
　　b: Pierre ne regarde que lui (-même)
　　　　Peter is looking only at himself

[23] *a:* Pierre s'admire
        Peter admires himself
     b: Pierre n'admire que lui (-même)
        Peter admires only himself

However, the following sentences are ungrammatical:

[24] *les manifestants n'ont dispersé qu'eux (-mêmes)

[25] *l'équipe n'a réuni qu'elle (-même)

[26] *le brouillard n'a dissipé que lui (-même)

Facts of the same kind are found in cleft sentences (*cf* Moreau, 1970): non-clitic reflexives are possible in *focus* position (for this term, *cf* Akmajian, 1970, Chomsky, 1971):

[27] *a:* Pierre se regarde dans le miroir
        Peter is looking at himself in the mirror
     b: ce n'est pas lui-même que Pierre regardait dans le miroir, mais
        Marie
        it was not himself that Peter was looking at in the mirror, but
        Mary

[28] *a:* Pierre s'est nui (à lui-même)
        Peter has harmed himself
     b: ce n'est pas à lui-même que Pierre a nui, mais à Marie
        it is not himself that Peter has harmed, but Mary

But [29–30] are impossible:

[29] *ce n'est pas elle-même que l'équipe de football a réunie, mais celle
      de rugby
     *it was not itself that the soccer team assembled, but the rugby team

[30] *ce n'est pas eux-mêmes que les manifestants ont dispersés, mais les
      policiers
     *it was not themselves that the demonstrators dispersed, but the
     police

Further, in general when a pronominal construction is possible with a reflexive implication, it can also have a reciprocal implication, *cf* [31–32]:

[31] Pierre et Paul se sont lavés l'un l'autre
     Peter and Paul washed one another

[32] Juliette et Justine s'admirent l'une l'autre
     Juliet and Justine admire one another

However, it is impossible to have:

[33] *les deux équipes se sont réunies l'une l'autre[5]
    *the two teams assembled one another

and if [34] is possible, it is really because [20a] is ambiguous as between a 'neutral' sense (see below) and a reciprocal sense:

[34] les manifestants se sont dispersés les uns les autres
    the demonstrators dispersed each other

These facts suggest that any distinction between our examples that might be based on the possibility or impossibility of the subject and the object of the transitive construction belonging to the same selectional class and which would result in grouping some of these examples with the 'true reflexives' would be superficial. In fact, my aim is to demonstrate that we must indeed distinguish at least two main groups among examples [4–12], but that the dividing line lies elsewhere. On the one hand, we must distinguish examples of the type of [10–12], which from now on I shall call the 'middle' constructions, using a classic term, and, on the other hand, examples of the type of [4–9], which I shall call 'neutral' pronominal constructions, for want of a better term.

3

I shall not here undertake to describe in detail the differences between the middle and the neutral constructions; in any case these differences will progressively become clear in the course of our exposition. Traditional grammarians (Grevisse, Martinon, Sandfeld, Blinkenberg, Stéfanini) have discussed semantic differences between the two constructions at length; they say, in the main, that the constructions that I call middle have 'a passive sense', which means that they are apprehended as implying the presence of an agent, not expressed and different from the surface subject, whereas the presence of such an agent is not apprehended in the case of the neutrals. Independently of these semantic considerations, for the moment I shall simply say that the possibility of having a neutral construction depends on very varied constraints of a lexical nature, whereas the middle construction, which is very productive, is subject to certain syntactic and semantic constraints of a general character. Later on I shall give examples of the lexical limitations to which the neutral construction is subject; the middle construction can be found with a very large number of verbs, but it is, for example, subject to time constraints which do not exist in the case of the neutrals; the middle construction is impossible with an indication of a precise point in time, *cf:*

[35] *a:* ces lunettes se nettoient facilement
          these glasses clean easily
      b: *ces lunettes se sont nettoyées hier à huit heures et quart
          *these glasses cleaned yesterday at a quarter past eight

in comparison with:

[36] *a:* on a nettoyé ces lunettes hier à huit heures et quart
          someone cleaned these glasses yesterday at a quarter past eight
      b: ces lunettes ont été nettoyées hier à huit heures et quart
          these glasses were cleaned yesterday at a quarter past eight

Similarly:

[37] *a:* ce genre de livre se vend surtout aux bonnes soeurs
          this sort of book sells mainly to nuns
      b: ce livre $\left\{\begin{array}{l}\text{*s'est}\\\text{a été}\end{array}\right\}$ vendu hier à une bonne soeur

          this book $\left\{\begin{array}{l}\text{*sold}\\\text{was sold}\end{array}\right\}$ yesterday to a nun

Notice the contrast between [35*b*] and [38], which is a typical example of the neutral construction:

[38] cette branche s'est cassée hier à huit heures et quart
      this branch broke yesterday at a quarter past eight

Generally speaking, the middle construction cannot be employed to indicate a particular event taking place at a point in time; instead it can have habitual, normative or generic implications. This is no doubt the explanation of the fact which the traditional grammarians also noticed, that it is frequently found with certain adverbs, like *facilement* in [35*a*], or *fréquemment* (frequently) in the sentence that I am writing now,† or with the subject *cela* or *ça;* the latter frequently appears, in fact, in generic constructions such as:

[39] *a:* $\left.\begin{array}{l}\text{les femmes}\\\text{*Justine}\end{array}\right\}$, ça bavarde sans arrêt

          $\left.\begin{array}{l}\text{women}\\\text{*Justine}\end{array}\right\}$, they chatter ceaselessly

† 'elle se rencontre fréquemment avec certains adverbes' is the French text. [*Translator's note*]

b: les femmes⎱ , c'est inconstant
    *Justine⎰

   women⎱ , they're a fickle lot
   *Justine⎰

c: *les femmes, ça a bavardé hier soir
   *women, they chattered yesterday evening

and generic middle constructions of this type are very common, *cf:*

[40] les maximanteaux⎱ , ça se porte sur une minijupe
     un maximanteau⎰

   maxi-coats, they're ⎱ worn over a mini-skirt
   a maxi-coat, that's ⎰

[41] les patrons, ça se séquestre
     bosses get isolated

[42]   les erreurs⎱ , ça se paie
       une erreur pareille⎰

     mistakes, they have⎱ to be paid for
     a mistake like that, it has⎰

It should be noted that the presence of adverbs like *facilement*, etc, or the presence of *cela* or *ça*, is not by itself a sufficient condition for having the middle construction, *cf* the ungrammaticalness of:

[43] *ces lunettes se sont facilement nettoyées hier à huit heures et quart
   *these glasses cleaned easily yesterday at a quarter past eight

[44] *cette cravate, ça s'est porté hier pendant toute la soirée
   *this tie, it was worn yesterday throughout the whole evening

The presence of these elements is simply a frequent corollary of the generic or habitual implication of a sentence. Another observation of the traditional grammarians, according to whom the middle constructions are more acceptable with non-animate surface subjects (*cf* [10–12]), is contradicted by example [41] (see also below [52–54]). If, in certain cases, there is a tendency to avoid middle constructions with an animate surface subject, this is perhaps for reasons of performance, insofar as these constructions are often ambiguous (see below).

Furthermore, Richie Kayne and Hans Obenauer have intimated to me that there might be semantic constraints on the understood agent of the middle constructions: this would always have to be interpreted as animate, and even, more precisely, as human. If [45] and [46] are equally possible, in [47] the understood agent could not be interpreted as being *l'orage* (the storm); in the same way, [48] would be bizarre, given that *laper* (to lap) can normally only be used of an animal:

[45]   les soldats ont détruit le pont
       the soldiers destroyed the bridge

[46]   l'orage a détruit le pont
       the storm destroyed the bridge

[47]   les ponts, ça se détruit facilement
       bridges are easily destroyed

[48]   le lait, ça se lape facilement
       milk is easily lapped up

Nevertheless, I am not convinced of the reality of this restriction on the understood agent, insofar as the following sentences seem to me entirely natural:

[49]   un pont, ça se détruit facilement, il y suffit d'un gros orage
       a bridge is easily destroyed; it only needs a bad storm

[50]   une barrière pareille, ça se renverse facilement, il y suffit d'un peu de
          vent
       a barrier like that is easily overturned; it only needs a little wind

[51]   pour un chat⎫
          si on est un chat⎭, le lait, ça se lape facilement
          for a cat⎫
          if you're a cat⎭, milk is easily lapped up

At all events, this point needs to be looked into more closely.

The productivity of the middle construction results in the fact that a very large number of pronominal constructions are ambiguous. Thus, [52a] can be interpreted as middle (sadism), reflexive (masochism) or reciprocal (sado-masochism): [52b] is impossible, because of its generic implication, [52c] can only be reciprocal or reflexive, and [52d] can only be reflexive (*fouetter* (to whip) is not possible as a neutral verb):

[52]   *a:* les femmes, ça se fouette
          women get whipped/whip themselves/whip each other
       b: *Justine, ça se fouette

    c: les femmes se sont fouettées hier soir
       the women whipped each other yesterday evening/
       the women whipped themselves yesterday evening
    d: Justine s'est fouettée hier soir
       Justine whipped herself yesterday evening

Similarly, [53*a*] can be either middle, or reflexive or reciprocal, but [53*b*] is only reflexive or reciprocal:

[53] *a:* les enfants, ça se lave en dix minutes
       children can be washed in ten minutes/children wash themselves
       in ten minutes/children wash each other in ten minutes
    b: les enfants se sont lavés en dix minutes
       the children washed themselves in ten minutes/the children
       washed each other in ten minutes

Lastly, [54*a*] and [55*a*] can be either neutral or middle (in the case of [54*a*], either the crowd disperses by itself or else it is dispersed, for example, by the police), whereas [54*b*] and [55*b*] can only be neutral:

[54] *a:* une foule, ça se disperse aisément
       a crowd disperses easily/a crowd is easily dispersed
    b: la foule s'est dispersée vers huit heures
       the crowd dispersed about eight o'clock

[55] *a:* ce genre de branche se casse facilement
       this sort of branch breaks easily/this sort of branch can be easily
       broken
    b: cette branche s'est cassée hier matin
       this branch broke yesterday morning

Despite its productive character, the middle construction allows certain exceptions, but these are of a very different kind from those that the neutral construction allows. The latter are typically capricious, and subject to all sorts of dialectal, idiolectal and diachronic variations (*cf* below, section 5). On the other hand, the exceptions to the middle construction are themselves an indication of underlying regularities. For example, Jean-Paul Boons and Maurice Gross have pointed out to me that the verb *comporter* (to comprise, include, entail) cannot be put into the middle, *cf:*

[56] *a:* le gouvernement comporte dix-sept ministres
       the Government comprises seventeen ministers
    b: *des ministres, ça se comporte

But, in the first place, notice that this verb also prohibits other operations, such as the PASSIVE or OBJECT-RAISING, cf:

[57] a: *dix-sept ministres sont comportés par le gouvernement
          *seventeen ministers are comprised by the Government
      b: il est difficile à un gouvernement de comporter plus de dix-sept
          ministres
          it is difficult for a Government to comprise more than seventeen
          ministers
      c: *plus de dix-sept ministres sont difficiles à comporter pour un
          gouvernement
          *more than seventeen ministers are difficult to comprise for a
          Government

Further, it is clear that the subject of *comporter*, in [56a], is not an agent (*cf* on this notion Chapter 4). Now, it certainly appears that the understood complement of middle sentences can only be interpreted as an agent[6] (whether or not it is also subject to restrictions in terms of the feature human/non-human). And, in fact, all the verbs whose subject normally has a non-agentive interpretation seem to permit the middle construction very uneasily, *cf*:

[58] a: Don Juan adorait les femmes
          Don Juan adored women
      b: ?les femmes, ça s'adore
          ?women get adored

[59] a: les bandes dessinées amusent les enfants
          strip-cartoons amuse children
      b: ?les enfants, ça s'amuse difficilement[7]
          children are difficult to amuse

[60] a: Pierre m'a touché (par sa prévenance)
          Peter touched me (by his attentiveness)
      b: *les gens susceptibles, ça se touche difficilement
          *easily-offended people are difficult to touch

(compare [60b] with the sentence *cette cible, ça se touche difficilement* (that target is difficult to hit), where *toucher* is taken in a physical sense, with an understood agent).

The fact that I make a difference, in terms of acceptability, between [58b–59b] on the one hand, and [60b] on the other hand, is because *toucher* (in the psychological sense) never has an agentive interpretation, whereas *adorer* or *amuser* can have that interpretation (*cf* Chapter 5); and, in fact, sentences analogous to [58*b*] seem to me to be acceptable under appropriate conditions, imposing a 'voluntarist' interpretation, *cf:*

[61] les impérialistes, ça se déteste
       Imperialists get (themselves) hated

[62] les mouchards, ça se méprise
       informers get (themselves) despised

The exceptions to the middle construction, then, can be shown to have a regularity in common, which can be accounted for by imposing on this construction the condition that the understood complement is always interpreted as an agent. These exceptions are thus of a very different status from that of the exceptions to the neutral construction, which, as we shall see in section 5, most often display the character of accidental gaps.

4

These distinctions having been made, the question now arises what type of derivation we must give our two constructions, neutral and middle, if we wish to account for the facts of selection noted at the start. My hypothesis is that the middle constructions must be derived transformationally, by means of rule [13], whilst the neutral constructions will be generated directly in the base by rule [14], and the regularities of selection that they show will be treated by means of lexical redundancy rules of the type of [15].

Let it be said at once that one of the best arguments that one can usually invoke in favour of a transformational derivation cannot be used here, either in the case of the neutrals or of the middles. The introduction of a transformation is justified if it enables us to simplify the rules of the base in a significant manner; this is the sort of classic argument which justifies the transformations which form the interrogatives (*cf* Kayne, 1972), the relatives, the rule of affix movement, that of DO-SUPPORT in English (*cf* Chomsky, 1957), etc. Now in French there exists a fairly large number of 'intrinsically' pronominal verbs, such as *s'évanouir* (to faint, to vanish), *se désister* (to withdraw, to stand down), *s'imaginer* (to think, to fancy), etc, which, unlike the reflexives, the reciprocals, the neutrals and the middles, it is impossible to connect with any transitive construction (direct or indirect), *cf* for example:

[63] *a:* Pierre s'est évanoui
       Peter fainted

b: *Pierre a évanoui Paul
*Peter fainted Paul

c: *Pierre a évanoui à Paul

d: *le choc a évanoui Pierre
*the shock fainted Peter

e: *Pierre n'a évanoui $\begin{Bmatrix} \text{que lui-même} \\ \text{qu'à lui-même} \end{Bmatrix}$
*Peter fainted only himself

f: *c'est (à) lui-même que Pierre a évanoui
*it was himself that Peter fainted

The facts of [63] do seem to indicate that there is no reason not to introduce *s'évanouir*, as it stands, directly in the base; more exactly, *évanouir* would be introduced in the base with the obligatory subcategorization feature [$+se \ldots$ ——].[8] Nevertheless, before choosing this solution, it would be advisable to consider another possibility. We could, also, treat *évanouir* as an ordinary transitive verb, but one subject to the condition that its subject and its object are obligatorily coreferential. This is the solution suggested by Jackendoff (1969*b*) for English, to account for sentences such as:

[64] John $\begin{Bmatrix} \text{behaved} \\ \text{perjured} \end{Bmatrix} \begin{Bmatrix} \text{himself} \\ \text{*Bill} \end{Bmatrix}$

In English, this solution is reasonable insofar as *himself* appears in effect in the position of direct object. In French, things are less plain. Certainly, as [63] shows, there is no positive trace of the existence of an object, direct or indirect, of a verb like *évanouir*. But this by itself is not enough to justify the introduction of *se* into the base and to eliminate the 'English' solution. In fact, starting from a base structure *Pierre$_i$ a évanoui Pierre$_i$* (or *Pierre$_i$ a évanoui lui$_i$*, depending on whether one introduces the pronouns transformationally or directly in the base), we would obtain [63*a*] by the usual rules for the formation of *se* in the case of the reflexives. Moreover, the impossibility of [63*e–f*] is only at first sight a counter-argument to the idea that *évanouir* has a direct object in the base. Semantic considerations would in fact lead us to see in this impossibility no more than a consequence of the obligatory coreferentiality of the subject and the object of *évanouir*. Consider sentences such as:

[65] c'est Marie que Pierre a embrassée
it was Mary that Peter kissed

[66] Hamlet n'a aimé qu'Ophélie
Hamlet loved only Ophelia

Semantically, these sentences contain a presupposed part (respectively, 'Pierre a embrassé quelqu'un' ('Peter kissed someone')), and 'Hamlet a aimé quelqu'un' ('Hamlet loved someone'), and an asserted part (respectively '... Marie' ('... Mary') and '... seulement Ophélie' ('... only Ophelia')) (on the notion of presupposition, see especially Ducrot, 1972). It is clear that this interplay of presupposition and assertion is only possible if there is a certain liberty in the choice of objects of the verbs *embrasser* and *aimer*: Peter and Hamlet can in principle love or kiss several different persons. Now, it is clear that, if a verb is specified in the lexicon as taking obligatorily coreferential subject and object, all liberty in the choice of object becomes impossible, and with it, the interplay of presupposition and assertion. In this perspective, [63e–f] would thus be semantically absurd rather than ungrammatical and would not constitute an argument against the derivation of [63a] from a transitive construction.

R. S. Kayne (1969, forthcoming) has nevertheless noted some facts that indicate that at least some of the 'intrinsically' pronominal verbs must be introduced as such in the base. This is the case with *s'imaginer* (where the *se* is felt as 'dative' rather than as a direct object). If [67] were really derived from [68]:

[67] Jean se l'imagine
    John imagines it

[68] *Jean$_i$ l'imagine à lui$_i$-(même)

it would be difficult to understand why it is impossible to have [69] parallel to [70], and [71] parallel to [72]:

[69] *Jean m'imagine à lui-même
    *John imagines me to himself

[70] Jean me présentera à elle
    John will introduce me to her

[71] *Jean se l'imagine à lui-même

[72] Jean se l'est dit à lui-même
    John said it to himself

These facts, which are independent of any semantic consideration, are enough to show that at least some of the 'intrinsic' pronominals cannot be derived from transitive constructions (indirect in this case) and must appear as they are in the base (this would also be the case for verbs such as *s'en aller* (to go away), which show two intrinsic clitics, *se* and *en*). The principle of simplicity, in the absence of positive arguments to the contrary, then induces us to treat the other intrinsics, such as *s'évanouir*, in the same way.

Notice that the foregoing discussion (relating to [63*e–f*]) does not invalidate the line of argument that we used, in section 2, to distinguish the neutrals from the reflexives, and which was specifically based on examples of restrictive and cleft sentences. In fact, verbs such as *disperser*, *réunir*, etc, obviously allow various objects. The type of semantic explanation which enables us to account for the impossibility of [63*e–f*] is not valid for [24–26] or [29–30].

Once certain intrinsic pronominals are introduced in the base, whatever the exact nature of the mechanism that introduces them, it is clear that this mechanism is available to be used if necessary to introduce the middles and/or the neutrals. The introduction of a transformation (of the type of [13]) to account for these constructions would not in any case entail any simplification of the base rules. If such a transformation should prove to be necessary for other reasons, it would then be a case of a 'structure-preserving' transformation, in Emonds' sense (1970) (see Chapter 1).

5

As far as the neutrals are concerned, there are a certain number of indications in favour of a lexical rather than a transformational solution. I said earlier on that the possibility of a verb appearing in a neutral construction was subject to restrictions of a lexical nature, and we have seen examples of verbs (*manger*, *vendre*, *nettoyer*, *fouetter*, etc) which, while appearing in transitive and middle constructions, cannot appear in the neutral construction. In fact, one is struck by the capricious and idiosyncratic character of the correspondences between the neutral and transitive constructions. If we derived the first from the second transformationally (by rule [13]), we would expect a regular correspondence (*cf* Chomsky, 1970), and, if there are restrictions on the transformation, that it would be a matter of restrictions of a general character, indicating that, in certain general conditions, the transformation does not apply. In other words, we would expect to have cases, predictable in general terms, where NP_2 V NP_1 exists, and where NP_1 *se* V does not exist. We have seen that this is what happens in the case of the middle construction (this fact is clearly not in itself an argument in favour of a transformational derivation of the middles; it is only 'consistent' with such a solution).

For the neutrals, the facts are very different. We meet a large number of verbs appearing in the construction NP_1 *se* V and not appearing in the construction NP_2 V NP_1, and this despite their great semantic similarity to verbs which appear in both constructions, and without our being able to formulate any generalizations as to the reason for these 'gaps'. Here are some examples (notice that the ungrammatical sentences here are all perfectly comprehensible; there is therefore no general semantic reason for excluding these sentences):

[73] *a:* Marie a $\begin{Bmatrix} \text{*évanoui} \\ \text{endormi} \end{Bmatrix}$ Pierre

      Mary $\begin{cases} \text{*fainted Peter} \\ \text{put Peter to sleep} \end{cases}$

   b: Pierre s'est $\begin{cases} \text{évanoui} \\ \text{endormi} \end{cases}$

      Peter $\begin{cases} \text{fainted} \\ \text{fell asleep} \end{cases}$

[74] *a:* Irène a $\begin{Bmatrix} \text{?*levé} \\ \text{couché} \end{Bmatrix}$ les enfants

      Irene $\begin{cases} \text{got the children up} \\ \text{put the children to bed} \end{cases}$

   b: les enfants se sont $\begin{cases} \text{levés} \\ \text{couchés} \end{cases}$

      the children $\begin{cases} \text{got up} \\ \text{went to bed} \end{cases}$

[75] *a:* les prêtres ont $\begin{Bmatrix} \text{assis} \\ \text{agenouillé} \\ \text{?accroupi} \\ \text{?prosterné} \\ \text{*affalé} \\ \text{*affaissé} \end{Bmatrix}$ la victime de force

      the priests forced the victim to $\begin{cases} \text{sit} \\ \text{kneel} \\ \text{crouch} \\ \text{prostrate himself} \\ \text{sink down} \\ \text{sag over} \end{cases}$

b: la victime s'est
$$\begin{cases} \text{assise} \\ \text{agenouillée} \\ \text{accroupie} \\ \text{prosternée} \\ \text{affalée} \\ \text{affaissée} \end{cases}$$

the victim
$$\begin{cases} \text{sat down} \\ \text{knelt down} \\ \text{crouched (down)} \\ \text{prostrated himself} \\ \text{sank down} \\ \text{sagged over} \end{cases}$$

[76] *a:* Hélène $\begin{cases} \text{*empiffre} \\ \text{gave} \end{cases}$ ses enfants de bonbons

Helen $\begin{cases} \text{*gorges} \\ \text{crams} \end{cases}$ her children with sweets

b: les enfants $\begin{cases} \text{s'empiffrent} \\ \text{se gavent} \end{cases}$ de bonbons

the children $\begin{cases} \text{gorge themselves} \\ \text{cram themselves} \end{cases}$ with sweets

[77] *a:* ?*les policiers ont attroupé les passants   (compare with [5])
?the police gathered the passers-by together
b: les passants se sont attroupés
the passers-by gathered together

[78] *a:* *le poids des marchandises a $\begin{cases} \text{écroulé} \\ \text{effondré} \end{cases}$ le plancher

*the weight of the goods $\begin{cases} \text{collapsed} \\ \text{caved in} \end{cases}$ the floor

b: le plancher s'est $\begin{cases} \text{écroulé} \\ \text{effondré} \end{cases}$ (compare with [9])

the floor $\begin{cases} \text{collapsed} \\ \text{caved in} \end{cases}$

[79] *a:* Pierre a $\begin{cases} \text{engueulé} \\ \text{*querellé} \\ \text{?*disputé} \end{cases}$ Paul

Peter $\begin{Bmatrix} \text{went for} \\ \text{*quarrelled} \\ \text{*argued} \end{Bmatrix}$ Paul

b: Pierre s'est $\begin{Bmatrix} \text{engueulé} \\ \text{querellé} \\ \text{disputé} \end{Bmatrix}$ avec Paul

Peter $\begin{Bmatrix} \text{had a row} \\ \text{quarrelled} \\ \text{argued} \end{Bmatrix}$ with Paul

As I have already pointed out, we are in a domain here where many variations from one dialect to another may be expected. I have met speakers who accept *Irène a levé les enfants* (*cf* [74]) or *Pierre a querellé Paul* (*cf* [79]), and I should not be surprised if some speakers accept [77a] (to me, *l'accident a attroupé les passants* (the accident drew the passers-by together), with an inanimate subject, is acceptable). In the same way, we would expect fluctuations in the course of the history of the language. Haase (1965, 136*ff*) gives some examples from the seventeenth century of *prosterner* used transitively (*cf* [75]), and, conversely, of *se démanger* (to itch) (' Il se gratte où il se démange ' (' He scratches where he itches ') Molière), where modern French tends to allow only the transitive construction (*sa cicatrice le démange* (his scar is itching)). All these fluctuations (which are also found in the relationships between pronominal and non-pronominal neutrals (see below)) are clearly in accordance with a lexicalist theory of the neutrals.

It might be useful to point out, as R. Kayne has suggested to me, that the standard dictionaries (*Petit Larousse, Dictionnaire Larousse du Français contemporain, Mansion's French-English Dictionary*) habitually list the neutrals, with their own meaning, separately from the transitives, whereas they give no special entry for *se nettoyer, se vendre, se manger*, etc. This obviously corresponds to the intuitive recognition on the one hand of the regularity of the process of formation of the middles, and on the other hand of the frequently idiosyncratic character of the neutrals, from the syntactic as well as the semantic point of view.

It will be seen that the distinction that I made, for reasons of exposition, between the intrinsics and the neutrals, is artificial. Apparently, the only difference between the two constructions stems from the fact that some pronominal verbs, but not all, are found also in direct transitive constructions. But this is not all. We notice also that some verbs, which are possible in both constructions, are subject to particular selectional

constraints in one construction which do not apply to them in the other,
cf:

[80] *a:* le cuisinier a éparpillé les petits pois
          the cook scattered the peas

      b: les petits pois se sont éparpillés
          the peas scattered

      c: ?*les policiers ont éparpillé les manifestants
          ?*the police scattered the demonstrators

      d: les manifestants se sont éparpillés
          the demonstrators scattered

[81] *a:* on a écoulé l'eau de pluie par cette canalisation
          they ran rain-water through this piping

      b: l'eau de pluie s'est écoulée par cette canalisation
          rain-water ran through this piping

      c: *le temps écoule $\left\{\begin{array}{l}\text{la rivière}\\\text{la journée}\end{array}\right.$

          *time rolls on $\left\{\begin{array}{l}\text{the river}\\\text{the day}\end{array}\right.$

      d: $\left.\begin{array}{l}\text{la rivière}\\\text{la journée}\end{array}\right\}$ s'écoule

          $\left.\begin{array}{l}\text{the river}\\\text{the day}\end{array}\right\}$ rolls on

[82] *a:* on a tassé $\left\{\begin{array}{l}\text{la farine}\\\text{*les désaccords}\end{array}\right.$

          they heaped up $\left\{\begin{array}{l}\text{the flour}\\\text{*dissensions}\end{array}\right.$

      b: $\left.\begin{array}{l}\text{la farine s'est}\\\text{les désaccords se sont}\end{array}\right\}$ tassé(e)(s)

          the flour piled up
          dissensions accumulated

In all these cases, the constraints apply to the transitive construction;
here is another case where, in contrast, it is the pronominal construction
which is subject to additional restrictions (see also Chapter 5):

[83] *a:* Pierre remplit le tonneau de bière
          Peter filled the cask with beer

      b: le tonneau se remplit de bière
          the cask filled with beer

[84] *a:* cette nouvelle remplit Paul de joie
      this news filled Paul with joy
   b: *Paul se remplit de joie
     *Paul filled with joy

Facts of this kind, together with the semantic differences (to which I shall return; see Chapter 4) between the transitive construction and the neutral construction, seem to me important indications that the latter must be generated in the base, and that the regularities that connect it with the transitive construction will be adequately expressed by redundancy rules of the type of [15]. Other types of facts support this hypothesis.

In the first place, there is the problem of the existence or absence of certain idiomatic expressions. We know that the grammaticalness of sentences such as:

[85] *a:* le roi a rendu justice sous un chêne
      the king dispensed justice under an oak-tree
   b: justice a été rendue par le roi
     justice was dispensed by the king
   c: en ces temps troublés, justice est difficile à rendre
     in these troubled times, justice is difficult to dispense

has been taken as an argument in favour of a transformational derivation of [85*b*] and [85*c*] from [85*a*] (*cf* Chomsky, 1970, Perlmutter, 1970, and Chapter 2 of this book); in other words, the surface subjects of [85*b*–*c*] are objects in deep structure. Now, it is striking that corresponding idioms are not found in the neutral constructions, *cf:*

[86] *justice s'est rendue hier à huit heures du soir
     *justice dispensed yesterday at eight o'clock in the evening

[87] *a:* nos troupes ont livré bataille ce matin
      our troops gave battle this morning
   b: bataille a été livrée ce matin
     battle was joined this morning
   c: *bataille s'est livrée ce matin

[88] *a:* le premier ministre nous a promis monts et merveilles
      the Prime Minister has promised us wonders
   b: monts et merveilles nous ont été promis par le premier ministre
     wonders have been promised us by the Prime Minister
   c: *monts et merveilles se sont promis

A second type of fact that is pertinent is connected with the existence of certain verbs – such as, in French, *oser* (to dare) or *daigner* (to condescend) – which take complements in the infinitive whose implied subject, understood as identical with the subject of the main verb, must, moreover, be a deep subject, not derived (*cf* Perlmutter, 1971). Thus we have the following facts:

[89] Justine a osé
  - gifler le marquis
  - *être caressée par le petit page
  - se faire caresser par le petit page
  - être insolente
  - *me sembler être une allumeuse
  - *sembler aimer un nègre

Justine dared
  - to slap the Marquis
  - *to be fondled by the little page
  - to have the little page fondle her
  - to be insolent
  - *to seem to me to be a flirt
  - *to seem to love a negro

All the excluded constructions are ones that we have good reason to think contain a subject derived transformationally, by PASSIVE or SUBJECT-RAISING (*cf* this book, Chapter 2). If the neutral constructions of the type of examples [4–9] were introduced by a transformation such as [13], we would expect not to find them embedded under verbs like *oser* or *daigner* If they are in the base, we would expect on the contrary that complex constructions of this type would be possible, and this is in fact what happens, *cf*:

[90] l'équipe a osé
  - *être réunie
  - se réunir

the team dared
  - *to be assembled
  - to assemble

[91] la foule a daigné
  - *être dispersée
  - se disperser

the crowd condescended
  - *to be dispersed
  - to disperse

Notice on the other hand that it is impossible to obtain a middle interpretation in these conditions, a fact which is consistent with the idea of a transformational derivation of the middles. If we refer back to examples

[52–53], which were ambiguous as between reflexive (or reciprocal) and middle interpretations, we note that, in [92–93], in spite of the generic or habitual function of these sentences, only the reflexive (or reciprocal) interpretation remains:

[92] les femmes, ça n'ose généralement pas se fouetter
       women, they don't generally dare to whip themselves / each other

[93] les enfants, ça n'ose pas se laver en dix minutes
       children, they don't dare to wash themselves / each other in ten minutes

We have facts of the same sort with verbs such as *forcer* (to force), which require their direct object to be identical with the understood subject of the infinitive complement, and which also require that this understood subject should be a deep subject, *cf*:

[94] le marquis a forcé Justine à $\begin{cases} \text{faire le ménage} \\ \text{*être caressée par le petit page} \\ \text{se faire caresser par le petit page} \\ \text{se quereller avec Juliette} \\ \text{s'empiffrer de foie gras} \end{cases}$

       the Marquis forced Justine to $\begin{cases} \text{do the housework} \\ \text{*to be fondled by the little page} \\ \text{have the little page fondle her} \\ \text{quarrel with Juliet} \\ \text{stuff herself with } foie\ gras \end{cases}$

[95] les policiers ont forcé la foule à $\begin{cases} \text{se disperser} \\ \text{s'attrouper} \end{cases}$

       the police forced the crowd to $\begin{cases} \text{disperse} \\ \text{gather together} \end{cases}$

[96] le président a contraint le conseil à se réunir à cinq heures du matin
       the President compelled the council to meet at five o'clock in the morning

Furthermore, R. Kayne has drawn my attention to a case that, though not directly pertinent insofar as the transformational versus lexical derivation of the neutrals is concerned, is nonetheless an instance of neutrals behaving like the intrinsics, and at the same time being differentiated both from the reflexives and reciprocals and from the middles. We know that, in certain conditions (embedding under certain verbs such as *faire, laisser*, etc), it happens that *se* alternates with Ø; now, this alternation is possible only for certain intrinsics, *cf: faites-le taire* (make him be silent), and for certain neutrals, *cf: je les ai fait asseoir* (I made them sit down), *j'ai envoyé les enfants promener* (I sent the children for a walk). It is impossible for the reflexives and the reciprocals: in no case can *j'ai fait laver les enfants* (I had the children washed), *j'ai fait détester Pierre et Marie* (I caused Peter and Mary to be hated) be interpreted as synonymous with *j'ai fait se laver les enfants* (I made the children wash themselves/each other), *j'ai fait se détester Pierre et Marie* (I made Mary and Peter hate each other). As for the middles, we know (*cf* Gross, 1968) that it is impossible, no doubt because of their generic or habitual interpretation, to embed them under *faire* or *laisser* (*cf *j'ai fait se nettoyer ma veste*). The idiomatic and residual nature of these expressions obviously limits the scope of this observation, but it is useful to remark that, in the seventeenth century, when this alternation between *se* and Ø was more frequent, it was also limited to the neutrals and intrinsics, to the exclusion of the reflexives and reciprocals (*cf* Haase, 1965, 144*ff*).[9]

6

If we now pass on to the middle constructions, we find that it is not very easy to discover decisive arguments in favour of a transformational solution, bearing in mind that such a solution does not in this case help to simplify the base rules. Nevertheless we have already seen some points – notably the regularity and productivity of the middle – which constitute a presumption in favour of a transformational derivation, but without providing a decisive argument (a redundancy rule can be very general and productive).

As we have seen, the traditional grammarians noticed the semantic similarities between the middle and the passive. It would be tempting, if we derive the middle constructions by means of rule [13], to see in this rule – at least in the part of it which places the NP object in subject position – the same rule as the part of the PASSIVE rule that places the object in subject position (the NP-PREPOSING rule proposed by Chomsky, 1970). This possibility was considered by H. G. Obenauer (in a Master's thesis of the Université de Paris VIII), but certain facts go against this identification. For example, we know that certain verbs with indirect object, *obéir* (to obey) and *pardonner* (to forgive), can be put into the passive (*cf* [97*a*–*b*], [98*a*–*b*]); but [97*c*], [98*c*] seem to me very doubtful, whereas we should expect to have them if the middles and the passives were derived by the same rule of NP-PREPOSING:

[97] *a:* le caporal a obéi au colonel
  the corporal obeyed the colonel
 b: le colonel a été obéi par le caporal
  the colonel was obeyed by the corporal
 c: ?*un chef pareil, ça ne s'obéit pas
  ?a leader like that does not get obeyed

[98] *a:* un chrétien pardonne à ses ennemis
  a Christian forgives his enemies
 b: nos ennemis seront pardonnés
  our enemies will be forgiven
 c: ?* les ennemis, ça ne se pardonne pas
  ?enemies, they don't get forgiven

(All the same, Maurice Gross tells me that he accepts these middle sentences.)

On the other hand, certain constructions which are impossible in the passive, are perhaps acceptable in the middle (though the data are rather doubtful here), *cf:*

[99] *a:* on a tiré sur les policiers
  someone fired on the police
 b: les policiers, on leur a tiré dessus
  the police were fired on
 c: *les policiers ont été tirés dessus
 d: ?les policiers, ça se tire dessus à vue
  ?the police, they're fired on at sight

We shall see below (section 6.1) two cases where the passive and middle constructions behave in an altogether different way. Further, we know that the phrase in *par NP*, corresponding to the agent of passive sentences, which used to be found in the middle constructions, is no longer grammatical in these constructions in modern French; [100], which was acceptable in the eighteenth century (*cf* Martinon, 1927, 302), is impossible today:

[100] *cela se dit par le peuple
  this is said by the people

Sentences such as [101–102] have sometimes (*cf* Stéfanini, 1962, 126) been put forward as counter-examples to this restriction:

[101] l'éducation du coeur se fait par les mères
  emotional discipline is instilled through the mother

[102] ce genre de liaison se rompt par le départ
this kind of attachment is broken off by separation

But here the phrases in *par NP* are actually not agents but instrumentals, as is proved by the fact that they can be questioned by means of *comment* (how); compare, from this point of view, [103–104] with [105*b*]:

[103] comment se fait l'éducation du coeur? – par les mères
how is emotional discipline instilled? – through the mother

[104] comment se rompt ce genre de liaison? – par le départ
how is this kind of attachment broken off? – by separation

[105] *a:* Pierre a été frappé $\begin{cases} \text{par Paul} \\ \text{avec une matraque} \end{cases}$

Peter was struck $\begin{cases} \text{by Paul} \\ \text{with a club} \end{cases}$

b: comment Pierre a-t-il été frappé? – $\begin{cases} \text{*par Paul} \\ \text{avec une matraque} \end{cases}$

how was Peter struck? – $\begin{cases} \text{*by Paul} \\ \text{with a club} \end{cases}$

Notice also the possibility of having the phrases in *par NP* of [101–102] in active sentences, with an expressed subject, which is not possible for the *par NP* phrase of [105*a*]; compare [106–107] with [108]:

[106] on fait l'éducation du coeur par les mères
one instils emotional discipline through the mother

[107] on rompt ce genre de liaison par le départ
one breaks off this kind of attachment by separation

[108] on a frappé Pierre $\begin{cases} \text{*par Paul} \\ \text{avec une matraque} \end{cases}$

someone hit Peter $\begin{cases} \text{*by Paul} \\ \text{with a club} \end{cases}$

The confusion arises from the possibility of having the same phrases functioning sometimes as agents (and occupying especially the subject position) and sometimes as instrumentals, *cf:*

[109] les mères font l'éducation du coeur
mothers instil emotional discipline

[110] le départ rompt ce genre de liaison
      separation breaks up this kind of attachment

In parenthesis, this discussion shows that, contrary to Fillmore's opinion (1968; see also Chomsky's criticism, 1972, and that of Dougherty, 1970a), it is not possible to equate the distinction between agents and instrumentals with that between animate and inanimate noun phrases. Examples [101], [103], [106] show that some animate NPs can function as instrumentals. Conversely, if various inanimates can function as agents (cf [110], as well as [111–112]), some are impossible, or very unnatural, with the function of instrumentals (compare [113] with [114]):

[111] le feu a détruit le pont
      fire destroyed the bridge

[112] le vent a renversé la barrière
      the wind overturned the barrier

[113] a: on a détruit le pont par le feu
           they destroyed the bridge by fire
       b: un pont, ça se détruit par le feu
           a bridge, that's destroyed by fire   .

[114] a: *on a renversé la barrière par le vent
           *they overturned the barrier by the wind
       b: *une barrière, ça se renverse par le vent
           *a barrier, that's overturned by the wind

The truth is that an NP, animate or inanimate, can be interpreted as agent if it participates in an autonomous way in the action expressed by the verb (for more details, see Chapter 4), and, conversely, one of the conditions of its being able to be interpreted as an instrumental depends on the possibility of interpreting its role in the action as non-autonomous. If the sentences of [114] – as opposed to those of [113] – are so unnatural, it is because it is difficult to imagine situations where the wind is used as a means in a given action. If we manage to imagine some such situations, sentences of this kind become possible, cf:

[115] Zeus a détruit la flotte d'Ulysse par le vent et la tempête
      Zeus destroyed Ulysses' fleet by wind and tempest

[116] quand on est un dieu en colère, les villes, ça se détruit par le vent et
      la tempête
      when you're an angry god, towns get destroyed by wind and
      tempest

6.1

Let us try to find other arguments in favour of a transformational derivation of the middles. The argument based on idiomatic expressions is not
very conclusive. The examples given by Kayne (1969, 162) as grammatical I find rather doubtful. If they seem to me less good than the corresponding passives, they are nonetheless apparently better than the neutrals
(*cf* [86–88]):

[117] ?assistance se porterait facilement à une si belle fille
       help would readily be given to such a beautiful girl

[118] ?justice se rendrait facilement dans ces conditions
       justice could easily be done in these conditions

One of the most decisive arguments that could be given in favour of a
transformational derivation (*cf* Chomsky, 1970) is to show that the rule or
rules concerned must be capable of being applied, not only to the base
structures, but also to structures of which one has reason to know that
they must be derived by transformation. Some of the best arguments
advanced in favour of rules such as PASSIVE, EQUI, RAISING, etc (*cf*
Chapter 2), are of this type; they imply a crucial resort to the order of the
transformational rules. If, as far as the neutrals are concerned, it is impossible to invoke facts of this sort – which is a negative argument
against a transformational derivation of the neutrals – the facts are less
clear in the matter of the middles.

Let us first of all consider a verb such as *juger* (to judge). This verb
appears in the constructions NP V NP (*cf* [119*a*]), NP V [$_S$ NP VP]$_S$
(*cf* [120*a*]), and NP V AP (*cf* [120*b*]). Some linguists (Gross, 1968,
Fauconnier, 1971) have accepted that the last of these constructions was
derived from the second by a transformation (OBJECT FORMATION)
which converts the subordinate subject into the object of the main verb:
[120*b*] would be derived from [120*a*] by OBJECT FORMATION, followed
by a transformation which deletes the subordinate verb *être*. Subsequently, the application of PASSIVE in the main clause gives [120*c*] on the same
basis as [119*b*]. The problem is as follows: if it is to be expected that
[120*d*] – the neutral construction – would be ungrammatical, a transformational derivation of the middles would predict that [120*e*] would be
grammatical. But [120*e*] is just as bad as [120*d*]:

[119] *a:* on a jugé ce criminel
       they have judged this criminal

  b: ce criminel a été jugé
   this criminal has been judged
  c: un criminel pareil, ça se juge
   a criminal like that, he's judged

[120] *a:* on a jugé que cet acte était odieux
   people judged that this action was odious
  b: on a jugé cet acte odieux
   people judged this action odious
  c: cet acte a été jugé odieux
   this action has been judged odious
  d: *cet acte s'est jugé odieux
  e: *un acte pareil, ça se juge odieux

All this is far from conclusive. In any event, it is not certain that the OBJECT FORMATION rule is justified. However this may be, we have here one more fact that distinguishes the middle sentences from the passive sentences.

A more interesting case is provided by sentences showing an inter-action of the middle and factitive constructions. At least some speakers accept sentences such as [121a], [122a], while rejecting [121b], [122b]. In a general way, if for many speakers examples (*a*) are rather doubtful, they are always felt to be better than the corresponding (*b*) examples – another difference between the neutrals and the middles:

[121] *a:* ?les enfants, ça se fait taire difficilement
   children are difficult to keep quiet
  b: *les enfants se sont fait taire difficilement hier soir
   *children kept quiet with difficulty yesterday evening

[122] *a:* ?les pommes de terre, ça se fait manger difficilement aux enfants
   ?potatoes are difficult to get children to eat
  b: *les pommes de terre se sont fait manger difficilement aux en-fants hier soir
   *potatoes got eaten by children with difficulty yesterday evening

It seems that we may well have an argument here for a transformational derivation of the middles. In fact, the base structure of [122a], for example, would be [123a], which is converted, by the rules for the forma-tion of factitives (*cf* Kayne, 1969, forthcoming), into [123b]; then, the MIDDLE-SE rule [13], reformulated so that it can operate over

the sequence *faire* V, will on the second cycle convert [123*b*] into
[122*a*]:

[123] *a:* Δ faire [$_S$ les enfants mangent difficilement les pommes de
              terre $_S$]
        b: Δ faire manger difficilement les pommes de terre aux enfants

As for the neutrals [121*b*] and [122*b*], they would be automatically
excluded if the neutrals are generated directly in the base, given the
absence in the base of a construction NP *se faire* S. Notice also, again, a
difference in behaviour between middle and passive sentences: in contrast with the relative acceptability of [121*a* – 122*a*], the corresponding
passives are excluded, *cf:*

[124] *les enfants ont été fait taire

[125] *les pommes de terre ont été fait manger

In this case, then, it is the passive sentences which are subject to a
restriction from which the middle sentences are apparently exempt. It is
exactly the opposite situation to what we had in examples [119–120].

6.2

Certain facts, which were drawn to my attention by R. Kayne, suggest
another argument in favour of the derivation of the middle sentences by
rule [13]. They concern the distribution of the pronouns *soi* and *soi-
même*. We know that, in modern French (*cf* Sandfeld, 1962, and Kayne,
1969, forthcoming), *soi* is no longer the stressed form corresponding to
the clitic reflexive *se*, but an object pronoun corresponding to an indefinite subject pronoun, usually *on* (sometimes also *chacun* (each one) or
tout le monde (everyone)), *cf:*

[126] en période troublée $\left\{\begin{array}{l}\text{on}\\\text{chacun}\end{array}\right\}$ ne pense qu'à soi

        in troubled times $\left\{\begin{array}{l}\text{one thinks only of oneself}\\\text{each thinks only of himself}\end{array}\right.$

Beside *soi*, we find *soi-même*, the distribution of which is subject to
restrictions similar to those which govern the distribution of the other
reflexives in *-même:*

[127] Pierre parle trop souvent de lui(-même)
        Peter talks too often about himself

[128] quand on parle trop souvent de soi(-même), on risque de faire fuir
     ses amis
    when one talks too often about oneself, one risks driving one's
    friends away

[129] Pierre croit que Marie est amoureuse de lui (*-même)
    Peter believes that Mary is in love with him(*self)

[130] quand on croit qu'une jolie femme est amoureuse de soi (*-même),
    on est prêt à faire toutes les folies
    when one thinks that a pretty woman is in love with one(*self),
    one is ready to commit any folly

Briefly, the forms in PRO-*même* are possible if they are coreferential
with an NP, provided that this NP is found in the same simple clause as
the form in PRO-*même*; the non-compound personal pronouns are not
subject to this restriction. *Lui-même* is possible in [127] because it is
coreferential with *Pierre*, the subject of the same simple clause, but
lui-même is impossible in [129] because the NP which is coreferential
with it, *Pierre* again, is not in the same simple clause (the subordinate).
We have the same restrictions on *soi-même* in [128] and [130].

Now, we have the following facts:

[131] cela se dit facilement de soi-même
    this is easily said of oneself

[132] ce genre d'objet s'achète facilement pour soi-même
    this sort of thing is readily bought for oneself

but:

[133] quand tout s'effondre autour de soi (*-même), on perd la tête
    when everything is collapsing around one(*self), one loses one's
    head

[131] and [132] are middle sentences; *s'effondrer*, in the subordinate
clause of [133], is a neutral verb. If the neutrals and the middles had the
same deep structure, we could not understand the differences in the
distribution of *soi(-même)*. On the other hand everything is explained
naturally if the deep structures that we have proposed are accepted – provided that it is also accepted that the 'empty' subject Δ that we placed
in the deep structure in [13] allows the coreference with *soi(-même)* just
like *on;* if it proved (*cf* section 3) that the understood agent of the middles
must be human, this empty subject could be replaced in [13] by a pronoun marked with the feature [+ HUMAN], and thus close to *on*.

In effect, [131], for example, will then have the following deep structure:

[134] Δ dit facilement cela de PRO (but see note 4)

This structure will be converted into [131] by the successive application of the REFLEXIVIZATION rule, introducing *soi-même* in place of PRO, by coreference with Δ (*cf* Kayne, 1969, forthcoming), and of the MIDDLE-SE rule. On the other hand, [133] will have as deep structure [135]:

[135] quand tout s'effondre autour de PRO, on perd la tête

PRO being coreferential with *on*, which is not in the same simple clause, the REFLEXIVIZATION rule, which introduces *soi-même*, cannot be applied. Only the PRONOMINALIZATION rule, introducing *soi*, which is not subject to this restriction on simple clauses, can be applied.

More briefly, if we consider only simple clauses, the difference between [131–132] on the one hand, and [136–137] on the other hand, can be explained if we assume the deep structures postulated:

[136] *tout s'est effondré autour de soi (-même)
       *everything has collapsed around one(self)

[137] *tous les amis se sont réunis autour de soi(-même)
       *all friends have gathered round one(self)

The neutrals being generated as such in the base, there is in [136] or [137] no NP (*on*, or *chacun*, or *tout le monde*, or Δ) capable of being coreferential with *soi(-même)*. If *soi* is possible in the subordinate clause of [133], it is because *soi*, unlike *soi-même*, can be coreferential with an NP not appearing in the same simple clause.

7

I come now to a final argument, of a very different type, which indicates that the middles must be treated transformationally, and which at the same time confirms that the neutrals must be generated in the base. This argument rests on considerations bearing on the relationships between certain categories of adverbials and the subjects of sentences.

It has often been noticed (*cf* Fodor, 1970) that certain adverbials are interpreted as referring to the subject of the sentence in deep structure. Thus, in [138]:

[138] les policiers ont dispersé les étudiants $\begin{cases} \text{avec enthousiasme} \\ \text{à regret} \end{cases}$

       the police dispersed the students $\begin{cases} \text{with enthusiasm} \\ \text{regretfully} \end{cases}$

the complements of manner refer to the subject: it is clear that it is the police and not the students who, as the case may be, show enthusiasm or regret. The important point is that this relationship remains intact if the deep structure has undergone transformations, for example the PASSIVE, as in [139]:

[139] les étudiants ont été dispersés par les policiers $\begin{cases} \text{avec enthousiasme} \\ \text{à regret} \end{cases}$

the students were dispersed by the police $\begin{cases} \text{with enthusiasm} \\ \text{regretfully} \end{cases}$

Parenthetically, I shall not here express an opinion as to the exact way in which the adverbials should be represented in deep structure; perhaps there is, underlying *avec enthousiasme* in [138], an embedded sentence (*cf* Kuroda, 1970), whose subject is subsequently deleted by identity with the main subject; underlying [138], we should then have something like:

[140] les policiers ont dispersé les étudiants [s les policiers avaient de l'enthousiasme]

the police dispersed the students [s the police had enthusiasm]

In this case, the selectional constraints that we observe between the subject and the adverbial would be treated within the embedded sentence. Perhaps on the contrary the adverbials are generated as they are in the base, and some interpretative mechanism attaches them to the subject, at the same time accounting for the selectional restrictions. This alternative does not bear directly on the point that concerns us here.

Furthermore, if it is clear in all the examples given and in those that will follow that the adverbials refer to the deep subjects, it must be said that the possibility of obtaining derived structures when some of these adverbials are present is subject to certain restrictions. Thus, the passive sentences are not always possible, *cf* the ungrammaticalness of [141]:

[141] *les étudiants ont été dispersés par les policiers en utilisant des matraques

*the students were dispersed by the police by using clubs

The conditions in which a derived structure containing adverbials is possible are, it seems, fairly complex, and bring various factors into play, such as the internal structure of the adverbial, the nature (animate or inanimate) of the derived subject, the presence or absence of an expressed agent complement, etc. These conditions would require a special study on their own, which I shall not undertake here. In any case, they do not bear on the point that concerns us, namely that these adverbials, when they are possible, always refer to the deep subject.

Let us now consider the following examples:

[142] *a:* les étudiants se sont dispersés $\begin{cases} \text{avec enthousiasme} \\ \text{à regret} \end{cases}$

   the students dispersed $\begin{cases} \text{with enthusiasm} \\ \text{regretfully} \end{cases}$

   b: les étudiants, ça se disperse $\begin{cases} \text{avec enthousiasme} \\ \text{à regret} \end{cases}$

   students, they disperse/ $\begin{cases} \text{with enthusiasm} \\ \text{regretfully} \end{cases}$
      are dispersed

It is evident i: that in [142*a*], it is the students, and not some indeterminate agent, who show enthusiasm or regret, ii: that [142*b*] is ambiguous (*cf* above examples [52–55]), and can be interpreted with the adverbs modifying either *les étudiants* or a non-specified agent. The facts are still clearer in [143], where *les vitres*, being [−ANIMATE], cannot be modified by a manner adverbial such as *avec enthousiasme*:

[143] *a:* les manifestants ont brisé les vitres avec enthousiasme
      the demonstrators broke the windows with enthusiasm
   b: les vitres ont été brisées (par les manifestants) avec enthousiasme
      the windows were broken (by the demonstrators) with enthusiasm
   c: *les vitres se sont brisées avec enthousiasme
      *the windows broke with enthusiasm
   d: les vitres, ça se brise avec enthousiasme
      windows get broken with enthusiasm

This time, [143*c*], which is neutral, is ungrammatical, and [143*d*] is not ambiguous and is interpreted as a middle.

These facts are not limited to the adverbials of manner, but are equally valid for the instrumental adverbials, *cf* [144–145], and for those of purpose, *cf* [146]:

[144] *a:* j'ai cassé cette branche $\begin{cases} \text{*sous son propre poids} \\ \text{d'une seule main} \\ \text{à coups de hache} \end{cases}$

   I broke this branch $\begin{cases} \text{*under its own weight} \\ \text{with one hand} \\ \text{with an axe} \end{cases}$

b: cette branche a été cassée { *sous son propre poids / d'une seule main / à coups de hache

this branch was broken { *under its own weight / with one hand / with an axe

c: cette branche s'est cassée { sous son propre poids / *d'une seule main / *à coups de hache

this branch broke { under its own weight / *with one hand / *with an axe

d: une branche comme ça, ça se casse { sous son propre poids[10] / d'une seule main / à coups de hache

a branch like that breaks under its own weight

a branch like that can be broken { with one hand / with an axe

[145] a: les policiers ont dispersé les étudiants à coups de matraques
           the police dispersed the students with clubs
        b: les étudiants ont été dispersés (par les policiers) à coups de
           matraques
           the students were dispersed (by the police) with clubs
        c: *les étudiants se sont dispersés à coups de matraques[11]
           *the students dispersed with clubs
        d: les étudiants, ça se disperse à coups de matraques
           students are dispersed with clubs

[146] a: nous avons cassé les branches mortes pour faire du feu
           we broke the dead branches to make a fire
        b: les branches mortes ont été cassées pour faire du feu
           the dead branches were broken to make a fire
        c: *les branches mortes se sont cassées pour faire du feu
           *the dead branches broke to make a fire
        d: les branches mortes, ça se casse pour faire du feu
           dead branches can be broken to make a fire

Let us agree that adverbials of manner, of purpose and the instrumentals,[12] are generated (as in Chomsky, 1965) in deep structure, either as

they are, or under the form of embedded sentences, in the same positions as those that they occupy in surface structure (this concept was rejected by Lakoff, 1968a, 1970c, in favour of the idea that the adverbials are predicates of higher sentences, but his arguments are unconvincing; for a critique of Lakoff, 1968a, see Bresnan, 1968); the constraints which connect them with the subject will also be determined at this level. With this concept, all the facts that we have looked at follow naturally from the hypothesis that the neutral constructions are basic and that the middles, on the other hand, are derived transformationally. Just consider the sentences of [143]. The deep structure of [143a–b] will be something like [147] (I am simplifying, retaining only those aspects of the structure which are pertinent to our argument):

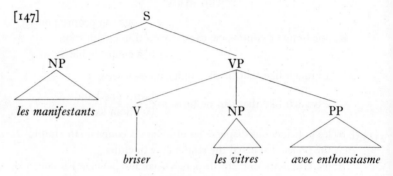

[147]

The deep subject, *les manifestants*, being [+ ANIMATE], satisfies the constraints on the occurrence of the manner adverbial *avec enthousiasme*, hence the grammaticalness both of [143a] and of [143b]. In the cases of [143c] and [143d], these will have respectively, as deep structures, [148] and [149]:

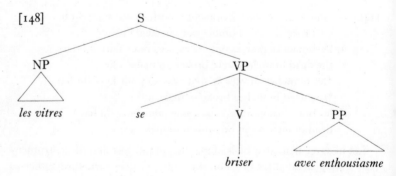

[148]

[149]

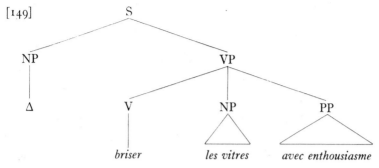

It is apparent that, if [143c] is excluded it is because, in [148], the selectional restrictions between the subject and the adverbial are violated. In the case of [143d], the 'empty' subject of [149] is, by definition, non-distinct (*cf* Chomsky, 1965, 81) from a subject satisfying the selectional restrictions imposed by the adverbial. Alternatively, if we put a human pronoun in place of the 'empty' subject, this will equally well satisfy these selectional restrictions. Thus [143d] is grammatical.

In the same way, [142a] (in the neutral, not the reciprocal, interpretation) will have [150] as deep structure, and [142b], which is ambiguous between a neutral and a middle interpretation, will have as deep structure, either, in the first case, [150] also, or, in the second, [151 overleaf]:

[150]

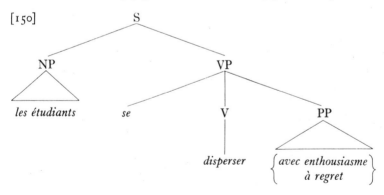

We see that, if [142a] and [142b] are equally grammatical, and if [142b] is ambiguous, it is because, on the one hand, in [150], *les étudiants*, being [+ ANIMATE], satisfies the selectional restrictions of the adverbial *avec enthousiasme* or *à regret*, while, on the other hand, in [151], we have the same conditions as in [149], the 'empty' subject being non-distinct from a subject satisfying these selectional restrictions.[13]

[151]

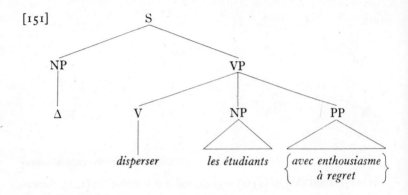

8

It is important to note that certain non-pronominal verbs, which are traditionally called middle, in fact generally behave like the neutrals. I am thinking of sentences such as [152b–154b]:

[152]   *a:* Pierre a cassé la branche
           Peter broke the branch
        b: la branche a cassé
           the branch broke

[153]   *a:* Adèle cuit le ragoût
           Adèle cooks the stew
        b: le ragoût cuit
           the stew cooks

[154]   *a:* le médecin a accouché Madeleine hier à six heures du soir
           the doctor delivered Madeleine yesterday at six o'clock in the
               evening
        b: Madeleine a accouché hier à six heures du soir
           Madeleine was delivered yesterday at six o'clock in the evening

As can be seen (*cf* especially [154]), these sentences are not subject to the time constraints characteristic of the middle constructions. Also, they show very idiosyncratic relationships with the corresponding transitive constructions, as well as with the neutral pronominal constructions. *Cf* for example, on the one hand:

[155]   *a:* ??Adèle marine les maquereaux (compare with [153])
           Adèle souses the mackerel
        b: les maquereaux marinent
           the mackerel are sousing

[156] *a:* l'ennemi a coulé le cuirassé
the enemy sank the battleship
b: le cuirassé a coulé
the battleship sank

[157] *a:* *l'ennemi a sombré le cuirassé
*the enemy foundered the battleship
b: le cuirassé a sombré
the battleship foundered

[158] *a:* ? ?le médecin a avorté Iphigénie (compare with [154])
? ?the doctor miscarried Iphigenia
b: Iphigénie a avorté
Iphigenia miscarried

[159] *a:* *Pierre a trébuché Paul
*Peter stumbled Paul
b: Paul a trébuché
Paul stumbled

And, on the other hand:

[160] *a:* la branche a cassé
the branch broke
b: la branche s'est cassée
the branch broke

[161] *a:* *la branche a brisé
b: la branche s'est brisée
the branch shattered

[162] *a:* Madeleine a accouché
Madeleine was delivered
b: *Madeleine s'est accouchée

In both cases, dialectal variations are to be expected. There are dialects in which [162*b*], and perhaps also [155*a*], [158*a*], are grammatical.

The subjects of these constructions – which might be called non-pronominal neutrals – also have all the properties of deep subjects, as is proved by the fact that they can be embedded as complements of certain verbs:

[163] Madeleine a daigné accoucher à l'heure prévue
Madeleine condescended to give birth at the due time

[164] le médecin a forcé Madeleine à accoucher prématurément
the doctor forced Madeleine to give birth prematurely

and by the constraints on the adverbials:

[165] *a:* Pierre a cassé la branche $\left\{\begin{array}{l}\text{pour faire du feu} \\ \text{*sous son propre poids}^{14} \\ \text{d'une seule main}\end{array}\right.$

Peter broke the branch $\left\{\begin{array}{l}\text{to make a fire} \\ \text{*under its own weight} \\ \text{with one hand}\end{array}\right.$

b: la branche a cassé $\left\{\begin{array}{l}\text{*pour faire du feu} \\ \text{sous son propre poids} \\ \text{*d'une seule main}\end{array}\right.$

the branch broke $\left\{\begin{array}{l}\text{*to make a fire} \\ \text{under its own weight} \\ \text{*with one hand}\end{array}\right.$

[166] *a:* Adèle a cuit le canard $\left\{\begin{array}{l}\text{avec précaution} \\ \text{tout en lisant} \\ \text{*en grésillant}\end{array}\right.$

Adèle cooked the duck $\left\{\begin{array}{l}\text{carefully} \\ \text{while reading} \\ \text{*sputteringly}\end{array}\right.$

b: le canard a cuit $\left\{\begin{array}{l}\text{*avec précaution} \\ \text{*tout en lisant} \\ \text{en grésillant}\end{array}\right.$

the duck cooked $\left\{\begin{array}{l}\text{*carefully} \\ \text{*while reading} \\ \text{sputteringly}\end{array}\right.$

The absence of a non-pronominal middle (in our sense) construction is clearly seen if we compare [167a] and [167b]. [167a] is an ordinary example of a middle construction, and [167b] is ungrammatical:

[167] *a:* un rôti, ça se cuit tout en lisant
　　　　a roast can be cooked while reading
　　　b: *un rôti, ça cuit tout en lisant
　　　　*a roast cooks while reading

Notes

1   I am leaving aside here sentences such as *Pierre se répète* (Peter repeats himself), *Paul s'est exprimé avec clarté* (Paul expressed himself with clarity), *la rivière se déroulait devant nos yeux* (the river stretched out before our eyes), etc, which, as Maurice Gross has pointed out to me (personal communication), pose special problems. Verbs like *répéter*, etc, in fact appear in the two frames NP_1 *se* — X and NP_1 — NP_2 X, but, in contrast with the case of the reflexives and the reciprocals, the possible NP_1s are not here a subset of the possible NP_2s. In fact, we have:

[I]   *a:* Paul ⎫
       Pierre ⎬ se répète sans arrêt

     Paul ⎫
     Peter ⎬ repeats himself continually

   b: *Pierre répète Paul sans arrêt
     *Peter repeats Paul continually
   c: Pierre répète sans arrêt les mêmes idées
     Peter repeats the same ideas continually

[II] *a:* Paul s'est exprimé avec clarté
     Paul expressed himself with clarity
   b: *Pierre a exprimé Paul avec clarté
     *Peter expressed Paul with clarity
   c: Pierre a exprimé ⎰ ses idées   ⎱ avec clarté
               ⎱ les idées de Paul ⎰

     Peter expressed ⎰ his ideas   ⎱ with clarity
               ⎱ Paul's ideas ⎰

[III] *a:* la rivière ⎫
      la route ⎬ se déroulait devant nos yeux

     the river ⎫
     the road ⎬ stretched out before our eyes

   b: *la rivière déroulait la route devant nos yeux
     *the river stretched out the road before our eyes
   c: la rivière déroulait ses méandres devant nos yeux
     the river stretched out its windings before our eyes

We see that the sentences of type (*a*) can be approximately paraphrased by sentences of type (*c*), those of type (*b*) being impossible. In the sentences of type (*c*), there is a possible coreferentiality relationship, not between the subject and the object (which would characterize the underlying structure of the true reflexives), but between the subject and an element of the determiner of the object. I shall leave aside here the question as to whether sentences of type (*a*) should be derived from constructions of type (*c*), or whether on the other hand verbs of type (*a*) should be treated as 'intrinsic' pronominals (see later in this chapter). I hope to return to this question elsewhere.

2   *Ce sapin s'admire* (this fir-tree is admired) is no doubt possible, but then it is a question of a middle construction (see further on).

3   For a modification and an improvement of rule [15], see Chapter 4.

4   I shall not here take a stand on the much-debated question as to whether the reflexive constructions are derived from deep structures by substitution of the reflexive pronoun for a 'full' NP, identical with another coreferential NP (in this case [16] would be derived from [17*c*]) (*cf* Lees and Klima, 1963), or whether the reflexive pronouns are generated in the base in the position of

NP, either directly under their stressed form (*lui-même*, etc), or under the form of an abstract pronoun (PRO), to be subsequently marked coreferential with other NPs by rules of semantic interpretation (this is Jackendoff's position, 1969b). This point does not affect my argument. It will be seen later that, for reasons of exposition, I choose to represent the pronouns in the base by an abstract form PRO.

5 Notice that *les deux équipes se sont réunies l'une à l'autre* (the two teams joined up with one another) is possible, but this is another construction, NP *se réunir à* NP.

6 At first sight, the verb *subir* (to undergo) provides a counter-example to this generalization, *cf:*

[I] les tortures, ça se subit sans broncher
     tortures are undergone without flinching

It seems difficult to interpret the subject of *subir* as an agent. In fact, it seems to me that *subir* is ambiguous, and that it allows an agentive or non-agentive interpretation of its subject, *cf:*

[II] *a:* Pierre a forcé Paul à subir un interrogatoire serré
         Peter forced Paul to undergo a close interrogation

$$
b:\ \text{Paul a} \left\{ \begin{array}{l} \text{stoïquement} \\ \text{de son plein gré} \\ \text{volontairement} \\ \text{joyeusement} \end{array} \right\} \text{subi} \left\{ \begin{array}{l} \text{d'horribles tortures} \\ \text{un interrogatoire serré} \end{array} \right.
$$

$$
\text{Paul} \left\{ \begin{array}{l} \text{stoically} \\ \text{of his own accord} \\ \text{voluntarily} \\ \text{blithely} \end{array} \right\} \text{underwent} \left\{ \begin{array}{l} \text{horrible tortures} \\ \text{a close interrogation} \end{array} \right.
$$

In [IIa], *subir* is embedded as complement of a verb that normally imposes an agentive interpretation on the subordinate subject (deleted by EQUI by coreference with the main direct object); in [IIb], we see that *subir* allows typical adverbs of agentive constructions. For more details on the notion of agent, see Chapters 4 and 5.

7 Of course, [59b] is possible in its neutral interpretation. On verbs of the class of *amuser, toucher*, etc, see Chapter 5.

8 More exactly, *évanouir* will be marked in the lexicon with the features $[+se\dots\text{——}]$ and $[+[A\text{——}pé]_A]$, the latter to account for sentences such as *Pierre est évanoui* (Peter is in a faint).

9 R. Kayne draws my attention to yet another difference between neutrals and middles, of a rather mysterious nature. In the neutral constructions, the presence of the clitic *se* prevents the placing of the dative pronoun in clitic position, in the manner of the ordinary clitics, *cf* [I]–[II]:

[I] *a:* cela s'est révélé à moi
         this was revealed to me
     b: *cela se m'est révélé

[II] *a:* je me suis déclaré à elle
          I declared myself to her
      b: *je me lui suis déclaré

In the middle constructions, on the other hand, we have the following paradigm:

[III] Δ achète ça pour soi → ça s'achète pour soi
       Δ buys that for oneself → that is bought for oneself

[IV] Δ achète ça à soi → *ça s'achète à soi

[V] Δ dit ça de soi → ça se dit de soi
Δ says that of oneself → that is said of oneself

[VI] Δ dit ça à soi → *ça se dit à soi
Δ says that to oneself → *that is said to oneself

In other words, if we have *soi* (or *soi-même*) in positions (*cf* [III], [V]) which are not sources of clitic pronouns, the middle sentences are grammatical. But if, as in [IV] and in [VI], *soi(-même)* is generated in a position which is the source of a dative clitic pronoun, it is impossible to obtain a well-formed surface structure corresponding to the deep structure source: the pronoun, apparently, cannot remain in its base position, and further, *ça se s'achète, *ça se se dit*, are excluded by the general constraint which forbids any sequence of *se se, se me, se lui*, etc. It seems then that the presence of a *se* of middle origin, contrary to the general rule, is not associated with blocking of the clitic-placing rule.

10 [144*d*] is grammatical, whatever adverbial is chosen, for the following reason: *une branche comme ça, ça se casse* is ambiguous (*cf* [52–55]); *une branche comme ça, ça se casse sous son propre poids* (a branch like that breaks under its own weight) is then interpreted as a neutral construction, and the two other sentences are taken as cases of middles.

11 Of course, [145*c*] is grammatical if this sentence is interpreted in a reciprocal sense (*cf* [34]).

12 It is important to note that the obligation to interpret an adverbial as referring to the deep subject does not apply to all types of adverbials. As Fodor has noted (1970), it does not apply to adverbials of time, *cf*:

[I] la police a arrêté Pierre avant de fusiller Paul
the police arrested Peter before shooting Paul

[II] Paul a été arrêté (par la police) avant d'avoir pu finir son repas
Paul was arrested (by the police) before being able to finish his meal

In [I] it is *la police* (both deep and surface subject) which is interpreted as the subject of *fusiller*, but in [II] it is *Paul*, the surface subject, which is interpreted as the subject of *avoir pu finir*. Other cases are less clear, as for example that of the 'gerunds' of the form *en* V-*ant* X. If, in certain cases, they behave like manner adverbials or instrumentals:

[III] les policiers ont dispersé les manifestants en hurlant
the police dispersed the demonstrators, yelling

[IV] les manifestants, ça se disperse en hurlant
demonstrators can be dispersed by yelling

[V] ?les manifestants ont été dispersés (par les policiers) en hurlant
?the demonstrators were dispersed (by the police) by yelling

(notice the difference in acceptability between the middle construction and the passive), in other cases, we find them referring either to surface subjects [VI], or to non-subject phrases [VII] which are not necessarily expressed:

[VI] *a:* j'ai été convaincu en lisant Chomsky
I was convinced by reading Chomsky
b: ?Marie a été violée en prenant son bain
?Mary was raped taking a bath

[VII] *a:* l'appétit vient en mangeant
         the appetite grows with eating
      b: cette idée m'est venue en dormant
         this idea came to me while sleeping

Note also

[VIII] Pierre a été arrêté sans savoir pourquoi
       Peter was arrested without knowing why

These facts would require a deeper study. As far as the 'gerunds' are concerned, these elements seem very ambiguous: they can be interpreted just as well as manner adverbials, as instrumentals or as adverbials of time, which would perhaps explain the variations in their behaviour. The character of agent or of non-agent of the subject also doubtless plays a part (in [VII] the subjects are not agents).

Notice also, regarding the adverbials of purpose, that, in certain conditions, their presence blocks the passive transformation, *cf:*

[IX] on a torturé Pierre $\begin{cases} \text{pour sauver la France} \\ \text{pour le faire parler} \end{cases}$

they tortured Peter $\begin{cases} \text{to save France} \\ \text{to make him talk} \end{cases}$

[X] Pierre a été torturé $\begin{cases} \text{pour sauver la France} \\ \text{*pour le faire parler} \end{cases}$

Peter was tortured $\begin{cases} \text{to save France} \\ \text{to make him talk} \end{cases}$

This should perhaps be compared with the constraints relating to the verb *menacer* noted in Chapter 2, note 11.

13 The same type of argument that we have just used with reference to the adverbials which necessarily relate to the deep subject, could be reproduced when it is a question of adverbials which relate to the deep object. In fact we have the following sentences:

[I] *a:* Philip Marlowe boit toujours son whisky sec
        Philip Marlowe always drinks his whisky neat
    b: Marie-Hélène a pris son bain très chaud
        Marie-Hélène took her bath very hot
    c: Rodrigue a embrassé Chimène dans le cou
        Rodrigue kissed Chimène on the neck

[II] *a:* ce whisky a été bu sec
         this whisky was drunk neat
     b: ce bain a été pris trop chaud (par Marie-Hélène)
         this bath was taken too hot (by Marie-Hélène)
     c: Chimène a été embrassée dans le cou par Rodrigue
         Chimène was kissed on the neck by Rodrigue

As expected, the middle constructions allow these adverbials, relating to the surface subject, *ie* the deep object, *cf:*

[III] *a:* un whisky de douze ans d'âge, ça se boit sec
          a twelve-year-old whisky is drunk neat
      b: un bon bain, ça se prend très chaud
          a good bath is taken very hot

c: les filles⎱
   une fille comme ça⎰, ça s'embrasse dans le cou

    girls are⎱ kissed on the neck
  a girl like that is⎰

14 The sentence *Pierre a cassé la branche sous son propre poids* (Peter broke the branch under his own weight) is no doubt grammatical if we agree that it means Peter's own weight, and not that of the branch. This confirms that the adverbial modifies the deep subject.

Chapter 4

Factitive constructions*

Of the discussions which currently range the supporters of 'generative semantics' against those of 'standard' generative theory or those of the 'extended standard theory' (on these distinctions, see especially Chomsky 1971, 1972), a large proportion hinge on the question whether, in the representation of the sentences of a language, it is legitimate to propose a level of *deep structure* distinct both from the level of surface structure and from that of the semantic representation of sentences. As we know, this level plays a central role in standard theory (see Chomsky, 1965).

Though extended standard theory (see Chomsky, 1971, 1972, Jackendoff, 1969b, Dougherty, 1969, etc), has abandoned the hypothesis that only the syntactic information contained in the deep structure is relevant for the semantic interpretation, and though it allows that some aspects of the surface structure (and perhaps also of certain other intermediate levels) contribute to the semantic interpretation, it nonetheless maintains the level of deep structure. It continues, in particular, to affirm that, on the one hand, the deep structure is characterized by the fact that all the lexical items have been inserted into the phrase-markers generated by the base rules (in other words, all the (transformational) rules of lexical insertion are ordered before the syntactic transformations), and that, on the other hand, at least as far as the semantic role of the grammatical relations and functions (as they are defined in Chomsky, 1965) is concerned, only the grammatical relations and functions defined in deep structure contribute to the semantic interpretation.

* Revised version of 'Défense de la structure profonde: les constructions factitives en français', *Scritti e Ricerche di Grammatica Italiana*, Trieste, Editrice Lint, 1972.

The supporters of generative semantics on their side (*cf* McCawley, 1968*b*, 1968*c*, Postal, 1970*a*, Lakoff, 1970*a*, 1971), assert that this intermediate level is superfluous. For them, the base rules, similar to the rules of a logical calculus, generate semantic representations, which are converted into surface structures by means of rules of a single type, which are transformations.

More precisely, in its most recent versions (*cf* various works by Lakoff, especially 1971), generative semantics conceives the derivation of a sentence as a sequence of phrase-markers $I_1, \ldots, I_n$, where I_1 is the semantic representation of the sentence and I_n its surface structure, a sequence which is subject to 'derivational constraints' which define well-formedness conditions on configurations of corresponding nodes in phrase-markers; these are not necessarily adjacent. The transformations are then conceived as particular cases of these derivational constraints: they are 'local' constraints, in the sense that they define well-formedness conditions on adjacent phrase-markers; there would also be 'global' constraints, defining well-formedness conditions on non-adjacent phrase-markers. For a discussion of this notion of global derivational constraints, whose descriptive power is enormous, and on the question whether it is legitimate to equate transformations with local derivational constraints, see Chomsky, 1972.

A crucial point is that, for generative semantics, lexical transformations, instead of substituting, as in Chomsky (1965), lexical items (represented by matrices of syntactic, semantic and phonological features) for occurrences of the dummy symbol Δ, substitute phonological representations of lexical items for (semantic) configurations in phrase-markers, and they are not necessarily ordered before the syntactic transformations.[1]

As Chomsky (1971, 1972) and Katz (1970, 1971) have tried to show, a large part of these discussions is purely terminological, and it seems that, at least on certain points, generative semantics is no more than a notational variant of the standard theory. Nevertheless, I shall not follow Katz in completely equating the two theories (an equation which to a large extent results in depriving the notion of deep structure of its content). If Katz is right in holding that it is not legitimate to talk of two distinct *theories* in the strict sense, certain differences of emphasis seem to me more interesting than the resemblances, and I shall try to suggest that a theory which includes a level of deep structure is better equipped to handle some types of facts, certain of which are of a semantic order, than a theory which has no place for this level.

We know that the development of generative semantics is the logical result of a tendency which had led certain linguists, considering it established that transformations do not change meaning, to propose more and more abstract deep structures (*ie* more and more distant from the surface) (*cf* for example, Lakoff, 1968*a*); correlatively, these linguists proposed to introduce into the grammar a certain number of new transformations, with properties which were often bizarre, which were intended to convert these very abstract structures into more familiar structures. These new transformations were then made use of more and more frequently to justify more and more abstract syntactic analyses. It would not be an exaggeration to say that the entire edifice of generative semantics rests on the hypothesis that three or four particular transformations have a privileged status in grammars. But linguists are far from being all agreed on the legitimacy of these transformations. For one thing, several of these transformations (*cf* Chomsky, 1972, Hasegawa, 1970) have formal properties that are not very desirable. Further, if we look back to the type of arguments, of a purely syntactic kind, which were traditionally invoked to justify the introduction of any particular transformation into a grammar (regularization of the paradigms, simplification of the base structure, arguments of order, etc, *cf* Chomsky, 1970, and Chapters 2 and 3 of this book, etc), we see that in general this type of argument is lacking when it comes to justifying the proposed new transformations. As has been pointed out, especially by Chomsky (1970) and Jackendoff (1969b), the types of facts invoked, when they are not of a purely semantic nature, can often be handled by means of mechanisms other than transformational ones (for example, lexical redundancy rules), mechanisms which are available in the standard theory.

My intention, in this chapter and the following one, is to consider types of facts, to handle which the generative semanticists have proposed to introduce transformations that have subsequently been used in a large number of other analyses. The syntactic arguments invoked in their favour are rather weak, and have already often been discussed elsewhere, at least for English (the facts concerned are fairly similar in French and English). I shall endeavour especially to show that certain aspects, of a lexical or semantic order, of the constructions in question do not only pose problems for generative semantics, but seem likely to be treated in a more revealing way within the framework of standard theory or of extended standard theory (here it will not be a question of the types of facts which led Chomsky and other linguists to abandon standard theory in favour of extended standard theory).

1

In the preceding chapter, I proposed to treat the relationship between the neutral pronominal constructions and the transitive constructions, not by deriving the first from the second by the MIDDLE-SE transformation (*cf* Chapter 3, [13]), but by means of redundancy rules (*cf* Chapter 3, [15]), of which the general form would be:

[1] $[+V], [+ \underline{\quad} NP \ X], [+ \underline{\quad} [\alpha F]] \rightarrow [+V], [+ [\alpha F] \ se \ldots \underline{\quad} X]$

(where $[\alpha F]$ represents the features of the object NP relevant for the selection of the transitive verb).

In fact, this formulation now seems to me incorrect, and I should like to replace rule [1] by the following rule:

[2] $[+V], [+ (se) \ldots \underline{\quad} X], [+ [\alpha F] \ldots \underline{\quad}] \rightarrow [+V], [+ CAUSE],$
$[+ \underline{\quad} NP \ X], [+ \underline{\quad} [\alpha F]]$

This reformulation amounts to introducing the verbs into the lexicon no longer as transitive but as intransitive, and accounting for their transitive use by the redundancy rule [2]. A verb such as *réunir* will then appear in the lexicon with the features $[+V], [+ se \ldots \underline{\quad}], [+ [- SEM \ SING]$ $\ldots \underline{\quad}]$, which accounts for *l'équipe se réunit* (the team assembles), *les soldats se réunissent* (the soldiers assemble), *Pierre se réunit (*Peter assembles), etc, and it will be rule [2] which will account for its transitive uses, in *l'entraîneur a réuni l'équipe* (the trainer assembled the team), *le chef a réuni les soldats* (the leader assembled the soldiers), **le chef a réuni Pierre* (*the leader assembled Peter), etc.

The reasons for this modification (which is based on the formulation suggested by Chomsky, 1970) are as follows. Firstly, rule [2] distinguishes the selectional features $([+ [\alpha F] \ldots \underline{\quad}])$ from the strict subcategorization features $([+ (se) \ldots \underline{\quad}])$, whereas rule [1] did not distinguish them. Further, by means of the introduction of the feature $[+ CAUSE]$, it accounts for the systematic semantic difference between the neutral verbs and the corresponding transitives, the latter being interpreted as causatives of the former. Lastly, it allows a better treatment of the differences between pronominal and non-pronominal intransitives. I had in fact indicated (Chapter 3, section 8) that the non-pronominal intransitive constructions, which have the same properties as the neutral pronominal constructions, should be treated in the same way, *cf* the paradigms:

[3] l'équipe s'est réunie
the team assembled

[4] la branche s'est brisée
    the branch broke

[5] le chef a réuni l'équipe
    the leader assembled the team

[6] Pierre a brisé la branche
    Peter broke the branch

[7] la branche a cassé
    the branch broke

[8] le ragoût cuit
    the stew is cooking

[9] ce galopin a cassé la branche
    this urchin broke the branch

[10] Adèle cuit le ragoût
     Adèle is cooking the stew

Now, as I also noted, there are many idiosyncrasies in the occurrence of pronominal and non-pronominal features in the intransitives (*cf: la branche se casse, la branche se brise*, compared with *la branche casse*, *la branche brise). The natural place to treat these idiosyncrasies is the lexical entry for these verbs. Thus, if we accept the formulation of [2], *casser* will be introduced into the lexicon with the feature $[+(se) \ldots \text{---} \#]$, *se briser* with only the feature $[+se \ldots \text{---} \#]$, and *cuire* with only the feature $[+ \text{---} \#]$; the transitive verbs *casser, briser, cuire*, will all be introduced by rule [2]. If on the other hand we introduced the transitives directly in the lexicon and if we obtained the intransitives by means of rules such as [1], we would be obliged to complicate these rules, in order to account for the capricious distribution of the pronominal and non-pronominal intransitives. To introduce the non-pronominals, another rule would be necessary,

[11] $[+V], [+ \text{---} NP \ X], [+ \text{---} [\alpha F]] \rightarrow [+V], [+[\alpha F] \ldots \text{---} X]$,

and we would need to mark the verbs as being subject to [1] and [11] equally (as in the case of *casser*), or as subject only to [1] (*briser*), or only to [11] (*cuire*).

There is nevertheless, *a priori*, another possible transformational solution for relating the intransitive constructions of [3], [4], [7], [8], to the corresponding transitive constructions [5], [6], [9], [10]. This solution consists, not in deriving the intransitive constructions from the transitives by means of MIDDLE-SE (or by a similar rule not introducing the *se* in the case of [7–8]), but, on the contrary, in deriving the transitive constructions from complex sentences in which an intransitive sentence is embedded as complement of a causative verb; as we see at once, this solution also allows us to formulate the selectional restrictions in one statement, but, whereas the MIDDLE-SE solution amounted to formulating them on the level of the relations between the verb and the object in the transitive sentences, this solution amounts to formulating them on the level of the relations between the subject and the verb in the intransitive sentences. Like the lexical solution, this second solution would have the advantage of removing the problem which existed for the MIDDLE-SE solution, namely that the subjects of sentences such as [3–4] behave in all respects like deep subjects.

This second transformational solution has in fact been proposed, for English, by Lakoff (1970c), who suggests deriving [12] from an underlying structure analogous to that of [13]:

[12] Floyd melted the glass

[13] Floyd caused the glass to melt

This solution was subsequently taken up by McCawley (1968c), and extended to cases where morphemic identity of the two verbs, the transitive and intransitive, is not found; in this way McCawley proposes to derive [14] from [15]:

[14] John killed Mary

[15] John caused Mary to die

More precisely, Lakoff and McCawley propose to derive [12] and [13], on the one hand, and [14] and [15], on the other hand, from semantic structures such as [16] and [17],[2] where the terminal elements, written in capital letters, are considered to represent semantic primitives:

[16] FLOYD CAUSE [$_S$ THE GLASS MELT]

[17] JOHN CAUSE [$_S$ MARY DIE]

The surface structures [12] and [14] are derived from these underlying structures by means of two transformational rules: (a) first there is a rule, called PREDICATE RAISING, which extracts the verb from the subordinate clause and places it on the right of the main verb, giving the intermediate structures:

[18] FLOYD CAUSE-TO-MELT THE GLASS

[19] JOHN CAUSE-TO-DIE MARY

(b) then there is an operation of LEXICALIZATION, which substitutes a lexical item, more precisely a morphophonological form, *melt* or *kill*, for the sequence of semantic elements constituted by the causative verb and the subordinate verb. The PREDICATE-RAISING rule is optional; if it does not operate, the operations of LEXICALIZATION will have different results; MELT will be spelled out as *melt*, DIE *die*, and the causative verb will become *cause;* we then obtain the surface structures [13] and [15].

This analysis, if it were correct, would have important theoretical consequences. It implies in effect that certain syntactic transformations (in this instance PREDICATE-RAISING) can apply before the lexical insertion transformations, which involves abandoning one of the essential hypotheses relating to the status of deep structure. At first sight, as far as French is concerned, it may appear attractive. Let us look again at example [10]. We see that, beside [10], there exists a factitive sentence such as [20], which is of a very common type, and which, moreover, is apparently in a relationship of paraphrase with [10]:

[10] Adèle cuit le ragoût
     Adèle cooks the stew

[20] Adèle fait cuire le ragoût
     Adèle causes the stew to cook

We could then suggest, after Lakoff and McCawley, deriving [10] and [20] from the same underlying structure, say [21]:

[21] ADÈLE CAUSE [$_S$ LE RAGOÛT CUIRE]

In fact, still at first sight, French even shows a more favourable situation for this analysis than English. Indeed, Chomsky (1972) has shown that, in English, the PREDICATE-RAISING rule, as it is formulated by McCawley, is entirely *ad hoc;* it has no reason for existence other than to make possible this analysis of transitive sentences starting from complex sentences, and especially to create conditions such that the sequence of (semantic) elements for which a lexical item (*kill* for example in [19]) is substituted can be a constituent. McCawley in fact admits that the LEXICALIZATION rule can only substitute a lexical item for a sequence of terminal elements if that sequence is a constituent. Now, R. S. Kayne (1969) has shown that, if we wish to describe the syntax of French factitive constructions of the type of [20], we are, for entirely independent reasons, led to derive them from deep structures such as [22]:

[22] Adèle fait [$_S$ le ragoût cuire]

by means, in particular, of a transformation (called by Kayne FAIRE-ATTRACTION) which attaches the subordinate verb to the right of the main verb *faire* (this has various important syntactic consequences, which do not concern us here), and so is in form close to PREDICATE-RAISING. If FAIRE-ATTRACTION was ordered before LEXICALIZA-TION, an important part of the derivation of [10] from [21] would then be justified in an independent way, and the only new thing would be the choice, on the level of LEXICALIZATION, between the replacement of CAUSE + CUIRE by *cuire* and its replacement by *faire + cuire*.

Actually, as Kayne formulates it, the FAIRE-ATTRACTION rule does not resolve the difficulty raised by Chomsky: in fact, according to Kayne, the derived structure resulting from FAIRE-ATTRACTION is either [23a] or [23b]:

[23]

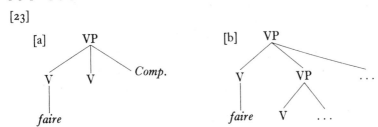

We see that, in one case as in the other, the sequence *faire* + V is not a constituent, and that, in order to make it so, a new operation, otherwise totally unjustified, would be necessary.

Nonetheless, if this represents a difficulty for McCawley's 'extended' analysis (the one which has the most important theoretical implications), it is not a difficulty for the analysis (compatible with the traditional conception of deep structure), which would consider, not [21] (a purely semantic structure), but [22] (a deep syntactic structure, where the lexical items have already been inserted), as the underlying structure of [10]. [10] would be obtained by the successive application of FAIRE-ATTRAC-TION and of a rule which would substitute, not a morphophonological form for a sequence of semantic elements, but simply the subordinate verb for the main verb *faire;* this transformation, which is of a more traditional type, could be formulated as follows:

[24] FAIRE-SUBSTITUTION (optional):

$$
\begin{array}{ccccc}
X & - faire & - V & - Y \\
1 & 2 & 3 & 4 \\
\Rightarrow 1 & 3 & \emptyset & 4
\end{array}
$$

In fact, the objections which are to follow are just as valid against this restricted conception as against the extended conception, independently of the additional difficulties that the latter meets in other respects; my conclusion will be, then, that whatever formulation is given to it a transformational solution is inadequate to treat the regularities of selection which relate intransitive sentences like [3], [4], [8] to transitive sentences like [5], [6], [10]. So, in the framework of the present theory, only the possibility of treating these regularities in terms of lexical redundancy rules remains. This might suggest (*cf* also Jackendoff's remarks, 1969b (Introduction) and those of Fodor, 1970) that it would be necessary to constrain, more severely than in the standard theory, the types of transformational operations which can affect lexical items. We could for example rule out transformations which, like [24], substitute for one another items belonging to one of the lexical categories N, V, A (*cf* Chomsky, 1965, 74 and *passim*).

2

The analysis of Lakoff and McCawley has already evoked various criticisms in relation to English (*cf* Chomsky, 1971, 1972, Hall-Partee, 1971, and especially Fodor, 1970). I shall look at some of these criticisms in passing, shall propose others, and shall suggest a means of treating the several types of facts invoked in a uniform manner.

I shall not dwell on the fact that the classic arguments in favour of a transformational solution do not apply here. Short of showing that all direct transitive constructions can be traced to complex constructions in which intransitive constructions are embedded (which no one, to my knowledge, has tried to do up to the present), the proposed analysis cannot result in any simplification of the base rules.[3] No well-established transformation seems to precede the rules of PREDICATE-RAISING, LEXICALIZATION or FAIRE-SUBSTITUTION.[4] Again, for a large number of verbs, the two constructions do not both exist, and, for a certain number of these verbs at all events, it appears impossible to reduce these lacunae to any syntactic or semantic regularity (*cf* Chapter 3), which is a strong indication that a lexical solution is preferable.

Lakoff (1970c) considered that he had found certain facts involving pronouns, for which a transformational analysis of the sort that he proposes would provide an explanation, but Fodor (1970) has criticized this convincingly, and has suggested another solution remaining within the framework of the 'lexicalist' analysis; moreover, apparently, the facts invoked by Lakoff are often of rather doubtful grammaticality, and even more markedly so in French than in English.

Lakoff's examples are of the following type:

[25] Floyd melted the glass, and *it* surprised me

(where *it* is ambiguous, meaning either 'that Floyd melted the glass' or 'that the glass melted')

[26] Floyd melted the glass, though it surprised me that $\begin{Bmatrix} he \\ it \end{Bmatrix}$ would do so

(where *he would do so* = 'Floyd melted the glass', and *it would do so* = 'the glass melted')

Given a transformational analysis of pronouns, which obtains them by substitution for full NPs (or VPs), under conditions of identity with an antecedent, the transformationalist theory would explain the ambiguity of [25] and the possibility of having either *he* or *it* in [26]. But this transformational theory of pronouns is itself very unreliable (see Dougherty, 1969, Jackendoff, 1969b), and Fodor suggests another solution for dealing with these facts. In French, facts of this sort seem to me even more marginal and more limited than in English. Thus, keeping to Lakoff's theory, if [27] were derived from [28],

[27] les policiers ont dispersé les trotskystes
      the police dispersed the Trotskyites

[28] les policiers ont fait se disperser les trotskystes
      the police made the Trotskyites disperse

we would expect to have [30] beside [29] (and with the same meaning of *en faire autant* (to do the same)); but [30] is impossible in this reading:

[29] les maoïstes se sont dispersés et les trotskystes en ont fait autant
      the Maoists dispersed and the Trotskyites did so too

[30] *les policiers ont dispersé les maoïstes, et les trotskystes en ont fait autant
      *the police dispersed the Maoists, and the Trotskyites did so too

It is clear that [30] is only acceptable with the reading that the Trotskyites collaborated with the police to disperse the Maoists; the impossibility of [30] in the other reading is still more obvious if we substitute *là pluie* (the rain) for *les policiers*. In the same way:

[31] ?la porte de devant s'est ouverte, et celle de derrière en a fait autant
      ?the front door opened, and the back door did the same

[32] *Jules a ouvert la porte de devant, et celle de derrière en a fait autant
*Julius opened the front door, and the back door did so too

Nevertheless there are certain cases where sentences of this sort seem more or less acceptable, as, for example:

[33] ?Graham Hill a calé le moteur de la Lotus, et tout de suite après celui de la Ferrari en a fait autant
?Graham Hill stalled the engine of the Lotus, and immediately afterwards the Ferrari engine did the same

Fodor suggests that, in certain conditions, an anaphoric element (perhaps generated directly in the base) which refers to a transitive verb, can also refer to the intransitive verb of the same morphophonological form (in fact, these anaphoric phenomena are impossible if the two verbs are of different phonological form, *cf: *John killed Mary, and Susan did so too*). It seems that, in French, this identity of the morphophonological form should be understood in a very strict sense; in fact, example [33], in contrast to examples [30] and [32], is characterized by the fact that *caler* (to stall), intransitive, is non-pronominal, and so is not phonologically (morphologically) distinguished from the transitive verb, which is not the case with *disperser / se disperser, ouvrir / s'ouvrir*.

In the main, Fodor's arguments (1970) are as valid for French as for English. I shall not therefore dwell on this too much, contenting myself with giving examples and referring the reader to Fodor's demonstration. In particular, he shows that, in a complex factitive sentence, it is sometimes possible to have different adverbials of time, referring to different moments of time, in the main clause and in the subordinate clause [*cf* [34]], which is impossible in a simple sentence (*cf* [35]); now, a simple sentence with a factitive transitive verb, such as [36], is as unacceptable as [35], whereas Lakoff's transformational analysis would predict that it would be grammatical, and could only exclude it by recourse to an *ad hoc* condition on PREDICATE-RAISING or on FAIRE-SUBSTITUTION:

[34] le médecin a fait accoucher Madeleine dimanche en lui donnant un médicament samedi
the doctor caused Madeleine to give birth on Sunday by giving her medicine on Saturday

[35] *l'astronome a observé la comète dimanche en regardant dans le télescope samedi
*the astronomer observed the comet on Sunday by looking through the telescope on Saturday

[36] *le médecin a accouché Madeleine dimanche en lui donnant un
médicament samedi
*the doctor delivered Madeleine on Sunday by giving her medicine
on Saturday

A second argument of Fodor's concerns the property that instrumental
adverbs have (see also Chapter 3 of this book) of always relating to their
deep subject. If [37] were derived from [38]:

[37] John killed Bill

[38] John caused Bill to die

we should expect that [39] would be ambiguous, like [40], since these two
sentences could just as well have [41] as [42] for deep structure; but [39]
is not ambiguous, and its interpretation corresponds only to that of [41].
This follows naturally from the hypothesis that [39] is in deep structure,
but could only be treated in an *ad hoc* manner by the transformational
analysis:[5]

[39] John killed Bill by swallowing his tongue (John a tué Bill en avalant
sa langue)

[40] John caused Bill to die by swallowing his tongue

[41] John caused [Bill die] by [John swallow Bill's tongue]

[42] John caused [Bill die by [Bill swallow Bill's tongue]]

[43] Jean a fait mourir Pierre en avalant sa langue
John caused Peter to die by swallowing his tongue

In French, the argument might, at first sight, be weakened insofar as it
is rather difficult to perceive the ambiguity of the sentence corresponding
to [40], namely [43] (it is difficult to conceive a reading in which it is
Pierre who swallows his tongue); apparently, adverbs of the form *en*
V-*ant* X are not very acceptable in sentences embedded under *faire*. In
any case, the fact that it is a matter of a fairly superficial phenomenon is
clear if we modify the order of the elements:

[44] les C.R.S. ont fait se disperser les étudiants en hurlant†
the C.R.S. caused the students to disperse, shouting

[45] en hurlant, les C.R.S. ont fait se disperser les étudiants
shouting, the C.R.S. caused the students to disperse

† C.R.S. = Compagnies Républicaines de Sécurité (mobile police units). [*Translator's note*]

[46] les C.R.S. ont fait se disperser en hurlant les étudiants
     the C.R.S. caused the students to disperse shouting

[47] les C.R.S. ont dispersé les étudiants en hurlant
     the C.R.S. dispersed the students, shouting

[48] les étudiants se sont dispersés en hurlant
     the students dispersed, shouting

The ambiguity of [44] doubtless does not appear very clearly; but the fact that this sentence is in effect ambiguous is seen if we consider [45], where it is clearly the C.R.S. who shout, and [46] where it is, preferably, the students (*cf* [48]). The crucial point is that [47] only has the reading corresponding to [45], whereas the transformational analysis of the factitive transitives would predict its ambiguity. Another very clear example is the following:

[49] Pierre a hissé Paul d'une seule main sur le cheval
     Peter hoisted Paul on to the horse with one hand

[50] Pierre a fait se hisser Paul d'une seule main sur le cheval
     Peter caused Paul to hoist himself on to the horse with one hand

It is clear that [49] cannot have the interpretation corresponding to [50]; the instrumental in [49] relates to *Pierre;* in [50], it relates to *Paul.*

3

Let us pass on to other types of arguments, not considered by Fodor.[6] Firstly, the selectional restrictions imposed on the surface subject or object are not the same in the two types of construction, the simple transitives and those in *faire* + V. Let us consider first the case of the surface object. Whereas [51a and b] are equally possible, in the same way as [52a and b], only [53a] is grammatical; [53b] is excluded:

[51] *a:* la voiture est entrée dans le garage
          the car entered the garage
     b: les invités sont entrés au salon
          the guests entered the drawing-room

[52] *a:* Delphine a fait entrer la voiture dans le garage
          Delphine got the car into the garage
     b: Delphine a fait entrer les invités au salon
          Delphine showed the guests into the drawing-room

[53] *a:* Delphine a entré la voiture dans le garage
      Delphine put the car in the garage
   b: *Delphine a entré les invités au salon
      ? Delphine put the guests in the drawing-room

Here it is a case, not of an idiosyncrasy like those noted in Chapter 3, section 8, but of a fairly general phenomenon which prohibits a human object in the simple transitive construction if the verb is a verb of motion, such as *entrer, sortir, monter, descendre,* etc. (This is a simplification, see below.)

Conversely, there are a certain number of cases where the construction in *faire* + V is impossible if the surface object is inanimate, *cf:*

[54] *a:* Roman a sorti la bouteille de vodka du frigidaire
      Roman got the bottle of vodka out of the refrigerator
   b: *Roman a fait sortir la bouteille de vodka du frigidaire[7]

[55] *a:* Fritz a monté les provisions de la cave
      Fritz brought the stores up out of the cellar
   b: *Fritz a fait monter les provisions de la cave

A particularly clear case of this restriction is that of sentences with a surface object designating a part of the body of the person indicated by the subject (generally speaking, an inalienable property), *cf:*

[56] *a:* Barbe-Bleue a froncé ses terribles sourcils
      Bluebeard knitted his fearsome brows
   b: ?*Barbe-Bleue a fait (se) froncer ses terribles sourcils
   c: les terribles sourcils de Barbe-Bleue se sont froncés
      Bluebeard's fearsome brows knitted

[57] *a:* Irène a baissé ses beaux yeux bleus
      Irene lowered her lovely blue eyes
   b: ?*Irène a fait (se) baisser ses beaux yeux bleus
   c: les yeux d'Irène se sont baissés
      Irene's eyes dropped

There are also different selectional restrictions on the subject, *cf:*

[58] *a:* l'amiral a fait échouer le cuirassé
      the Admiral caused the battleship to run aground
   b: l'amiral a échoué le cuirassé
      the Admiral ran the battleship aground

[59] *a:* cette manoeuvre stupide a fait échouer le cuirassé
        that stupid manoeuvre caused the battleship to run aground
      b: *cette manoeuvre stupide a échoué le cuirassé

[60] *a:* le médecin a fait accoucher Madeleine
        the doctor caused Madeleine to give birth
      b: le médecin a accouché Madeleine
        the doctor delivered Madeleine

[61] *a:* ce médicament a fait accoucher Madeleine
        this medicine caused Madeleine to give birth
      b: *ce médicament a accouché Madeleine

This time we see that, if the surface subject is inanimate, the simple transitive construction is excluded.

To account for these selectional restrictions, then, the analysis which derives simple transitive sentences from sentences in *faire* + V would have to multiply the conditions on the application of the PREDICATE-RAISING rule (or on that of FAIRE-SUBSTITUTION). In order to exclude [53*b*], the rule would have to be blocked if the subordinate subject is human; in order to exclude [59*b*] and [61*b*], it would also have to be blocked if the main subject is inanimate. On the other hand, in order to exclude [54*b*–57*b*], the rule would have to be made obligatory if the subordinate subject is inanimate. Examples [54–55] are particularly awkward for the transformational hypothesis, not only because [54*b*] and [55*b*] are excluded, but also because (in contrast to examples [56–57]) the simple sentences corresponding to the subordinate clause are also excluded, *cf:*

[62] ?*la bouteille de vodka sort du frigidaire
      ?*the bottle of vodka comes out of the refrigerator

[63] ?*les provisions montent de la cave
      ?*the stores come up out of the cellar

In order to be able to generate sentences [54*a*–55*a*], the transformational analysis, then, would be obliged not only to make the application of PREDICATE-RAISING obligatory, but also to find a means of excluding the simple sentences [62–63] (or to assign them a deviant interpretation). One might try to resolve the difficulty by considering that, underlying [54*a*], we do not have something like [54*b*], but rather [64]:

[64] Roman a fait [$_S$ la vodka être sortie du frigidaire]
      Roman caused [$_S$ the vodka to be out of the refrigerator]

where *être sortie* is the sequence *être* + adjective (*cf* the ambiguity of *Madame est sortie* (Madam is out / Madam went out), which appears if we compare *Madame est sortie hier soir à huit heures* (Madam went out yesterday at eight o'clock) and *Pour l'instant, Madame est sortie, elle est en train de faire ses courses* (At the moment, Madam is out, she is doing her shopping)), but, in any case, sentences such as:

[65] ?*la vodka est sortie du frigidaire

[66] ?*les provisions sont montées de la cave

seem to be very unnatural even if one interprets them in this way. The PREDICATE-RAISING rule would, then, be obligatory anyway in this case.

However this may be, to attempt to account for the selectional differences between the two constructions in terms of constraints on the application of PREDICATE-RAISING seems to me a hopeless undertaking, all the more so because the examples given up to now represent only relatively simple cases. There are far more complicated ones which, for example, it would be impossible to treat simply in terms of the distinction human/non-human. We have seen cases where the inanimate character of the surface object entails the simple transitive construction (*cf* [54–57]). Now, there are others where – independently of the nature of the subject – the presence of certain inanimate surface objects, on the contrary, prohibits the simple transitive construction, and prescribes the construction in *faire* + V. Thus, [67] presents a striking contrast with Lakoff's paradigmatic example [12–13]; other examples will be found in [68–71]:

[67] *a:* le colonel a fait fondre trois sucres dans son café
          ?the colonel made three lumps of sugar dissolve in his coffee
      b: *le colonel a fondu trois sucres dans son café
          the colonel dissolved three lumps of sugar in his coffee†

[68] *a:* les pluies ont fait monter le niveau de la rivière
          the rains caused the level of the river to rise
      b: *les pluies ont monté le niveau de la rivière

[69] *a:* en ouvrant les vannes du barrage, l'ingénieur a fait monter le niveau du lac
          by opening the flood-gates of the dam, the engineer caused the level of the lake to rise

† It will be observed that in these cases the English usage seems to be the reverse of the French. See also *pp.* 156 and 158. [*Translator's note*]

    b: *en ouvrant les vannes du barrage, l'ingénieur a monté le niveau
        du lac

[70] *a:* ce médicament a fait baisser la fièvre de Juliette
       this medicine caused Juliet's temperature to go down
     b: *ce médicament a baissé la fièvre de Juliette

[71] *a:* le médecin a stupidement fait monter la fièvre de Juliette
       the doctor stupidly caused Juliet's temperature to rise
     b: *le médecin a stupidement monté la fièvre de Juliette

The examples could be multiplied. But there are difficulties of another
order. Up to now I have agreed (or rather pretended to agree) that the
simple transitive constructions and those in *faire* + V were in a paraphrase
relationship, and, indeed, it does seem that [12] and [13], or [10] and [20]
are paraphrases of each other, the following sentences being contradictory:

[72] *a:* ⊄ Adèle a cuit le ragoût mais elle n'a pas fait cuire le ragoût
       ⊄ Adèle cooked the stew but she did not make the stew cook
     b: ⊄ Adèle a fait cuire le ragoût mais elle n'a pas cuit le ragoût
       ⊄ Adèle made the stew cook but she did not cook the stew
       (where ⊄ is the contradiction sign)

Lakoff's argument soon met with the objection (*cf* Chomsky, 1971)
that there is a slight difference of meaning between sentences such as
[12] and [13], the first implying a direct connection between the subject
and the object that the second does not imply; but Lakoff (1970c) had
replied in advance that all these sentences are equally ambiguous: the
ambiguity – direct connection versus indirect connection – being a
general property of the element CAUSE, common to the two constructions.

    In fact, in French, it is not difficult to find a whole group of cases where
it is clear that the sentences in *faire* + V are not paraphrases of the sentences with the simple verb, even if one takes the notion of paraphrase
only in the sense that there are the same truth values in the two sentences.
Consider, for example, the following sentences (note that they are an
exception to the selectional restrictions on the human object indicated
above):

[73] *a:* Alice a fait remonter Humpty Dumpty sur son mur
       Alice made Humpty Dumpty get back on his wall
     b: Alice a remonté Humpty Dumpty sur son mur
       Alice put Humpty Dumpty back on his wall

[74] *a:* Jean-Baptiste a fait plonger Jésus dans le Jourdain
John the Baptist caused Jesus to immerse Himself in the Jordan
    b: Jean-Baptiste a plongé Jésus dans le Jourdain
John the Baptist immersed Jesus in the Jordan

The absence of paraphrase between sentences (*a*) and (*b*) stands out clearly if we consider the following sentences:

[75] *a:* Alice a fait remonter Humpty Dumpty sur son mur, mais elle ne l'a pas remonté (elle-même)
Alice made Humpty Dumpty get back on his wall, but she did not put him back (herself)
    b: ∉ Alice a remonté Humpty Dumpty sur son mur, mais elle ne l'a pas remonté (elle-même)
∉ Alice put Humpty Dumpty back on his wall, but she did not put him back (herself)

[76] *a:* Jean-Baptiste a fait plonger Jésus dans le Jourdain, mais il ne l'a pas plongé (lui-même) dedans
John the Baptist caused Jesus to be immersed in the Jordan, but he did not immerse Him (himself)
    b: ∉ Jean-Baptiste a plongé Jésus dans le Jourdain, mais il ne l'a pas plongé (lui-même) dedans
∉ John the Baptist immersed Jesus in the Jordan, but he did not immerse Him (himself)

Clearly, the (*b*) examples are contradictory, but the (*a*) examples are not. Sentence [73*a*], for example, can mean that Alice persuaded Humpty Dumpty to get back on the wall by himself, by talking to him, by urging him, by promising to kiss him if he did so, etc, but it does not in any way imply that she acted herself directly and physically, for example by taking Humpty Dumpty in her arms and putting him on the wall. On the other hand, [73*b*] can only mean one thing: that such a physical action indeed took place, Humpty Dumpty then playing a purely passive role. It ensues from this that [75*a*] is not contradictory, whereas [75*b*] is. The same remarks hold for [74] and [76], and one could easily multiply observations of this sort.[8]

In view of these examples, it is clear that Lakoff's position, on the general ambiguity of the element C A U S E, is untenable, and that the distinction between direct action, implied by the simple transitive construction, and indirect action, possible only in the complex construction, must be considered valid, the more so as we immediately find other cases where this distinction obtains in a more subtle form.

In contrast with the examples that we have just seen, the two sentences of [77], like [12–13] or [10–20], seem indeed to be in a paraphrase relationship, as [78] seems to prove:

[77] *a:* Graham Hill a fait caler le moteur de sa Lotus
             Graham Hill made the engine of his Lotus stall
       b: Graham Hill a calé le moteur de sa Lotus
             Graham Hill stalled the engine of his Lotus

[78] *a:* ⊄ Graham Hill a fait caler le moteur de sa Lotus, mais il ne l'a pas
                 calé
             ⊄ Graham Hill made the engine of his Lotus stall, but he did not
                 stall it
       b: ⊄ Graham Hill a calé le moteur de sa Lotus, mais il ne l'a pas fait
                 caler
             ⊄ Graham Hill stalled the engine of his Lotus, but he did not
                 make it stall

Yet consider the following examples:

[79] *a:* en voulant la dépasser, Graham Hill a fait caler le moteur de la
                 Ferrari de Jacky Ickx
             in trying to pass it, Graham Hill made the engine of Jacky Ickx's
                 Ferrari stall
       b: *en voulant la dépasser, Graham Hill a calé le moteur de la
                 Ferrari de Jacky Ickx
             *in trying to pass it, Graham Hill stalled the engine of Jacky
                 Ickx's Ferrari

[79a] is grammatical, but [79b] is excluded; clearly, it is not a question of selectional restrictions here. The difference between [77a] and [77b] – and this is what explains why [79b] is excluded – is that [77b] implies that Graham Hill is at the wheel of the Lotus, whereas [77a] implies nothing of the sort.[9] In fact, a sentence such as [80]:

[80] Graham Hill a calé le moteur de la Ferrari de Jacky Ickx
       Graham Hill stalled the engine of Jacky Ickx's Ferrari

implies that, at the moment when the engine stalled, Graham Hill was at the wheel of Ickx's Ferrari, having borrowed or bought it from him, etc. So here, from another aspect, we again find the difference between direct connection and indirect connection, and still in the same way: the simple transitive construction implies a direct action of the subject on the object, whereas the construction in *faire*+V does not necessarily imply such a direct action.[10]

4

Perhaps it is possible to describe all these facts in the framework of generative semantics, given the enormous power of this theory. Nevertheless, it seems more interesting to me to consider what the standard theory (or the extended standard theory) has to say on the question. We recall that standard theory allows two different deep structures to be assigned to sentences (*a*) and (*b*) of the preceding examples, deep structures which would be, schematically, [81] for the constructions with simple transitive verb, and [82] for the constructions in *faire*+V:

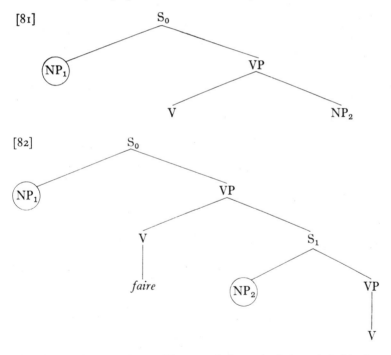

Further, standard theory (like extended standard theory), holds that grammatical relations and functions – defined derivatively by reference to phrase-marker configurations in deep structure (for example, 'subject-of' = [NP, S], 'direct object-of' = [NP, VP], etc; *cf* Chomsky, 1965, 68*ff*) –

help to determine the semantic interpretation of sentences. This idea has not been well understood. If we consider sentences such as:

[83] Pierre a battu Paul
      Peter beat Paul

[84] Pierre a subi un interrogatoire (examples from Rohrer, 1971)
      Peter underwent an interrogation

to which standard theory would attribute a deep structure identical (on the points which concern us) with their surface structure, it is quite clear, and was well known to the traditional grammarians, that the semantic relationship between the subject and the verb (or that between the object and the verb) is not at all the same in the two cases (*cf* also, of course, all the examples of the type of [3] as compared with [5], etc).[11] From this it was concluded rather hastily (*cf* Lakoff and Ross, 1966; Fillmore, 1968; Rohrer, 1971) that the grammatical relations and functions defined at the level of relatively less 'abstract' deep structures in the sense of Chomsky (1965) had no semantic relevance.

It must be said that Chomsky (1965) is not very explicit on the way in which the relations and functions of the base determine the semantic interpretation.[12] On the other hand, the purely combinative conception of the semantic projection rules according to Katz and Fodor (1963) did not, at first sight, make it possible to account for semantic differences as evident as those illustrated by [83–84] or [3–5]. More recently, however, the conception of the semantic component has been refined (*cf* Jackendoff, 1969b), and Chomsky himself (1971, 1972) has defined his position (see also Anderson, 1971). All depends on the way in which the role of the semantic interpretation rules is conceived. If these rules do not consist simply of a direct projection of grammatical relations, and if it is a question of complex rules which 'bring in something new', from various sources, among them those provided by grammatical relations, we can begin to understand how far the grammatical relations contribute to the semantic interpretation. No doubt examples such as [83–84] or [3–5] prevent us from directly translating the grammatical subject-verb relation as a semantic relation such as, for example, 'agent'-'action'; but it is perfectly possible, *a priori*, that such a grammatical relation contributes to the semantic interpretation in a more indirect, subtle and abstract way – in other words, that whenever we have a subject-verb relation, and if, besides, certain conditions are fulfilled, we can formulate some interesting generalizations from the semantic point of view. The question whether it is worth while to envisage the semantic role of grammatical relations in this way is a strictly empirical question, and it is the factitive constructions that seem to me to provide a good illustration of the semantic role that the grammatical relations are called upon to play.

We might suggest informally that, among the rules that interpret semantically the grammatical configurations of deep structure, are the following:

[A] Any NP defined as the 'subject-of' a given verb can be interpreted as designating the 'agent' of the action expressed by the verb – *provided that* certain additional conditions are fulfilled.

[B] Only an NP defined as the 'subject-of' a given verb can be interpreted as designating the 'agent' of the action expressed by that verb; in particular, an NP defined as the 'direct object-of' a given verb can never be interpreted as an 'agent'.

[C] Any configuration $[_S$ NP $[_{VP}$ V NP X]] is interpreted as indicating that a 'direct connection' is established, between the referent of the subject NP and the referent of the direct object NP; in particular, if the verb is marked [+CAUSE], if the subject is defined as 'agent', and if the verb is a verb of motion or a change-of-state verb, this configuration $[_S$ NP$[_{VP}$ V NP X]] is interpreted as expressing a 'direct action' of the referent of the subject NP on the referent of the direct object NP.

These rules call for some commentary. I shall confine myself here to certain indications.

Firstly, if we consider [A], it would be necessary to define the semantic notion of 'agent', and to determine in what conditions a subject can, must, or cannot be interpreted as an agent. Despite the interesting remarks on this subject that can be found in Gruber (1965), Jackendoff (1969b), Fillmore (1968), etc, it cannot be said that we possess here and now a satisfactory definition of the notion of 'agent'. There have been many attempts to define the agent by 'a semantic reading which attributes to the [subject, N.R.] NP will or volition towards the action expressed by the sentence. Hence only animate NP's can function as Agents' (Jackendoff, 1969b, 78; also, *ibid*, note 8 of Chapter 2; see also Fillmore, *op cit*, and Gruber, *op cit*). But this conception is too restrictive. Chomsky (1972) and Dougherty (1970a), criticizing Fillmore (1968), gave examples of sentences in which inanimate subjects behave as agents. I have myself pointed out other cases of this sort in Chapter 3, section 6. It is clear, intuitively, that, in sentences such as:

[85] le vent a renversé la barrière
      the wind overturned the barrier

[86] la Lotus a sorti la Ferrari de la route
      the Lotus sent the Ferrari off the track

le vent and *la Lotus* are interpreted as agents (and, notably, have no connection with instrumentals). On the other hand, it is not sufficient for a subject to be animate for it to be interpreted automatically as an agent, *cf*:

[87] Fritz frappe Raoul par sa maîtrise (*cf* Chapter 5)
      Fritz impresses Raoul by his mastery

[88] Julie dort
      Julie is sleeping

Furthermore, discussions on the notion of agent generally relate to transitive sentences (direct or indirect), whereas the concept should be extended to take intransitive sentences into account, such as:

[89] les manifestants se sont dispersés
      the demonstrators dispersed

[90] Pierre vient de sortir
      Peter has just gone out

[91] le train va partir
      the train is about to leave

But again, one would hesitate to extend it to sentences such as:

[92] la branche a cassé
      the branch broke

[93] le sucre a fondu
      the sugar dissolved

[94] le moteur de la Ferrari a calé
      the engine of the Ferrari stalled

Apparently, the conditions necessary for a subject to be interpreted as an agent are complex. They depend on the semantic reading of the verb: for example, verbs of motion allow it, change-of-state verbs (*cuire* (to cook), *casser* (to break), *caler* (to stall), *fondre* (to melt, dissolve)) require it if they are transitive but do not necessarily require it if they are intransitive (*cf* [92–94]); at least some stative verbs exclude it (*cf* [87]; on this notion of stative verbs, see Lakoff, 1966). These conditions depend also on the semantic reading of the subject and especially on the semantic content of the head noun of the subject.

A necessary condition (but not a sufficient one, if we refuse to see agents in the subjects of [92–94]) for the interpretation of the subject as an agent depends on the possibility of considering that subject as 'capable of intervening in an autonomous way' in the activity expressed by the verb. I understand by this the ability that we have of conceiving the role of a being or an object in a motion, a change-of-state, etc, as intervening quite apart from any external cause – that that being or that object itself undergoes the motion or change-of-state or that it induces it in another. This is what makes the difference between sentences such as [85–86], [89–94], on the one hand, and, on the other hand, sentences such as [95–96] (*cf* [54–55]):

[95] *les provisions montent de la cave
     *the stores come up out of the cellar

[96] *la vodka sort du frigidaire
     *the vodka goes out of the refrigerator

Determining which NPs can be interpreted as agents or as being capable of autonomous activity undoubtedly depends in large part on the native speakers' knowledge of the world and representation of the world. In the last analysis, it depends on anthropological observation. No doubt it will vary between cultures, and according to the 'universe of discourse' envisaged. Sentences such as [95–96] might be natural in the 'universe' of fairy stories, or if they are used metaphorically.

Gruber, Jackendoff and Fillmore have tried to find syntactic criteria, such as the possibilities of co-occurrence with certain adverbials, to define agents. These criteria are very imperfect and it is not my intention to review them here. But, for example, human agents allow co-occurrence with adverbials of intention, such as *de façon à* . . . (in such a way as to . . .) *dans le but de* . . . (with the intention of . . .), *intentionnellement* (intentionally), *volontairement* (voluntarily), etc, whereas non-agentive human NPs do not allow them, *cf* the contrast between [97] and [98]:

[97] les manifestants se sont dispersés
$$\begin{cases} \text{de leur propre chef} \\ \text{volontairement} \\ \text{dans le but de tromper la} \\ \quad \text{police} \end{cases}$$

the demonstrators dispersed $\begin{cases} \text{of their own volition} \\ \text{voluntarily} \\ \text{with the aim of deceiving the police} \end{cases}$

[98] *Marie a frappé Paul $\begin{cases} \text{intentionnellement} \\ \text{dans le but de faire sa conquête} \end{cases}$
      par son intelligence

      *Mary impressed Paul $\begin{cases} \text{intentionally} \\ \text{with the aim of making a conquest of him} \end{cases}$
      by her intelligence

Clearly, the same criteria are not valid for non-human subject NPs, but sometimes it is possible to distinguish NPs capable of autonomous activity from those that are not, by their co-occurrence with adverbs such as *de lui-même* for example, *cf:*

[99] la branche a cassé d'elle-même
     the branch broke of its own accord

[100] la balle a glissé d'elle-même le long de la pente
      the ball glided down the slope of its own accord

[101] *Marie a frappé d'elle-même Paul par sa stupidité
      *Mary impressed Paul of her own accord by her stupidity

[102] Julie $\begin{cases} \text{*sait} \\ \text{a appris} \end{cases}$ sa leçon d'elle-même

      Julie $\begin{cases} \text{*knows} \\ \text{learned} \end{cases}$ her lesson of her own accord

Whatever may be said of the difficulties in defining the notion of agent and the related notion of being or object endowed with autonomous activity, what is important above all for our present enquiry is rule [B] (which is clearly linked with the hypothesis that the agent complement of passive sentences and the understood subject of middle sentences are subjects in deep structure; see Chapter 3). The crucial point is the impossibility of interpreting a direct object as an agent, or even as participating in an autonomous way in the action expressed by the verb. If the tests of co-occurrence with adverbials such as *intentionnellement*, *de lui-même*, etc, are not sufficient to define subject agents, they give very clear results when we consider the relationships of these adverbials with direct objects. Adverbials of this type can never relate to direct objects; in particular, all the following sentences are excluded:

[103] *l'entraîneur a réuni l'équipe d'elle-même
      *the trainer assembled the team of its own accord

[104] *Marie frappe Paul de lui-même par sa stupidité
*Mary impresses Paul of his own accord by her stupidity

[105] *cette idée m'est venue de moi-même en dormant
*this idea came to me of my own accord while I slept

[106] Pierre a $\left\{\begin{array}{l}\text{épousé}\\\text{rencontré}\\\text{embrassé}\end{array}\right\}$ Marie $\left\{\begin{array}{l}\text{de lui-même}\\\text{*d'elle-même}\end{array}\right.$

Peter $\left\{\begin{array}{l}\text{married}\\\text{met}\\\text{kissed}\end{array}\right\}$ Mary $\left\{\begin{array}{l}\text{of his own accord}\\\text{*of her own accord}\end{array}\right.$

[107] *Graham Hill a sorti la Ferrari d'elle-même de la route
*Graham Hill sent the Ferrari off the track of its own accord

This point is crucial insofar as a true counter-example to the theory outlined here would be a case of a transitive sentence in which it is clear that the direct object is interpreted as an agent. To my knowledge, such counter-examples do not exist.[13] On the other hand we see, in comparing [98] and [104], that verbs exist which can in no case have an agent attributed to them.

Rule [C] would necessitate defining the notion of 'direct connection'. The essential point is that the process or the action expressed by the verb is conceived as a global and unitary process, especially from the point of view of time. This process cannot be broken down into several processes linked to each other by relations of cause and effect, and occurring at distinct moments of time. As we have seen, depending on the verb this direct connection will assume a different content (see [77–79], and also note 10).

Rule [C] should no doubt be extended to account for constructions with an indirect object. It certainly seems that, in [108], there is a direct connection not only between the subject and the direct object, but also between the subject and the indirect object, as well as between the direct object and the indirect object (see below, section 7):

[108] Debussy a $\left\{\begin{array}{l}\text{donné}\\\text{montré}\end{array}\right\}$ la partition du *Martyre* à Stravinsky

Debussy $\left\{\begin{array}{l}\text{gave}\\\text{showed}\end{array}\right\}$ the score of the *Martyre* to Stravinsky

5

Let us return now to the problem of the factitive constructions, and try to see how much light is shed on it by the preceding considerations.

Let us go back to [81–82], which represent the deep structures that standard theory would allow us to attribute, respectively, to simple transitive constructions and to complex factitive constructions. In these representations, I have circled the NPs which fulfil the structural conditions enabling them to be assigned an agent interpretation, all other things being equal.

The difference between [81] and [82] is obvious. Whereas, in both cases, NP_1 can be interpreted as an agent, NP_2 can only be so interpreted in [82], where it is defined as 'subject-of' S_1. In [81], NP_2, which is defined as 'direct object-of' the VP, can in no case, by reason of [B] above, be interpreted as an agent.

Notice, again, that an NP defined as 'subject-of' a sentence S is not necessarily to be interpreted as an agent. The complex factitives, in particular, are generally ambiguous from this point of view, *faire* S allowing an agentive or non-agentive reading of the subject; thus, [109a] is ambiguous, and can be interpreted in the sense of [109b] (agentive) or in that of [109c] (non-agentive):

[109] *a:* Pierre a fait pleurer Marie
             Peter made Mary cry
         b: Pierre a sciemment fait pleurer Marie
             Peter knowingly made Mary cry

         c: le comportement⎱ de Pierre a fait pleurer Marie
             l'attitude⎰

             Peter's ⎰behaviour⎱ made Mary cry
                     ⎱attitude⎰

Similarly, [110a] can be interpreted in an agentive sense (*cf* [110b]) or in a non-agentive sense (*cf* [110c]):

[110] *a:* Pierre a fait tomber Paul
             Peter made Paul fall over
         b: Pierre a (sciemment) fait tomber Paul (en lui faisant un croc-en-jambe)
             Peter (knowingly) made Paul fall over (by tripping him up)
         c: la maladresse de Pierre a fait tomber Paul
             Peter's clumsiness made Paul fall over

What is correct in Lakoff's observation (1970c) noted above, on the ambiguity of the element CAUSE ('direct connection'/'indirect connection') amounts, I think, to this ambiguity ('agentive'/'non-agentive') of the construction in *faire* + V. If the same ambiguity is found in certain simple transitive causative verbs, with a psychological connotation (*cf* [111] and Chapter 5):

[111] Pierre amuse Paul
      Peter amuses Paul

it is excluded for all transitive verbs of motion or of physical change-of-state (*cf* the examples of section 3).

In the last analysis, I would say that it is the difference between the deep structures [81] and [82] which, in conjunction with rules [A–C], will enable us to account for the divergences indicated in section 3 between the simple transitive constructions and the complex factitives. Let us look again at the examples of section 3.

We saw that, when the surface object of the two constructions is human, we find, either selectional constraints on the simple transitive construction which do not exist in the complex factitive (*cf* [51–53]), or distinct differences of meaning between the two constructions (*cf* [73–76]). We can now see that it is a question of one and the same phenomenon, of a semantic nature, which arises from the attribution of different deep structures to the two constructions, and from the application of the interpretation rules [A–C], jointly.

Consider the examples of [51–53] and of [73], which, for the sake of convenience, I shall repeat as [112–113]:

[112] *a:* Delphine a $\left\{ \begin{array}{l} \text{i: fait entrer} \\ \text{ii: entré} \end{array} \right\}$ la voiture dans le garage

Delphine $\left\{ \begin{array}{l} \text{i: got the car into the garage} \\ \text{ii: put the car in the garage} \end{array} \right.$

b: Delphine a $\left\{ \begin{array}{l} \text{i: fait entrer} \\ \text{ii: *entré} \end{array} \right\}$ les invités au salon

Delphine $\left\{ \begin{array}{l} \text{i: showed the guests into the drawing-room} \\ \text{ii: ?put the guests in the drawing-room} \end{array} \right.$

[113] Alice a $\left\{ \begin{array}{l} \text{i: fait remonter} \\ \text{ii: remonté} \end{array} \right\}$ Humpty Dumpty sur son mur

Alice $\left\{ \begin{array}{l} \text{i: made Humpty Dumpty get back on his wall} \\ \text{ii: put Humpty Dumpty back on his wall} \end{array} \right.$

Examples (i) and (ii) having different deep structures (respectively, of the type [82] and [81]), rule [A] allows us to interpret *la voiture*, *les invités*, *Humpty Dumpty*, in examples (i) as agents; rule [B] prevents us from interpreting these same NPs as agents in examples (ii). Now, a human being is, by definition, capable of autonomous activity and of volition; on the other hand, there are numerous actions in which a human being can take part in a non-active way: one can put a child to bed, put someone back on a wall, immerse him in water (*cf* [74]), hoist him on to a horse (*cf* [49]). Of these same actions, there are many also in which a human being can take part in an autonomous and active way – hence the differences of meaning encountered in [113i] and [113ii]. And again, there are circumstances which prohibit treating a human being as a passive object: if Delphine has guests, by definition she treats them as free beings – hence the anomaly of [112*b*ii].

We see that the distinction made in section 3 between semantic facts and facts relating to selectional restrictions is artificial. It will not be necessary to impose special selectional restrictions on *entrer* transitive, etc, in terms of the feature $[+ \underline{\quad\quad} [\pm \text{HUMAN}]]$. All the sentences of [112–113], etc, will be generated by the grammar, and it will be the interpretative mechanism outlined in [A–C] (more precisely rule [B]), which will, at the same time, account for the differences of meaning between [113i] and [113ii], and mark [112*b*ii] as anomalous. Note that this anomaly of [112*b*ii], in the final analysis, involves the native speakers' knowledge of the world (or of the usages of 'civilised' society).

In fact, we find verbs, semantically similar to *entrer*, for which the transitive construction with a human object is possible, but an idea of coercion, exercised by the subject upon the object, comes in, which is not necessarily present in the corresponding complex factitive, and which can be explained in terms of rules [A–C], *cf*:

[114]   Cassius Clay a tombé Sonny Liston au troisième round
        Cassius Clay downed Sonny Liston in the third round

[115]   le videur du bar a sorti l'ivrogne à coups de pied au cul
        the chucker-out kicked out the drunkard

The following facts are particularly interesting from this point of view.†
Verbs such as *se suicider* (to commit suicide), or *démissionner* (to resign),

---

† See the Grammaire Larousse du XX° siècle, Paris, 1936, para 369 (*Échange des voix*), where this transitive use of pronominal or intransitive verbs is noted, and described as 'une incorrection voulue'. [*Translator's note*]

by definition relate to free and autonomous agents. But, in a substandard style of French, fairly common in the newspapers, one comes across sentences such as [116a], [117a]:

[116] a: le Président a démissionné le ministre des Finances
            the President 'resigned' the Finance Minister
        b: le Président a fait démissioner le ministre des Finances
            the President made the Finance Minister resign

[117] a: la police a suicidé Stavisky
            the police 'suicided' Stavisky
        b: la police a fait se suicider Stavisky
            the police made Stavisky commit suicide

These sentences are not at all synonymous with the corresponding (b) examples: whereas, in the (b) cases, the President simply put pressure on the Minister, and the police on Stavisky, so as to lead them to resign or to commit suicide, [116a] means in plain terms that the President dismissed the Minister, letting it appear as a voluntary resignation, and [117a] means that the police killed Stavisky and disguised the murder as suicide. No doubt, this is a question of figurative and marginal usages, but they are not surprising if looked at in the framewok of the theory outlined here on the relationship between the simple transitive construction and the factitive construction: bearing in mind the lexical content of *se suicider* or of *démissionner*, on the one hand, and rule [B], on the other hand, sentences such as [116a–117a] cannot be other than deviant; if they are interpretable, they can only receive a special interpretation, and the one that they in fact receive safeguards the idea of direct action of the subject on the object (*cf* [C]). No doubt, we still lack a suitable theory for the interpretation of deviant sentences of this sort, but we can discern the possibility of integrating it with the standard theory. On the other hand, I do not see how generative semantics could represent as being other than a coincidence the fact that these sentences differ from examples (b) in the way indicated.[14]

If we now pass on to the constraints concerning the inanimate surface object (*cf* [54–55]), we see that the impossibility of having [54b–55b] is a consequence of the impossibility of having [62–63] (or [95–96]), which in turn results from the fact that stores or a bottle of vodka are by nature inert objects, incapable of autonomous motion. As for the possibility of having [54a–55a], this poses no problem, the direct object of these constructions being unable to have the character of agent. It will be noted that this leads to not formulating selectional restrictions, in terms of the feature [±ANIMATE], on the object of the transitive verb, any more than on the subject of the intransitive verb: the anomaly of [62–63] ([95–96]) will be due to the interpretative principle which requires of the subjects of verbs of motion that they should be capable of autonomous movement.

The case of inalienable objects (cf [56–57]) is different, insofar as they can appear as subjects of intransitive sentences (cf [56c–57c]). The (a) examples do not pose any problem, but why are the (b) examples excluded? The answer seems to me to stem from the very nature of inalienable properties, and from the difficulty that one has in conceiving the breaking down of an action which involves a subject and its inalienable properties. This breaking down does not occur in the (a) examples or in the (c) examples.[15] For me, too, [56b–57b] 'sound' bizarre and pleonastic rather than ungrammatical. I must add that, as Maurice Borel has pointed out to me, there are cases with an inalienable object in which the two constructions are equally possible, and even in which the complex factitive is more natural than the simple transitive, cf:

[118] Pierre a $\begin{cases} \text{fait claquer ses doigts (sa langue)} \\ \text{?claqué les doigts (la langue)} \end{cases}$

Peter $\begin{cases} \text{?made his fingers (his tongue) click†} \\ \text{clicked his fingers (his tongue)} \end{cases}$

[119] Pierre a $\begin{cases} \text{fait remuer ses oreilles} \\ \text{?remué les oreilles} \end{cases}$

Peter $\begin{cases} \text{?made his ears wiggle†} \\ \text{wiggled his ears} \end{cases}$

[120] Pierre a $\begin{cases} \text{fait craquer ses articulations} \\ \text{*craqué} \begin{cases} \text{ses} \\ \text{les} \end{cases} \text{articulations} \end{cases}$

Peter $\begin{cases} \text{?made his joints crack†} \\ \text{cracked his joints} \end{cases}$

It seems that what counts here is the degree of naturalness of the action expressed by the verb and of the connection between the subject and the object: it is natural to lower one's eyes or to knit one's brows (or to raise one's arm, etc); it is much less natural to crack one's joints or to wiggle

† In these examples, too, the English usage seems to be a mirror image of the French. (Cf note to example [67].) [Translator's note]

one's ears – in fact many people cannot do these things. This perhaps would explain the possibility, which is suggested by the complex factitive, of breaking down the process into two phases.

In general, the two constructions, direct transitive and complex factitive, are equally possible when the surface object belongs to that special class of inanimates which includes vehicles, certain machines, etc, cf [51–53], [77–80]. The possibility of complex factitives depends on the possibility of conceiving this type of inanimates as agents, or at least as capable of autonomous activity. In the case of [77–80], I have already discussed some semantic differences between the two constructions. Analogous differences are also found in the other sentences of the same type. It is easy to see that these differences always come down to a difference between direct action of the subject upon the object, implied by the transitive construction, and indirect action, permitted by the complex factitive construction. Thus, [53a] implies that Delphine has exercised a direct physical action upon the car, either in being at the steering-wheel, or in pushing it with her hand. In contrast, [52a] implies nothing of the sort: someone else could be at the steering-wheel, and Delphine could, for example, simply open the garage door or make a sign to the driver. If the most plausible interpretation is often almost the same in the two cases (Delphine being at the steering-wheel), this stems from the possibility of conceiving the action of the driver on the car equally well as either direct or indirect (through the medium of the steering-wheel, the engine, the wheels, etc).

In the same way, the most natural interpretation of [58b] would be that in which the admiral is at the helm of the battleship, or at least that in which he has direct responsibility for its navigation. [58a], by contrast, implies nothing of the sort. Examples could be multiplied. Here is yet another, which can be interpreted in the same way:

[121] *a:* le pilote a fait atterrir le Boeing 747
       the pilot made the Boeing 747 land
   b: le pilote a atterri le Boeing 747
       the pilot landed the Boeing 747

[122] *a:* la tour de contrôle a fait atterrir le Boeing 747
       the control tower made the Boeing 747 land
   b: ??la tour de contrôle a atterri le Boeing 747
       ??the control tower landed the Boeing 747

The difference depends on the fact that the action of the pilot on his aircraft can be conceived equally well as direct or indirect, whereas the action of the control tower can only be indirect (through the medium of the pilot's role). In all these examples, the opposition between direct action and indirect action seems to be linked to the presence (versus the absence) of spatial contiguity between the subject and the object, but I do not claim that this connection is always required.

Example [67] – as opposed to [12–13] – seems to me especially interesting, I give it again here:

[67] *a:* le colonel a fait fondre trois sucres dans son café
            ?the colonel made three lumps of sugar dissolve in his coffee
      b: *le colonel a fondu trois sucres dans son café
            the colonel dissolved three lumps of sugar in his coffee†

beside:

[123] *a:* le chimiste (le métallurgiste) a fait fondre le métal
            the chemist (the metallurgist) caused the metal to melt
       b: le chimiste (le métallurgiste) a fondu le métal
            the chemist (the metallurgist) melted the metal

The anomalous character of [67*b*] again seems to me to be due to the impossibility of considering the melting of the sugar in the coffee as resulting from a direct action of the colonel on the sugar. The opposition between direct and indirect action here seems to be connected with the presence (versus the absence) of continuous control (or mastery) of the subject over the process to which the object is subjected. In [67], the colonel's part in the process consists solely in the fact that he put some sugar in his coffee; the fact that the sugar has dissolved depends on causes beyond his control. *Trois sucres* in [67*a*] is difficult to take as an agent, but in a sense it participates in the process expressed by the verb *fondre* in an autonomous way, in any case in a way beyond the colonel's control. It is a different matter in [123], where it may be considered that the chemist or the metallurgist keeps direct and continuous control over the operation of metal-melting. Other similar examples, in which the surface object, even in the complex factitive construction, cannot be taken as an agent in the proper sense of the term, but in which the distinction between direct action and indirect action persists, are easy to find. Consider:[16]

[124] Graham Hill a $\begin{Bmatrix} a: \text{gonflé} \\ b: \text{*fait gonfler} \end{Bmatrix}$ les pneus de sa Lotus

        Graham Hill $\begin{Bmatrix} a: \text{inflated the tyres of his Lotus} \\ b: \text{*caused the tyres of his Lotus to inflate} \end{Bmatrix}$

† See note on *p* 141.

[125] le boulanger a $\begin{Bmatrix} a: \text{?gonflé} \\ b: \text{fait gonfler} \end{Bmatrix}$ la pâte (en y mettant de la levure)

the baker $\begin{Bmatrix} a: \text{? raised the dough} \\ b: \text{made the dough rise} \end{Bmatrix}$ (by putting yeast in it)

Let us go on to the cases where the simple transitive construction is impossible or hardly natural if the subject is inanimate (cf [58–61]). Many of these cases are explained if it is admitted that transitive verbs and physical change-of-state verbs normally impose an agentive interpretation on their subject. This is what excludes the (b) cases in the following examples:

[59] cette manoeuvre stupide a $\begin{Bmatrix} a: \text{fait échouer} \\ b: \text{*échoué} \end{Bmatrix}$ le cuirassé

this stupid manoeuvre $\begin{Bmatrix} a: \text{caused the battleship to run aground} \\ b: \text{*ran the battleship aground} \end{Bmatrix}$

[126] $\begin{Bmatrix} \text{la maladresse} \\ \text{un simple geste} \end{Bmatrix}$ de Delphine a $\begin{Bmatrix} \text{fait entrer} \\ \text{*entré} \end{Bmatrix}$ la voiture dans le garage

$\begin{Bmatrix} \text{Delphine's clumsiness} \\ \text{a mere sign by Delphine} \end{Bmatrix}$ $\begin{Bmatrix} \text{caused the car to enter the garage} \\ \text{*put the car in the garage} \end{Bmatrix}$

[127] l'indifférence d'Alice a $\begin{Bmatrix} a: \text{fait remonter} \\ b: \text{*remonté} \end{Bmatrix}$ Humpty Dumpty sur son mur

Alice's unconcern $\begin{Bmatrix} a: \text{caused Humpty Dumpty to get back onto} \\ \text{his wall} \\ b: \text{*put Humpty Dumpty back on his wall} \end{Bmatrix}$

That it is not the [± ANIMATE] character of the subject, but rather the possibility of interpreting it as an agent, which counts is clearly seen if we compare these examples with [128–129]:

[128] le vent a cassé les branches
the wind broke off the branches

[129] la pluie a dispersé les manifestants
the rain dispersed the demonstrators

Nevertheless, some difficulties remain, notably concerning the treatment of examples [68–71] above. I cannot quite see what makes the difference between [129] and [68b], which I repeat:

[68] a: les pluies ont fait monter le niveau de la rivière
the rains caused the level of the river to rise
b: *les pluies ont monté le niveau de la rivière

None of the conditions that I have given seems to be able to prohibit [68b], and the same assessment applies to [69–71]. There is, at first sight, a difference between [68–71] and the other sentences that we have considered, a difference that is clear if we look at the following paradigm:

[130]   *a:* le métal a fondu (*cf* [123])
           the metal melted
        b: le métal est fondu
           the metal is melted

[131]   *a:* le poulet a cuit
           the chicken cooked
        b: le poulet est cuit
           the chicken is cooked

[132]   *a:* le niveau de la rivière a monté
           the level of the river has risen
        b: *le niveau de la rivière est monté
           *the level of the river is risen

[133]   *a:* la fièvre de Juliette a baissé (*cf* [70–71])
           Juliet's temperature has fallen
        b: *la fiévre de Juliette est baissée
           *Juliet's temperature is fallen

At first sight, it seems that, when the simple transitive construction is possible, there is a possibility also of a simple intransitive construction and equally of a construction with stative adjective, of the form NP *être* [$_A$ V-*é*], illustrated by [130b–131b] (on this point, see also Chapter 5). Now, these constructions with stative adjective are impossible in the cases considered here. On the other hand, it is a fact that, from the semantic point of view, there is a relationship of implication between the simple transitive sentence and the sentence with stative adjective (between [123b] and [130b] for example), a relationship that can be schematized as follows

[134] NP$_1$ V NP$_2$ (at time t_i) ⊃ NP$_2$ *est* [$_A$ V-*é*] (at time t_j)
        (where $i < j$)

In other words, the fact that the chemist melts the metal at a given moment implies that, at a later moment, the metal is melted. We might, then, be tempted to connect the impossibility of sentences [68b–71b] with the impossibility of having corresponding constructions with stative adjective. Unfortunately, there are verbs that allow the transitive construction, while not allowing the construction with stative adjective. This is the case with *remonter* (and with *monter* in similar examples), *cf* [73] and [135]:

[135] *pour l'instant, Humpty Dumpty est (re)monté sur son mur
      *for the moment, Humpty Dumpty is put (back) on his wall

Of course, a sentence such as [136] is possible, but, as is indicated by the presence of the adverbial, this is not a stative sentence, but a sentence with compound past tense, where *être* is the past auxiliary:

[136] à huit heures moins le quart, Humpty Dumpty est (re)monté sur
      son mur
      at a quarter to eight, Humpty Dumpty got (back) on his wall

In short, the only difference that seems to hold between sentences such as those of [73] or [123], on the one hand, and those of [68–71], on the other hand, is that the first group can have corresponding intransitive sentences with *être* (whether it is a case of stative sentences, as in the case of [123], or of sentences with *être* as an auxiliary, as with [73]), whereas the second group do not have corresponding sentences with *être*. Perhaps it is in this direction that we must look for an explanation, but I confess that I cannot find it at the moment.[17]

6

Now I should like to consider a rather different type of argument. If there are, on the one hand, idiosyncratic differences, and, on the other hand, systematic semantic differences between the simple transitive construction and the complex factitive construction, they also show a systematic difference on another level, which is that of strict subcategorization restrictions (*cf* Chomsky, 1965, 90*ff*).

Let us first recall some facts concerning the derivation of complex factitive constructions. We know (*cf*, for further details, Kayne, 1969) that, when the sentence embedded under *faire* is a direct transitive, its deep subject is obligatorily preceded by the preposition *à* in surface structure, *cf*:

[137] Pierre a fait dormir $\left\{ {*\grave{a} \atop \emptyset} \right\}$ Paul

      Peter made Paul sleep

[138] Pierre a fait manger un steak $\left\{ {\grave{a} \atop *\emptyset} \right\}$ Paul

      Peter made Paul eat a steak

Transitive verbs with deletable (or optional) object, such as *manger* (to eat), when their object is absent on the surface, behave like intransitives, *cf:*

[139] Pierre a fait manger $\begin{Bmatrix} *\text{à} \\ \text{Ø} \end{Bmatrix}$ Paul

Peter made Paul eat

which means that, at the stage of the derivation when the transformation or transformations (À-INSERTION, in fact, *cf* Kayne, 1969) which account for the surface structure of factitive constructions take place, the direct object of verbs such as *manger* is absent.

Let us now consider sentences such as [140–142], which are fairly close semantically, and which differ syntactically only in the optional presence of a prepositional versus direct object – or, in terms of standard theory, in a strict subcategorization feature:

[140] Madeleine a accouché (d'un gros garçon)
Madeleine gave birth (to a fine boy)

[141] Jules a vomi (tout son repas)
Julius vomited (his entire meal)

[142] la poule a pondu (un bel oeuf)
the hen laid (a nice egg)

Let us see what happens if, on the one hand, we construct factitives in which [140–142] are embedded under *faire*, and, on the other hand, if we construct the corresponding simple transitives. We obtain the following results:

[143] le médecin a fait accoucher Madeleine (d'un gros garçon)
the doctor made Madeleine give birth (to a fine boy)

[144] le médecin a accouché Madeleine (d'un gros garçon)
the doctor delivered Madeleine (of a fine boy)

[145] *a:* Irène a fait vomir Jules
Irene made Julius vomit
b: Irène a fait vomir tout son repas à Jules
Irene made Julius vomit his entire meal

[146] *a:* *Irène a vomi Jules
b: *Irène a vomi tout son repas à Jules

[147] *a:* le fermier a fait pondre la poule
        the farmer made the hen lay
     b: le fermier a fait pondre un bel oeuf à la poule
        the farmer made the hen lay a nice egg

[148] *a:* *le fermier a pondu la poule
     b: *le fermier a pondu un bel oeuf à la poule

We see that it is impossible to obtain a simple factitive transitive if the subordinate verb of the complex factitives is a transitive verb, and this is so whether the direct object is present (*cf* [146*b*], [148*b*]), or absent (*cf* [146*a*], [148*a*]). Here we have a fact which is very common, *cf* again:

[149] *a:* le roi a abdiqué (le pouvoir)
        the king abdicated (his power)

     b: les révolutionnaires ont fait abdiquer $\begin{cases} \text{le roi} \\ \text{le pouvoir au roi} \end{cases}$

        the revolutionaries made the king $\begin{cases} \text{abdicate} \\ \text{abdicate his power} \end{cases}$

     c: *les révolutionnaires ont abdiqué $\begin{cases} \text{le roi} \\ \text{le pouvoir au roi} \end{cases}$

[150] *a:* les prisonniers ont hurlé (des injures)
        the prisoners shouted (insults)

     b: par leurs tortures, les SS ont fait hurler $\begin{cases} \text{les prisonniers} \\ \text{des injures aux} \\ \quad \text{prisonniers} \end{cases}$

        by their torture, the SS made the prisoners $\begin{cases} \text{shout} \\ \text{shout insults} \end{cases}$

     c: *par leurs tortures, les SS ont hurlé $\begin{cases} \text{les prisonniers} \\ \text{des injures aux} \\ \quad \text{prisonniers} \end{cases}$

It is clear that we have a problem here for the transformational analysis. As [143–144] show, there is no general constraint which would prevent FAIRE-SUBSTITUTION (or PREDICATE-RAISING) from operating in the presence of a complement of the subordinate verb. The transformational analysis would in fact predict the grammaticality of [146*a–b*], etc. So it would be necessary to impose on FAIRE-SUBSTITUTION an *ad hoc* constraint blocking this transformation if the subordinate verb is transitive. What is worse, this constraint could not make use of the mention of

the presence of an NP in term 4 of the structure index of the transformation (*cf* [24]). In fact, we have just seen, on the one hand, that FAIRE-
SUBSTITUTION must be blocked, whether the deep direct object of the
verb is present or not (*cf* [146], [148], etc), and, on the other hand, (*cf*
[137–139]) that the direct object is absent at the time of the operation of
À-INSERTION, which should be ordered before FAIRE-SUBSTITUTION.
At best, we should then have to resort to a global derivational constraint,
mentioning, on the one hand, a stage when [143] is distinct from [145],
and, on the other hand, the stage when FAIRE-SUBSTITUTION applies.
This constraint would have no explanatory value.

Obviously, we could try to get over this in various ways. Firstly, we
could invoke the semantic differences mentioned in section 5: one might
argue that, when the subordinate verb is transitive, it is impossible to
conceive direct action by the main subject on the subordinate subject.
The semantic closeness of [140], [141], [142], makes this explanation
suspect. In the same way, [149c] and [150c] seem capable of being interpreted naturally in terms of direct action: compare, especially, [149e] with
[116a], which is very close to it in meaning; even in the style in which
[116a] is possible, with its particular interpretation, [149c] seems to me
to be entirely excluded.

On the other hand, we might make use of the fact that sentences of the
same surface structure as [146], etc, are often grammatical, but with
another interpretation. Thus, [146a] is possible, in a rather substandard
dialect, and means approximately that Julius violently disgusts Irene.
Similarly, [150c] (with the direct object present) has a quite natural
interpretation.† We might then consider resorting to a perceptual
strategy (*cf* Klima, 1970, and Chapter 6 of this book) which, in certain
conditions, would eliminate one reading of a sentence if it is in com-
petition with another. But it is soon evident that this recourse is excluded. In the first place, the ambiguity of sentences like [146a] is not
at all of the same type (absolute structural ambiguity) as those which
seem to necessitate recourse to perceptual strategies, and besides, in
French there are comparable ambiguities which are perfectly well
tolerated, *cf* that of [151], in which *Marie* can be understood as being
either the recipient, or the 'source' of the action (the bookseller, in this
case):

[151] Pierre a acheté un livre à Marie
        Peter bought a book for Mary/Peter bought a book from Mary

† 'the SS shouted insults at the prisoners'. [*Translator's note*]

Secondly, in cases where resort to perceptual strategies is justified, one of the two readings is not excluded purely and simply; rather there is a hierarchy of possible readings (*cf* Chapter 6). Here on the contrary, it is clear that, for example, the reading of [146a] corresponding to [145a] is entirely excluded. Furthermore, structures of the type of [146], etc, are not always ambiguous; for example, [149c] in fact has no other possible reading. Lastly, it is sometimes only the construction with direct object present on the surface (*cf* [150c]), and sometimes only the construction without a direct object (*cf* [146a]) which has another possible reading. Resort to a perceptual strategy would not explain why all the constructions of [146], [148], etc, are impossible, whether the direct object is present or not, and whether the sentence has another possible reading or not.

We must therefore seek another explanation. Now, standard theory offers us one which is entirely natural. Consider rule [2], which I repeat here:

[2] $[+\text{V}]$, $[+(se)\ldots\text{---}\text{X}]$, $[+[\alpha\text{F}]\ldots] \rightarrow [+\text{V}]$, $[+\text{CAUSE}]$,
    $[+\text{---}\text{NP X}]$, $[+\text{---}[\alpha\text{F}]]$

This rule, remember, establishes a correspondence between deep structures. In particular, the sequences (NP) X which appear on the right in the subcategorization features of the verbs can only, by definition, be sequences of categories that can be generated by the base rules. Now we know that, in French, there is no rule VP → V (NP) (NP); a sequence of two NPs is therefore excluded. In other words, the X which appears in [2] cannot be of the form NP Y, whereas it can perfectly well be of the form PP Y (*cf* the rule VP → V(NP) (PP)). In short, it is therefore this constraint on the base rules of French which explains why [146] is excluded while [144] is allowed.

Nevertheless, there is still a further specification to be made. Standard theory offers *a priori* several means of treating transitive verbs with an optional object such as *vomir*, *manger*, *abdiquer*, etc. We can subcategorize them in terms of $[+\text{---}\text{NP}]$, and then delete an indefinite or dummy object NP by means of a transformation; this is the traditional solution. If we choose this solution, clearly there is no problem. But this is not the only possibility. As there is no syntactic indication (*cf* [137–139]) that these object NPs are ever present at any stage of the derivation of sentences in which they do not appear on the surface,[18] we might content ourselves with subcategorizing *vomir*, etc, in terms of the features $[+\text{---}\text{NP}]$ and $[+\text{---}\#]$, and we could dispense with the deletion transformation. In this case, if sentences of the type [146*b*] are always excluded by the joint operation of the base rules and of [2], it is no longer apparent, at first sight, how to block the derivation of [146*a*], which would not then differ from, for example, [10], *Adèle cuit le ragoût*.

There remains yet another possibility, which consists in subcategorizing *vomir*, etc, not in terms of the independent features [+ —— NP] and [+ —— #], but in terms of the feature [+ —— (NP)]; in other words, we would make the parentheses play a crucial role. In this case, if we wanted to apply the part of rule [2] which concerns us to verbs such as *vomir*, that part of the rule would be:

[152] [+ V], [+ —— (NP)], . . . → . . . , [+ —— NP (NP)], . . .

and we see that the right-hand side of the rule shows a sequence which cannot be generated by the base rules. There would therefore no longer be a problem, as in the solution by deletion. Supposing that the solution in terms of subcategorization to the problem posed by verbs with optional object is preferable to the solution by deletion, the facts of [143–150] seem to me to be simply an additional empirical justification of the parenthesis notation (*cf* Chomsky, 1965, Chapter 1, § 7).[19]

But there are one or two exceptions to the generalization that has just been formulated. These exceptions concern the verbs *paître* and *apprendre*, *cf*:

[153] *a:* les brebis paissent (l'herbe)
              the sheep feed (on grass)
       b: i: le berger fait paître les brebis
                  the shepherd makes the sheep feed
             ii: le berger fait paître l'herbe aux brebis
                  the shepherd makes the sheep feed on grass
       c: i: le berger paît les brebis
                  the shepherd feeds the sheep
             ii: *le berger paît l'herbe aux brebis

[154] *a:* Pierre apprend le violon
              Peter is learning the violin
       b: Paul fait apprendre le violon à Pierre
              Paul is making Peter learn the violin
       c: Paul apprend le violon à Pierre
              Paul is teaching Peter the violin

In the conception that I am advocating, I shall be obliged to distinguish two lexical entries for *paître* and for *apprendre*. Note that *paître* is rather an archaic verb. Of the constructions of [153], only the intransitive of [153*a*] is given by the *Dictionnaire Larousse du Français contemporain* (Dubois *et al*, 1966). But they are all found in Littré, and apparently they all belong to the same dialect of French. Further, *paître* is an irregular, defective verb (it has no past participle). Moreover, it is not clear (*cf* [155]) that the object of *paître* is a true direct object; *paître* might be closer to a verb like *habiter* (*cf Pierre habite (à) Paris* (Peter lives in Paris)) than to a verb like *brouter* (to browse, to graze), which (*cf* [156]) behaves in accordance with the generalization that we have just formulated:

[155] les brebis paissent dans l'herbe
   the sheep feed in the grass

[156] *a:* les brebis broutent (l'herbe)
   the sheep graze (the grass)

  b: le berger a fait brouter $\begin{cases} \text{l'herbe aux brebis} \\ \text{les brebis} \end{cases}$

   the shepherd made the sheep $\begin{cases} \text{graze the grass} \\ \text{graze} \end{cases}$

  c: *le berger a brouté $\begin{cases} \text{l'herbe aux brebis} \\ \text{les brebis} \end{cases}$

If the object of *paître* was in fact a PP in deep structure, this would explain the possibility of having [153*ci*]. But the impossibility of having the passive (due to the absence of the past participle), as well as my absence of intuition on sentences such as [157] (*cf* [158]), prevents me from drawing any conclusion on the exact nature of the complement of *paître* (*l'herbe* in [153*a*]):

[157] les brebis la paissent, cette herbe
   the sheep feed on it, this grass

[158] *Pierre l'habite, cette ville

In any case, then, *paître* has very special characteristics. What is important is that the transformational analysis, in terms of FAIRE-SUBSTI-TUTION, would predict the grammaticalness of [153*cii*]. Yet this sentence is altogether excluded.

The verb *apprendre* is different: [154*c*] – which corresponds to [153*cii*] – would in fact be predicted by FAIRE-SUBSTITUTION, and is grammatical. Moreover, if we cannot deduce much from the impossibility of [159c] – given the doubtful character of sentences where *apprendre* is intransitive,

[159] *a:* ?Pierre apprend
          Peter learns
       b: ?Paul fait apprendre Pierre
          Paul makes Peter learn
       c: *Paul apprend Pierre

the analysis by FAIRE-SUBSTITUTION would predict that it is equally possible to derive from [160a] the grammatical [160b], and the excluded [160c]:

[160] *a:* Paul fait [s Pierre apprendre le violon avec Menuhin]
          Paul causes [s Peter learn the violin with Menuhin]
       b: Paul fait apprendre le violon à Pierre avec Menuhin
          Paul causes Peter to learn the violin with Menuhin
       c: *Paul apprend le violon à Pierre avec Menuhin

[160c] clearly being grammatical in the reading in which 'Paul, en collaboration avec Menuhin, apprend le violon à Pierre' (Paul, in collaboration with Menuhin, teaches Peter the violin), *cf: les Anglais ont battu les Allemands avec les Américains* (the English beat the Germans with the Americans).

Finally, then, there is no transitive verb whose behaviour is entirely predicted by FAIRE-SUBSTITUTION. The solution which consists in keeping the generalization based on redundancy rule [2], combined with the attribution of two distinct lexical entries to *paître* and to *apprendre*, is decidedly preferable.

7

All the preceding arguments tend to show that an analysis relating simple factitive transitive sentences to complex factitive sentences by lexical redundancy rules is preferable to a transformational analysis which derives the first from the second by FAIRE-SUBSTITUTION. These arguments tell even more strongly against McCawley's analysis using PREDICATE-RAISING (*cf* section 1). I should like to revert briefly to some additional difficulties raised by McCawley's analysis (see also Fodor's criticisms, 1970).

For McCawley, sentences such as [161a], [162a], would be derived, respectively, from structures underlying [161*b*], [162*b*], by PREDICATE-RAISING and LEXICALIZATION:

[161] *a:* Stéphane a donné le *Livre* à Arthur
Stéphane gave the *Livre* to Arthur
b: Stéphane a fait avoir le *Livre* à Arthur
Stéphane caused Arthur to have the *Livre*

[162] *a:* Claude a montré la partition du *Martyre* à Igor
Claude showed the score of the *Martyre* to Igor
b: Claude a fait voir la partition du *Martyre* à Igor
Claude caused Igor to see the score of the *Martyre*

At first sight, there would be a syntactic argument in favour of this analysis. In fact, by ordering LEXICALIZATION after the rule that inserts the preposition *à* in [161*b*], [162*b*] (À-INSERTION, *cf* Kayne, 1969), we could account in one step for the presence of this preposition in examples (*a*) and in examples (*b*). But this benefit is illusory. Indeed, we see at once that, as many constructions with an indirect object in *à* do not seem to be derivable in this way, *cf:*

[163] Roman a présenté Morris à Noam (see note 3)
Roman introduced Morris to Noam

it would in any case be necessary to introduce *à* in the base, independently of À-INSERTION.

There is a more serious objection still. We have just seen in section 6 that, if we retain the analysis by FAIRE-SUBSTITUTION, we are obliged to introduce an *ad hoc* condition which blocks the application of this rule if the subordinate verb is a direct transitive. The same condition is necessary if one turns to PREDICATE-RAISING.

Now, if we uphold the derivation by PREDICATE-RAISING of sentences [161*a*], [162*a*], we find ourselves in a paradoxical position: the PREDICATE-RAISING rule, blocked if [146] and [148] are to be excluded, where the verbs concerned (*pondre, vomir*) are morphologically identical in the simple transitive and in the complex factitive, must be allowed in the case of [161], [162], where the verbs (*avoir* and *donner*, *voir* and *montrer*) are morphologically differentiated. This condition is bizarre, to say the least – it does not obtain if the subordinate verb (*cuire, fondre, mourir/tuer*) is intransitive. One could get round the difficulty by introducing a global constraint, combined with that mentioned in section 6, which would give the stages of the derivation corresponding, on the one hand, to the input of PREDICATE-RAISING, and, on the other hand, to the output of LEXICALIZATION. But the least that one could say is that such a formulation would not be very enlightening.

In any case, it is not true, generally speaking, that the distribution of prepositions is the same in simple and complex constructions which are, like [161a–b], [162a–b], more or less in a paraphrase relation. Ronat (1972) has recently proposed a criticism of Postal's analysis of the verb *remind* (see this book, Chapter 1, section 3.2, and Chapter 5, section 8). In particular it shows (though subsequently rejecting this solution) that it is possible, within the framework of generative semantics, to give an analysis of the verb *remind* different from Postal's and having certain advantages over it: this analysis amounts to deriving [164a] from [164b]:

[164] *a:* John reminds me of Bill
       b: John makes me think of Bill

This solution has the advantage, notably, of introducing in one step the preposition *of*, which, in Postal's solution, had to be treated in an *ad hoc* way. This, then, is an argument of the same nature as the one which we have just described in connection with [161 – 162]. Now, if we consider the French equivalent of [164], namely [165], to which the same type of derivation could be applied just as well (or just as badly):

[165] *a:* le sourire de Marilyn rappelle à Raoul celui de Mona Lisa
           Marilyn's smile reminds Raoul of the Mona Lisa's
       b: le sourire de Marilyn fait penser Raoul à celui de Mona Lisa
           Marilyn's smile makes Raoul think of the Mona Lisa's

we see that the distribution of the prepositions is not at all what would be predicted by the PREDICATE-RAISING analysis; this would in fact predict [166], which is ungrammatical:[20]

[166] *le sourire de Marilyn rappelle Raoul à celui de Mona Lisa

As I said at the beginning of this section, then, we find the same differences between the sentences of [161a and b], [162a and b], in terms of 'direct connection'/'indirect connection' of which we spoke earlier on. The difference between [161a] and [161b], for example, is comparable to that obtaining between [73b] and [73a], as the coordination test shows: [167a] is contradictory, but [167b] is not:

[167] *a:* ∉ Stéphane a donné le *Livre* à Arthur mais il ne le lui a pas donné
           (lui-même)
       ∉ Stéphane gave the *Livre* to Arthur but he did not give it to
           him (himself)

b: Stéphane a fait avoir le *Livre* à Arthur, mais il ne le lui a pas
donné (lui-même)

Stéphane caused Arthur to have the *Livre*, but he did not give
it to him (himself)

In short, the use of *donner* in [161a] implies that *le Livre* was in the
possession of *Stéphane*, whereas the use of *faire avoir* in [161b] does not
necessarily imply that *le Livre* was in the possession of *Stéphane*. (It is
quite another question to say, with Bierwisch (1970), that something
like FAIRE AVOIR, with other elements, forms part of the semantic
representation of *donner*: the important thing is that the notion of 'direct
connection' is related to the deep structure $[_S NP[_{VP} VNP X]]$). Moreover,
as I pointed out earlier (see the end of section 4), this idea of direct connection is extended here to the relationship which links the subject and
the indirect object: [161a] suggests a direct relation between *Stéphane* and
Arthur, and will have as its most natural interpretation that Stéphane
himself hands over the book to Arthur, whereas this idea is not present
in [161b].

One more remark. We have seen (*cf* [140], [143]) that certain prepositional complements are found both in transitive constructions and in the
corresponding intransitive constructions. If [161a] were derived from
[161b], we should expect to have [169] parallel to [168]; but [169] is
excluded:

[168]   *a:* Arthur a eu le *Livre* par Victor
Arthur had the *Livre* through Victor

b: Stéphane a fait avoir le *Livre* à Arthur par Victor
Stéphane caused Arthur to have the *Livre* through Victor

[169]   *Stéphane a donné le *Livre* à Arthur par Victor
*Stéphane gave the *Livre* to Arthur through Victor

8

In note 7, I pointed out that sentences such as [20]

[20]   Adèle fait cuire le ragoût
Adèle gets the stew cooked

are ambiguous. They correspond either to a deep structure of the type
[170], or to a deep structure of the type [171] (*cf* [172]):

[170]   Adèle fait $[_S$ le ragoût cuire]
Adèle causes $[_S$ the stew cook]

[171] Adèle fait [$_S$ Δ cuire le ragoût]
       Adèle causes [$_S$ Δ cook the stew]

[172] Adèle fait cuire le ragoût par sa cuisinière
       Adèle gets the stew cooked by her cook

Up to now I have left aside the cases in which sentences of the type of [20] have the reading which corresponds to the deep structure [171]. (A study of these constructions and of their relations with the PASSIVE will be found in Kayne, 1969, forthcoming). However, Dubois (1969, 34 ff) has observed that sentences such as [173] can be interpreted either with the meaning of [174], or with that of [175]:

[173] mes amis construisent une maison
       my friends are building a house

[174] mes amis construisent une maison (de leurs propres mains)
       my friends are building a house (with their own hands)

[175] mes amis font construire une maison (par des ouvriers)
       my friends are having a house built (by workmen)

Dubois thus distinguishes an 'active' sense of *construire* – that of [174] – and a 'factitive' sense – that of [175], which he also sees in [176]:

[176] l'architecte a construit une maison
       the architect built a house

'This difference of meaning', says Dubois, 'which must be accounted for syntactically, does not appear to be inherent in the verb itself, but in the deep structure'. So he proposes to derive [173], in the 'factitive' sense, from something like [175]. He is not very explicit as to the derivation that he proposes, and the derivation that one can reconstruct from the indications that he gives would entail certain difficulties as shown by Kayne (1969). But, taking into account the analysis proposed by Kayne[21] for the derivation of constructions in *faire* V NP *par* NP, we might suggest the following derivation:

[177] *a:* BASE: mes amis font [$_S$ Δ construire une maison par Δ]
              → AGENT-POSTPOSING →
       b: mes amis font [$_S$ construire une maison par Δ]
              → AGENT-DELETION →
       c: mes amis font construire une maison
              → FAIRE-SUBSTITUTION →
       d: mes amis construisent une maison

This analysis, then, would bring in the FAIRE-SUBSTITUTION rule (*cf* [24]), which I tried to show did not come into the derivation of simple transitives.

In fact, this analysis poses several serious problems. Firstly, it is not clear that these facts must be accounted for in syntactic terms, in particular in transformational terms. The fact that a construction is ambiguous is not generally enough to justify a syntactic treatment of the ambiguity, nor to propose two distinct deep structures (*cf* Jackendoff, 1969b, Chomsky, 1970, 1971, and Chapter 1 of this book). It is always necessary, as I have endeavoured to show several times in this book, to have had recourse to strictly syntactic arguments for other reasons. Yet not only does Dubois not propose syntactic arguments, but his analysis gives rise to certain difficulties at this level.

In fact, we saw in section 6 that, when certain prepositional complements accompany the subordinate verb in a factitive sentence of the surface form NP_1 *faire* V NP_2 PP, they are also sometimes found in the corresponding transitive construction, NP_1 V NP_2 PP (*cf* [143]), [144]). It is possible to treat these facts in terms of redundancy rule [2], as we have seen. On the other hand, there are various types of complements which appear in the subordinate clause of the factitive construction and which cannot appear in the simple transitive. One of the general difficulties of the analysis by FAIRE-SUBSTITUTION (or by PREDICATE-RAISING) is that it imposes *ad hoc* constraints to prevent transitive sentences with these complements from being generated (*cf* Fodor, 1970, and this chapter, section 2 and the end of section 7). Now, if we adopt Dubois' analysis, we come up against a difficulty of this very type. If the sentences of the type of [173], in their 'factitive' sense, were derived in the manner of [177], we should expect to have [178b], [179b], beside [178a], [179a] – in other words, we should expect to find agent complements in the simple transitives, as in the complex factitives. But examples (*b*) are ungrammatical:

[178] *a:* mon ami fait construire sa maison par un maçon qualifié
      my friend is having his house built by a skilled mason
    b: *mon ami construit sa maison par un maçon qualifié
      *my friend is building his house by a skilled mason

[179] *a:* Néron a fait brûler Rome par ses sbires
      Nero had Rome burned by his sbirri
    b: *Néron a brûlé Rome par ses sbires
      *Nero burned Rome by his sbirri

A grammar which considers [173] as basic, whatever its precise meaning may be, would have no difficulty in excluding [178b–179b]: these sentences are simply a particular case of the general constraint which excludes having an agent complement in *par* NP in co-occurrence with an expressed subject, *cf* [180–181]:

[180] *Gary a embrassé Marilyn par Clark
       *Gary kissed Marilyn by Clark

[181] *Claude a présenté Igor à Arnold par Alban
       *Claude introduced Igor to Arnold by Alban

All these facts are treated naturally by the usual formulation of the PASSIVE rule (whether or not it is broken down into two steps).

In contrast, Dubois' analysis would have to impose an independent and *ad hoc* constraint to exclude sentences such as [178b–179b].

On the semantic level, also, Dubois' analysis raises difficulties. Firstly, Dubois concludes too hastily, it seems to me, that the ambiguity 'is not inherent in the verb itself'. The ambiguity, if ambiguity there is, seems in any case to be limited to a certain class of verbs (*construire*, *détruire*, *brûler*, etc), and it is clear that sentences such as [182a], [183a], for example, cannot in any case be interpreted as paraphrases of [182b], [183b]:

[182] *a:* Gary a embrassé Marilyn
            Gary kissed Marilyn
       b: Gary a fait embrasser Marilyn (par quelqu'un)
            Gary had Marilyn kissed (by someone)

[183] *a:* Claude a présenté Igor à Arnold
            Claude introduced Igor to Arnold
       b: Claude a fait présenter Igor à Arnold (par quelqu'un)
            Claude had Igor introduced to Arnold (by someone)

In the second place, all the following sentences are equally possible:

[184]   mon ami ⎫
        l'architecte ⎬ construit la maison
      l'entrepreneur ⎪
          le maçon ⎭

        my friend ⎫
      the architect ⎬ is building the house
      the contractor ⎪
         the mason ⎭

[185] mon ami fait construire la maison par $\begin{cases} \text{l'architecte} \\ \text{l'entrepreneur} \\ \text{le maçon} \end{cases}$

my friend is having the house built by $\begin{cases} \text{the architect} \\ \text{the contractor} \\ \text{the mason} \end{cases}$

[186] l'architecte fait construire la maison par $\begin{cases} \text{l'entrepreneur} \\ \text{le maçon} \end{cases}$

the architect is having the house built by $\begin{cases} \text{the contractor} \\ \text{the mason} \end{cases}$

[187] l'entrepreneur fait construire la maison par $\begin{cases} \text{l'architecte} \\ \text{le maçon} \end{cases}$

the contractor is having the house built by $\begin{cases} \text{the architect} \\ \text{the mason} \end{cases}$

As, for Dubois, *construire* only has the 'active' meaning if it is taken in the entirely concrete and physical sense of *les maçons construisent la maison* (the masons are building the house), it follows that most of these sentences ought to be ambiguous, which does not seem to accord with intuition. Also there would be nothing to prevent one from deriving [173], not only from [177a], but for example from [188a or b]:

[188] *a:* mes amis font [$_{S1}$ Δ faire [$_{S2}$ Δ construire une maison par Δ]]

     b: mes amis font [$_{S1}$ Δ faire [$_{S2}$ Δ faire [$_{S3}$ Δ construire une maison par Δ]]]

In other words, we should have the problem posed by the possibility of the infinite recursion of the factitive construction: a sentence such as [173] would theoretically be infinitely ambiguous. If this consequence is to be avoided, it would once again be necessary to introduce an *ad hoc* constraint prohibiting this infinite recursion.

Finally, between [173], even taken in the 'non-concrete' or 'non-active' sense, and [175] there is a difference of meaning, which is similar to those that we pointed out between the simple transitives and the complex factitives: [175] propounds explicitly that the house is built (in a sense which is not necessarily specified as 'concrete active') by someone other than *mes amis;* 'my friends' are the external cause of an action which is carried out by someone else. [173] on the contrary shows *mes amis* as the direct cause of the building process, even if the precise nature of this process is not specified. In other words, we again have here the distinction between direct connection and indirect connection, even if the direct connection is not necessarily interpreted here in the sense of a concrete spatial connection.

In view of these difficulties, then, we are in a position to cast doubt on the ambiguity of [173]. It might be asked whether this sentence is not 'indeterminate' (or 'vague'; on this distinction, see Ducrot and Todorov, 304), rather than ambiguous. Many linguistic expressions leave all sorts of aspects of the situation indeterminate, without what might properly be called ambiguity. For example, the sentence *Pierre a levé le bras* (Peter raised his arm) leaves indeterminate the question whether Peter raised his right arm or his left arm, but there would be no ground for talking of ambiguity. Could one not simply say that, in a sentence like [173], *construire* requires its subject to be interpreted as the agent responsible for the action, leaving indeterminate the concrete modality in which the action is realized? The semantic component could, besides, include an interpretative principle, perhaps of quite general application, saying that, for verbs of a certain class, the precise modality of the action for which the subject is responsible can be understood in different ways, of which one implies a physical action, and the other simply the idea of responsibility. We should then understand the various nuances in the meaning of the verbs *battre*, *tuer*, *brûler*, in the following sentences:[22]

[189] *a:* Napoléon a battu les Russes à Austerlitz
        Napoleon beat the Russians at Austerlitz
    b: le Réal Madrid a battu l'Inter par 2 à 1
        Real Madrid beat Inter by 2 to 1
    c: Pierre bat sa femme tous les soirs
        Peter beats his wife every evening

[190] *a:* Charles d'Anjou a défait et tué Manfred à Bénévent
        Charles d'Anjou defeated and killed Manfred at Benevento
    b: les cinquante conjurés ont tué César
        the fifty conspirators killed Caesar
    c: Pat Garrett a tué Billy the Kid d'une balle en plein coeur
        Pat Garrett killed Billy the Kid with a bullet to the heart

[191] *a:* Néron a brûlé Rome
        Nero burned Rome
    b: James Bond a brûlé les papiers compromettants dans sa cheminée
        James Bond burned the compromising papers in his fireplace

I shall leave this question in abeyance. The aim of this whole discussion is only to show that it is risky to propose any given syntactic derivation, in a case of this sort, without first considering the question of the semantic nature of the class of verbs which allows this kind of interpretation.

9 Résumé and conclusion

I have tried to show that there is no syntactic or semantic reason for deriving simple transitive factitive constructions from complex factitive constructions – even if one adheres to the restricted analysis, compatible with standard theory, which involves the FAIRE-SUBSTITUTION transformation. On the other hand, there are syntactic advantages in treating the systematic relations between the two types of construction in terms of redundancy rules (cf sections 2 and 6); as for the semantic and selectional differences which separate them, it seems that a more promising way of dealing with these would be by means of special interpretation rules (cf sections 4 and 5). The extensions of the transformational analysis proposed by McCawley (cf section 7) and by Dubois (cf section 8) encounter the same difficulties as the restricted transformational analysis, and raise additional ones.

Undoubtedly, the notions of agent, of autonomous activity, and of direct versus indirect connection would need to be defined more precisely. The main point is that, in a series of clear cases, the syntactic analysis proposed and the employment of these notions provide a way of accounting for the semantic differences between the transitive construction and the complex factitive. The cases of synonymy or near-synonymy between the two constructions (cf [10], [20]) can be understood, essentially, if we agree that a subject (in the event, the subordinate subject in the complex factitive construction) need not necessarily be interpreted as an agent: these cases, then, far from being paradigmatic, as Lakoff would have it, are limiting cases rather.[23] Moreover, there seem to be no counter-examples associating the complex factitive construction with the notion of direct connection and the transitive construction with the notion of indirect connection. In particular, the sentences which remain problematical (cf [68–71], and the discussion at the end of section 5), cannot be taken as counter-examples in this sense. Lastly, although it will doubtless be necessary (in order to account for sentences such as [190a], for example) to incorporate a theory of stylistic or metaphorical extensions of meaning into the analysis, it does not appear that this extension would be inconsistent with the proposed solution.

One more remark. In section 2 (*cf* examples [43–48]), I pointed out that some adverbials, which are excluded in a certain interpretation of the transitive construction, are rather unnatural in the complex factitive construction also. Similarly, if we consider the impossibility of [103] (section 4), which I repeat:

[103] *l'entraîneur a réuni l'équipe d'elle-même
       *the trainer assembled the team of its own accord

we notice that the corresponding complex factitive, [192], although better, is still not fully acceptable:

[192] ?l'entraîneur a fait se réunir l'équipe d'elle-même
       ?the trainer made the team assemble of its own accord

It therefore seems that if, semantically, the subordinate subject of the complex factitive has more independence than the object of a simple transitive, it is still subject to certain constraints, as is shown by the difficulty of modifying it by certain adverbials. In fact, by confining myself solely to the comparison of constructions in NP_1 V NP_2, on the one hand, and of those in NP_1 *faire* V NP_2, on the other hand, I have simplified the question. Constructions in which substantival clauses with finite verb are embedded under *faire*[24] should also be taken into account. A hierarchy in these constructions would then emerge, with regard to the autonomy of NP_2; in this hierarchy, constructions in NP_1 *faire* V NP_2 X would occupy an intermediate position between simple transitive constructions and constructions of the form NP_1 *faire que* [$_S$ NP_2 V X] or of the form NP_1 *faire en sorte que* [$_S$ NP_2 V X]. An indication of the existence of this hierarchy is apparent if we compare [103] and [192] with the following sentences:

[193] l'entraîneur a fait que l'équipe se réunisse d'elle-même
       the trainer saw (to it) that the team assembled of its own accord
[194] l'entraîneur a fait en sorte que l'équipe se réunisse d'elle-même
       the trainer arranged that the team should assemble of its own accord

If we consider these examples, we see that there seems to be a correlation between the greater or lesser degree of autonomy of the object or of the subordinate subject – or between the more or less direct character of the connection between NP_1 and NP_2 – and the complexity of the syntactic base structure. More precisely, the more or less direct character of the connection between NP_1 and NP_2 seems to be a function of the distance (calculated in terms of the number of nodes in the tree) which separates NP_1 from NP_2. This might induce speculation as to the role played by iconic aspects in the relations between syntax and semantics (on this subject see Jakobson's stimulating remarks, 1965).

Notes

1 On all these points, see Chapter 1.
2 These representations are very much simplified, but they are sufficient for what interests us here. McCawley (1968c) in fact derives *John killed Mary* from something like *John caused Mary to become not alive*, with several successive applications of the PREDICATE-RAISING rule.
3 It is difficult to see, for example, how sentences such as:

   [i] Claude a présenté Igor à Arnold
   Claude introduced Igor to Arnold

   [ii] l'astronome a observé la comète
   the astronomer observed the comet

   [iii] Gary a trompé Marlène (avec Greta)
   Gary deceived Marlene (with Greta)

   [iv] Dave a embrassé Debbie
   Dave kissed Debbie

   could be reduced to constructions of the form NP — *faire* — V — X.
4 Clearly, if we accept FAIRE-SUBSTITUTION, this rule must follow FAIRE-ATTRACTION and all the rules which precede the latter (see Kayne, 1969, forthcoming). But the fact is that there is no independent justification for this way of proceeding.
   The most important effort so far undertaken to find justification for the idea that certain syntactic transformations are ordered before lexical insertion is represented by Postal's work (1970a). However, this study has already been subjected to severe criticism (see Kimball, 1970; Ronat, 1972). I shall return later (section 7) to the problems raised for French by McCawley's 'extended' analysis, which involves PREDICATE-RAISING.
5 A similar argument was suggested to me by a remark of Miriam Lemle (personal communication). Take the sentences:

   [i] Adèle a fait cuire le cochon avec un citron dans la bouche
   Adele got the pig cooked with a lemon in its/her mouth

   [ii] Adèle a cuit le cochon avec un citron dans la bouche
   Adele cooked the pig with a lemon in her mouth

   Sentence [i] is ambiguous, insofar as it can correspond to the two underlying structures [iiia] and [iiib]:

   [iii] *a:* Adèle a fait [s le cochon cuire avec un citron dans la bouche]
        b: Adèle a fait [s le cochon cuire] avec un citron dans la bouche

   In [iiia], it is the pig which has a lemon in its mouth, and in [iiib], it is Adèle who has. Only the second reading, odd though it is, is possible in the case of [ii].
6 Hall-Partee (1971) briefly gives arguments of the same order for English.

7 As in the case of [20], sentences such as [54b] or [55b] have another reading in which they are acceptable, but which does not concern us here. This is the reading which corresponds to an underlying structure in which the sentence embedded under *faire* is a direct transitive sentence with an unexpressed subject. These embedded sentences are related to the passive, *cf: Adèle a fait cuire le ragoût par Amélie* (Adèle got the stew cooked by Amélie), *Fritz a fait monter les provisions de la cave par son assistant* (Fritz got the stores brought up out of the cellar by his assistant) (see Kayne, 1969, forthcoming). Let it be understood once and for all that, whenever I here consider a construction of the type NP_1 *faire* V NP_2 X, I mean a construction of which the deep structure is of the form NP_1 *faire* [$_S$ NP_2 V X], and not of the form NP_1 *faire* [$_S$ Δ V NP_2 X]. In section 8, I shall, however, return to the possible relations between sentences such as *je construis une maison* and *je fais construire une maison (par des maçons)*.

8 *Cf* [49–50] above. In general, the absence of a paraphrase relationship between the simple transitive construction and the complex factitive is much more evident in the case where it is a pronominal verb which is embedded under *faire*.

9 It follows that [78a], when looked at more closely, is not really contradictory (nor [72b], probably). [78a] only appears contradictory because, in the absence of other specifications, the most natural interpretation of [77a] tends to imply – in the sense of Grice's 'logic of conversation' (1967) – that Graham Hill is at the wheel of his Lotus.

10 Once again, examples could be multiplied. Thus, Roland Dachelet and Pierre Culand have pointed out to me that [1a] contrasts with [1b] insofar as [1a] implies that Hill's car came into physical contact with Ickx's; [1b] implies nothing of the kind:

[1] *a:* en voulant la dépasser, Graham Hill a $\left\{ \begin{array}{l} \text{sorti de la route} \\ \text{dévié} \end{array} \right\}$

la Ferrari de Jacky Ickx

in trying to pass it, Graham Hill $\left\{ \begin{array}{l} \text{sent} \\ \text{diverted} \end{array} \right\}$

Jacky Ickx's Ferrari off the track

b: en voulant la dépasser, Graham Hill a fait $\left\{ \begin{array}{l} \text{dévier} \\ \text{sortir de la route} \end{array} \right\}$

la Ferrari de Jacky Ickx

in trying to pass it, Graham Hill made Jacky Ickx's Ferrari

$\left\{ \begin{array}{l} \text{diverge from} \\ \text{leave} \end{array} \right\}$ the track

We see that the precise content of what is implied varies in accordance with the verbs (and with the type of adverbials present). But, in all cases, the transitive construction implies a direct connection, which the complex factitive construction does not in principle imply.

11 See also the difference between verbs of the class of *mépriser* and those of the class of *degoûter*, studied in Chapter 5.

12 Moreover, it should be remembered that Chomsky has always cautioned against a too hasty identification of syntactic categories and mechanisms with semantic categories and mechanisms (*cf* Chomsky, 1957, 100f).

13 Symmetric verbs such as *épouser, rencontrer*, etc (*cf* [106]) might lead one to think that the subject and the object are both interpreted as agents, and some

linguists (*cf* Lakoff and Peters, 1969) have indeed proposed deriving a sentence like [1*a*] from [1*b*]:

[I] *a:* Pierre a rencontré Marie
      Peter met Mary
    b: Pierre et Marie se sont rencontrés
      Peter and Mary met each other

But Dougherty (1970*b*) showed convincingly that such a derivation was incorrect: [1*a*] and [1*b*] must both be generated in the base. Example [106] itself shows that the subject and the object of *rencontrer* are not on the same level. Similarly, in [II]:

[II] Pierre a (intentionellement) rencontré Marie (dans le but de faire en-
    rager Paul)
    Peter (intentionally) met Mary (with the aim of annoying Paul)

the adverbials of intention or purpose, characteristically relating to agents, refer unambiguously to the subject only. Note that an adverbial such as *contre son gré* (against one's will) is not under the same constraints: it can refer equally to the subject and the object, hence the ambiguity of:

[III] l'entraîneur a réuni l'équipe contre son gré
     the trainer assembled the team against his/its will

[IV] Pierre a $\left\{\begin{array}{l}\text{rencontré}\\ \text{épousé}\end{array}\right\}$ Marie contre son gré

    Peter $\left\{\begin{array}{l}\text{met}\\ \text{married}\end{array}\right\}$ Mary against his/her will

14 One test to verify the validity of the proposed distinction between direct action and indirect action would be to submit to native speakers sentences such as [1*b*] and [II*b*], which we have seen (*cf* the end of Chapter 3) to be ungrammatical:

[I] *a:* l'amiral a fait sombrer le cuirassé
      the Admiral caused the battleship to founder
    b: *l'amiral a sombré le cuirassé
      *the Admiral foundered the battleship

[II] *a:* Pierre a fait trébucher Paul
      Peter made Paul stumble
    b: *Pierre a trébuché Paul
      *Peter stumbled Paul

The task imposed on the native speakers would be to find an interpretation for these sentences. It seems to me that these interpretations would not simply amount to a paraphrase in the form of [1*a*] or [II*a*], but would bring in the notion of direct action in one way or another. Personally, if I am ob- liged to find an interpretation for [II*b*], I could not do other than exclude a non-agentive interpretation of the subject (in the manner of [110*c*]); the only interpretation possible will be that in which, by a deliberate and direct action, Peter caused Paul to stumble (by pushing him, by tripping him up, etc).

15 Another example, which also brings into play an inalienable relation between the subject and the object, but which does not concern parts of the body, is that of [I] in contrast with [II]:

[I] *a:* Pierre a raté son coup
      Peter missed his shot

> b: *Pierre a fait rater son coup (where *son* is coreferential with *Pierre*)
> *Peter caused his shot to miss

[II] a: *Pierre a raté l'enterprise de Paul
> *Peter failed Paul's enterprise
> b: Pierre a fait rater l'enterprise de Paul
> Peter caused Paul's enterprise to fail

Notice that here the 'direct connection' between the subject and the object cannot be interpreted in terms of 'direct action' of the subject on the object, *rater* not being a verb of motion or a change-of-state verb.

16 [124b] obviously has a perfectly natural reading corresponding to *Graham Hill a fait gonfler les pneus de sa Lotus (par son mécanicien)* (Graham Hill had the tyres of his Lotus inflated (by his mechanic)). See note 7, and section 8 below.

17 I thank Maurice Gross and Jean-Paul Boons, who drew my attention to the connection between these sentences and the restrictions on the auxiliaries.

18 Jean-Claude Milner has pointed out to me (personal communication) that an argument in this sense would be the impossibility of submitting the subjects of transitive verbs without an expressed object to INDEFINITE NP EXTRA-POSITION, the rule deriving [1b] from [1a]:

[I] a: quelqu'un est venu
> someone has come
> b: il est venu quelqu'un
> there has come someone

Now, we do not have sentences such as [IIb], [IIIb]:

[II] a: quelqu'un a mangé
> someone has eaten
> b: *il a mangé quelqu'un
> *there has eaten someone

[III] a: quelqu'un a vomi
> someone has vomited
> b: *il a vomi quelqu'un
> *there has vomited someone

Moreover, sentences such as [IVb] are excluded by Emonds' constraints on 'structure-preserving' transformations (*cf* Emonds, 1970; see this book, Chapter 1, section 2.2):

[IV] a: quelqu'un a mangé ce gâteau
> someone has eaten this cake
>
> b: *il a mangé $\begin{cases} \text{ce gâteau quelqu'un} \\ \text{quelqu'un ce gâteau} \end{cases}$
>
> *there has eaten $\begin{cases} \text{this cake someone} \\ \text{someone this cake} \end{cases}$

If, in [IIa] or [IIIa], the indefinite object is indeed present at the stage when INDEFINITE NP EXTRAPOSITION is applied, the ungrammaticalness of [IIb–IIIb] would be explained by the same principle which excludes [IVb]. This argument is, however, weakened by the fact that the INDEFINITE NP EXTRAPOSITION rule is subject to other constraints, and notably that many purely intransitive verbs do not allow it, *cf*:

[V] a: *il dégénéra une discussion apparemment très agitée
> *there 'lowered the tone' an apparently very excited discussion

b: *il maigrissait la plupart des prisonniers
  *there were growing thin most of the prisoners
c: ?il a dormi quelqu'un ici
  *there has slept someone here

For a discussion of INDEFINITE NP EXTRAPOSITION (called the 'impersonal transformation' in the *Introduction à la grammaire générative*), see, besides Kayne (1969), Gaatone (1970) and Martin (1970), from whom I have borrowed examples [v*a* and *b*].

19 The facts discussed in this section militate in favour of making a distinction very early on (at the base structure stage) between noun phrases and prepositional phrases, and so run counter to the theory (*cf* for example Ross, 1969, and Postal, 1971) which makes a difference between these two categories only at a fairly late stage in the derivation.

20 *Rappeler* can appear in the frame of [166], but it would then be a case of idiomatic expressions which have nothing to do with the facts discussed, *cf: Pierre a rappelé Paul à l'ordre (à ses devoirs)* (Peter called Paul to order, Peter recalled Paul to the path of duty).

21 Kayne (1969) has shown that constructions in *faire* V NP *par* NP are, unlike those in *faire* V NP *à* NP, related to passive sentences. Kayne takes up the analysis proposed for English by Chomsky (1970), and breaks down the PASSIVE rule into two rules, one, called AGENT-POSTPOSING, which moves the deep subject into the position of agent complement, and the other, called NP-PREPOSING, which moves the deep object into the subject position (and which perhaps introduces the passive auxiliary at the same time). Kayne suggests that only the first of these rules comes into play in the derivation of constructions in *faire* V NP *par* NP, the deep object NP remaining in its position on the right of the verb, and the auxiliary not being introduced (*cf* the ungrammaticalness of **Pierre a fait être battu Paul par Jean*).

22 Other facts of indeterminacy will be noticed in these sentences. For example, [190*b*] in no way implies that each of the fifty conspirators dealt Caesar a death blow, but this sentence could certainly not be paraphrased by *les cinquante conjurés ont fait tuer César (par certains d'entre eux)* (the fifty conspirators caused Caesar to be killed (by some of their number)). [190*a*] is particularly interesting: all that this sentence asserts is that Charles d'Anjou is directly responsible for Manfred's death, but the exact manner of Manfred's death (whether he was killed by Charles with his own hands or by one of Charles' soldiers, whether he died from a fall from his horse in the course of the battle, or whether he was drowned while fleeing, etc) remains undetermined. This sentence cannot be paraphrased either by *Charles d'Anjou a défait et fait tuer Manfred à Bénévent* (Charles d'Anjou defeated Manfred at Benevento and had him killed) (which tends to imply that Charles explicitly gave the order to kill Manfred) or by *Charles d'Anjou a défait et fait mourir Manfred à Bénévent* (Charles d'Anjou defeated Manfred at Benevento and caused his death), in which the idea of a direct connection is lacking.

23 Even sentences such as [10] and [20], that I have myself considered (*cf* [72]) as being in a paraphrase relationship, show different shades of meaning, which are clearly seen if they are put into the imperative, as in cookery recipes; compare:

[1] faites cuire le poulet pendant dix minutes
  let the chicken cook for ten minutes

[11] cuisez le poulet pendant dix minutes
  cook the chicken for ten minutes

Sentence [II] seems to me slightly odd, insofar as it suggests a continuous action of the subject (the cook) on the chicken for ten minutes, this nuance being absent from [I]. In passing it may be noted that in cookery recipes we practically only find sentences of type [I], and almost never those of type [II]. (But in English it is the other way round. [*Translator's note*])

24 We must also take into account sentences of the type of [III] as against [I] and [II]:

[I]   Pierre a tué Paul
      Peter killed Paul

[II] Pierre a fait mourir Paul
      Peter caused Paul to die

[III] Pierre a $\begin{Bmatrix}\text{causé}\\\text{provoqué}\end{Bmatrix}$ la mort de Paul

      Peter $\begin{Bmatrix}\text{caused}\\\text{brought about}\end{Bmatrix}$ Paul's death

These sentences of type [III], again, have different properties, *cf* for example:

[IV] *a:* Pierre a fait mourir Paul à petit feu
          Peter killed Paul by inches/Peter kept Paul on tenter-hooks
      b: ?*Pierre a causé (provoqué) la mort de Paul à petit feu
          ?*Peter caused (brought about) Paul's death by inches

[V]   *a:* Adèle a fait cuire le poulet
          Adèle cooked the chicken
      b: ?Adèle a causé (provoqué) la cuisson du poulet
          ?Adèle caused (brought about) the cooking of the chicken

Chapter 5

On a class of 'psychological' verbs*

1

Consider the following examples

[1] $\left.\begin{array}{r}\text{Pierre}\\ \text{*ce rocher}\\ \text{*la sincérité}\end{array}\right\}$ méprise $\left\{\begin{array}{l}\text{les femmes}\\ \text{l'argent}\\ \text{les idées de Paul}\end{array}\right.$

$\left.\begin{array}{r}\text{Peter}\\ \text{*this rock}\\ \text{*sincerity}\end{array}\right\}$ despises $\left\{\begin{array}{l}\text{women}\\ \text{money}\\ \text{Paul's ideas}\end{array}\right.$

[2] $\left.\begin{array}{r}\text{les femmes}\\ \text{l'argent}\\ \text{les idées de Paul}\end{array}\right\}$ dégoûte(nt) $\left\{\begin{array}{l}\text{Pierre}\\ \text{*ce rocher}\\ \text{*la sincérité}\end{array}\right.$

$\left.\begin{array}{r}\text{women}\\ \text{money}\\ \text{Paul's ideas}\end{array}\right\}$ disgust(s) $\left\{\begin{array}{l}\text{Peter}\\ \text{*this rock}\\ \text{*sincerity}\end{array}\right.$

We see that *mépriser* and *degoûter*, which are both direct transitive verbs, have almost exactly opposite selectional restrictions on subject and object.[1] While *mépriser* requires a human subject and imposes practically no selectional restrictions on its object, *dégoûter*, on the other hand, requires a human object and imposes practically no restrictions on its subject.[2] As selectional restrictions on verbs are, in general, an indication of semantic constraints, this amounts to saying that, at least from a certain point of view, the semantic relation between *mépriser* and its

* Not previously published.

object is analogous to that between *dégouter* and its subject, and that the semantic relation between *mépriser* and its subject is analogous to that between *degoûter* and its object. How will a generative grammar account both for these resemblances and for these differences?

A priori, there are (at least) two possibilities. We might consider that – from the point of view that interests us here and other things being equal – the sentences of [1] and [2] have deep structures identical with their surface structures (the subjects and the objects occupying the same positions relatively to the verb in deep structure as in surface structure). In this case, we should be obliged to have different rules of semantic interpretation for [1] and [2]. Or else we could consider that the surface structures of [1] and [2] do not directly reflect their deep structures. The deep structures would be much closer to each other, and, in particular, the surface subject of [1] and the surface object of [2] would occupy the same positions in deep structure; so would the surface object of [1] and the surface subject of [2]. The surface differences between [1] and [2] would then be treated in transformational terms, by means of one or more transformations which would permute the subject and the object in one case but not the other. *A priori*, there is nothing to choose between the two solutions: one amounts to complicating the semantic component, the other to complicating the transformational component. There would be no reason to say, *a priori*, that one is simpler than the other.

The second solution, which I shall call the transformational solution, has been adopted by a certain number of linguists (Rosenbaum, 1967, Chapin, 1967, Lakoff, 1970c, Postal, 1971; see also Chomsky, 1970). They have proposed, for reasons that we shall consider later, to take the subject-verb-object order of [1] as fundamental, and to derive constructions of the type of [2] by means of a transformation which permutes the subject and the object. Note that, a *priori*, there is another possible transformational solution consisting in taking the order of [2] as fundamental and deriving the sentences of [1] by a permutation rule. But as no one has considered this solution,[3] I shall leave it aside.

Let us be more specific. According to this transformational hypothesis, the deep structures of [1] and [2], reduced to their essential elements, would be respectively [3] and [4]:

[3] Pierre — mépriser — l'argent
      Peter — despise — money

[4] Pierre — dégoûter — l'argent
      Peter — disgust — money

Then, a transformation which I shall call PSYCH-MOVEMENT,[4] after Postal (1971), would convert [4] into [2]. It could be formulated as follows:

[5] PSYCH-MVT: NP — V — NP — X

$$1 \quad 2 \quad 3 \quad 4 \Rightarrow 3 - 2 - 1 - 4$$

This solution, obviously, requires us not only to introduce a new transformation into the grammar, but also to mark the different verbs as allowing or not allowing this rule to be applied. In other words, recourse to rule features in Lakoff's sense (1970c) is necessary. The lexical entries for *mépriser* and *dégoûter* would then include the following features:

[6] *mépriser:* [+V], [+ —— NP], [+[+HUMAN] ——],
      [−PSYCH-MVT], ...

[7] *dégoûter:* [+V], [+—— NP], [+[+ HUMAN] ——],
      [+PSYCH-MVT], ...

I have said that another solution is possible, which I shall call the semantic solution. It makes use of the theory of 'thematic' functions outlined by Gruber (1965) and taken up by Jackendoff (1969b, 1972). As this theory is less familiar than classic transformational theory, I shall start by saying a few words about it, following Jackendoff (1969b) in particular.

2

Gruber and Jackendoff consider a system of semantic functions that noun phrases or prepositional phrases can carry out in sentences, functions distinct from the syntactic functions of subject, direct object, indirect object, etc. This system of semantic functions, called 'thematic functions', is designed, essentially, to formalize traditional notions such as those of agent, patient, beneficiary of an action, instrumental, etc. These functions 'are treated as properties of semantic interpretations, related to the grammatical relations (subject, object, etc) by projection rules'[5] (Jackendoff, 1969b, 75).

I shall here consider only some of the main thematic functions: 'theme', 'location', 'source', 'goal' and 'agent'.

The most fundamental, and at the same time the most neutral thematic function, *ie* the least marked, is that of 'theme'. Every sentence contains a theme, which is the subject in the case of sentences with a purely intransitive verb (an apparent exception being impersonal sentences with 'weather' verbs, such as *il pleut* (it is raining), *il neige* (it is snowing), where we could no doubt speak of incorporation of the theme in the verb). In sentences with verbs of motion, the theme is the NP designating the object which undergoes the motion (*cf Pierre* and *la voiture* in [8]); in sentences with verbs of 'location', the theme is the NP designating the object whose location is being asserted (*cf: le livre* in [9]):

[8] *a:* la voiture⎫
               ⎬ ira à Paris
         Pierre⎭

       the car⎫
              ⎬ will go to Paris
        Peter⎭

     b: Paul a conduit la voiture de Rome à Paris
          Paul drove the car from Rome to Paris
     c: Jacques a envoyé Pierre chez Marie
          James sent Peter to Mary's

[9] *a:* le livre est resté sur l'étagère
          the book remained on the shelf
     b: Pierre a gardé le livre sur l'étagère
          Peter kept the book on the shelf

As the theme in these examples is sometimes subject and sometimes object, we see straight away that thematic functions do not directly coincide with syntactic functions. Other thematic functions are fulfilled by the other NPs and PPs of [8–9]. For example, *à Paris* is 'goal' in [8*a*] and [8*b*]; similarly, *chez Marie* is 'goal' in [8*c*]; *de Rome* is source in [8*b*]. In [9], *sur l'étagère* is 'location'.

Two important principles come into play in the theory of thematic functions. One is that, in sentences related in terms of co-occurrence of elements, but distributionally different, morphologically related elements fulfil the same thematic functions. Consider for example:

[10] *a:* le jardin grouille de vermine
           the garden is swarming with vermin
      b: la vermine grouille dans le jardin
           vermin is swarming in the garden

As, in [10*b*], it is clear that *dans le jardin* is 'location' and that therefore *la vermine* is 'theme', we extend these concepts to [10*a*], where *le jardin* will be 'location' and *de vermine* 'theme'.

The second principle is the extension of the concepts of 'theme', 'location', etc, to sentences of more or less abstract meaning. This principle is based on the idea that the sense of a verb is fundamentally the same in its various usages. Thus, beside sentences like [9a–b], where *rester* and *garder* are used in a sense of spatial location, we find sentences such as:

[11] *a:* Pierre est resté $\begin{cases} \text{de glace} \\ \text{ferme} \end{cases}$

Peter remained $\begin{cases} \text{icy} \\ \text{firm} \end{cases}$

  b: Paul a gardé la tête froide
  Paul kept a cool head

We then extend the application of thematic functions to these cases and say that *de glace* or *ferme* function as abstract 'locations' in [11a] – *Pierre* being 'theme'. In [11b], *la tête* would be 'theme' and *froide* would be 'location'. Adjectives and expressions like *de glace* are considered as 'locations', as if they meant 'in the abstract domain (of "quality space") containing those things which are *Adj.*' (Jackendoff, *op cit*, 77 and 1972, 31). Another example of extension, parallel this time to the sentences of [8], is [12], where *de déceptions* is 'source' and *en déceptions* is 'goal':

[12] Pierre est allé de déceptions en déceptions
    Peter went from disappointment to disappointment

In the same way, the notion of possession is conceived of as an abstract 'location'. In [13], *ce livre* and *Pierre* are respectively 'theme' and 'location'; and further, in [14], *Pierre* is 'source', *ce livre* is 'theme' and *Jacques* is 'goal':

[13] *a:* ce livre appartient à Pierre
      this book belongs to Peter
    b: Pierre possède ce livre
      Peter owns this book

[14] *a:* Pierre a vendu ce livre à Jacques
      Peter sold this book to James
    b: Jacques a acheté ce livre à Pierre
      James bought this book from Peter

These sentences provide further illustration of the fact that phrases with a given thematic function do not necessarily occupy the same syntactic positions in all cases.

The thematic function of 'agent', which we saw in Chapter 4 to be associated in a special way with the syntactic function of subject, is often superimposed on other thematic functions. Thus, in [8a], *Pierre* is simultaneously 'theme' and 'agent'. Similarly, while in [15a] the functions of 'theme' and 'agent' are dissociated, *la police* being 'agent' and *les manifestants* 'theme', in [15b] *les manifestants* is both 'theme' and 'agent':

[15] *a:* la police a dispersé les manifestants
        the police dispersed the demonstrators
      b: les manifestants se sont dispersés
        the demonstrators dispersed

Again, in [14a], *Pierre* is both 'source' and 'agent', while in [14b] *Jacques* is both 'goal' and 'agent' (*cf* the possibility in both cases of attaching adverbials such as *intentionnellement* to the subject).

Explained rapidly like this, the theory of thematic functions might not appear to go beyond a very banal level of observation, well known to traditional grammarians. Nevertheless, Gruber obtained some very interesting results by applying it to the analysis of a whole series of verb classes. He also set himself to define the syntactic criteria for determining the thematic functions of phrases in certain conditions (co-occurrence with certain prepositions, with certain adverbials, etc). Jackendoff, too, used this theory to formulate certain constraints on coreferentiality, which we shall refer to later (see section 6.2).

Yet this theory is still rather nebulous in some respects, and many problems arise: it is not clear, for example, that the notions of 'location' on the one hand, 'source' and 'goal' on the other hand, represent primitive and independent semantic terms, and one may often hesitate over the attribution of one or the other of these functions to a given phrase. The merit of this theory is that it proposes an approach to semantic functions distinct both from a theory of case in Fillmore's sense (1968) and from a reduction of these semantic functions to terms of abstract syntax, in the manner of generative semantics. Above all, it adumbrates a means of representing in a consistent manner what there is in common between concrete and abstract processes, between physical and psychological actions.

Let us go back to sentences [1–2] and see how we could describe them in terms of thematic functions. Jackendoff (1969b, 84 *ff*) discusses constructions of the type of [2]; for him, in [2], the subject would be theme and the object a sort of goal. He does not discuss examples analogous to [1]; but we could extend the analysis proposed for [2] to [1]: in [1], the subject would be goal and the object would be theme. Nevertheless, it seems more natural to me to attribute the thematic function of 'location' to the subject in [1] and to the object in [2]: *Pierre* would be the 'location' of a certain psychological process (*dégoût, mépris*) which has as its theme *l'argent, les femmes*, etc. A syntactic indication of this locative character of *Pierre* in [1–2] is given by the following sentences, where *Pierre* is governed by prepositions of a clearly locative nature:

[16] il y a $\begin{Bmatrix} \text{en} \\ \text{chez} \end{Bmatrix}$ Pierre un profond mépris de l'argent

    there is in Peter a deep disdain of money

[17] il y a $\begin{Bmatrix} \text{chez} \\ \text{en} \end{Bmatrix}$ Pierre un profond dégoût de l'argent

    there is in Peter a deep disgust for money

Note that sentences [16–17], like the nominalizations [18–19], are evidence of the relatedness of constructions of types [1] and [2]: contrary to what happens in [1] and [2], the NP themes and locations are found, in [16–17] and in [18–19], in the same syntactic positions.

[18] le $\begin{Bmatrix} \text{mépris} \\ \text{dégoût} \end{Bmatrix}$ de Pierre pour l'argent

[19] le $\begin{Bmatrix} \text{mépris} \\ \text{dégoût} \end{Bmatrix}$ de l'argent de Pierre

The idea that *Pierre* in [1–2] is a 'psychological location' corresponds to certain traditional intuitions, like that of Clédat (1900, 227), according to whom 'the subject who experiences an emotion is not the true agent of it, but the location. *Aimer, admirer, redouter*, etc, are not, properly speaking, actions'. However this may be, what is important is that the subject in [1] and the object in [2] have the same thematic function attributed to them.

If we accept the analysis of [1–2] in terms of thematic functions, we see that it is possible to describe the relationship between them in non-transformational terms. It will be sufficient for the lexical entry for *mépriser* and *dégoûter* to specify that the function of the location of the psychological processes that these verbs express is performed, in one case by the subject, and in the other by the object. Instead of having the lexical entries [6–7], these two verbs would then have the following entries:[6]

[20] *mépriser*: [+V], [+ —— NP], [+[+HUMAN] ——],
        [+[+LOCATION] ——]

[21] *dégoûter:* [+V], [+ —— NP], [+[—— +HUMAN]],
            [+ —— [+LOCATION]]

If we compare the entries in [6–7] and [20–21], we see that they are comparable in terms of the complexity of the formal apparatus that they imply: it is clear that, in order to choose between them, we must have recourse to other empirical arguments.

My proposal in this chapter will be to try to show that the semantic or thematic solution is preferable to the transformational solution. Since, of all the linguists who have suggested adopting the transformational solution, Postal (1971) has been the most concerned to justify it by empirical arguments (but without considering the possibility of the other solution), I shall begin by reviewing his arguments, and I shall endeavour to show to what extent they are unconvincing. Then I shall present a positive argument in favour of the semantic solution. Postal's analysis refers, of course, to English, but I think that the French occurrences are close enough to the English for us to be able to take up his arguments and discuss them with reference to French examples.

3

Above all, it is important to demonstrate for French, as Postal has done for English, that this phenomenon of contrastive distribution of 'location' and 'theme', far from being an isolated curiosity, is on the contrary very widespread. There are a large number of verbs, verbal expressions and adjectives, often semantically close to one another, and sometimes homonyms, of which some behave like *mépriser* and others like *dégoûter*. I shall give some examples of this.

Firstly, there are two large series of direct transitive verbs; *mépriser* belongs to one series, *dégoûter* to the other. The verbs of these two series are the most regular and the most productive cases, and they will be the ones that we shall especially consider.[7] On the one hand we have:

[22] mépriser, aimer, adorer, admirer, détester, supporter, déplorer,
        redouter, regretter, estimer, apprécier, . . .
        to despise, to love, to adore, to admire, to hate, to tolerate, to deplore,
        to dread, to regret, to consider, to appreciate, . . .

[23] dégoûter, amuser, intéresser, agacer, ennuyer, effrayer, gêner,
        terrifier, horrifier, humilier, surprendre, étonner, impressionner,
        préoccuper, . . .

to disgust, to amuse, to interest, to annoy, to bore, to frighten, to inconvenience, to terrify, to horrify, to humiliate, to surprise, to astonish, to impress, to preoccupy, . . .

Then there are verbs which in the main take a clause as theme, and which are found in surface constructions of which some have undergone transformations such as EXTRAPOSITION, SUBJECT-RAISING and OBJECT-FORMATION (insofar as this last rule exists).[8] Thus, beside:

[24] *a:* Pierre croit que la fin du monde est proche
       Peter believes that the end of the world is near
     b: Pierre croit la fin du monde proche (derived from (*a*) by OBJECT-
          FORMATION?)
          Peter believes the end of the world near

[25] *a:* Justine trouve que le ragoût est trop salé
       Justine finds that the stew is too salty
     b: Justine trouve le ragoût trop salé
       Justine finds the stew too salty

we have:

[26] *a:* il me semble que le coût de la vie a augmenté
       it seems to me that the cost of living has increased
     b: le coût de la vie me semble avoir augmenté (derived from (*a*) by
          SUBJECT-RAISING)
          the cost of living seems to me to have increased

[27] *a:* il se trouve que cette information est fausse
       it turns out that this information is false
     b: cette information se trouve être fausse
       this information turns out to be false

In the thematic hypothesis, the subject *Pierre* in [24] and the indirect object *me* (or rather *moi* in deep structure) in [26] would be assigned the function of 'location', the object or subject substantival clauses being 'themes'.

In Postal's transformational hypothesis, [24] and [26] would have similar underlying structures, say [28] and [29]:

[28] Pierre — croit — [$_{NP}$ [$_S$ la fin du monde est proche]]

[29] moi — semble — [$_{NP}$ [$_S$ le coût de la vie a augmenté]]

To obtain [24*a*], [28] would undergo only transformations which do not concern us here. As for [24*b*], it would be reached from [28] by the

OBJECT-FORMATION rule, which converts a subordinate subject into
the object of the main verb, plus a rule deleting *être* (see Gross, 1968).

[29] would undergo one or other of the two following derivations.
Either it would undergo PSYCH-MOVEMENT, with the object clause,
dominated by NP in this hypothesis, assuming the subject position:

[30] [$_{NP}$ [$_S$ le coût de la vie a augmenté]] — semble — à moi

Then, the EXTRAPOSITION rule would apply obligatorily, followed by
CLITIC-PLACING, which would give [26a]; or else [29] would first
undergo OBJECT-FORMATION, giving [31]:

[31] moi — semble — [$_{NP}$ le coût de la vie] — [$_{VP}$ avoir augmenté]

Then the PSYCH-MOVEMENT rule would apply, permuting the subject
and the new object created by the application of the preceding rule. The
subsequent application of CLITIC-PLACING would give [26b]. Similar
derivations would be ascribed by the two theories to [25] on the one hand,
and to [27] on the other.

We see that Postal's analysis, apart from the use of PSYCH-MOVE-
MENT, implies an analysis of the facts involved in 'subject-raising' which
is different from that which I proposed in Chapter 2. The RAISING rule
does not directly form subjects, but is reduced to an OBJECT-FORMA-
TION rule. I shall return later to the difficulties of this formulation (*cf*
section 7).

As well as these two sorts of examples, we also find sentences containing
adjectives (some of them homonyms) which contrast with each other in
the same way as *mépriser* and *dégoûter* or as *croire* and *sembler*, *cf* on the
one hand:

[32] Jacques est $\begin{Bmatrix} \text{malheureux} \\ \text{content} \end{Bmatrix}$ de devoir partir

James is $\begin{Bmatrix} \text{unhappy} \\ \text{pleased} \end{Bmatrix}$ at having to leave

[33] la sage-femme est heureuse que Madeleine ait accouché sans
    douleur
    the midwife is happy (fortunate) that Madeleine has given birth
    without pain

[34] Alfred est $\begin{Bmatrix} \text{sûr} \\ \text{certain} \end{Bmatrix}$ que Mao dit la vérité

Alfred is $\begin{Bmatrix} \text{sure} \\ \text{certain} \end{Bmatrix}$ that Mao speaks the truth and, on the other hand:

[35] il est $\left\{\begin{matrix}\text{pénible}\\\text{agréable}\end{matrix}\right\}$ (pour Jacques) de devoir partir

it is $\left\{\begin{matrix}\text{painful}\\\text{pleasant}\end{matrix}\right\}$ (for James) to have to leave

[36] il est heureux (pour la sage-femme) que Madeleine ait accouché sans
douleur
it is fortunate (for the midwife) that Madeleine has given birth without pain

[37] il est $\left\{\begin{matrix}\text{certain}\\\text{clair}\\\text{probable}\\\text{evident}\\\text{sûr}\end{matrix}\right\}$ (pour nous) que le fascisme ne passera pas

it is $\left\{\begin{matrix}\text{certain}\\\text{clear}\\\text{probable}\\\text{evident}\\\text{sure}\end{matrix}\right\}$ (to/for us) that Fascism will not pass

Here again, the thematic solution would attribute the function of
'location'[9] to the subjects, in [32–34], and to the complements in *pour*,
in [35–37], and the function of 'theme' to the substantival clauses, whereas Postal would derive [35–37] transformationally by PSYCH-MOVE-
MENT, from sentences whose structure would be similar to that of [32–
34].

Postal also speaks at some length of what he calls, on one hand 'perception predicates', and on the other hand 'sensation predicates'. I
shall say correspondingly less on this aspect as the very idiosyncratic
character of these predicates seems to be even more marked in French
than in English. Examples of the first type are verbs such as *sentir*, *goûter*,
sonner, etc, *cf* for example:

[38] *a:* Mélisande sentait cette rose
Mélisande smelled that rose
b: cette rose sentait bon
that rose smelled nice

[39] *a:* le caporal a sonné (de) la trompette
the corporal sounded the trumpet

    b: cette trompette sonne faux
       this trumpet sounds out of tune

As examples of 'sensation predicates', we might cite expressions such as:

[40] *a:* j'ai mal à la tête
     I have a headache
    b: la tête me fait mal
     my head aches

  Here again we have a whole series of pairs of sentences; in every case in examples (*a*), in the thematic hypothesis it is the 'location' which is in the subject position, and in examples (*b*) it is the 'theme'. Postal would derive examples (*b*) by PSYCH-MOVEMENT from underlying structures similar to examples (*a*):

[41] *a:* Jesse James possède un troupeau de mille taureaux
     Jesse James owns a herd of a thousand bulls
    b: ce troupeau de mille taureaux appartient à Jesse James
     this herd of a thousand bulls belongs to Jesse James

[42] *a:* j'ai manqué de temps pour terminer cet article
     I lacked the time to finish this article
    b: le temps m'a manqué pour terminer cet article[10]
     time was lacking for me to finish this article

[43] *a:* Merckx a $\left\{\begin{array}{l}\text{profité}\\\text{bénéficié}\end{array}\right\}$ de l'abandon d'Ocana

     Merckx $\left\{\begin{array}{l}\text{profited}\\\text{benefited}\end{array}\right\}$ from Ocana's withdrawal

    b: l'abandon d'Ocana a $\left\{\begin{array}{l}\text{profité}\\\text{bénéficié}\end{array}\right\}$ à Merckx

     Ocana's withdrawal benefited Merckx

[44] *a:* Pierre répugne aux travaux pénibles
     Peter feels repugnance for laborious work
    b: les travaux pénibles répugnent à Pierre
     laborious work is repugnant to Peter

[45] *a:* Stravinsky s'est souvent inspiré des musiques du passé
     Stravinsky was often inspired by the music of the past
    b: les musiques du passé ont souvent inspiré Stravinsky
     the music of the past often inspired Stravinsky

  Lastly, to say nothing of variations between languages (compare the English *I miss you* with the French *vous me manquez*), there are diachronic or dialectal variations; a predicate which, in a certain dialect or at a certain period of the language, has a 'location' as subject and a 'theme' as object, will have the relationship reversed in another dialect or at a different period. Thus, in the eighteenth century [46b], archaic today, and [46a] were equally current:

[46] a: je me souviens du temps des cerises
          I remember cherry-time
       b: il me souvient du temps des cerises

In [46a], the subject je is 'location', and the indirect object, du temps des cerises, is 'theme'; in [46b], the 'location' is in the position of indirect object (me), and du temps des cerises could pass for a sort of 'logical subject'.

Another example of variation is shown in Belgian French, which has the construction [47a], as compared with the standard construction [47b]:

[47] a: Pierre a $\left\{\begin{array}{l}\text{facile}\\\text{difficile}\end{array}\right\}$ de travailler

       b: il est $\left\{\begin{array}{l}\text{facile}\\\text{difficile}\end{array}\right\}$ à Pierre de travailler

          it is $\left\{\begin{array}{l}\text{easy}\\\text{difficult}\end{array}\right\}$ for Peter to work

In this case, while in the standard language, the 'location' is in the position of indirect object (the subject 'theme' being placed in the post-verbal position by EXTRAPOSITION), in Belgian French the 'location' is in the subject position; obviously, there is also a change of verb, avoir instead of être (compare this construction with the standard construction Pierre a de la difficulté à travailler (Peter has difficulty in working)). These fluctuations seem to indicate that the distinction between the two constructions is of a relatively superficial nature.

It is important to note, as Postal does, that the regularity of contrast between the two types of construction is often masked by syntactic differences. Thus, while mépriser and dégoûter are both direct transitive verbs and differ only in the contrastive distribution of themes and locations, some of the verbs of our examples have prepositional objects (cf [26], [35–37], [41–44]), and the prepositions vary according to the verbs. Sometimes, one of two homonymous verbs is pronominal and the other is not (cf [25] and [27], [45]). It also happens that verbs which require a theme in subject position do not have (or do not necessarily have) a surface complement expressing location (cf [27], [37], [38–39]).

The two solutions, transformational and thematic, will also diverge in the way in which they treat these differences. For Postal, it is a question of differences in surface structure: the presence or absence of such and such a preposition, the pronominal or non-pronominal character of a verb, the presence or absence of an expressed 'location' PP, result from the application of certain transformations depending, like PSYCH-MOVEMENT, on 'rule features' provided in the lexical entries of the verbs. The underlying structures, for example of [34] and [37], or of [45a and b], would not show these surface differences. Thus, in cases where a 'location' complement is missing on the surface, there would always be a subject in the underlying structure and, after the application of PSYCH-MOVEMENT, it would be deleted. Or again, a preposition, absent at a certain stage in the derivation, would be 'spelled out' after the application of PSYCH-MOVEMENT.

In the thematic hypothesis, on the other hand, all these differences would be found in the deep structure, and they would be treated in terms of strict subcategorization features (see Chomsky, 1965, Chapter 2) on the verbs. Thus, the verb *trouver*, sometimes pronominal and sometimes non-pronominal, would be treated in the same way, as, in Chapter 3, verbs which are sometimes neutral and sometimes transitive are treated. Or again, a verb like *manquer* (*cf* [42]), would have the two following entries:

[48] *manquer:* (i) [+V], [+ —— *de* NP], [+[+HUMAN] ——],
                       [+[+LOCATION] ——], . . .
                 (ii) [+V], [+ —— *à* NP], [+ —— [+HUMAN]],
                       [+ —— [+LOCATION]], . . .

As for the absence of a 'location' PP, this would be treated either by a deletion rule as in Postal, or by a strict subcategorization feature of the type (+ —— (PP)).

Here I shall not linger over the role that these syntactic differences could play in a comparison of the merits of the two theories. The power of mechanisms which resort to 'rule features' is such that it would certainly render the transformational solution observationally adequate. I shall nevertheless point out certain difficulties that some of these differences raise for the transformational treatment in Postal's way.

First, there is the question of 'location' complements absent on the surface. In the thematic hypothesis, this is something that is quite natural: we know of many other examples where prepositional complements are optional (*cf: j'ai dit (à Pierre) que S*, etc). But, if we assume that these elements are subjects in deep structure, obligatorily present, it is not certain that the reconstruction of these underlying subjects can always be justified. Syntactic arguments are lacking. As for the semantic argument that sentences such as *il est évident que S*, etc, imply reference to a being (human and indefinite) for whom *que S est évident*, this is not without difficulties. Consider the following paradigm:

[49] *a:* il m'est agréable de partir
         I'm agreeable to leaving
       b: pour moi, il est agréable de partir
         as far as I can see, it's all right to leave

[50] *a:* *il m'est évident (sûr, probable, certain) que Pierre est fou
       b: pour moi, il est évident (sûr, probable, certain) que Pierre est fou
         to me, it is evident (sure, probable, certain) that Peter is mad

We see that, while *agréable* allows two types of prepositional complement, in *à NP* and in *pour NP*, *évident*, *sûr* etc, allow only complements in *pour NP*. If there were no other differences, this would be no problem in the transformational solution, which would simply mark *agréable* and *évident* with partially different rule features. The problem arises from the fact that there is a difference of meaning between [49*a*] and [49*b*]: in [49*a*], *je* is the implied subject of *partir*, while [49*b*] is not necessarily understood in this way; [49*b*] means, approximately, '*à mon avis, il est agréable de partir*' ('in my opinion, it is all right to leave'), and the subject of *partir* is left indeterminate. Now in [50], we have an interpretation close to that of [49*b*]. If we consider that *me*, in [49*a*] is the 'location' of the psychological process, and hence the deep subject according to Postal, the absence of [50*a*] and this difference of meaning tend to preclude the possibility of interpreting *pour moi* in [50*b*] in the same way. Complements of this type in *pour moi*, contrary to what we said at first, would have a function other than that of psychological 'location' and could not be considered the deep subjects of *agréable*, *évident*, etc. We would then be obliged to reconstitute another ('location') deep subject, which, in view of the impossibility of [50*a*], would be syntactically very arbitrary. Note that, in the case of *agréable*, the two complements in *à NP* and in *pour NP* can co-exist in the same sentence, *cf:*

[51] pour moi, il est agréable à Pierre de partir
       as far as I can see, Peter is agreeable to leaving

We have similar problems with the sentences of [27]. Besides the fact that *se trouver* must probably in any case be treated as a neutral (see Chapter 3), it does not allow an indirect object (*cf* [52]), and [27*a*] is certainly not synonymous with [53]:

[52] *il se trouve à Pierre que le coût de la vie a augmenté

[53]   on⎫
       quelqu'un⎭ trouve que cette information est fausse

       it is thought   ⎫
       someone thinks ⎭ that this information is false

The reconstitution of an underlying subject which would be indefinite and different from *on* or from *quelqu'un* is therefore rather problematical.

These difficulties are perhaps not insurmountable for the transformational theory, but it must be said that they do not arise in the thematic theory: the differences in syntactic behaviour between *agréable* and *évident*, and between *sembler* and *se trouver*, will be treated in terms of strict subcategorization features, and as for the differences of meaning indicated, we can hope to relate them in a systematic way to precisely these differences of form (presence or absence of certain complements, choice of different prepositions, different positions in the underlying structure of complements in *à NP* and of those in *pour NP*).

A different problem is raised for Postal's analysis by the sentences of [26*a*] and [46*b*], which I give again here:

[26] *a:* il me semble que le coût de la vie a augmenté

[46] *b:* il me souvient du temps des cerises

We have seen that Postal derives [26*a*] from [29]:

[29] moi — semble — [$_{NP}$ [$_{S}$ le coût de la vie a augmenté]]

by PSYCH-MOVEMENT and obligatory EXTRAPOSITION. By analogy, we could derive [46*b*] from [54] by PSYCH-MOVEMENT, giving the intermediate stage [55], and EXTRAPOSITION:

[54] moi — souviens — le temps des cerises

[55] le temps des cerises — souvient — (à) moi

(CLITIC-PLACING giving the correct form of indirect object).

The problem is that, in the case of sentences derived by EXTRAPOSITION (see Gross, 1968), it is normally impossible to have sentences containing clitic pronouns corresponding to extraposed complements, *cf:*

[56] *a:* travailler est facile à Pierre ($\to$ EXTRAPOSITION $\to$)
       b: il est facile à Pierre de travailler ($\to$ CLITIC-PLACING $\to$)
       c: *il en est facile à Pierre

[57] *a:* que Pierre parte est probable ($\to$ EXTRAPOSITION $\to$)
       b: il est probable que Pierre partira ($\to$ CLITIC-PLACING $\to$)
       c: *il l'est (probable que Pierre partira)

Moreover, as these examples show, EXTRAPOSITION is normally optional. But not only must Postal's analysis say that, for *sembler* and *souvenir*, EXTRAPOSITION is obligatory,[11] but, in addition, the substantival clause *que S* in [26a], and the *de NP* in [46b], are possible sources of clitic pronouns, *cf:*

[58] il me le semble

[59] il m'en souvient

These facts are explained naturally if we assume that the deep structures of [26a] and [46b] are, respectively:

[60] Δ — semble — [$_{NP}$ [$_S$ le coût de la vie a augmenté]] — à moi

[61] Δ — souvient [$_{PP}$ de [$_{NP}$ le temps des cerises]] — à moi

(where the impersonal subject *il* will be introduced by a late insertion rule). These sentences would then have no lexical subject in deep structure, the indirect object would be marked as 'location', and the substantival clause or the *de NP* as 'theme'.

If we wish to keep Postal's transformational analysis, it is not impossible to account for these facts, but it would be necessary then to modify the PSYCH-MOVEMENT rule. We should start from the following underlying structures:

[62] moi — semble — [$_{NP}$ [$_S$ le coût de la vie a augmenté]]

[63] moi — souvenir — [$_{PP}$ de [$_{NP}$ le temps des cerises]]

Then, the PSYCH-MOVEMENT rule would be decomposed into two steps, i: subject postposing, and ii: object preposing into the subject position. Only the first of these rules would apply in the case of *sembler* and *souvenir*. I shall not here consider the consequences that might in general follow from this decomposition of PSYCH-MOVEMENT into two steps, which is reminiscent of the decomposition of the PASSIVE proposed by Chomsky (1970).

4

The verbs in series [23] show a number of syntactic and semantic peculiarities which it is important to bear in mind. They have been described in part by Gross (1968, 1969). Firstly, when the subject of these verbs is human, the sentence is in general ambiguous. Thus, the following sentence:

[64] Jean amuse Pierre
      John amuses Peter

'is interpreted i: either with an 'active' subject – John carries out a *voluntary* action which causes Peter's enjoyment; ii: or else with a 'non-active' subject – it so happens that John behaves in such a way (*involuntarily*) that he amuses Peter' (Gross, 1968, 70). In the second interpretation, [64] is comparable with [65]:

[65] le comportement de Jean amuse Pierre
      John's behaviour amuses Peter

This second interpretation is the only one possible when the subject is non-human. Continuing with the terminology of thematic functions, I shall say that, in the case of (ii) the subject is simply the 'theme' of the process expressed by the sentence, whereas in the case of (i) it is also the 'agent' of this process. The agentive interpretation of the subject appears clearly in sentences such as:

[66] Jean a délibérément amusé Pierre
      John deliberately amused Peter

[67] Jean a de lui-même amusé Pierre
      John of his own accord amused Peter

[68] Paul a forcé Jean à amuser Pierre
      Paul forced John to amuse Peter

The two interpretations are not always possible, however. Besides the fact that, in certain general syntactico-semantic conditions, the agentive interpretation of the subject is excluded (*cf* [71], [72], [77] below, or constructions of the type of [93], even if the subject is human), there are certain verbs in class [23] for which the agentive interpretation seems very artificial or is even excluded: this is the case for *préoccuper*, and for *frapper* and *toucher* (in their psychological sense, see below, section 8), *cf:*

[69] *Jean a délibérément $\left\{\begin{array}{l}\text{frappé}\\ \text{touché}\end{array}\right\}$ (l'esprit de) Pierre

   *John deliberately $\left\{\begin{array}{l}\text{struck}\\ \text{touched}\end{array}\right\}$ Peter (Peter's sensibilities)

   On the syntactic plane, the verbs of [23] appear in surface structure in a variety of syntactic frames other than that of [2] or of [64]. Besides the case of passive sentences (cf [70]), we have first (cf Gross, 1969, 38–39), sentences containing pseudo-instrumental adverbials, cf [71–75]:

[70] Pierre a été $\left\{\begin{array}{l}\text{amusé}\\ \text{impressionné}\end{array}\right\}$ par Jean

   Peter was $\left\{\begin{array}{l}\text{amused}\\ \text{impressed}\end{array}\right\}$ by John

[71] Pierre impressionne Paul par son intelligence
    Peter impresses Paul by his intelligence

[72] Pierre ennuie Paul à toujours parler de ses soucis
    Peter bores Paul by always talking about his worries

[73] *par sa fatuité, Pierre ennuie Paul à toujours parler de ses soucis
    *by his self-centredness, Peter bores Paul by always talking about his worries

[74] *Paul a été impressionné par Pierre par son intelligence
    *Paul was impressed by Peter by his intelligence

[75] *Pierre est ennuyé par Paul à toujours parler de ses soucis
    *Peter is bored by Paul by always talking about his worries

   As we see, these pseudo-instrumentals are incompatible with one another, and with the passive. Moreover, they are subject to coreferentiality constraints with the subject, cf:

[76] *Pierre impressionne Paul par l'intelligence de Marie
    *Peter impresses Paul by Mary's intelligence

   Note that, in [71–72], the subject cannot have an agentive interpretation, cf:

[77] *Pierre a délibérément ennuyé Paul $\left\{\begin{array}{l}\text{par sa fatuité}\\ \text{à parler de ses soucis}\end{array}\right.$

   *Peter deliberately bored Paul $\left\{\begin{array}{l}\text{by his self-centredness}\\ \text{by talking about his worries}\end{array}\right.$

This distinguishes these constructions with pseudo-instrumentals from other constructions which are superficially identical with them, such as:

[78] Jules nous a (délibérément) amusés par un discours très enlevé
      Julius (deliberately) entertained us by a very lively speech

The complement in *par NP* of [78] seems closer to a true instrumental: the agentive interpretation is possible, and these complements, in contrast to those of [71–72], can be interrogativized with *comment, cf:*

[79]   Comment Jules   ⎧*Par son intelligence
        vous a-t-il amusés? ⎩Par un discours très enlevé

       How did Julius   ⎧*By his intelligence
         entertain you?   ⎩By a very lively speech

Then, as we can see, the complement in *par NP* of [78] allows determiners in the NP that those of the type of [71] do not allow.

Further, most of these verbs have corresponding adjectival forms, generally of the form V-*ant*, which appear in constructions like those of [81]:

[80]   le froid⎫ ⎧gêne ⎫
          ce que raconte Paul⎭ ⎩ennuie⎭ Marie

                 the cold⎫ ⎧upsets⎫
           what Paul is relating⎭ ⎩vexes ⎭ Mary

[81]   le froid⎫ est ⎧gênant   ⎫ pour Marie
          ce que raconte Paul⎭   ⎩ennuyeux⎭

                 the cold⎫ is ⎧upsetting⎫ for Mary
           what Paul is relating⎭   ⎩vexing   ⎭

These types of construction, which have been studied by Lélia Picabia (1970), could be the subject of various lines of comment. We must at least point out that if, in [81], *Marie* can have the same semantic relationship (that of 'location') with the verbal adjective that the direct object has with the verb in [80], this is not generally so, especially if the subject is human. Thus, [82] seems to me not at all natural, and, in [83], the *pour NP* is not the equivalent of a direct object; its interpretation is, rather, of the type discussed above in connection with [49–50]:

[82] ?Jean est amusant pour Paul (spoken with normal sentence intonation)

[83] pour Paul, Jean est amusant
      in Paul's opinion, John is amusing

We could approximately paraphrase [83] by 'in Paul's opinion, John has the characteristic of being amusing' (where the 'location' is altogether indeterminate). Thus it will be necessary to divide the verbs of class [23] into those that allow a 'location' of the form *pour NP* in constructions of the type of [81], and those that do not allow it. Note that verbs which allow this complement, like *gêner*, can appear with two complements in *pour NP*:

[84] pour Paul $\begin{Bmatrix} \text{Jean} \\ \text{le froid} \end{Bmatrix}$ est gênant pour Marie

     in Paul's opinion $\begin{Bmatrix} \text{John} \\ \text{the cold} \end{Bmatrix}$ is upsetting for Mary

Lastly, most of these verbs can appear in either of two constructions which are illustrated, respectively, by [86] and [87]:

[85] $\left.\begin{matrix} \text{Paul} \\ \text{cette table} \\ \text{le bruit qu'on fait sur cette histoire} \\ \text{que Jules soit sorti} \end{matrix}\right\}$ étonne Marie

$\left.\begin{matrix} \text{Paul} \\ \text{this table} \\ \text{the fuss they are making about this story} \\ \text{that Julius has gone out} \end{matrix}\right\}$ astonishes Mary

[86] Marie s'étonne $\left\{\begin{matrix} \text{*de Paul} \\ \text{*de cette table} \\ \text{du bruit qu'on fait sur cette histoire} \\ \text{(de ce) que Jules soit sorti} \end{matrix}\right.$

Mary is astonished $\left\{\begin{matrix} \text{*at Paul} \\ \text{*at this table} \\ \text{at the fuss they are making about this story} \\ \text{that Julius has gone out} \end{matrix}\right.$

[87] Marie est étonnée $\left\{\begin{matrix} \text{*de Paul} \\ \text{*de cette table} \\ \text{du bruit qu'on fait sur cette histoire} \\ \text{(de ce) que Jules soit sorti} \end{matrix}\right.$

One of the striking features of these constructions – one pronominal, the other with a 'passive' verbal adjective – is that in general they do not have the same selectional restrictions as the corresponding simple transitive constructions; human NPs, and also concrete non-human NPs, are, in general, barred from the complement position in [86] and [87].[12] In fact, there are many variations in this respect between the verbs, and some verbs, such as *dégoûter* itself, are not subject to these selectional restrictions; compare [88] with [86–87]:

[88] Marie $\begin{Bmatrix} \text{est dégoûtee} \\ \text{se dégoûte} \end{Bmatrix}$ $\begin{Bmatrix} \text{de Pierre} \\ \text{de la bière} \\ \text{de ce que raconte Jules} \end{Bmatrix}$

     Mary $\begin{Bmatrix} \text{is disgusted} \\ \text{(grows disgusted)} \end{Bmatrix}$ $\begin{Bmatrix} \text{with Peter} \\ \text{with beer} \\ \text{with what Julius is recounting} \end{Bmatrix}$

Furthermore, these verbs do not all appear indiscriminately in these various constructions. For example, some are barred from the pronominal construction illustrated by [86],[13] *cf*:

[89] Marie $\begin{Bmatrix} \text{*se gêne} \\ \text{est gênée} \end{Bmatrix}$ de ce que raconte Paul

     Mary is upset at what Paul is recounting

[90] Marie $\begin{Bmatrix} \text{*se tente} \\ \text{est tentée} \end{Bmatrix}$ d'acheter cette robe

     Mary is tempted to buy that dress

Others, in addition, do not allow the construction with a 'passive' verbal adjective and a complement in *de*, *cf*:

[91] Marie $\left\{ \begin{matrix} \begin{Bmatrix} \text{*s'impressionne} \\ \text{*est impressionnée} \end{Bmatrix} \text{de cette histoire} \\ \text{est impressionnée par cette histoire} \end{matrix} \right.$

     Mary is impressed by this story

Let us represent the various constructions that we have just reviewed by the following syntactic frames:

[92] $NP_1 \text{ V } NP_2$
     (simple transitive construction)

[93] NP_1 *être* $[_A \text{ V-}ant]$ $[pour \text{ } NP_2]$
     (construction with 'active' verbal adjective)

[94] NP_2 *être* V-*é par* NP_1
  (passive construction)

[95] NP_2 *être* [$_A$ V-*é*] *de* NP_1
  (construction with 'passive' verbal adjective)

[96] NP_2 *se* V *de* NP_1
  (pronominal construction)

The relationships between these various constructions pose all sorts of problems that I cannot attempt to resolve here. What is striking is that the sentences illustrating these constructions form two groups which contrast with each other in the same way as the examples of [1] and [2] from which we started. In the cases of [92] and [93], we have (in thematic terminology) a 'theme' (NP_1) in the subject position, and a 'location' in the post-verbal position. In the cases of [94–96], we have a 'location' (NP_2) in the subject position, and a 'theme' in the post-verbal position. It is important, therefore, to take these various constructions into account, and not only those of [92], if we wish to give an adequate treatment of the problem which concerns us.

A priori, once more, we can imagine all sorts of ways of treating the regularities which relate these various constructions to one another. We could treat the whole question in transformational terms, or, conversely, in terms of redundancy rules; there could also be intermediate solutions, linking together some of the constructions of [92–96] by transformations, and others by redundancy rules. Maurice Gross seems to suggest deriving all the constructions [93–96] from a deep structure of the form [92], and in particular he would consider [94] and [95] as varieties of the passive; he also considers [96] as a sort of passive, 'where the reflexive particle corresponds to the auxiliary *être* of the usual passive' (Gross, 1969, 38).

In English, the facts are slightly different: there is no construction corresponding to the pronominal construction [96], but sentences such as [97], [98], and [99] are examples of constructions which correspond approximately to [93], [94] and [95] respectively:

[97] Bill's stories are amusing to me

[98] I was amused by Bill's stories

[99] I am amused at Bill's stories

As we have already seen in part, Postal would derive [92], and also [93], by PSYCH-MOVEMENT from underlying structures where the order of the elements is fundamentally that of [95–96]. Moreover, he makes a sharp distinction between passive sentences of the type of [98], which he derives from active structures according to the classic solution, and forms of the type of [99], which for him are basic. It does appear that, for English, everyone in fact agrees to consider these sentences of the type of [99] as basic (*cf* Chapin, 1967, Lakoff, 1970c, and also Chomsky, 1970), and the only question, therefore, is that of the derived status, or otherwise, of active sentences with the 'theme' in subject position.

I shall not go into the relations between [92] and [93]. In my opinion, there is no reason for deriving [93] from [92] by transformation, and, if [92] is basic [93] is so too. But this issue is secondary to the point of view which concerns us. I agree with Postal that [92] and [93] show the same order of NP_1 and NP_2 relative to the verb in deep structure. The question at issue is whether, *from this point of view*, the deep structure of [92–93] is different from their surface structure.

As for [96], I think that constructions of this type belong to the class of neutral constructions, studied in Chapter 3. It would be easy to confirm that the arguments used in Chapter 3 to demonstrate the basic character of the pronominal neutrals apply equally to constructions of the type [96]: we find the same capricious character in the relationship between transitive sentences and pronominal sentences (*cf* [89–91]), the semantic differences between the two constructions (*cf* below, section 5), the possibility of inserting neutral pronominal constructions under verbs such as *daigner* or *forcer*, etc (*cf* [100–101]):

[100] Pierre a daigné s'étonner de l'absence de Paul
       Peter condescended to wonder at Paul's absence

[101] l'absence de Paul a forcé Pierre à s'amuser tout seul
       Paul's absence forced Peter to amuse himself alone

Certain facts that were drawn to my attention by Maurice Gross suggest another argument in favour of introducing pronominals of the type of [96] in deep structure. Constructions of the type of [96] allow, for some verbs at least, complements that those of the type of [92] do not allow; thus we have [102] but not [103]:

[102] Pierre s'est $\begin{Bmatrix} \text{inquiété} \\ \text{étonné} \end{Bmatrix}$ auprès de Jean de l'absence de Paul

       Peter $\begin{Bmatrix} \text{made enquiries of John about} \\ \text{expressed his surprise to John at} \end{Bmatrix}$ Paul's absence

[103] *l'absence de Paul a $\left\{\begin{matrix} \text{inquiété} \\ \text{étonné} \end{matrix}\right\}$ Pierre auprès de Jean

The ungrammaticalness of [103] makes a derivation of [102] from a construction of the form [92] very difficult. On the other hand, if the two types of construction, [92] and [96], are equally basic, the possibility or impossibility of having complements in *auprès de NP* can be dealt with naturally by means of subcategorization features. In the matter of the semantic relationship linking the complement in *auprès de NP* with the verb and the subject, a relationship which also occurs in sentences with non-pronominal verbs, *cf:*

[104] Pierre a signalé l'absence de Paul auprès des autorités compétentes
     Peter reported Paul's absence to the competent authorities

[105] Pierre a fait des démarches pressantes auprès des autorités
     Peter made urgent approaches to the authorities

this will be dealt with by means of interpretation rules for base component grammatical relations.

My analysis of [96] would thus be similar to that proposed by Postal and by Chomsky (1970) for English sentences of the type of [99]: both would be basic.

The most delicate problem is that posed by the relations between constructions [94] and [95], and also their respective relations with the active construction [92]. It is clear that, at least for certain verbs (of a class other than class [23], *présenter* for example), sentences of the form [94] must be derived transformationally, by PASSIVE, from structures underlying active constructions; R. S. Kayne has argued convincingly for this view (see Kayne, 1969, forthcoming). On the other hand, as François Dell (1970) has emphasized, in the case of many constructions of the form of [95], there is no positive reason to indicate a transformational derivation by means of PASSIVE, for example [106] compared with [107]:

[106] Pierre est (intimement) persuadé $\left\{\begin{matrix} \text{de son bon droit} \\ \text{que Paul ment} \end{matrix}\right.$

 Peter is (inwardly) persuaded $\left\{\begin{matrix} \text{of his own right} \\ \text{that Paul is lying} \end{matrix}\right.$

[107] Pierre a été (?? intimement) persuadé par Marie $\left.\begin{matrix} \\ \end{matrix}\right\}$ de son bon droit que Paul mentait

 Peter was (?? inwardly) persuaded by Mary $\left\{\begin{matrix} \text{of his own right} \\ \text{that Paul was lying} \end{matrix}\right.$

The sequences V-$é$ are true adjectives here, and it is reasonable to regard these constructions as basic.

But if we take the verbs one by one, it seems to be more difficult than in English (compare [98] with [99]), to determine whether we are dealing with a true passive or a construction with a basic verbal adjective. In this respect, the table of forms [92–96] offers a deceptive simplification, in the sense that there are certain verbs (cf [91]), which allow a complement in *par NP* and yet appear to be nearer to constructions of the type [95] than to true passives. Tests involving co-occurrence with adverbs such as *très* (versus *beaucoup*) and *si* (versus *tant*) give no clear result.[14]

I shall not try to solve these difficulties here. I shall only point out that, as in English, there seem to be two types of construction, at least in the clear cases. In some instances (certain 'passives' in *par*), there is obviously a transformational derivation from active forms. In other cases, which perhaps include constructions in *NP être V-é par NP* as well as constructions in *NP être V-é de NP*, it appears that these constructions must be generated in the base, the V-$é$ having the status of a true adjective. However this may be, if we leave aside the true passives, we have two types of construction, [92–93] on one hand, [95–96] on the other hand. What concerns us is the status of the relation between these two groups, and more especially the question whether constructions of the type [92–93] should be derived from underlying structures related to [95–96] by means of the PSYCH-MOVEMENT transformation.

5

Before embarking on a critique of Postal's arguments, we must first draw attention to a confusion that must be avoided. By saying that the various sentences of [80–81], [85–87], or the pairs of sentences of [41–45], etc, are related, and that this relationship must be systematically described in the grammar, we do not in any way imply that these related sentences are synonymous with each other. Clearly this is not the case in general, even if there is a systematic semantic relationship between the sentences, which we have schematized in terms of thematic functions ('location' and 'theme').

On certain points, the differences are evident: there are differences of aspect; the theme in subject position can be an agent, while the theme in object position can never be an agent; the constructions of [95] are stative, while those of [92] are non-stative (cf Lakoff, 1966), etc. A very clear example of another sort, where the difference is of a lexical order, is found when we compare [33] and [36] above; I repeat them here:

[33] la sage-femme est heureuse que Madeleine ait accouché sans douleur

[36] il est heureux pour la sage-femme que Madeleine ait accouché sans douleur

From the point of view of meaning, [36] would be more like [108]:

[108] la sage-femme a de la chance que Madeleine ait accouché sans douleur

the midwife is lucky that Madeleine has given birth without pain

In fact, if we add '... et pourtant, la sage-femme n'en est pas heureuse' ('... and yet, the midwife is not happy about it') to [33] and to [36], we get a contradictory sentence in the first case, but not in the second.

Other semantic differences are more subtle, like those which differentiate some of the constructions of [92–96]. Thus, [85] and [87] are distinct from [86]. In contrast to [85] and to [87], [86] implies in effect that Mary displays her astonishment (by words, usually), and this is clearly apparent when we consider the following sentences:

[109] *a:* que Jules soit sorti étonne Marie ⎫ mais elle
b: Marie est étonnée que Jules soit sorti ⎬ n'en laisse
c: ??Marie s'étonne que Jules soit sorti ⎭ rien paraître

a: that Julius has gone out astonishes Mary ⎫ but she
b: Mary is astonished that Julius has gone out ⎬ gives no
c: ??Mary is (obviously) astonished that Julius ⎭ sign of it
has gone out

Sentences (*a*) and (*b*) are perfectly natural, but [109*c*] is odd, and even seems contradictory.

A similar case is shown in the following sentences:

[110] *a:* la conduite de Mélisande est gênante pour Golaud
Mélisande's behaviour is embarrassing for Golaud

b: Golaud est gêné de la conduite de Mélisande
Golaud is embarrassed by Mélisande's behaviour

[111] *a:* le fait qu'il va devoir payer tellement d'impôts est ennuyeux pour Oscar
the fact that he is going to have to pay so much tax is annoying for Oscar

b: Oscar est ennuyé {du fait / de ce} qu'il va devoir payer tellement d'impôts[15]

Oscar is annoyed that he is going to have to pay so much tax

In the (*b*) examples, Golaud and Oscar are necessarily conscious of the annoyance (*gêne* or *ennui*) which the situation expressed by the complement entails for them. This is not necessarily the case in the (*a*) examples, which could be simply statements by an outside observer who is objectively assessing a certain situation and judges that it is annoying (*gênant* or *ennuyeux*) for a particular individual, even if that individual is not himself aware of the fact. In this way, [111*a*] could be uttered by Oscar's bank manager, who is aware of the amount of his tax and of his financial position – while Oscar is travelling and is unaware of the situation. This sort of interpretation is impossible for [111*b*]. In the same way, we could quite naturally add 'mais, le pauvre, il ne se doute de rien' ('but, poor man, he is quite unsuspecting') to [110*a*]; this addition would be impossible in the case of [110*b*].[16]

I stress these semantic differences for the following reason. Postal, of course, has also pointed out that the related constructions in question, for example those of [97–99], are not in general synonymous. He emphasizes this most explicitly (*cf* Postal, 1971, 40, 42). As, for him, all semantic differences must be reflected in the underlying syntactic structure of the sentences, this means that, for example, [97] and [99] do not have the same underlying structure.

But, on the other hand, the analysis proposed by Postal, which brings PSYCH-MOVEMENT into the derivation of [97], results in close, if not identical, underlying structures for [97] and [99], which are both then something like [112]:

[112] [_{NP} I] [_V amuse] [_{NP} Bill's stories]

Postal says explicitly that [112] is not *the* underlying structure of [97] and [99]; this structure, for him, only represents what [97] and [99] have in common. But he completely leaves aside the question of how the differences of meaning between [97] and [99] should be represented.

I do not claim, at this stage, that it is not possible, within the framework of generative semantics, to represent these differences in a way that would be compatible with the idea that [97] and [99] share the structure represented in [112], as an essential part of their underlying structure. I wish only to make an observation which seems to me important from the methodological point of view. In [97] and [99] – or in [40] and [41], [110] and [111], etc – we are dealing with sentences which show syntactic differences, on the one hand, and semantic differences on the other hand. Postal's solution, which aims at accounting for certain resemblances, amounts to leaving aside the syntactic differences at an early stage without specifying how they will be accounted for (except by having recourse to 'rule features', and this is not specified in detail), and deferring until later the question of how the semantic differences will be treated. But this procedure tends to overlook a question which must be asked: is there a correlation between these syntactic differences and the semantic differences, and if there is, how should it be treated?

6

Let us go on to look at Postal's arguments in favour of PSYCH-MOVE-MENT. We have already seen that the fact that this solution allows us to unify the treatment of selectional restrictions and grammatical relations in [1] and in [2] cannot be taken as an argument specifically in its favour. The semantic solution sketched out in section 2 succeeds just as well. Nevertheless, it seems that, with Postal, the analysis by PSYCH-MOVE-MENT is implicitly linked with the idea that there is a sort of natural bond between human (or animate) NPs and the (deep) subject position. Many linguists (for example Hall, 1965) have noted that a very large number of verbs have human subjects – more precisely that, when a verb has selectional restrictions that relate to neighbouring [±HUMAN) NPs, it is often the subject that is marked [+HUMAN]. This is clearly not a general fact, and the verbs that concern us represent precisely the most important class of exceptions to any such generalization that one might be tempted to make. If there were serious and independent arguments of another provenance in favour of PSYCH-MOVEMENT, this class of exceptions would be eliminated, and it could be a step towards a definition of the notion of subject in terms of the feature [+HUMAN], or something of that sort. But it is clear that this regularization of the distribution of the feature [+HUMAN] cannot by itself count as a justification of PSYCH-MOVEMENT, without involving a circular argument.

This point is worth some attention, because there often seems to be confusion – and not only on the part of linguists who propose the analysis by PSYCH-MOVEMENT for the constructions considered here – between three notions which sometimes overlap, but which are nevertheless quite distinct: they are the notions of deep subject, agent, and human or animate NP. I have already dealt with this problem in Chapter 4, but I will return to it briefly. The following examples will be sufficient to show that it is not possible to establish a unity of these three notions:

[113] Maurice mange un gâteau
       Maurice is eating a cake

[114] Pierre a subi un dur interrogatoire
      Peter underwent a severe interrogation

[115] Alfred a reçu un coup de poing en pleine figure
      Alfred received a punch full in the face

[116] le vent a renversé la clôture
      the wind blew the fence down

[117] la voiture a cassé la fenêtre avec son pare-chocs
      the car broke the window with its bumper

[64] Jean amuse Pierre
     John amuses Peter

[1] Pierre méprise les femmes
    Peter despises women

If, in [113], the subject NP is indeed a human agent, in [114] and in [115] (which have approximately the same selectional restrictions as [113] on the subject and the object, in terms of the feature [± HUMAN]), it is not apparent that the human subject is an agent (but see Chapters 3 and 4). In [116] and [117], the subject is non-human, and Chomsky (1972), as well as Dougherty (1970a), have clearly shown that these non-human subjects have the properties of agent, and that it is not possible, for example, to reduce them to a type of instrumental. The human subject of [64], as we have seen, may or may not be interpreted as an agent. And lastly, what the human object of [64] and the human subject of [1] have in common semantically, has nothing to do with the notion of agent; it is what I have characterized by the notion of 'location' of a psychological process.

No doubt there is something systematic in the relations between these notions of deep subject, agent and human NP. But the best way to characterize this relation is, in my opinion, (see Chapter 4, and also Chomsky, 1972 and Dougherty, 1970a) to define the semantic notion of agent derivatively, by means of possibly complex rules of semantic interpretation, from the function of (deep) subject: in certain conditions, an NP which appears, in deep structure, in the configuration which defines a subject, can, must, or cannot be interpreted as an agent (and moreover only a deep subject can be interpreted as an agent). That deep subjects may often be human NPs then appears as simply a consequence of the fact that human beings are, in a general way, more capable of 'autonomous activity' (see Chapter 4) than inanimate objects. We see that this concep-

tion, if it is justified, far from supporting the analysis by PSYCH-MOVE-
MENT, helps rather to refute it. In effect, analysis by PSYCH-MOVEMENT
would not enable us to express directly why *Pierre*, in [64], cannot in any
reading be interpreted as an agent, or why *Jean* can be.

In fact, these considerations can serve as an illustration to the question
that I asked at the end of the preceding section, on the correlations between syntax and semantics. If we agree, in accordance with the thematic
hypothesis, that all the constructions of [92–96] are generated in deep
structure (except for [94], which will be derived from [92] by PASSIVE),
two very simple rules allow us to predict the distribution of agents:

  i: Only a deep subject can be interpreted as an agent
  ii: The deep subject of *être* can never be interpreted as an agent[17]

Rule (i) predicts that the subject of [92] or of [96] can be an agent,
without saying that it must always be so. At the same time it excludes any
of the post-verbal complements of [92–96] (with the exception, once
again, of the 'agent complements' of passive sentences of the type [94])
from being interpreted as an agent. Rule (ii) excludes the agentive interpretation of both the subject of [93] and that of [95].

Note that the same rules predict that the subjects of verbs such as
mépriser, etc, can also be interpreted as agents (but not necessarily). We
have characterized these subjects as the 'locations' of psychological
processes (in the same way as the objects of verbs like *dégoûter*). Clédat
(1900; see above, section 2) noted that sentences of the type of [1] can
be ambiguous. Thus, [118] usually means that the grandfather 'experiences a feeling for his grandson', while in [119], 'the peoples perform
acts of worship' (Clédat, 1900, 225):

[118] son grand-père adore cet enfant
      his grandfather worships that child

[119] certains peuples adorent les animaux
      certain peoples worship animals

In fact, both these sentences are ambiguous, although the most natural
interpretation is not the same in both cases. We see, then, that the thematic function of agent can be superimposed on the function of 'location',
as in [118–119], or on that of theme, as in [64]. This is exactly what is
predicted by the analysis that we propose, while the fact remains unexplained in Postal's formulation.

6.1

Postal's second argument is of the same order. It concerns 'the behaviour of the curious adverb *personally*'. In the analysis by PSYCH-MOVEMENT, '*personally* may be said to accompany the logical subject. Otherwise its occurrence must be given disjunctively in some manner' (Postal, 1971, 42). Postal quotes the following examples, among others, in support:

[120] *a:* I personally am annoyed with Jack
    b: *Jack is annoyed with me personally

[121] *a:* Jack is annoying to me personally
    b: *I personally am annoying to Jack

In other words, for Postal the occurrence of *personally* is related to the presence in the sentence of a deep subject in the first person singular. Examples in French comparable to [120–121] can be found, although judgments on their grammaticality seem to me less definite:

[122] *a:* personnellement, je suis dégoûté de Marie
        personally, I am disgusted with Mary
    b: ?*personellement, Marie est degoûtée de moi
        *personally, Mary is disgusted with me

[123] *a:* personnellement, Marie me dégoûte
        personally Mary disgusts me
    b: ?personnellement, je dégoûte Marie
        ?personally, I disgust Mary

In the case of a sentence of the type of [1], we have the following distribution:

[124] *a:* personnellement, je méprise Marie
        personally, I despise Mary
    b: ?*personnellement, Marie me méprise
        *personally, Mary despises me

Let us assume that the facts are as simple as Postal says. They can just as well be treated in the framework of the thematic solution. We should only need a rule of semantic interpretation linking *personnellement* to an NP marked [+LOCATION] which is in the first person singular; any sentence not containing an NP fulfilling these conditions would be considered semantically ill-formed. This solution would even be distinctly preferable if the following sentences turned out to be cases of true passives:

[125] 'Personnellement,' dit Stravinsky, 'j'ai été influencé par Gesualdo'
'Personally,' said Stravinsky, 'I have been influenced by Gesualdo'

[126] 'Personellement,' dit Cécile, 'j'ai été $\begin{Bmatrix} \text{complètement} \\ \text{??très} \end{Bmatrix}$ pervertie
par Valmont'

'Personally,' said Cécile, 'I have been $\begin{Bmatrix} \text{completely} \\ \text{?? very} \end{Bmatrix}$ corrupted
by Valmont'

If these sentences are true passives, in fact, the subject *je* is only a surface subject, not a deep one, but it can undoubtedly be characterized as the 'psychological location' of a certain process. Postal's analysis could not account for these sentences, or would be obliged to have recourse to a 'disjunctive' formulation.

Furthermore, if Postal's generalization is to hold good, independently of the cases of [125–126], it would have to be shown that all the following sentences have a deep subject in the first person singular, which is very far from evident:

[127] personnellement, $\begin{cases} \text{la lecture de Chomsky m'a beaucoup aidé} \\ \text{cette fille a conquis mon cœur} \\ \text{ceci a} \begin{cases} \text{retenu} \\ \text{éveillé} \\ \text{attiré} \end{cases} \text{mon attention} \\ \text{ces faits répondent à mon attente} \\ \text{ceci ne me dit rien qui vaille} \\ \text{mon foie me donne du souci} \\ \text{la révolution est le cadet de mes soucis} \end{cases}$

personally, $\begin{cases} \text{reading Chomsky helped me a lot} \\ \text{that girl has won my heart} \\ \text{this} \begin{cases} \text{kept} \\ \text{aroused} \\ \text{attracted} \end{cases} \text{my attention} \\ \text{these facts correspond to my expectations} \\ \text{this tells me nothing of any value} \\ \text{my liver is giving me concern} \\ \text{the revolution is the least of my worries} \end{cases}$

On the other hand, these sentences pose no problems for the thematic analysis, inasmuch as thematic functions are not in principle linked to particular syntactic functions.

But, actually, the facts concerning *personnellement*[18] seem to be even more complex. If we consider sentences such as:

[128] personnellement, ce chien m'obéit toujours
      personally, this dog always obeys me

[129] personnellement, dans cette bagarre, j'ai été blessé par les policiers
      personally, in that scuffle, I was wounded by the policemen

[130] ?personnellement, dans cette bagarre, les policiers m'ont blessé
      ?personally, in that scuffle, the policemen wounded me

it seems that we must give up any attempt to formulate the constraints on *personnellement* in a simple manner, whether it be in terms of co-occurrence with a deep subject or in terms of linking it with an NP marked [+LOCATION]. Perhaps we should adopt a fairly loose formulation indicating that *personnellement* is possible if the process expressed by the verb 'affects' the subject of the enunciation (*je*) in some manner, provided that this is present in surface structure. Further, the difference between [129] and [130], somewhat subtle in other respects, seems to indicate that, in certain cases, the nature of the derived subject plays a part. However it may be, these facts cannot be considered as providing arguments for the analysis by PSYCH-MOVEMENT.

Incidentally, although we must exercise great caution in a question which remains shrouded in all kinds of obscurity, we could derive an argument against the analysis by PSYCH-MOVEMENT from the distribution of certain adverbs of manner. We know (*cf* Chapter 3) that certain adverbs of manner are linked to the deep subject, *cf*:

[131] les SS ont férocement battu les résistants
      the SS beat the Resistance men savagely

[132] les résistants ont été férocement battus par les SS
      the Resistance men were savagely beaten by the SS

In [132], as in [131], it is the SS, and not the Resistance men, who display their savagery. If the analysis by PSYCH-MOVEMENT was justified, one might expect to find, in sentences of the form of [2], etc, adverbs of manner relating to the surface object, since this would be a deep subject in fact. But nothing of the sort happens, *cf*:

[133] *a*: je m'amuse comme un fou
          I'm enjoying myself like a lord (*literally*, like mad)
      b: *cette histoire m'amuse comme un fou
          *this story amuses me like a lord

[134] *a:* don Juan aimait les femmes $\begin{cases} \text{tendrement} \\ \text{avec passion} \\ \text{à la folie} \end{cases}$

Don Juan loved women $\begin{cases} \text{tenderly} \\ \text{with passion} \\ \text{to distraction} \end{cases}$

b: les femmes plaisaient $\begin{cases} \text{*tendrement} \\ \text{*avec passion} \\ \text{?? à la folie} \end{cases}$ à don Juan

women attracted Don Juan $\begin{cases} \text{*tenderly} \\ \text{*with passion} \\ \text{?? to distraction} \end{cases}$

[135] *a:* Pierre a délibérément profité de l'inattention de Paul
       Peter deliberately took advantage of Paul's inattention

   b: *l'inattention de Paul a délibérément profité à Pierre
       *Paul's inattention deliberately advantaged Peter

6.2

Finally, the only argument of Postal's which should detain us is that relating to 'Cross-Over' constraints, which are in fact the principal concern of his book (1971). To account for facts like the following, for example:[19]

[136] Charley stabbed himself
       'Charley s'est poignardé lui-même'

[137] *Charley was stabbed by himself
       'Charley a été poignardé par lui-même'

[138] *himself was stabbed by Charley
       'lui-même a été poignardé par Charley'
       (where *himself* is coreferential with *Charley*)

Postal proposes submitting grammars to a universal constraint, called the Cross-Over Principle (here abbreviated as COP), a constraint which, in certain conditions, blocks the application of movement transformations in cases where such transformations would result in crossing one NP over another coreferential NP. If, for example, [137] is ungrammatical, according to Postal this is because this principle has been violated. Effectively, the passive transformation – in whatever manner it is formulated –

amounts to crossing two NPs (the deep subject and object); now in [137] (and in [138]), the two NPs concerned in the PASSIVE rule, *Charley* and *himself*, are coreferential.

Postal finds further facts of the same sort in a variety of constructions involving well-known movement transformations. In sentences of the type that concern us, he finds similar facts, but with a distribution of grammaticality and ungrammaticalness which is the reverse of what we find in passive sentences. It is thus, according to him, that we have the following facts (*cf* Postal, 1971, 47):

[139] *a:* I am amused at myself (*cf* [97–99])
         b: *I am amusing to myself

[140] *a:* I was horrified at myself
         b: *I was horrifying to myself

If we agree (*cf* [112]) that [139*a*] and [139*b*] are derived from related deep structures, *grosso modo* of the form [141]:

[141] [$_{NP}$ I] [$_V$ amuse] [$_{NP}$ I]

and if we agree moreover that [139*a*] directly reflects this base structure, while [139*b*] is derived from it by PSYCH-MOVEMENT, we see a way of explaining the facts: PSYCH-MOVEMENT, like PASSIVE, has the effect of crossing one NP over another, and the COP would block its application in the case of [139*b*]; [139*a*], not having undergone any such transformation, would be derived from [141] by the normal application of the REFLEXIVIZATION rule.

In French, the selectional restrictions which in general exclude a human object in constructions of the form [95] or [96] (*cf* [85–87]) limit the possibility of finding exact equivalents for sentences [139–140]. Nevertheless there are more complex cases which show the existence of similar constraints on sentences containing coreferential NPs. Thus, for me [142] – which is itself rather odd – is better than [143]:

[142] ?Ernest s'admire (lui-même) pour sa constance
         ?Ernest admires himself for his constancy

[143] ??Ernest s'impressionne (lui-même) par sa constance
         ??Ernest impresses himself by his constancy

Another example, where one's intuitions are more definite, is provided by the contrast between [144*b*] and [145*b*] (*cf* [24–26] above):

[144] *a:* je crois que je suis malade
         I believe that I am ill

      b: je me crois malade
         I believe myself (to be) ill

[145] *a:* il me semble que je suis malade
         it seems to me that I am ill
     b: *je me semble malade
         *I seem to myself (to be) ill

Whatever the analyses proposed for deriving constructions of type (*b*) (see above, section 3, and also Chapter 2), in general they imply that, in [144*b*], the *me*, which is coreferential with the subject, never has to cross it in the course of the derivation, whilst the *je* of [145*b*] has to cross the main indirect object *me*, either by the operation of SUBJECT-RAISING (*cf* Chapter 2) or by the application of PSYCH-MOVEMENT following on OBJECT-FORMATION (*cf* Postal's analysis summarized in section 3).[20]

I shall not deal in detail with the general problem of COP here. In the formulation that Postal gives of it (1971), it is accompanied by so many restrictive conditions that its explanatory value may be doubted. In any case, Postal himself has recently given up this principle as a general explanatory principle for constraints on coreference (*cf* Postal, 1970a, 1972, as well as the preface of Postal, 1971, itself);[21] he now thinks that this principle should be replaced by global constraints on derivations. This weakens the hypothesis that a movement transformation of PSYCH-MOVEMENT exists.

On the other hand, Ray Jackendoff (1969b), taking up the facts discussed by Postal (1971), has suggested a purely semantic means of treating these coreference constraints; this solution is compatible with the semantic solution that I proposed at the beginning of this chapter for dealing with the facts which concern us. In brief, Jackendoff suggests considering the thematic functions as forming a hierarchy, as follows, in an ascending order: (1) 'theme', (2) 'goal', 'source', 'location', (3) 'agent'. He then proposes the principle that a reflexive cannot be coreferential with an NP lower down in the hierarchy. Thus, [137] is excluded because *himself*, which is an 'agent', is higher in the hierarchy than *Charley*, which is 'theme' or perhaps 'goal'. Conversely, [139*a*] is possible because *myself*, being 'theme', is lower in the hierarchy than *I*, which is 'location' (or 'goal'); and [139*b*] is excluded because *myself* ('location' or 'goal') is higher in the hierarchy than *I*, which is 'theme'.

Jackendoff's principle predicts, correctly, the difference between [142] and [143]. In fact, in [142], *Ernest*, 'location' or 'goal', is higher in the hierarchy than *se*, 'theme', whilst, in [143], *Ernest* is 'theme' and *se* is 'location' or 'goal'. As for the ungrammaticalness of [145*b*], this is pre-dicted by an additional principle which says that any NP which has been extracted from its deep structure sentence by a RAISING transforma-tion is 'down-graded' from its place in the hierarchy and placed at the lowest level: in [145*b*], *je*, whatever its original function in [145*a*], is thus lower in the hierarchy than *me*, which is 'location' or 'goal'.

In French, in any case, there are certain very clear counter-examples to Postal's theory; one of these counter-examples involves the very verb that we took as a paradigmatic example, *dégoûter*. In fact, [146*a*] and [146*b*] are equally acceptable:

[146] *a:* Pierre se dégoûte (lui-même)
           Peter disgusts himself
       b: Pierre est dégoûté de lui-même
           Peter is disgusted with himself

Notice that, in [146*a*], *lui-même* is understood (just as in *Pierre s'aime lui-même* (Peter loves himself)) as being the object of *dégoûter* (whereas in *Pierre se lave lui-même* (Peter washes himself) for example, *lui-même* can be understood as an 'emphatic reflexive' referring to the subject). The facts of [146] are incompatible with any analysis which maintains at one and the same time (*a*) the validity of COP, and (*b*) a transformational derivation of [146*a*] and [146*b*] from a common source. In particular, whatever the precise manner in which the reflexive pronouns (*se* and *lui-même*)[22] are accounted for, if we assume that [146*b*] represents the order of the elements in deep structure and that [146*a*] is derived from a similar deep structure by means of PSYCH-MOVEMENT, the COP would predict that [146*a*] is ungrammatical. And conversely, if we agree to the hypothesis that [146*a*] represents the base order, and that [146*b*] is derived by PASSIVE or a similar rule (*cf* Gross, 1969), then it is [146*b*] which is the problem and which ought to be blocked by virtue of COP. Here then is a case where retaining COP would lead us to con-sider that [146*a*] and [146*b*] both appear, as they are, in the base.

On the other hand, the question arises whether [146] is not just as much a counter-example to Jackendoff's theory. Note that, even if this is the case, this point has no direct bearing on what concerns me at the moment, namely to show that the analysis by PSYCH-MOVEMENT has no positive advantage over the thematic analysis. It would simply be a case of one of the numerous problems which remain unexplained, whatever theoretical framework one adopts. But, as Jackendoff's theory on the hierarchy of thematic functions is consistent with my hypothesis on the derivation of sentences of type [2], it may be interesting to look more closely at what this theory has to say on sentences like those of [146].

As far as [146b] is concerned, there is no problem. [146b] is grammatical for the same reasons as [139a]: *Pierre* is 'location' and *lui-même* is 'theme' (remember that rule (ii) above prevents *Pierre* from being interpreted here as 'agent'). It is [146a] which poses the problem, as for Postal. If (*cf* [139b]) *Pierre* is 'theme' here and *se* ... *lui-même* is 'location', [146a] violates the hierarchic principle and ought to be excluded.

Let us recall that, in certain conditions, the subject 'theme' of sentences of the type of [2] can at the same time also be an 'agent'. If we agree that, when two thematic functions are assumed by one phrase, the function that is higher in Jackendoff's hierarchy takes precedence over the other, we might expect to find sentences of the type of [146a] that are acceptable, inasmuch as the subject is interpreted as an agent in them, and is therefore higher in the hierarchy than the object, which is a 'location'. This seems to be what happens in the following sentences, where the *se* is a true reflexive, in contrast to constructions of the type of [96]:

[147] Pierre s'amuse lui-même
       Peter amuses himself

[148] Paul essaie de s'impressionner lui-même
       Paul tries to impress himself

[149] Marie joue à $\begin{cases} \text{s'impressionner elle-même} \\ \text{se faire peur (à elle-même)} \end{cases}$

       Mary is playing at $\begin{cases} \text{impressing herself} \\ \text{frightening herself} \end{cases}$

The possibility of interpreting the subjects of these sentences as agents would explain why they are more acceptable than [143], for example, where, as we have seen, the presence of a complement in the pseudo-instrumental *par NP* excludes an agentive interpretation of the subject. If, in addition, the English sentence [139b] is excluded, it is because rule (ii) above excludes an agentive interpretation of the subject of the verb *to be*. The same reason explains the contrast between the following sentences:

[150] *a:* Pierre se gêne lui-même
           Peter annoys himself
       b: ??Pierre est gênant pour lui-même
           ??Peter is annoying to himself

(where, we may recall, the *pour NP* behaves like a true 'location').

The problem is that a sentence like [146a] is acceptable, whether we interpret the subject as an agent, or only as a theme. So the problem remains. Perhaps we should complicate Jackendoff's hierarchy by a supplementary principle saying that, if a sentence is ambiguous insofar as its subject may or may not be interpretable as an agent, and if no indication arises in any other way to exclude this agentive interpretation, the subject in question is automatically put into the highest position in the hierarchy. But this is rather a strange principle and remains *ad hoc*. I shall therefore say no more on this question for the moment.

7

We see that none of the positive arguments that Postal believed he could advance in favour of the existence of a PSYCH-MOVEMENT transformation is convincing. I shall not dwell on the negative arguments that could be invoked against this analysis. On sentences of the type of [2], we could develop arguments of the same order as those that Chomsky applied to the analysis of derived nominals in English (*cf* Chomsky, 1970, and Chapter 1 of this book), or those that I myself used (*cf* Chapter 3), to show that 'neutral' pronominal constructions are not transformationally derived. Besides the semantic differences between related constructions, referred to in section 5, let us note that the sentences supposedly derived by PSYCH-MOVEMENT have an internal phrase structure identical with that of sentences generated directly in the base (compare [1] and [2]). To derive them transformationally would not contribute towards simplifying the phrase structure component of the grammar. Moreover, as we saw in section 3, the connection between constructions supposedly related by PSYCH-MOVEMENT is often of a very idiosyncratic nature, which leads to a presumption in favour of a lexical, rather than a transformational, treatment of the connection between them.

An indirect argument in favour of PSYCH-MOVEMENT might be suggested by the problems posed by the derivation of sentences such as [24b–26b] above, which I repeat here:

[24] *a:* Pierre croit que la fin du monde est proche
       Peter believes that the end of the world is near
      b: Pierre croit la fin du monde proche
       Peter believes the end of the world near

[26] *a:* il me semble que le coût de la vie a augmenté
       it seems to me that the cost of living has increased
      b: le coût de la vie me semble avoir augmenté
       the cost of living seems to me to have increased

I showed in Chapter 2 that sentences such as [26b] must be derived by
SUBJECT-RAISING from sentences such as [26a]. Further, several
linguists (Rosenbaum, 1967, Gross, 1968, Fauconnier, 1971) have proposed deriving sentences of the type of [24b] from sentences of the type of
[24a] by the OBJECT-FORMATION rule. As they are generally formulated, these two transformations present strong formal analogies; both
extract a subordinate subject and convert it, either into a subject, or into
an object of the main clause. So it would apparently be desirable to unify
them under one rule. But, if their traditional formulation is kept, such a
unification poses rather serious formal problems (cf Ross, 1967, Mc-
Cawley, 1970). Yet, if we accept Postal's idea that PSYCH-MOVEMENT
intervenes in the derivation of sentences such as [26] (cf section 3), we
perceive a means of unifying these two rules into one rule, without formal
complications: the rule of RAISING into subject position would be
reduced to the rule of OBJECT-FORMATION.

Unfortunately, the unification of SUBJECT-RAISING and OBJECT-
FORMATION into a single rule runs into other difficulties, not formal this
time, but of an empirical kind. In this respect the parallelism between
[24] and [26] is deceptive. In the first place, it is not certain that the
OBJECT-FORMATION rule is justified. None of the arguments that I was
able to adduce in Chapter 2 in favour of SUBJECT-RAISING can clearly
be applied in the case of OBJECT-FORMATION.[23] I shall not discuss the
question here, but there appear to be several ways of treating the connection between [24a] and [24b] without recourse to a rule which extracts
the subject of a subordinate clause to convert it into an object. For
English, moreover, Helke (1970) and Chomsky (1973) propose a derivation for sentences such as:

[151] John expects $\left\{ \begin{array}{l} \text{Bill} \\ \text{(himself)} \end{array} \right\}$ to be arrested by the police

which does not involve OBJECT-FORMATION. However this may be,
and even supposing that OBJECT-FORMATION could be justified, it
seems impossible to unify this rule and that of SUBJECT-RAISING into
one single rule, for the good reason that the conditions of their application
are different. Let us consider the following facts:

[152] a: il me semble que Pierre $\left\{ \begin{array}{l} \text{est fou} \\ \text{est sorti hier soir} \\ \text{a compris la démonstration} \\ \text{peut faire ce travail} \end{array} \right.$

it seems to me that Peter $\begin{cases} \text{is mad} \\ \text{went out yesterday evening} \\ \text{understood the demonstration} \\ \text{can do this work} \end{cases}$

b: Pierre me semble $\begin{cases} \text{(être) fou} \\ \text{être sorti hier soir} \\ \text{avoir compris la démonstration} \\ \text{pouvoir faire ce travail} \end{cases}$

Peter seems to me $\begin{cases} \text{(to be) mad} \\ \text{to have gone out yesterday evening} \\ \text{to have understood the demonstration} \\ \text{to be able to do this work} \end{cases}$

[153] *a:* je crois que Pierre $\begin{cases} \text{est fou} \\ \text{est sorti hier soir} \\ \text{a compris la démonstration} \\ \text{peut faire ce travail} \end{cases}$

I believe that Peter $\begin{cases} \text{is mad} \\ \text{went out yesterday evening} \\ \text{understood the demonstration} \\ \text{can do this work} \end{cases}$

b: je crois Pierre $\begin{cases} \text{(*être) fou} \\ \text{(*être) *sorti hier soir} \\ \text{*avoir compris la démonstration} \\ \text{*pouvoir faire ce travail} \end{cases}$

We see that the SUBJECT-RAISING rule is not subject to any special constraint. But in contrast, the application of OBJECT-FORMATION is subject to severe restrictions; it is only possible if the subordinate verb is *être*, and in fact the past auxiliary *être* is excluded even so;[24] furthermore, *être* must be deleted obligatorily, whereas in the case of SUBJECT-RAISING this deletion is optional.

If we were to retain Postal's analysis, which derives sentences of the type of [152*b*] by successive application of OBJECT-FORMATION and PSYCH-MOVEMENT, we would be obliged to introduce a very strange condition into the grammar: OBJECT-FORMATION could not be applied without restriction unless the main verb is marked as having subsequently to undergo the application of PSYCH-MOVEMENT (this is the case with *sembler*). If on the other hand the verb is marked as being unable to undergo PSYCH-MOVEMENT (this is the case with *croire*), the OBJECT-FOR-

MATION rule would be subject to the restrictions that we have observed. No doubt it is possible to formulate such a condition, but to say the least, this would be rather undesirable and extremely *ad hoc*.

8

All the preceding discussion has shown that the PSYCH-MOVEMENT analysis of the constructions that concern us has no particular advantage over the analysis in thematic terms. But the arguments invoked up to now have been of a predominantly negative character. At best they suggest that the thematic solution is more reasonable than the transformational solution. But now I should like to proceed to a positive argument in favour of the thematic solution. This argument is interesting in that it holds good for the class of verbs in list [23] – the verbs which appear normally in the various constructions of [92–96]. This is the class of verbs for which the relation between constructions of the form $NP_1 \ldots V \ldots NP_2$ (*cf* [92–93]) and those of the form $NP_2 \ldots V \ldots NP_1$ (*cf* [95–96]) is the most regular and the most productive, which, other things being equal, would be a presumption in favour of a transformational treatment (*cf* Chomsky, 1970; but see also the discussion in sections 4 and 5).

In *Aspects*, Chomsky remarks in passing (1965, 229) that in English there are several lexical elements *strike* which differ from each other in their strict subcategorization features; this is notably the case with the verbs *strike* which appear, respectively, in [154] and [155]:

[154] John strikes me as pompous
    'John me frappe par sa suffisance'

[155] he struck me
    'il m'a frappé'

For Postal (*cf* especially 1970a, 43 *f*), the verb *strike* which appears in [154] is in fact one of those verbs in whose derivation the PSYCH-MOVEMENT rule figures, preceded by the OBJECT-FORMATION rule. This derivation is outlined in [156], and [156a] would then be the underlying structure of [154]:

[156]   *a:* I strike [S John be pompous]
                    $\to$ OBJECT-FORMATION $\to$
        b: I strike John [? be pompous]
                    $\to$ PSYCH-MOVEMENT $\to$
        c: John strike me [? be pompous]
                    $\to$ other rules $\to$ [154]

Postal does not mention the existence of the homonymous verb *strike* which appears in [155], but it is clear that he would agree in considering that, from the point of view that concerns us, its underlying structure is essentially identical with its surface structure. We see, then, that an essential difference between [154] and [155] consists in the fact that the element *me*, which, in surface structure, appears in both cases in the object position, only appears in this position in deep structure in the case of [155]; in the deep structure of [154], it appears in the subject position.

Further, it seems that, for Postal, the homonymy of the two verbs *strike* would be a pure coincidence, of the same order, no doubt, as the homonymy of the two nouns *bank* ('banking-house' versus 'river-bank') or that, in French, of the two verbs *voler* ('to fly' versus 'to steal'). In actual fact, Postal does not mention the homonymy of the two verbs *strike*, and it may seem unfair to attribute this idea to him. Nonetheless, in his long study of the verb *remind* (Postal, 1970a; see also in this book, Chapter 1, section 3.2) which poses very similar problems, and in the derivation of which he makes PSYCH-MOVEMENT play a crucial part, he says explicitly (*ibid*, 38) that 'there are really several verbs in English whose phonological shape is *remind*'. He says that he is considering only the one which appears in sentences such as *Harry reminds me of Fred Astaire*, a sentence that he paraphrases by, and derives from, something like *I perceive that Harry is similar to Fred Astaire*. According to him, this verb 'must be kept distinct from a homonym which means roughly "cause to remember"' (and which) is illustrated in *Harry reminded Betty to visit her sick uncle*'.[25] The similarity between the cases of *remind* and *strike* allows me to argue that it will not be falsifying Postal's thinking to attribute to him the idea of a pure coincidence of homonymy between the two verbs *strike*. We must point out, moreover, that several linguists (Chomsky, 1972, Ronat, 1972, etc) have criticized Postal on precisely this point. For them, the homonymy of the two verbs *remind* – which is also found in French,[26] *cf* [179] below – cannot be a coincidence.

As the translation of the English examples has already shown, French likewise has two verbs *frapper*, which, at first sight, display clear semantic, selectional and distributional differences. One, which corresponds to the *strike* of [155], appears in [157]; henceforth I shall call it *frapper*ₐ; this is an active verb, expressing a physical action, the subject of which is clearly an 'agent', and the subject and object of which must be concrete entities, though not necessarily animate. The other, which roughly corresponds to the *strike* of [154], appears in [158]; I shall call it *frapper*ᵦ; this is a stative verb, expressing a psychological process, with non-restricted subject and human object, and the properties of which are similar to those of verbs of class [23], the class of *amuser, étonner*, etc:

[157] *a:* Brutus a frappé César $\begin{cases} \text{par inadvertance} \\ \text{avec sauvagerie} \\ \text{d'un coup de poignard} \\ \text{au visage} \end{cases}$

Brutus struck Caesar $\begin{cases} \text{by mistake} \\ \text{savagely} \\ \text{with his dagger} \\ \text{in the face} \end{cases}$

b: les marteaux viennent frapper les touches du piano
the hammers come up to meet the piano-keys
·: la flèche a frappé la cible avec un bruit sec
the arrow struck the target with a dull thud

[158] *a:* Brutus a frappé César par son ambition
Brutus struck Caesar by his ambition
b: les idées de Mao ont⎫
⎬ beaucoup frappé Marie-Claire
la lecture de Freud a⎭
Mao's ideas ⎫
⎬ greatly struck Marie-Claire
reading Freud⎭
c: ça me frappe, que Marie-Claire se soit convertie au maoïsme
I'm struck (by the fact) that Marie-Claire has been converted
  to Maoism
d: la ressemblance entre Tweedledum et Tweedledee est frappante
the resemblance between Tweedledum and Tweedledee is
  striking
e: je suis frappé de la beauté de ce paysage
I am struck by the beauty of this countryside

The difference between these two verbs stands out clearly if we consider:

i: the different choice of prepositions in the instrumental or 'pseudo-instrumental' adverbials:

[159] Brutus a frappé César $\begin{cases} \begin{Bmatrix} \text{*par} \\ \text{de} \end{Bmatrix} \text{son poignard} \\ \begin{Bmatrix} \text{*de} \\ \text{par} \end{Bmatrix} \text{son ambition} \end{cases}$

$$\text{Brutus struck Caesar} \begin{cases} \begin{Bmatrix} \text{*by} \\ \text{with} \end{Bmatrix} \text{his dagger} \\ \begin{Bmatrix} \text{*with} \\ \text{by} \end{Bmatrix} \text{his ambition} \end{cases}$$

ii: the differences of behaviour in the imperative and the progressive:

[160] *a:* frappez-le au visage!
       strike him in the face!
    b: ??frappe-le par ton intelligence!
       ??strike him by your intelligence!

[161] *a:* le marquis est en train de frapper Justine à coups de fouet
       the Marquis is in the act of striking Justine with a whip
    b: ?*ce paysage est en train de me frapper par sa beauté
       ?*this countryside is in the act of striking me by its beauty

iii: the possibility or impossibility of co-occurrence with the adverbs *très* or *si . . . que S* in constructions of the form *NP être V-é par NP* (see section 4 and note 14):

[162] *a:* *la cible a été $\begin{cases} \text{très frappée par cette flèche} \\ \text{si frappée par cette flèche qu'elle} \\ \quad \text{a été percée de part en part} \end{cases}$

       *the target was $\begin{cases} \text{very struck by that arrow} \\ \text{so struck by that arrow that it was pierced} \\ \quad \text{through and through} \end{cases}$

    b: Paul-Émile a été $\begin{cases} \text{très frappé par ces événements} \\ \text{si frappé par ces événements qu'il s'est} \\ \quad \text{immédiatement inscrit au Parti} \end{cases}$

       Paul-Émile was $\begin{cases} \text{very struck by these events} \\ \text{so struck by these events that he at once} \\ \quad \text{joined the Party} \end{cases}$

iv: the impossibility of having the interpretation corresponding to *frapper*ₐ in constructions with a verbal adjective in *-ant:* [163] can only have the interpretation corresponding to *frapper*ᵦ:

[163] ces flèches sont frappantes $\begin{cases} \text{par leur longueur} \\ \text{*avec un bruit sec} \end{cases}$

    these arrows are striking $\begin{cases} \text{in (respect of) their length} \\ \text{*with a dull thud} \end{cases}$

What is correct in Postal's observations relating to the behaviour of
personally and to coreferentiality constraints likewise distinguishes
frapper$_a$ from *frapper*$_b$, cf:

[164] *a:* ?personnellement, Pierre m'a frappé au visage
            ?personally, Peter struck me in the face
        b: personnellement, Pierre me frappe par son intelligence
            personally, Peter strikes me by his intelligence

[165] *a:* ?*Pierre a été frappé par lui-même d'un coup de poignard
            ?*Peter was struck by himself with a dagger
        b: Pierre s'est frappé lui-même d'un coup de poignard
            Peter stabbed himself with a dagger

[166] ?*Pierre se frappe par son imagination
        ?*Peter is struck by his imagination

The differences between *frapper*$_a$ and *frapper*$_b$ are therefore evident.
The problem is that, in French, it is impossible to regard the homonymy
of these two verbs as a pure coincidence, for the good reason that this is
not an isolated phenomenon. There are hundreds of homonymous verbs
in French which display, broadly speaking,[27] the same characteristics as
frapper$_a$ and *frapper*$_b$. These homonymies are much more numerous than
those we listed in section 3. In view of the extent of the phenomenon, I
shall give a large number of examples. First, here are some which involve
verbs in very common use. Examples (*a*) show verbs behaving like
frapper$_a$, and I shall call this class of verbs class A; examples (*b*) show
verbs behaving like *frapper*$_b$, and this class I shall call class B:

[167] *a:* Porthos a blessé Aramis d'un coup d'épée à l'épaule
            Porthos wounded Aramis with a sword-thrust in the shoulder
        b: les remontrances du roi sont très blessantes pour d'Artagnan
            the King's remonstrances are very wounding for d'Artagnan

[168] *a:* le Bismarck a touché le Hood de trois coups au but
            the Bismarck scored three direct hits on the Hood
        b: la famille du défunt est très touchée des nombreuses marques
            de sympathie qu'elle a reçues
            the deceased's family is very touched by the many expressions of
            sympathy received

[169] *a:* en voulant la dépasser dans le virage, la Ferrari a heurté la
            roue de la Lotus
            in trying to pass it on the bend, the Ferrari bumped the wheel of
            the Lotus

    b: les idées du Women's Lib heurtent Jacques dans ses convictions
       les plus intimes
      the ideas of Women's Lib offend James's deepest convictions

[170] *a:* les C.R.S. ont assommé ce pauvre diable à coups de matraques
      the C.R.S. clubbed this poor devil down
    b: les films d'Antonioni me paraissent tout à fait assommants
      Antonioni's films seem to me utterly boring

[171] *a:* Porthos a dévoré trois faisans entiers en dix minutes
      Porthos devoured three whole pheasants in ten minutes
    b: Abélard était dévoré de passion pour Héloïse
      Abélard was devoured by passion for Héloïse

[172] *a:* les Byzantins avaient coutume d'aveugler leurs empereurs
      déchus
      the Byzantines customarily blinded their deposed Emperors
    b: la haine des Juifs aveuglait les Nazis
      hatred of the Jews blinded the Nazis

[173] *a:* Vince Stone a saisi brutalement Debbie à la gorge
      Vince Stone brutally gripped Debbie by the throat
    b: l'interprétation de James Cagney dans *White Heat* est saisissante
      (de vérité)
      James Cagney's interpretation in *White Heat* is gripping (in its
      truth)

[174] *a:* le serpent a fasciné sa proie, puis lui a sauté dessus
      the snake fascinated its prey, then leapt upon it
    b: la beauté d'Ava Gardner {fascinait les spectateurs / était fascinante

      Ava Gardner's beauty {fascinated the audience / was fascinating

[175] *a:* la fumée troublait l'atmosphère de la pièce
      the smoke clouded the atmosphere of the room
    b: je suis très troublé de cette coïncidence
      I am very disturbed at this coincidence

And now here is a (very incomplete) list of verbs which appear in both
types of construction:

[176]   *agacer* (to irritate), *altérer* (to make thirsty, to change, to im-
      pair), *alanguir* (to enfeeble), *abasourdir* (to stun, to dumbfound),
      affaiblir (to weaken), *agiter* (to shake, to agitate), *anéantir* (to

annihilate), *aigrir* (to sour), *apaiser* (to pacify, to appease), *ahurir* (to daze), *atteindre* (to reach), *accrocher* (to hook), *affoler* (to madden), *attacher* (to attach), *attirer* (to attract), *affecter* (to affect), *achever* (to complete, to finish off/dispatch), *assombrir* (to darken), *bouleverser* (to overturn), *broyer* (to crush), *brûler* (to burn), *briser* (to break), *blinder* (to shield, to protect), *charmer* (to charm), *choquer* (to shock), *casser* (to break), *caresser* (to caress), *chiffonner* (to rumple, to vex), *coincer* (to wedge, to corner), *calmer* (to calm), *consumer* (to consume), *contracter* (to contract), *claquer* (to bang, to tire), *couler* (to glide, to sink), *crucifier* (to crucify), *chatouiller* (to tickle), *corrompre* (to corrupt), *débiliter* (to debilitate), *défoncer* (to smash in), *détourner* (to divert), *démanger* (to itch), *désemparer* (to disable), *disperser* (to disperse), *détruire* (to destroy), *défriser* (to uncurl, to vex), *détendre* (to loosen), *déchirer* (to tear up), *démonter* (to unseat, to disconcert), *dérouter* (to lead astray), *désorienter* (to disorientate), *déranger* (to disarrange, to disturb), *dégrader* (to degrade), *doucher* (to shower, to douse, to disappoint), *distraire* (to divert), *éblouir* (to dazzle), *exciter* (to excite), *épater* (to cripple the foot of (an animal), to astound), *énerver* (to hamstring, to enervate), *écraser* (to crush), *édifier* (to build, to edify), *embarrasser* (to encumber, to embarrass), *empoisonner* (to poison), *ensorceler* (to bewitch), *endormir* (to put to sleep, to benumb), *éreinter* (to break the back of, to exhaust, to vilify), *égarer* (to lead astray), *étouffer* (to smother), *emmerder* (to make dirty, to annoy), *étourdir* (to stun), *épuiser* (to exhaust), *exténuer* (to emaciate, to exhaust), *éprouver* (to test, to experience), *écarteler* (to quarter, to tear apart), *échauder* (to scald), *éclabousser* (to splash), *écorcher* (to flay), *effleurer* (to skim, to graze), *égratigner* (to scratch), *émousser* (to blunt), *empoigner* (to grasp), *encombrer* (to encumber), *emberlificoter* (to entangle, to wheedle), *embraser* (to set fire to), *enterrer* (to bury), *enfiévrer* (to make feverish), *enivrer* (to intoxicate), *envahir* (to invade), *étrangler* (to strangle), *enchanter* (to enchant), *ébranler* (to shake), *éclairer* (to illuminate), *emballer* (to pack, wrap up, to arrest (someone), to race (an engine), to excite, to reprimand), *foudroyer* (to blast, to strike (by lightning)), *fracasser* (to shatter), *froisser* (to bruise, crumple), *fatiguer* (to tire), *flatter* (to stroke, flatter), *foutre*[28] (obscene), *gêner* (to impede, hinder), *glacer* (to freeze), *griser* (to tint grey, to make tipsy), *irriter* (to irritate), *illuminer* (to illuminate), *inquiéter* (to disquiet), *lasser* (to weary), *miner* (to undermine), *marquer* (to mark), *mortifier* (to mortify), *mordre* (to bite), *nouer* (to knot, to tie together), *outrager* (to insult), *percer* (to pierce), *peler* (to depilate, peel, to strip (someone of his property)), *perturber* (to perturb), *pénétrer* (to penetrate), *prendre* (to take), *purifier* (to purify), *révolter* (to (induce to) revolt), *ruiner* (to ruin), *retourner* (to turn back), *ronger* (to gnaw), *renverser* (to upset, overturn), *remuer* (to move), *refroidir* (to cool), *rafraîchir* (to refresh), *rompre* (to break), *raser* (to shave, to skim, pass close to), *secouer* (to shake), *séduire* (to seduce), *surprendre* (to surprise), *saper* (to sap), *sonner* (to sound, to knock (someone's head)), *saouler* (to surfeit, to intoxicate), *suffoquer* (to suffocate), *submerger* (to submerge), *subjuguer* (to subjugate), *stupéfier* (to stupefy, bemuse), *tordre* (to twist), *tourmenter* (to torment), *torturer* (to torture), *tuer* (to kill), *tracasser* (to fuss, worry), *travailler* (to work, to torment), *tenailler* (to tear with pincers, to torture), *tripoter* (to finger, to meddle with, to paw (someone)), *trahir* (to betray), *troubler* (to make cloudy, to disturb), *tanner* (to tan, to bore, pester), *vanner* (to winnow, to tire out), *vider* (to empty, to tire or exhaust (someone)), etc.

We find the same duality in verbs which appear in other more or less complex syntactic constructions,[29] thus:

[177] *a:* Mélisande a souri tendrement à Pelléas
       Mélisande smiled tenderly at Pelléas
    b: personnellement, ce projet ne me sourit pas
       personally, this plan does not appeal to me

[178] *a:* Bacchus a rempli le tonneau d'hydromel
       Bacchus filled the cask with mead
    b: l'échec de ses entreprises avait rempli Philippe II d'amertume
       the failure of his undertakings had filled Philip II with bitterness

[179] *a:* la sécretaire a rappelé à son patron un rendez-vous urgent
       the secretary reminded her employer of an urgent appointment
    b: personnellement, la lagune de Venise me rappelle toujours
         l'*Invitation au Voyage*
       personally, the Lagoon of Venice always reminds me of the
         Invitation au Voyage

[180] *a:* Hercule a cassé le bras au titan
Hercules broke the Titan's arm

b: ça me casse les pieds de devoir écrire cet article
it's a terrible bore for me to have to write this article

[181] *a:* Oedipe s'est crevé les yeux avec la fibule d'or de Jocaste
Oedipus put out his eyes with Jocasta's golden fibula

b: ça crève les yeux, qu'il y a quelque chose de pourri au royaume de Danemark
it stares you in the face that something is rotten in the state of Denmark

[182] *a:* 'Qu'on leur coupe la tête à tous!' a dit le vainqueur
'Cut off everybody's head!' said the conqueror

b: la beauté du *Tombeau hindou*, ça vous coupe le souffle!
the beauty of *Le Tombeau hindou* takes your breath away!

[183] *a:* les C.R.S. lui ont tapé sur la tête, à ce pauvre diable
the C.R.S. hit him on the head, poor devil

b: personnellement, la lenteur de l'administration universitaire me tape sur les nerfs
personally, the slowness of the University administration gets on my nerves

[184] *a:* le médecin a fait vomir Madeleine en lui donnant un émétique
the doctor made Madeleine vomit by giving her an emetic

b: la laideur des films de Fellini me fait vomir
the ugliness of Fellini's films makes me sick

[185] *a:* Roméo a fait rire Juliette en lui chatouillant la plante des pieds avec un brin d'herbe
Romeo made Juliet laugh by tickling the soles of her feet with a blade of grass

b: ça me fait rire, qu'on prenne la traduction automatique au sérieux
it's absurd that machine translation is taken seriously

[186] *a:* 'Qu'est-ce que le marquis a fait à Justine?' – 'Il l'a fouettée jusqu'au sang'
'What did the Marquis do to Justine?' – 'He whipped her till the blood ran'

b: 'Qu'est-ce que ça te fait, que Marie te trompe avec Gustave?' – 'Ça m'ennuie horriblement'
'Do you care if Mary is deceiving you with Gustave?' – 'I mind terribly'

The reader can easily ascertain that, as a whole, the verbs of examples (*a*) behave like *frapper*_a syntactically and from the point of view of selectional restrictions, and those of examples (*b*) like *frapper*_b. This holds good, with the reservations made earlier, for the features described by Postal, like the behaviour of *personnellement* – *cf* [187], and also [177], [179], [183] – or the differences in the restrictions on the coreferentiality of the subject and the object – *cf* [188]:

[187] *a:* ??'Personnellement,' dit à Hamlet le spectre de son père, 'Claudius m'a empoisonné pendant mon sommeil'

        ??'Personally,' the ghost of Hamlet's father said to him, 'Claudius poisoned me while I slept'

    b: 'Personnellement,' dit à Hamlet le spectre de son père, 'ça m'empoisonne que Claudius couche avec ta mère'

        'Personally,' the ghost of Hamlet's father said to him, 'it embitters me that Claudius is sleeping with your mother'

[188] *a:* le tonneau s'est rempli de bière
       the cask filled with beer

    b: *Philippe II s'est rempli d'amertume
       *Philip II filled with bitterness

It is obvious that we have here a very general and productive phenomenon, and that there is a systematic relationship between verb classes A and B: a grammar of French which did not account for this would be inadequate. Furthermore, in the majority of cases, every native speaker of French has the intuition of a semantic relation between the two homonymous verbs. Broadly speaking, and in an impressionistic way, this relation can be expressed in the following way. In examples (*a*) as well as in examples (*b*), the verbs describe a process of which the subject NP designates the cause, and this process affects or has an effect in some way on the being or object designated by the object NP. The difference is that, in examples (*a*), the effect in question is of a purely physical order, whereas, in examples (*b*), the effect is psychological and mental. These verbs, then, whether they belong to class A or to class B (or, in a general way, to class [23]), are comparable with the factitives or causatives studied in the preceding chapter. Chomsky (1970) has in fact suggested treating a verb like *amuse* as a causative of *be amused at*. This semantic aspect of these verbs does not appear in the treatment by PSYCH-MOVEMENT.

Further, for all the productivity of the phenomenon, there can be all sorts of idiosyncratic differences between the homonymous verbs of type

A and of type B. Constructions [180–185], very productive in cases (*a*), nearly always have an idiosyncratic sense in cases (*b*). A verb like *impressionner*, typical of class [23]B, does exist as a verb of type A, but in a very restricted and technical sense, in the expression *impressionner une plaque photographique* (to make an impression on a photographic plate). In the same way, *énerver*$_b$, which is in very general use, is remote from *énerver*$_a$, which is somewhat archaic but is still given in dictionaries with the sense of 'inflicting the torture of hamstringing'. *Éblouir*$_a$ (*cf* [206] below) does not have the connotation of wonderment of *éblouir*$_b$ (*cf* [208]), etc. Many verbs of type B belong to a very familiar level of style, and their sense is often difficult to predict from the sense of the corresponding verb of type A: this is the case with *raser, peler, épater, emballer, doucher, sonner, tanner, vanner*, etc. Further, we know from their etymology that many verbs which are today principally or exclusively of type B, used to belong to type A. *Navrer*, which today is practically synonymous with *attrister* (to sadden or grieve), meant *blesser*$_a$ (to wound) in the Middle Ages; *étonner*, which is today synonymous with *surprendre*$_b$ (to surprise), used to have the sense of *foudroyer* (to thunder, to blast) (which itself exists today as a verb of type B, with a clear-cut metaphorical import); *tourmenter*, in earlier times synonymous with *torturer*$_a$, is now archaic in this sense and has taken on a specialized sense as type B, whereas *torturer*$_b$ is still felt as metaphorical. But these constant diachronic changes from type A to type B only serve to confirm the productivity of the phenomenon and its systematic character.

9

It is not easy to see how a grammar which has recourse to PSYCH-MOVEMENT to derive sentences of type B but not those of type A could account for the systematic correspondence that has just been described. Given the frequency of occurrence of homonymy in natural languages, it might be thought necessary to incorporate in general linguistic theory a principle which accords a higher value to a grammar which allows a fairly high proportion of homonyms than to a grammar which allows very few or none at all.[30] But, apart from the fact that it is not easy to see how to formulate this principle, it could not account for what is at issue here – namely the productivity of the phenomenon, and the systematic semantic correspondence between verbs of type A and verbs of type B. In a general way, such a principle would not enable us to account for the differences, intuitively perceived by native speakers, between various sorts of 'homonyms', such as, on the one hand, the difference between *voler* (to fly) and *voler* (to steal) (an accidental homonymy), and, on the other hand, the difference between *frapper*ₐ and *frapper*ᵦ.

A grammar incorporating PSYCH-MOVEMENT cannot account for this correspondence at the level of underlying structure, since it attributes radically different underlying structures to sentences with A verbs and sentences with B verbs. Neither can it account for it at the level of surface structure: in fact, in the theoretical frame which Postal adopts – that of generative semantics – the surface structure plays no part in the semantic interpretation of sentences, and all semantic differences and resemblances between sentences must be expressed in the underlying structure. In any case, even if we limit ourselves to accounting for the similarities of form, we cannot, as Chomsky notes in connection with the similar case of *remind* (see above), 'argue that some "output condition" on surface... structure requires this similarity of form for the various cases of *remind*, since the regularity illustrated ... is stateable only prior to transformational rules (such as passive) that yield surface...structures' (Chomsky, 1972).

It would be possible – assuming always that we limit ourselves to accounting for formal similarities – to imagine a principle operating at the level of lexical insertion. We could say, for example, that if a grammar contains, on the one hand, derivations generating sentences of type A (derivations in which no crucial transformation intervenes between the underlying structure and the surface structure), and, on the other hand, derivations generating sentences of type B (derivations in which PSYCH-MOVEMENT intervenes in a crucial manner), a principle governing lexical insertion predicts a high proportion of homonyms among the verbs appearing in these two types of derivation. But this principle would be no more natural than a principle predicting, for example, a high proportion of homonyms among verbs appearing in the derivation of sentences of type A, on the one hand, and verbs appearing in the derivation of sentences of the type of [1] (*cf* verbs of class [22], *mépriser, aimer*, etc), a derivation which does not involve PSYCH-MOVEMENT. In fact, such a principle could predict homonymies between two arbitrary classes of verbs, V_i and V_j, appearing in two arbitrary classes of derivations based on two classes of arbitrarily different underlying semantic structures.

Actually, the only natural way of accounting for the 'homonymy' between verbs of type A and those of type B consists in adopting the solution that we advocate. Some at least of the deep structures in which verbs A and B can appear are essentially identical (these are the ones that correspond to the frame [92] above). As grammatical relations determine a fundamental aspect of the semantic interpretation, it is not surprising that there should be something in common between the semantic interpretation of the relation between the verb and the object in the A cases and the semantic interpretation of the same relation in the B cases. On the other hand, that there should also be semantic differences is not surprising either, if we agree (*cf* Jackendoff, 1969b and Chapter 4 of this book) that the semantic representation of sentences is not a simple and direct projection of the deep syntactic structure, but that it is related to it by interpretation rules which can be quite complex.

In reality the facts are even more favourable to this solution than the examples given up to now and our brief comments on their interpretation might lead one to suppose. In fact, up to now, I have proceeded as though there were a sharp dichotomy between the A verbs and the B verbs. But this is a deceptive simplification. We have already seen that certain syntactic features characteristic of verbs of type B (for example, the possibility of occurrence in the frames [93], [95], [96]) are missing in a certain number of these verbs, even if these verbs describe psychological processes. Often the consequence of this is to bring the syntax of these verbs closer to that of the 'homonymous' verbs of type A. Consider, for example, a verb like *effleurer*. Facts like those of [189–190] indicate making a distinction between an *effleurer*$_a$, a verb of physical action, and an *effleurer*$_b$, a 'psychological' verb:

[189] *a:* la balle a effleuré $\begin{cases} \text{le mur} \\ \text{l'épaule de Clark Gable} \\ \text{*l'esprit de Hamlet} \end{cases}$

the bullet grazed $\begin{cases} \text{the wall} \\ \text{Clark Gable's shoulder} \\ \text{*Hamlet's mind} \end{cases}$

b: cette idée a effleuré $\begin{cases} \text{*le mur} \\ \text{*l'épaule de Clark Gable} \\ \text{l'esprit de Hamlet} \end{cases}$

this idea flitted across $\begin{cases} \text{*the wall} \\ \text{*Clark Gable's shoulder} \\ \text{Hamlet's mind} \end{cases}$

[190] *a:* ??personnellement, cette balle m'a effleuré
      ??personally, that bullet grazed me
   b: personnellement, cette idée ne m'a même pas effleuré
      personally, that idea never even occurred to me

But, apart from the fact that the subject of *effleurer*$_b$ is governed by fairly severe selectional restrictions[31] (it is not non-restricted in Gross's sense, 1968, 1969), we notice that all sorts of constructions, which are possible for *frapper*$_b$ and impossible for *frapper*$_a$, are equally impossible both for *effleurer*$_a$ and *effleurer*$_b$, cf:

[191] *a:* *cette balle est effleurante (pour Clark Gable)
      b: *cette idée est effleurante (pour Hamlet)

[192] *a:* Clark Gable a été (*très) effleuré par cette balle
          Clark Gable was (*very) grazed by that bullet
      b: Hamlet a été (*très) effleuré par cette idée
          Hamlet was (*very) visited by that idea

[193] *a:* *Clark Gable s'effleure d'une balle[32]
      b: *Hamlet s'effleure d'une drôle d'idée

As we see, *effleurer*$_b$ cannot appear in frames [93] (*cf* [191]) and [96] (*cf* [193]), any more than *effleurer*$_a$ can; as to the impossibility of having *très* (or *si . . . que S*) in [192], this indicates that both verbs behave in the same way in passive sentences (compare with [162] above). In fact, apart from the selectional differences noted in [189–190], one of the few differences between *effleurer*$_a$ and *effleurer*$_b$ lies in the fact that the latter can have a 'passive' in *de*, cf:[33]

[194] *a:* Clark Gable a été effleuré $\left\{ \begin{array}{l} \text{*d'} \\ \text{par} \end{array} \right\}$ une balle

          Clark Gable was grazed by a bullet

      b: Hamlet a été effleuré $\left\{ \begin{array}{l} \text{d'} \\ \text{par} \end{array} \right\}$ un terrible soupçon

          Hamlet was visited by a terrible suspicion

Effleurer is not the only verb to show characteristics of this sort. To take one property only, many verbs that other criteria lead us to assign to class B cannot appear in frame [93], *cf* the impossibility of:

[195] cette idée $\left\{ \begin{array}{l} \text{heurte} \\ \text{*est heurtante pour} \end{array} \right\}$ Paul

      this idea $\left\{ \begin{array}{l} \text{offends} \\ \text{*is offending for} \end{array} \right\}$ Paul

[196] la vue de tous ces cadavres $\left\{\begin{array}{l}\text{agite}\\ \text{*est agitante pour}\end{array}\right\}$ Attila

the sight of all these corpses $\left\{\begin{array}{l}\text{disturbs}\\ \text{*is disturbing for}\end{array}\right\}$ Attila

In short, the syntactic differences between A verbs and B verbs are not always as distinct as was at first stated. In the same way, from the semantic point of view, the dichotomy between physical and psychological processes is less well-marked than might be supposed. More precisely, for a large number of verbs, we find different shades of meaning which cannot be reduced simply to this dichotomy (differences that may also be accompanied by variations in syntactic properties). Thus, alongside *frapper*$_a$ and *frapper*$_b$, we find all sorts of uses of *frapper* which cannot be assigned to either of them, although having semantic elements in common with both of them, *cf:*

[197] un rayon de soleil frappait les bibelots
a ray of sunlight struck the ornaments

[198] un bruit étrange a frappé mes oreilles
a strange sound struck my ears

[199] le malheur a plusieurs fois frappé cette famille
misfortune has struck this family several times

[200] une taxe spéciale frappe les produits de luxe
a special tax falls on luxury articles

[201] les récentes mesures prises par Nixon frappent particulièrement
les Japonais
the measures recently taken by Nixon hit the Japanese particularly

Various differences in syntactic behaviour correspond to these differences of meaning, *cf:*[34]

[202] *a:* les bibelots sont frappés $\left\{\begin{array}{l}\text{?par}\\ \text{*d'}\end{array}\right\}$ un rayon de soleil

b: *le rayon de soleil est frappant pour les bibelots

[203] *a:* mes oreilles ont été brusquement (*très) frappées par un bruit
étrange
b: *ce bruit étrange est (très) frappant pour mes oreilles

[204] les produits de luxe sont frappés $\left\{\begin{array}{l}\text{par}\\ \text{d'}\end{array}\right\}$ une taxe spéciale

[205] *a:* *les récentes mesures prises par Nixon sont frappantes pour les
Japonais

b: les Japonais sont frappés $\left\{ \begin{array}{l} \text{par les} \\ \text{*des} \end{array} \right\}$ mesures prises par Nixon

Many of these verbs can express a perceptual process, a sensation
experienced by the referent of the object NP. Thus we have:

[206] *a:* les phares de la Ferrari ont brusquement ébloui le conducteur de
la 2CV
the headlights of the Ferrari suddenly dazzled the driver of the
2CV

b: le conducteur de la 2CV a été (délibérément) (*très) ébloui

$\left\{ \begin{array}{l} \text{par} \\ \text{*de} \end{array} \right\}$ celui de la Ferrari (avec ses phares)

the driver of the 2CV was (deliberately) (*very) dazzled by the
driver of the Ferrari (with his headlights)

c: ??personnellement, ces phares m'ont brusquement ébloui
??personally, those headlights suddenly dazzled me

[207] *a:* ces phares sont trop éblouissants
those headlights are too dazzling

b: *le conducteur de la 2CV est (très) ébloui de ces phares

c: personnellement, cette lumière m'éblouit
personally, that light dazzles me

[208] *a:* la beauté de Marlène était éblouissante
Marlene's beauty was dazzling

b: les spectateurs étaient (très) éblouis de la beauté de Marlène
the audience was (very) dazzled by Marlene's beauty

c: personnellement, la beauté de Marlène m'éblouit
personally, Marlene's beauty dazzles me

Clearly, in [208], *éblouir* belongs to type B; it is a 'psychological' verb.
On the other hand, in [206], *éblouir* belongs to type A; the sentences of
[206] are typical agentive sentences, as is shown by the possibility of
having instrumental or manner adverbials relating to the deep subject,
the impossibility of *très* and of the passive in *de*, and the somewhat unnatural character of *personnellement*. But [207] has an intermediate status.
From the point of view of its sense, it clearly belongs with [206], but
[207*a*] and [207*c*] are completely parallel with [208*a*] and [208*c*]. This
intermediate status is clearly apparent if we consider that the *éblouir* of

[207] can, like the B verbs, appear in frame [93] (with verbal adjective in -*ant*), but that, unlike the B verbs and like the A verbs, it cannot appear in frame [95] (with verbal adjective in -*é*) (*cf* [207*b*]). Postal included 'sensation predicates' among predicates subject to PSYCH-MOVEMENT (*cf* [38–40] above); this would entail putting the *éblouir* of [207] in the same class as that of [208], and in contrasting it with that of [206]. We see the arbitrariness of such a division.

Another example is that of the verb *gêner*, *cf*:

[209] *a:* Jack Brabham a (délibérément) (*très) gêné Pedro Rodriguez
dans le virage
Jack Brabham (deliberately) (*very) impeded Pedro Rodriguez
at the bend

b: cette voiture en stationnement interdit $\begin{Bmatrix} \text{gêne} \\ \text{est gênante pour} \end{Bmatrix}$

$\begin{Bmatrix} \text{la circulation} \\ \text{les usagers} \end{Bmatrix}$

this car in the no-parking area $\begin{Bmatrix} \text{obstructs} \\ \text{is in the way of} \end{Bmatrix}$

$\begin{Bmatrix} \text{the traffic} \\ \text{the road-users} \end{Bmatrix}$

c: ces souliers $\begin{Bmatrix} \text{me gênent} \\ \text{sont gênants} \end{Bmatrix}$ pour marcher

these shoes $\begin{Bmatrix} \text{pinch me·} \\ \text{are uncomfortable} \end{Bmatrix}$ for walking

d: personnellement, cette lumière trop vive me gêne
personally, that over-bright light bothers me

e: ça gêne Ursule, de devoir raconter toutes ces choses horribles à
son psychanalyste
it embarrasses Ursula to have to tell all these horrible things to
her psycho-analyst

The examples could be multiplied, but these will suffice. We see that it would be very difficult to establish a definite dichotomy that would be significant both from the syntactic and from the semantic point of view. If we insisted at all costs upon introducing PSYCH-MOVEMENT into the derivation of some of the sentences of [206–209], it is not easy to see where the dividing line could be drawn. But in contrast, if we give up PSYCH-MOVEMENT, this difficulty disappears. The deep structures of

[209a–e] are, essentially, similar to their surface structures, and the identity of the subject-verb and verb-object grammatical relations of the base enables us to account for the semantic similarities between all these sentences. As to the syntactic and semantic differences, the first could be treated in terms of strict subcategorization, and the second in terms of interpretation rules. In effect, these facts serve to confirm Chomsky's view that 'the properties of lexical items are formulable in terms of a set of phrase-markers that are defined by the categorial rules of the base' (Chomsky, 1972),

We may observe in passing that it is quite instructive to consider the way in which traditional dictionaries describe the various uses of the verbs in question. If the A and the B verbs constituted two distinct classes with, as Postal would have it, different derivational histories, we might expect to find that they would be classed as separate entries by the dictionaries in every instance. We saw in Chapter 3 that traditional dictionaries class related transitive and neutral (pronominal) verbs (*casser NP* versus *se casser*) as separate entries. Indeed, if we consult the *Dictionnaire du Français contemporain* by Dubois *et al* (1966), we see that this dictionary assigns two separate entries, for example, to *toucher*a and *toucher*b (*cf* [168]). Similarly, it gives two separate entries for *blesser*a and *blesser*b (*cf* [167]), but treats as a special case of *blesser*a the *blesser* which appears in sentences such as *ces couleurs criardes blessent la vue*, (these garish colours offend the eye), *cette musique de sauvages blesse nos oreilles*, (this jungle music offends our ears), when it clearly has features in common with *blesser*b (*cf: cette musique est blessante pour les oreilles; personnellement, ces couleurs blessent ma vue*, etc). It does not distinguish this *blesser* with a sensorial and perceptual content from the *blesser* which appears in *j'ai les pieds blessés par ces chaussures* (my feet have been hurt by these boots). As for *frapper*, although this dictionary distinguishes three main entries, two of which are idiomatic (*frapper monnaie* (to mint money), *frapper les touches d'une machine à écrire* (to strike the keys of a typewriter)), and are clearly connected with *frapper*a by metonymy, it classes all the cases in which we differentiated *frapper*a from *frapper*b, examples [197–201] included, under one entry only, as particular cases of one and the same verb. *Heurter*a and *heurter*b are likewise classed under a single entry. These hesitations and inconsistencies clearly cannot be taken, as such, as an argument in favour of a particular analysis. But, insofar as dictionary classifications reflect more or less faithfully the intuitions of native speakers, they seem to me to be an additional indication of the existence of a continuum between cases A and B.

10

It is not enough to have shown the unity underlying the differences between verbs of type A and type B, nor to have indicated that only a solution which excludes PSYCH-MOVEMENT and inserts these verbs in identical deep structures can account for this unity. Several problems still remain.

For some of the verbs of [167–176], such as *gêner, perturber, troubler*, one might indeed think that the difference between the homonymous verbs A and B depends solely on the physical, perceptual or psychological nature of the process expressed by the verb. An apparent solution would then be to have in each case a single verb *gêner, perturber, troubler*, etc, in the lexicon. A verb like *gêner* would then have the following lexical entry:

[210] *gêner:* [+V], [+ —— NP], [+ —— [+LOCATION]], . . . ,

ie essentially the same entry as *dégoûter* (*cf* [21]), but without the feature [+ —— [+HUMAN]].[35] The physical, perceptual or psychological nature of the process expressed would not be indicated in this entry, but would be given by lexical redundancy rules, which would be a function of the features appearing in [210]. The other differences (agentive or non-agentive interpretation of the subject, possibility of having non-restricted subjects, limitation of the object to [+HUMAN] NPs, possibility of appearing in certain of the frames of [92–96] etc) would be given in terms of other redundancy rules depending on the choice of features [+PHYSICAL], [+PERCEPTUAL], [+PSYCHOLOGICAL], introduced by this first redundancy rule. Some of these rules would perhaps be universal, and would not therefore have to appear in the grammar of French.

One difficulty that arises is as follows. For many of the verbs of [167–176], the relationship between type A and type B is perceived by native speakers as being a metaphorical one. In the case of *gêner, troubler*, etc, the various shades of meaning are to some extent on the same footing; they belong to the same level of standard style. But this is not general. Take for example the verb *tuer:*

[211] *a:* Hagen a tué Siegfried $\begin{cases} \text{par traîtrise} \\ \text{d'un coup de lance} \end{cases}$

Hagen killed Siegfried $\begin{cases} \text{by treachery} \\ \text{by a lance-thrust} \end{cases}$

    b: personnellement, ça me tue de devoir écouter l'intégrale de la
        Tétralogie par Furtwängler
    personally, it kills me to have to listen to the whole of the
    Tetralogy by Furtwängler

For me, [211*a*] and [211*b*] are not at all on the same plane as, for
example, [209*a*] on the one hand, and [209*d–e*] on the other hand. [211*b*]
contains a metaphorical element (whatever the exact meaning that one
gives to this notion),[36] which is not contained in [211*a*] nor in any of the
sentences of [209]. An indication of this metaphorical value is given by
the possibility of the adverb *littéralement* occurring in [211*b*], whereas the
presence of this adverb in [211*a*] would seem bizarre or redundant, *cf:*

[212] *a:* ? ?Hagen a littéralement tué Siegfried d'un coup de lance
      ? ?Hagen literally killed Siegfried with a lance-thrust
    b: ça me tue littéralement de devoir écouter l'intégrale de la
        Tétralogie par Furtwängler
      it literally kills me to have to listen to the whole of the *Tetralogy*
      by Furtwängler

If we put this adverb into sentences with type A verbs, on the one hand,
and into sentences with type B verbs on the other hand, we see:

  i: that in sentences with A verbs, the result is, generally, bizarre, as in
[212*a*], *cf:*

[213] ? ?la flèche a littéralement touché la cible
      ? ?the arrow literally hit the target

  ii: that in sentences with B verbs, sometimes the result is equally
bizarre, *cf:*

[214] ? ?Brutus frappait littéralement César par son ambition
      ? ?Brutus literally struck Caesar by his ambition
and sometimes the result is acceptable, *cf:*

[215] la passion aveuglait littéralement Isolde
      passion literally blinded Isolda

[216] *Le Désert rouge,* c'est littéralement assommant
      The Red Desert is literally exhausting

In some cases, that of *blesser,* for example, the presence of *littéralement*
shows up the metaphorical nature of *blesser*$_b$, whereas *blesser*$_a$ and *blesser*$_b$
are normally both perceived as being stylistically neutral. *Cf:*

[217] j'ai été littéralement blessé par cette remarque
      I was literally wounded by that remark

In cases of this sort, we might be tempted to consider the signification of type A ('physical process') as primary. We should then have only one lexical entry for *tuer, assommer*, etc. These verbs would appear in the lexicon with only the specification 'physical process', and the metaphorical usages would be described by means of 'transfer' rules, which would perhaps be universal also. We should then have two different mechanisms for treating related phenomena. Furthermore, the existence of intermediate cases like that of *blesser* would pose a problem.

But in any event, there remain the many cases of syntactic and/or semantic idiosyncrasy (special selectional restrictions on *effleurer*$_b$, the connotation of wonderment present in *éblouir*$_b$ or *fasciner*$_b$ and absent in the corresponding A verbs, possibility or impossibility of occurrence in the frame [93], technical sense of *impressionner*$_a$, etc). In a large number of cases, the sense of a B verb cannot be directly predicted from the sense of the corresponding A verb (and vice versa). In all these cases, it seems inevitable that we should have separate lexical entries for A verbs and for B verbs.

Another sizeable problem is posed by the apparent conflict between the analysis that I have proposed for the B verbs in thematic terms (*cf* [21], [210]), and the suggestion that they should be treated as causative verbs (*cf* the end of section 8), the corresponding A verbs being causative verbs as well. To understand the nature of this problem it will be useful to take up some remarks of Fillmore's (1970).

Fillmore has made a study of some English verbs which, according to our criteria, would be ranked in class A: *break* ('casser'), *hit* ('toucher', 'frapper', etc). He considers them in their 'basic' meaning – in which they express physical actions – and does not concern himself with their 'transferred' meanings. He divides these verbs into two semantic classes. Verbs like *break* are 'change-of-state' verbs; they 'assert that the object ... is understood as undergoing some kind of change of state'. The others, which are 'surface-contact' verbs, such as *hit*, 'assert the occurrence of some physical contact between two objects, but from the use of these verbs one cannot necessarily infer that the objects have undergone any essential change' (Fillmore, 1970, 125). Fillmore expresses these differences in the terms of his theory of case (*cf* Fillmore, 1968), which has certain points in common with the theory of thematic functions. He attributes different cases to the object NPs: for verbs of the first class, he postulates an 'objective' case, only 'for want of a better term', and for the others he suggests a 'locative' case – this latter term seems to be the equivalent of our thematic function of 'location'. In other words, only verbs of the first class would have a causative character: these verbs assert that the subject causes a change of state in the object.

Fillmore relates these semantic differences to syntactic differences which, at first sight, appear to be found in French also. Firstly, for the change-of-state verbs there are corresponding stative adjectives, homonyms of passive past participles, which assert that the subject is in the state resulting from the process expressed by the verb; such stative adjectives are impossible in the case of surface-contact verbs. The difference is plain if we compare [218b] and [219b]:

[218] a: ce voyou a cassé la vitre
            that hooligan broke the window
       b: la vitre est restée cassée tout l'hiver
            the window stayed broken all the winter

[219] a: la flèche a touché la cible
            the arrow hit the target
       b: *la cible est restée touchée tout l'après-midi
            *the target stayed hit all the afternoon

Further, 'when the *object* or *place* noun phrase is a possessed body-part noun [inalienable possession, N.R.]... the sentences with surface-contact verbs have paraphrases[37] in which the "possessor" appears as the direct object and the body-part noun appears in a "locative prepositional phrase"' (*ibid*, 126), cf:[38]

[220] a: j'ai touché $\begin{cases} \text{son dos} \\ \text{sa jambe} \end{cases}$

       I hit (touched) $\begin{cases} \text{his back} \\ \text{his leg} \end{cases}$

       b: je l'ai touché $\begin{cases} \text{dans le dos} \\ \text{à la jambe} \end{cases}$

       I hit him $\begin{cases} \text{on the back} \\ \text{on the leg} \end{cases}$

[221] a: je lui ai cassé la jambe
            I broke his leg
       b: *je l'ai cassé à la jambe
            *I broke him on the leg

These differences of behaviour between the two types of verbs seem to challenge the idea that the object could have the same thematic function in both cases. Furthermore, when we consider the corresponding type B verbs, the relations between verb and object seem to change. If *frapper*$_a$ or *toucher*$_a$ are 'surface-contact' verbs, and *blesser*$_a$ is a 'change-of-state' verb, it certainly seems that *frapper*$_b$, *toucher*$_b$ and *blesser*$_b$ are all 'psychological change-of-state' verbs, as is shown by the possibility of having stative adjectives for all of them, *cf:*

[222] Pierre est très $\begin{Bmatrix} \text{touché} \\ \text{frappé} \\ \text{blessé} \end{Bmatrix}$ de ce que tu lui as dit

Peter is very $\begin{Bmatrix} \text{touched} \\ \text{struck} \\ \text{hurt} \end{Bmatrix}$ by what you said to him

These differences apparently give additional cause to question both the internal unity of class A and the regularity of the semantic relationship linking class A with class B. But a deeper study of the facts shows us both, that from the syntactic as well as from the semantic point of view, the distinction between 'change-of-state' verbs and 'surface-contact' verbs is much less definite than Fillmore believes, and also that the distinctions and the properties that he has indicated are in fact found in both classes, A and B. This in effect accentuates the parallelism between the two classes even if, when we take the verbs one by one, the parallelism between a type A verb and the corresponding homonym of type B is not constant.

In the first place, Fillmore's generalization relative to constructions with locative prepositional complement does not hold good. We find 'change-of-state' verbs (of type A) which allow it (*cf* [223]) and 'surface-contact' verbs which allow it only doubtfully (*cf* [224]):

[223] *a:* Biron a blessé Lusignan au visage
       Biron wounded Lusignan in the face
    b: où Biron a-t-il blessé Lusignan?
       where did Biron wound Lusignan?

[224] *a:* ??la balle a effleuré Clark Gable à la joue
       ??the bullet grazed Clark Gable on the cheek
    b: ??où la balle a-t-elle effleuré Clark Gable?
       ??where did the bullet graze Clark Gable?

Again, we find verbs of type B in constructions with a 'pseudo-locative'[39] prepositional phrase which are parallel to the constructions of [220*b*] or of [223*a*], *cf* [225], but again this type of construction is not allowed by all verbs of type B, *cf* [226]:

[225] cet échec a $\left\{\begin{array}{l}\text{blessé}\\\text{frappé}\\\text{atteint}\end{array}\right\}$ Conrad $\left\{\begin{array}{l}\text{à un point sensible}\\\text{dans son orgueil}\\\text{dans ses affections}\end{array}\right.$

this setback $\left\{\begin{array}{l}\text{hurt}\\\text{hit}\\\text{wounded}\end{array}\right\}$ Conrad $\left\{\begin{array}{l}\text{in a sensitive spot}\\\text{in his pride}\\\text{in his affections}\end{array}\right.$

[226] *cette idée a effleuré Hamlet dans son esprit
    *this idea visited Hamlet in his mind

Furthermore, verbs of type B do not all allow corresponding stative adjectives, *cf* [227]:

[227] *Hamlet est resté effleuré d'un soupçon affreux
    *Hamlet remained visited by a terrible suspicion

If we keep this criterion for distinguishing 'change-of-state' verbs and 'surface-contact' verbs, we should be led to assert that there are also 'psychological surface-contact' verbs (whatever the exact semantic content attributable to this notion might be).

Lastly, many type A verbs that a superficial examination would characterize as 'surface-contact' verbs have uses which imply a 'change of state', *cf:*

[228] la radiographie a révélé que les poumons étaient gravement atteints[40]
    the X-rays showed that the lungs were seriously affected

[229] en l'observant à la longue-vue, Nelson a pu voir que le vaisseau amiral ennemi était sérieusement touché
    observing it through the telescope Nelson was able to see that the enemy flag-ship was badly hit

These facts throw doubt on the usefulness of a sharp distinction expressed in terms of case differences ('locative' versus 'objective') or thematic functions ('location' versus 'the affected'), between the objects of the different verbs. I would be inclined to think that all these verbs should be marked [+ —— [+LOCATION]], and that some of them, in certain conditions, imply a change of state in their object.[41]

Additionally, these facts confirm the overall parallelism of classes A and B, the same complications being found within both classes.

11

One cannot hope to resolve definitively all the problems outlined in the preceding section. I should simply like to suggest a solution which might be worth exploring more thoroughly. This solution relates to the theory of 'markedness', introduced in phonology by Chomsky and Halle (1968, Chapter 9), who were thus taking up some earlier ideas of the Prague School. For the sake of simplicity, I shall confine myself to verbs of type A (physical processes) and type B (psychological processes), not taking into account the intermediate cases that were noted, like the verbs (homonyms of A and/or B verbs) which express perceptual processes. But the solution proposed could also be extended to deal with these cases. I would also add that several of the features mentioned in the following discussion (for example [+CHANGE] to mark change-of-state verbs, [+PHYS] to designate 'physical processes', and [+PSYCH] to designate 'psychological processes') are *ad hoc* and would need to be analysed more deeply. Here I am interested in presenting a certain mechanism and in showing how it functions in simplified examples.

In the first place, we decide to assign a separate, fully specified lexical entry to every verb which has syntactic and/or semantic properties of its own. In other words, all the homonymous verbs considered receive separate lexical entries; for example, there are (at least) three verbs *toucher* – *toucher*$_{a1}$, a 'physical surface-contact' verb, *toucher*$_{a2}$, a 'physical change-of-state' verb, *toucher*$_{b}$, a 'psychological change-of-state' verb; in the same way, there are at least two verbs *impressionner*, and two *effleurer*, etc. Each property is specified, and we shall have the following entries, for instance, (where only some properties are specified, by way of example):

[230] *toucher*$_{a1}$: [+V], [+ —— NP], [+ —— [+LOCATION]],
 [+PHYS], [−CHANGE], [−NP *être* [$_A$ —— -*ant*]], . . .

[231] *toucher*$_{a2}$: [+V], [+ —— NP], [+ —— [+LOCATION]],
 [+PHYS], [+CHANGE], [−NP *être* [$_A$ —— -*ant*]], . . .

[232] *toucher*$_{b}$: [+V], [+ —— NP], [+ —— [+LOCATION]], [+PSYCH],
 [+CHANGE], [+NP *être* [$_A$ —— -*ant*]], . . .

[233] *effleurer*$_{a}$: [+V], [+ —— NP], [+ —— [+LOCATION]],
 [+PHYS], [−CHANGE], [−NP *être* [$_A$ —— -*ant*]], . . .

[234] *effleurer*$_{b}$: [+V], [+ —— NP], [+ —— [+LOCATION]],
 [+PSYCH], [−CHANGE], [−NP *être* [$_A$ —— -*ant*]], . . .

[235] *étonner*: $[+V]$, $[+ \text{——} NP]$, $[+ \text{——} [+\text{LOCATION}]]$, $[+\text{PSYCH}]$, $[+\text{CHANGE}]$, $[+ NP \ \text{être} [_A \text{——} -ant]]$, . . .

[236] *impressionner*$_a$: $[+V]$, $[+ \text{——} NP]$, $[+ \text{——} [+\text{LOCATION}]]$, $[+\text{PHYS}]$, $[+\text{CHANGE}]$, $[- NP \ \text{être} [_A \text{——} -ant]]$, [to produce an image on a photographic film], . . .

[237] *impressionner*$_b$: $[+V]$, $[+ \text{——} NP]$, $[+ \text{——} [+\text{LOCATION}]]$, $[+\text{PSYCH}]$, $[+\text{CHANGE}]$, $[+ NP \ \text{être} [_A \text{——} -ant]]$, . . .

Next, the grammar will include a certain number of conventions,[42] which fulfil the role hitherto assigned to the redundancy rules. Each of these conventions amounts to saying that under certain given conditions, a feature $[\alpha F]$ (where α is a variable ranging over $+$ or $-$) is interpreted as unmarked.[43] These conventions have the following general form:

[238] In conditions $C_1, \ldots, C_n$, $[\alpha F] \rightarrow [uF]$
    (where $u =$ unmarked)

Finally, we adopt the principle that the evaluation procedure, which measures the relative complexity of grammars in terms of length, *ie* in terms of the number of symbols appearing in the grammars (in practice, the number of features specified in the lexicon),[44] does not take unmarked features into account. The evaluation procedure does not apply directly to entries of the type of [230–237], but only to the entries which result from the application of conventions of the type [238] to these entries; only the features which, after application of the conventions, are still marked $[+F]$ or $[-F]$ will be counted by the evaluation procedure; $[uF]$ features do not count. This procedure results in a considerable economy of features in the lexicon, and a grammar containing such conventions is simpler, more highly valued, than a grammar which does not contain them. The more a grammar contains of these conventions (and the more general the conventions are), the more the grammar is considered as simple by the evaluation procedure.

By way of examples, here are some of the conventions which might be proposed. $[\alpha F, \ldots, \beta G]$ represents a matrix of phonological and morphological features.

[239] i: If the lexicon contains an entry *I* comprising the features $[\alpha F, \ldots, \beta G]$, $[+V]$, $[+ \text{——} NP]$, $[+ \text{——} [+\text{LOCATION}]]$, $[+\text{PHYS}]$, on the one hand, and an entry *J* comprising the features $[\alpha F, \ldots, \beta G]$, $[+V]$, $[+ \text{——} NP]$, $[+ \text{——} [+\text{LOCA-}$

TION]], [+PSYCH], on the other hand, the features [αF, . . . , βG], [+V], [+ —— NP], [+ —— [+LOCATION]], [+PSYCH], in $\mathcal{J}$, are unmarked.

ii: If the lexicon contains an entry I comprising the features [αF, . . . , βG], [+V], [+ —— NP], [+ —— [+LOCATION]], [+PHYS], on the one hand, and an entry $\mathcal{J}$ comprising the features [αF, . . . , βG], [+V], [+ —— NP], [+ —— [+LOCA-TION]], [+PHYS], [+CHANGE], on the other hand, the features [αF, . . . , βG], [+V], [+ —— NP], [+ —— [+LOCA-TION]], [+PHYS], [+CHANGE], in $\mathcal{J}$, are unmarked.

iii: If the lexicon contains an entry I comprising the features [+V], [+ —— NP], [+ —— [+LOCATION]], [+PSYCH], [+CHANGE], the feature [+CHANGE] in I is unmarked.

iv: If the lexicon contains an entry I comprising the features [+V], [+ —— NP], [+ —— [+LOCATION]], [+PSYCH], [+NP *être* [$_A$ —— *-ant*]], the feature [+NP *être* [$_A$ —— *-ant*]] in I is un-marked.

v: If the lexicon contains an entry I comprising the features [+V], [+ —— NP], [+ —— [+LOCATION]], [+PHYS], [−NP *être* [$_A$ —— *-ant*]], the feature [−NP *être* [$_A$ —— *-ant*]] in I is unmarked.

These conventions represent the following intuitions. [239i] amounts to saying that, if a transitive verb of physical action exists in the lexicon, there is normally an homonymous psychological transitive verb also. [239ii] amounts to saying that, if a verb whose object is 'location' exists in the lexicon, there is normally an homonymous verb expressing a change of state also; this convention is intended to account for the uses of *toucher* and *atteindre* as change-of-state verbs (*cf* [228–229]). [239iii] expresses the fact that a psychological verb of the class that concerns us is normally a change-of-state verb (*cf* [225]); a verb like *effleurer* (*cf* [233–234]) is exceptional from this point of view, and its exceptional character is reflected in the fact that the feature [−CHANGE] that it carries remains specified as such after the application of conventions [239i–iv]. [239iv] expresses the fact that it is normal for a psychological verb to appear in frame [93], a verb like *effleurer* again being exceptional from this point of view (in the same way as *heurter*, etc). Lastly, [239v] expresses the fact that a verb of physical action does not normally appear in frame [93] (*cf* [163]).

If we eliminate the unmarked features from the lexical entries, the entries taken into consideration by the evaluation procedure will no longer be [230–237], but [230′–237′]. It will be seen that the application of conventions [239i–v] allows a great economy in features. In the case of *toucher*~a2~ and *toucher*~b~, for example, only the syntactic and semantic features symbolized by . . . , and which are not treated by [239i–v], will still be taken into account. The line (——) in [231′], [232′], etc, indicates that the phonological and morphological features (*cf* [αF, . . . , βG] in [239i–ii]) will only count once for homonymous verbs such as *toucher*~a1~, *toucher*~a2~, *toucher*~b~, whereas, in cases of accidental homonymy (like *voler* (to fly) as opposed to *voler* (to steal)), these features would count twice, *voler* not being affected by these conventions.

[230′] *toucher*: [+V], [+ —— NP], [+ —— [+LOCATION]], [+PHYS], [−CHANGE],

[231′] ——: . . .

[232′] ——: . . .

[233′] *effleurer*: [+V], [+ —— NP], [+ —— [+LOCATION]], [+PHYS], [−CHANGE], . . .

[234′] ——: [−CHANGE], [−NP *être* [~A~ —— -*ant*]], . . .

[235′] *étonner*: [+V], [+ —— NP], [+ —— [+LOCATION]], [+PSYCH], . . .

[236′] *impressionner*: [+V], [+ —— NP], [+ —— [+LOCATION]], [+PHYS], [+CHANGE], [to produce an image on a photographic film], . . .

[237′] ——: . . .

The introduction of conventions such as [239i–v] in its turn poses a series of questions that it is not my intention to deal with here. These conventions should be supplemented by other conventions, and no doubt they should be recast in various ways. The important point is that these conventions themselves are such as to require justification; with the same formalization, one could in fact introduce all sorts of conventions having the same form as those of [239], but which would be entirely arbitrary, and which would predict non-existent facts. The conventions of markedness introduced in phonology by Chomsky and Halle (1968) are justified insofar as they have a precise phonetic content. For example, Chomsky and Halle consider the feature [+VOICED] as unmarked in vowels and marked in consonants; but this is because there are a number of phonetic arguments that it is natural that a vowel should be voiced and that a consonant should be unvoiced. No similar arguments as to the naturalness or otherwise of certain features or processes are available to us as yet, whether in syntax or semantics. Much work remains to be done before we can eliminate the remaining element of arbitrariness from our conventions. A case which seems promising is that of convention [239ii]: it seems quite natural to say that, if a verb expresses physical contact between two objects, this contact normally entails a change of state in one or the other of those objects.

Moreover, it will have been noticed that our conventions are silent as to the metaphorical character or otherwise of the 'psychological' verbs. At the moment I do not see any non-*ad hoc* means of accounting for these differences. The problem of metaphor is a central problem that has so far proved a stumbling-block for generative grammar. I hope to return to this question elsewhere, but it seems to me now that the notion of deep structure will play a crucial role here. Metaphorical processes, in fact, seem always to involve 'homonymous' lexical items appearing in two series of syntactic frames in deep structure with a common intersection.

Notes

1 This observation, as is usual in similar cases, entails a number of simplifica-
tions, but they do not affect the problem which directly concerns us. I have
not taken account of the *dégoûter* which appears in the frame NP — NP *de*
NP (*cf: Marie a dégoûté Pierre des femmes* (Mary disgusted Peter with women)). Furthermore, even in the frame that I am considering, there seem to
be greater restrictions on the object of *mépriser* than on the subject of *dégoûter*,
cf for example:

[I]   la couleur verte⎱
     que Paul ait pu dire une chose pareille⎰ dégoûte Pierre

         the colour green⎱
    that Paul could have said such a thing⎰ disgusts Peter

[II] Pierre méprise { ?la couleur verte
               { ?que Paul ait pu dire une chose pareille

   Peter despises { ?the colour green
             { *that Paul could have said such a thing

    Nevertheless there are a large number of verbs of the class of *mépriser*
(*cf* list [22]) which impose no selectional restrictions on their object.

2 The subject of *dégoûter*, and the object of *mépriser* (but see note 1), are 'non-
restricted' in Gross's sense (1968, 1969).

3 It might be asked why this possibility has never been considered. It is no
doubt due to certain more or less implicit ideas on the connection between
the deep subject position and the [+HUMAN] (or [+ANIMATE]) feature of
the NPs. See below, the beginning of section 6.

4 Postal chose this name because this transformation applies to verbs or adjectives which, nearly all, 'designate psychological states, processes or attributes' (Postal, 1971, 39). This rule had earlier been called FLIP by Lakoff (1970c).

5 In the sense of Katz-Fodor (1963). With Gruber, the manner in which thematic functions and grammatical relations are connected is treated differently, by the process of 'lexical incorporation' (cf Gruber, 1965, 1967).

6 In reality, as [+LOCATION] is not an intrinsic feature of the NPs (unlike [+HUMAN] in [6–7]), this representation is incorrect. I am only adopting it for reasons of exposition. The features [+[+LOCATION]——]] in [20] and [+——[+LOCATION]] in [21] simply mean that the projection rules which attribute the function of 'location' to an NP must be applied to the subject in [20] and to the direct object in [21]. I have not indicated that the object, in [20], and the subject in [21], are 'themes', inasmuch as this specification is redundant, once we have decided which NP is 'location'. Furthermore, if, as we shall see later on (cf section 11), verbs like mépriser and dégoûter are specified in the lexicon as expressing psychological processes, specification of the feature [+HUMAN] clearly also becomes redundant in [6–7] as in [20–21].

7 Gross (1969) has given long lists of these verbs, and has indexed their properties, in tables 6 and 4 respectively.

8 On these transformations, see Rosenbaum (1967), Gross (1968), and Chapter 2 of this book.

9 But see below, concerning the status of phrases in pour NP.

10 There are also many differences in selectional restrictions (cf note 1, and also [85–87]). With [42], compare the two following sentences:

[I] *j'ai manqué de Marie
[II] Marie m'a manqué
     I missed Mary

For the semantic differences between these related constructions, see section 5.

11 Moreover, we would have to say that, in the case of souvenir, the EXTRAPOSITION of an NP can apply to a 'definite' NP, which is not normally the case, cf: il est venu un garçon (there has come a boy) versus *il est venu ce garçon (*there has come this boy).

12 See also note 10.

13 It is essential to distinguish these pronominal constructions, which, in the terminology of Chapter 3, are 'neutrals', from the cases of true reflexives, found for example in [I] (cf [II]):

[I] Pierre s'est persuadé que la fin du monde était proche
    Peter persuaded himself that the end of the world was near
[II] Paul a persuadé Pierre que la fin du monde était proche
     Paul persuaded Peter that the end of the world was near

14 It is known that très and si . . . que S can accompany adjectives, whilst beaucoup and tant . . . que S modify verbs, cf:

[I] Pierre est $\left\{\begin{matrix} \text{très} \\ \text{*beaucoup} \end{matrix}\right\}$ intelligent

    Peter is very intelligent

[II] Pierre est $\left\{\begin{matrix} \text{si} \\ \text{*tant} \end{matrix}\right\}$ intelligent que tout le monde l'admire

     Peter is so intelligent that everyone admires him

[III] Pierre travaille $\begin{cases} \text{*très} \\ \text{beaucoup} \end{cases}$

Peter works a lot

[IV] Pierre travaille $\begin{cases} \text{*si} \\ \text{tant} \end{cases}$ qu'il va ruiner sa santé

Peter works so much that he is going to ruin his health

If we apply this test to *persuader* (*cf* [106–107]), we notice a fairly well-marked difference, *cf:*

[V] Pierre est $\begin{cases} \text{très persuadé de son bon droit} \\ \text{si persuadé de son bon droit qu'il va faire} \\ \text{un procès} \end{cases}$

Peter is $\begin{cases} \text{very convinced of his legal right} \\ \text{so convinced of his legal right that he is going to bring an action} \end{cases}$

[VI] ?*Pierre a été $\begin{cases} \text{très persuadé de son bon droit par Marie} \\ \text{si persuadé de son bon droit par Marie que ...} \end{cases}$

?*Peter was $\begin{cases} \text{very convinced of his legal right by Mary} \\ \text{so convinced of his legal right by Mary that ...} \end{cases}$

Furthermore, *impressionner* (*cf* [91]) allows *très* or *si ... que S* perfectly well, *cf:*

[VII] Pierre est $\begin{cases} \text{très impressionné par Paul} \\ \text{si impressionné par Paul que ...} \end{cases}$

Peter is $\begin{cases} \text{very impressed by Paul} \\ \text{so impressed by Paul that ...} \end{cases}$

But, in many other cases, the facts are not so clear. This question needs closer study. A good traditional study of the differences between 'passives' in *de* and 'passives' in *par* may be found in Clédat (1900).

15 [111b] has another reading, in which *du fait que . . .* has a causal sense. This reading does not concern us here.
16 Notice, too, the difference between [I] *les femmes dégoûtent Pierre* (women disgust Peter) and [II] *Pierre est dégoûté des femmes* (Peter is disgusted with women): [II] suggests that Peter has not always been disgusted with women, whilst [I] does not suggest anything of the kind.
17 Here the verb *être* (the copula) is meant, not the auxiliary which appears, for example, in *Pierre est parti* (Peter has left), *Pierre est arrivé* (Peter has arrived).
18 There are, in fact, several adverbs *personnellement*, which have quite distinct syntactic and semantic properties (see Ruwet, forthcoming).
19 In fact, Postal's judgements on these types of sentences and similar ones have often been challenged by linguists dealing with English (*cf* Kimball, 1970). The question which arises is whether the various degrees of oddity of sentences such as [137] should be treated in terms of ungrammaticalness, or whether they depend rather on semantic or indeed pragmatic considerations (*cf* Jackendoff, 1969b, Bar-Hillel, 1971).
20 In fact, if the deep structure of [145] is of the type of that proposed in [60] above, it is not apparent that the *je* arising from the subordinate clause has crossed the *me* arising from *à moi* (in [145b]). However there are several ways of envisaging the order of the transformations implied in the derivation of [145b], and one could perhaps maintain (*cf* Emonds, 1970) that, in deep structure, *à moi* is on the left of the substantival clause – which would entail a violation of the COP, in the application of SUBJECT-RAISING.

21 Here the dates of publication give rise to confusion. Postal's book, which appeared in 1971, dates from 1968, and is earlier than his article on *remind* (1970a). In his most recent article (1972), Postal says explicitly that the COP is not universal.

22 For a transformational analysis of the French reflexives, see Kayne (1969, forthcoming).

23 *Cf* the ungrammaticalness of:

[I] *je crois la solution en (être) excellente
[II] *quel crois-tu coupable?
[III] *je crois monts et merveilles promis par le Premier Ministre

24 It is the same for the auxiliary *être* of the 'true passive', *cf:*

[I] *je crois Pierre présenté à Marie par Paul

25 These examples may be translated:

[I] Harry me rappelle Fred Astaire
[II] Je perçois que Harry est semblable à Fred Astaire
[III] Harry a rappelé à Betty de rendre visite à son oncle malade

26 And in other languages, including Japanese. This simple fact demonstrates that it is not a coincidence, as in the case of accidental homonymies (*bank*, *voler*).

27 But see below, section 9.

28 See Gouet (1971), who raises a problem very similar to that considered here.

29 It is also found in intransitive verbs and adjectives, *cf* for example:

[I] *a:* le soleil brille
the sun is shining
b: cette idée est brillante
that idea is brilliant

[II] *a:* une bombe a éclaté boulevard Saint-Michel
a bomb exploded in the Boulevard Saint-Michel
b: la beauté de Gloria Grahame est éclatante
Gloria Grahame's beauty is dazzling

[III] *a:* cet appartement est très clair
this flat is very light
b: il est clair que tu n'as rien compris
it is clear that you have understood nothing

[IV] *a:* la neige était sale
the snow was dirty
b: cette idée est sale (*cf: cette idée est dégoûtante*)
that idea is dirty

30 The idea that it would be necessary to adopt such a principle was suggested to me by Wayles Browne (personal communication).

31 *Cf:*

[I]   la crainte de l'insuccès⎫
         *le départ de Marie   ⎬ avait à peine effleuré (l'esprit de) Pierre
     *(le fait) que Marie soit partie⎭

              fear of failure⎫
         *Mary's departure   ⎬ had hardly even crossed Peter's mind
     *(the fact) that Mary had gone⎭

The subject of *effleurer*ᵦ is apparently limited to NPs expressing ' inalienable psychological properties' of the referent of the object NP. These special selectional constraints on *effleurer*$_b$ were drawn to my attention by J. P. Boons.

32 Here the impossible construction is the one containing a neutral pronominal verb (*cf* [96]). [193*a*] seems possible after all if a true reflexive is involved with Clark Gable himself firing the bullet, and *d'une balle* being an instrumental.

33 Phrases in *de NP* are possible with *effleurer*$_a$, but then it is a question of instrumentals, *cf*: *le médecin a effleuré la blessure du bout des doigts* (the doctor lightly touched the wound with his finger-tips); this type of construction is impossible with *effleurer*$_b$, *cf*: **Claudius (cette idée) a effleuré Hamlet d'un terrible soupçon.*

34 [203*b*] is perhaps possible, but if so it is a case of *frapper*$_b$ (the 'psychological' *frapper*), and *mes oreilles* is taken in a figurative sense. In [204], *par une taxe* is an agent, but *d'une taxe* is an instrumental, and in this case there is an unexpressed agent, *cf*: *le gouvernement frappe ces produits d'une (*par une) taxe spéciale* (the Government burdens these products with a special tax). Dubois *et al* (see below) do not distinguish [204] and [205], although they show different syntactic behaviour: in [205], apparently, *mesure* cannot be an instrumental. Notice that [205*b*] is possible (with *par* as well as with *de*), as an instance of *frapper*$_b$.

35 As I have already pointed out (*cf* note 6), the feature [+ —— [+HUMAN]] is clearly redundant in the lexical entry for *dégoûter*, once this entry carries the indication that the verb expresses a psychological process (the feature [+PSYCH] of [239]). The difference between *gêner* and *dégoûter* would then depend only on the fact that the entry for *dégoûter* contains the feature [+PSYCH], whilst *gêner* is non-specified in terms of this feature. The anomalous character of sentences such as *l'argent dégoûte ce rocher* (*cf* [2]) would be predicted by a universal principle saying that only human (or animate) beings can be the location of psychological (or sensory) processes. There would then be no selectional restrictions in the strict sense on *dégoûter* in terms of the feature [±HUMAN]. Notice, on the other hand, that one cannot apparently eliminate selectional restrictions of this type when it is a question of accounting for restrictions on the object in [86–87] (*cf* **je suis étonné (amusé*, etc) *de Paul*, etc); in fact, these restrictions are not immediately understandable in semantic terms, and they are not universal (*cf* the English examples, [139–140]); even in French, they do not apply to all verbs (*cf* [88]).

36 Intuitively, there is a 'persistence' of the A sense in the B frame, but I do not see how one can account for it.

37 In fact there is really no paraphrase relation between sentences [220*a* and *b*], *cf* Dougherty (1970a) and Anderson (1971); but this point does not directly concern me here (see also Hatcher, 1944a, 1944b).

38 I am leaving aside the separate problem of constructions with the 'dative of the possessor' (*cf* [221*a*]), which are a characteristic of French. On this subject, see Hatcher (1944a, 1944b).

39 In speaking of 'pseudo-locatives', I mean that these complements do not have all the syntactic properties of the complement locatives of type A verbs. For example, the sentences of [225] (unlike those of [223*a*]) are not possible answers to the question: *où a-t-il été blessé (frappé, touché)?* (where was he hurt (struck, wounded)?). These pseudo-locatives seem to bear the same relationship to complement locatives of type A verbs as the 'pseudo-instrumentals' pointed out earlier (*cf* [71–72]) bear to true complement instrumentals of type A verbs (*cf* [159]). Once again, we encounter a partial

parallelism between A and B verbs, which it seems can only be described if we agree that the two types appear in similar deep structures (accepting locative complements, instrumental complements, etc), the differences having to be finally treated uniformly in terms of the semantic differences between physical processes and psychological processes.

40 The verb *atteindre* is another good example (see the end of section 9) of the difficulty that native speakers experience in establishing a clearly-marked boundary between A and B verbs. Dubois *et al* (1966) give two entries for this verb:

> 1. *Atteindre quelqu'un*, to succeed in wounding him, in seriously affecting him, in disturbing him morally: 'le coup de feu l'atteignit au bras' (the shot hit him in the arm) . . . 'Il est atteint dans ses convictions' (He is wounded in his convictions) . . . 'Ce reproche ne m'atteint pas' (that reproach does not affect me) . . .
>
> 2. 1 *Atteindre une personne, une chose*, to succeed in reaching them when they are distant or high up: 'Atteindre une cible, un but' (to reach a target, a goal) . . . 'Monter sur une chaise pour atteindre le haut de l'armoire' (to get up on a chair to reach the top of the cupboard) . . . 'Le fleuve a atteint un certain niveau' (the river reached a certain level) . . .
>
> 2 *Atteindre quelqu'un*, to get in touch with him: 'Je réussis à l'atteindre par téléphone avant son départ' (I succeeded in reaching him by telephone before he left) . . .

The main distinction made here corresponds to Fillmore's distinction between change-of-state verbs (1) and surface-contact verbs (2), but the A sense (physical process) and the B sense (psychological process) are merged in (1).

41 If we mark these verbs uniformly with the feature $[+ \underline{\quad} [+\text{LOCATION}]]$, it seems that we shall have difficulties with sentences such as [223], *Biron a blessé Lusignan au visage*, or [225], *cet échec a blessé Conrad dans son orgueil*. In fact, in these sentences, we would want to say that the prepositional phrase (*au visage, dans son orgueil*) is 'location'; in that case we should have two phrases classed as 'locations', the object NP and the PP. Actually, a more general problem is involved, which is found, for example, in time complements, *cf: je viendrai demain dans l'après-midi* (I shall come tomorrow in the afternoon). It seems to me that we can allow the presence in a sentence of more than one phrase having the same thematic function, if the second can be interpreted as a qualification of the first. This latitude could be limited to certain thematic functions, perhaps only that of 'location'.

42 I am leaving open the question whether these conventions, or some of them, are universal. In that case, they would appear in general theory, and the grammar of French would not have to specify them.

43 *Cf* Chomsky, 1965, Chapter 1, Chomsky and Halle, 1968.

44 This formulation is different from that of Chomsky and Halle (1968), who interpret convention [238] as meaning also that any feature $[-\alpha\text{F}] \rightarrow [m\text{F}]$ (where m = marked). The marked features, unlike the unmarked features, are counted by the evaluation procedure.

Chapter 6

How to deal with syntactic irregularities: constraints on transformations or perceptual strategies?*

Since the early days of generative grammar, linguists have been preoccupied with the following problem: a large number of transformational rules have a very widespread application, and yet, under certain conditions, their application is blocked (*cf* Chapter 1, section 2). This is especially so in the case of the various movement transformations which, by moving noun phrases or prepositional phrases, pronouns, etc, are involved in the formation of relatives, interrogatives, cleft sentences, clitic pronouns, etc. Here is an example of these restrictions. In French, a prepositional phrase of the form *de NP* can regularly be taken from its position in deep structure and either relativized, interrogativized, clefted or changed into a clitic pronoun, whether its position and function in the sentence be that of indirect object, adverbial complement, or noun complement, *cf*:

[1] *a:* je parle *de ce livre*
     I am speaking of this book
   b: le livre *dont* je parle
     the book of which I am speaking
   c: de quel livre parles-tu?
     of what book are you speaking?
   d: c'est *de ce livre* que je parle
     it is of this book that I am speaking
   e: j'*en* parle
     I am speaking of it

* Revised version of the French original of 'How to deal with syntactic irregularities: Conditions on transformations or perceptual strategies?' in Kiefer and Ruwet, eds, 1973, Dordrecht, Holland, Reidel Publishing Co.

[2] *a:* je viens *de Paris*
         I come from Paris
      b: l'endroit *d'où* je viens
         the place that I come from
      c: *de quelle ville* viens-tu?
         what town do you come from?
      d: c'est *de Paris* que je viens
         it's Paris that I come from
      e: j'*en* viens
         I come from there

[3] *a:* j'ai lu la préface *de ce livre*
         I read the preface of this book
      b: le livre *dont* j'ai lu la préface
         the book of which I read the preface
      c: de quel livre as-tu lu la préface?
         of what book did you read the preface?
      d: c'est *de ce livre* que j'ai lu la préface
         it's this book that I read the preface of
      e: j'*en* ai lu la préface
         I read the preface of it

In some circumstances, however, the movement of the *de NP* is not possible; thus from [4*a*] none of the operations mentioned above results in a grammatical sentence, *cf* [4*b*–4*e*]:

[4] *a:* je pense à la préface *de ce livre*
         I am thinking of the preface of this book
      b: *le livre *dont* je pense à la préface
      c: *de quel livre* penses-tu à la préface?
      d: *c'est *de ce livre* que je pense à la préface
      e: *j'*en* pense à la préface

It is important to realize that [4] is not an exception through any accidental, lexical reason; the exception is systematic and it can be formulated in general terms; namely, that any movement of a prepositional phrase of the type *de NP* is blocked if this phase is embedded in another prepositional phrase ('*à* la préface . . .'); compare also:

[5] *a:* j'habite *dans* la banlieue *de Paris*
         I live in the suburbs of Paris
      b: *j'*en* habite *dans* la banlieue

[6] *a:* je compte *sur* la préface *de* ce livre
       I am relying on the preface of this book
     *b: *j'en* compte *sur* la préface

(in [5] and [6], clitic placing is the only example given, but it is easy to verify that the other types of movement mentioned are also blocked).

Although the exception is of a systematic nature, it still constitutes 'a serious gap in the generality of a rule' (Klima, 1970). Even if it is often, but not always, possible to account for these exceptions by means of conditions on the application of specific movement rules, it is obvious that we cannot leave it at that if we want our account to have any explanatory value. If our aim is to construct a convincing model of language learning – in this case to account for the fact that a French child, after a few years of learning the language, rejects [4*b–e*], [5*b*], [6*b*], etc, while accepting without hesitation all the examples in [1–3] – we shall have to discover the general principles that account for these differences in grammaticalness.

Linguists have therefore been at pains to establish universal constraints of a very abstract nature, applying for example to movement transformations. In this way Chomsky (1964, 1968) proposed the 'A-over-A principle' which, as R. S. Kayne has shown (1969), can in particular be used to explain the aberrant behaviour of [4–6]. In many cases, however, the attempt to establish universal constraints has encountered great obstacles. We know, for example, that the universal validity of the 'A-over-A principle' has been disputed by Ross (1967), who proposed replacing this one principle by several independent constraints, whose explanatory power is unfortunately rather weak precisely because they are too specific. In some cases, too, even Ross's constraints have proved to be inadequate,[1] one fact among others which has recently led some linguists, for example Lakoff, to propose enriching the theory by introducing global derivational constraints (*cf* Lakoff, 1969, 1971) or even transderivational constraints (*cf* Lakoff, 1970b), which are so powerful that it may be asked whether a theory which includes them can still retain any interest (*cf* Chomsky, 1972).

With these problems in mind, E. S. Klima (1970) has recently proposed an entirely different way of approaching the question of restrictions on transformations; although Klima has as yet only outlined his proposal, it is worthy of serious consideration, and I should like to illustrate it here with some examples from French.

1 Factitive constructions

The syntax of factitive constructions in French shows many peculiarities; it has recently been the subject of a detailed study by R. S. Kayne (1969, forthcoming). To account for the facts presented in [7–10], Kayne proposes to assign deep structures such as [11] to factitive constructions, and to introduce three transformations, [12–14]:[2]

[7] *a:* je laisserai Jean partir
       I shall let John go
   b: je laisserai partir Jean
       as for (*a*)

[8] *a:* *je ferai Jean partir
    b: je ferai partir Jean
       I'll get John to go

[9] *a:* *je ferai Jean parler à Pierre
    b: je ferai parler Jean à Pierre
       I'll get John to speak to Peter

[10] *a:* *je ferai Jean lire ce livre
     b: *je ferai lire Jean ce livre
     c: *je ferai lire ce livre Jean
     d: je ferai lire ce livre à Jean
       I'll get John to read this book

[11] $NP - \begin{Bmatrix} \text{laisser} \\ \text{faire} \end{Bmatrix} - [_S \ NP - VP]$

[12] $T_1 : X - \text{faire} - NP - V - Y$

   $\quad$ 1 $\quad\quad$ 2 $\quad\quad$ 3 $\quad$ 4 $\quad$ 5

   $\quad\quad\quad\quad\quad\quad \Rightarrow 1 - 2 - 4 - 3 - 5$

[13] $T_2 : X - \text{faire} - V - NP - NP - Y$

   $\quad$ 1 $\quad\quad$ 2 $\quad\quad$ 3 $\quad$ 4 $\quad$ 5 $\quad$ 6

   $\quad\quad\quad\quad\quad\quad \Rightarrow 1 - 2 - 3 - à+4 - 5 - 6$

[14] $T_3 : X - \text{faire} - V - à \ NP - NP - Y$

   $\quad$ 1 $\quad\quad$ 2 $\quad\quad$ 3 $\quad$ 4 $\quad$ 5 $\quad$ 6

   $\quad\quad\quad\quad\quad\quad \Rightarrow 1 - 2 - 3 - 5 - 4 - 6$

Notice that [11–14] do not only predict the facts of [7–10], but would also mean that from the deep structure [15*a*], [15*b*], which is acceptable to at least some speakers, could be generated, and [15*c*], which is excluded.

Moreover, [15d], which is not directly generated by [11–14], is slightly better than [15c]:

[15] *a:* je ferai [s Jean porter ce message à Pierre]
          I shall make [s John take this message to Peter]
      b: ?je ferai porter à Jean ce message à Pierre
      c: *?je ferai porter ce message à Jean à Pierre
      d: ??je ferai porter ce message à Pierre à Jean

Perhaps [15d] is introduced by the rule (necessary for other reasons) which optionally permutes two adjacent prepositional phrases, *cf*:

[16] *a:* ce livre a été donné à Paul par Pierre
          this book was given to Paul by Peter
      b: ce livre a été donné par Pierre à Paul
          this book was given by Peter to Paul

[17] *a:* Pierre a parlé de ce problème à Paul
          Peter talked about this problem to Paul
      b: Pierre a parlé à Paul de ce problème
          Peter talked to Paul about this problem

I shall return later to the reasons for the varying degrees of unacceptability between [15b], [15c] and [15d]. In the case of [15c] and [15d], it is possible that an independent (? surface) constraint intervenes in any case, making unacceptable any sequence of two noun phrases of the form *à NP*, where both NPs are marked with the feature [+HUMAN].

However this may be, something like [15b], [15c] or [15d] must be postulated as an intermediate stage in the derivations of [18a–d], in which various movement transformations are involved:

[18] *a:* Jean, à qui je ferai porter ce message à Pierre, . . .
          John, whom I shall get to take this message to Peter, . . .
      b: à qui feras-tu porter ce message à Pierre?
          who will you get to take this message to Peter?
      c: c'est à Jean que je ferai porter ce message à Pierre
          it's John whom I shall get to take this message to Peter
      d: à Jean, je ferai porter ce message à Pierre
          John, I shall get to take this message to Peter

The interesting problem here is the following: while all the examples of [18] are grammatical (but see below), none of those of [19] is, apparently (granted, of course, that [19] is derived from [15a]; [19] would be grammatical if derived from *je ferai* [$_S$ *Pierre porter ce message à Jean*] (I shall make [$_S$ Peter take this message to John])):

[19] *a:* *Pierre, à qui je ferai porter ce message à Jean
       b: *à qui feras-tu porter ce message à Jean?
       c: *c'est à Pierre que je ferai porter ce message à Jean
       d: *à Pierre, je ferai porter ce message à Jean

In other words, given a structure such as [15*b*] (or [15*c*], [15*d*]), in which, following the operation of previous transformations (T$_1$ and T$_2$ above), two prepositional phrases of the form *à NP* occur, the one corresponding to the deep structure subject (*Jean*) can be moved by a movement transformation, but not the one corresponding to the deep structure indirect object (*Pierre*).

None of the universal constraints on transformations which have been proposed up to now accounts for the exclusion of the examples of [19], and these examples are all the more surprising in that they do not reflect any general constraint on the movement of the indirect object. The indirect object can be moved perfectly well under other conditions, for example in these same factitive constructions, when the subject appears in surface structure accompanied by the preposition *par* instead of *à, cf* [20]:[3]

[20] *a:* Pierre, à qui je ferai porter ce message par Jean
            Peter, to whom I shall get this message taken by John
       b: à qui feras-tu porter ce message par Jean?
            to whom will you get this message taken by John?
       c: c'est à Pierre que je ferai porter ce message par Jean
            it's to Peter that I shall get this message taken by John
       d: à Pierre, je ferai porter ce message par Jean
            to Peter, I shall get this message taken by John

In the absence of a universal constraint which would automatically exclude [19], we would be obliged, within the framework of classic transformational theory, to introduce a condition on movement transformations which would block them in cases corresponding to [19]. Let us agree that the general formulation for leftward movement rules is [21]:

$$[21] \quad Z - X - \begin{Bmatrix} NP \\ PP \end{Bmatrix} - Y$$
$$\quad\quad 1 \quad 2 \quad\quad 3 \quad\quad 4 \Rightarrow 1 \ 3+2 \ \emptyset \ 4$$

and, as a concrete example, take the cleft sentences [18*c*–19*c*]; their underlying structure, at the stage when [21] is applied, would be (*cf* [15*b*–*d*]), either [22*a*], [22*b*] or [22*c*] (see Moreau, 1970):

[22] *a:* c'est Δ [$_S$ je ferai porter à Jean ce message à Pierre]
          it is Δ [$_S$ I shall make John take this message to Peter]
      b: c'est Δ [$_S$ je ferai porter ce message à Jean à Pierre]
      c: c'est Δ [$_S$ je ferai porter ce message à Pierre à Jean]

According to whether it is [22*a*, *b* or *c*] that is the underlying structure, the condition on [21] blocking [19*c*] will be formulated as [23i], [23ii] or [23iii]:

[23]   i: *Condition*: [21] is blocked if
              a: 3 = *à NP*
              b: 2 = *W faire V à NP (NP)*

      ii: *Condition*: [21] is blocked if
              a: 3 = *à NP*
              b: 2 = *W faire V (NP) à NP*

     iii: *Condition*: [21] is blocked if
              a: 3 = *à NP*
              b: 2 = *W faire V (NP)*
              c: 4 = *à NP U*

The brackets round NP in [23] are there to account for sentences such as *c'est à Pierre que je ferai répondre à Jean, c'est à Pierre que je ferai penser à Jean*, which are ungrammatical in the reading in which *à Pierre* is the indirect object and *à Jean* the subject; for these sentences (which are grammatical with *à Pierre* as the subject and *à Jean* as the indirect object), an intermediate structure of the form *NP faire V à NP à NP*, with no direct object, must be postulated. Notice that sentences such as *c'est à Jean que je ferai parler de Pierre* and *c'est de Pierre que je ferai parler à Jean* are both of them grammatical and ambiguous. Let us repeat that the blocking of the movement of the indirect object results only from the occurrence in the same sequence of two phrases of the form *à NP*.

Condition [23] calls for some comment. In the first place, although it covers the facts of [18–19], it is clearly entirely *ad hoc*: it formulates the facts without explaining them. Next, it seems suspect that it has to be formulated in three different ways, according to whether [22*a*, *b* or *c*] is taken as the underlying structure to which [21] is applied: one feels intuitively that the respective positions of the two *à NP* phrases should not be a factor. At all events, the condition is rather a strange one, such as is found only rarely. More important is the fact that it would be just as easy (or difficult) to block the movement, not of the indirect object, but of the subject, in very similar terms. One would only have to posit the following condition (variants (i), (ii) and (iii) of which apply in the same conditions as those of [23]):

[24] i: *Condition*: [21] is blocked if
$$a: 3 = à\ NP$$
$$b: 2 = W\ faire\ V$$
$$c: 4 = (NP)\ à\ NP$$

ii: *Condition*: [21] is blocked if
$$a: 3 = à\ NP$$
$$b: 2 = W\ faire\ V\ (NP)$$
$$c: 4 = à\ NP$$

iii: *Condition*: [21] is blocked if
$$a: 3 = à\ NP$$
$$b: 2 = W\ faire\ V\ (NP)\ à\ NP$$

As is indicated by the grammaticalness of [18], movement of the subject is not blocked. But the point of this comparison between [23] and [24] is this: for the grammar of a language identical with French but for the sole difference that in it [18] would be ungrammatical and [19] would be grammatical, it would be neither more nor less difficult to formulate a condition (namely [24]) analogous to [23]. In other words, a grammar incorporating condition [23] in a sense asserts that it is an accident that the facts of French are as they are; if we allow conditions of the type of [23], we should equally well expect there to be languages that require instead condition [24]. This arises from the nature of transformations (and of conditions on transformations): these analyse terminal strings in terms of certain strings of categories and they ignore grammatical functions and relations; a transformation (or a condition on a transformation) can mention the sequence *à NP*, but it cannot refer to the functions of subject and indirect object. At the stage when the rules summarized in [21] apply, there is no phrase structure difference between a subject and an indirect object which are both of the form *à NP*. Now, one feels intuitively that the generalization underlying examples [18–19] is the following: 'The movement of the *à NP* indirect object is blocked if in the same sentence there is a subject of the same form *à NP*', and one would like to be able to say that it is not a matter of chance that it is the indirect object which cannot be moved, rather than the subject. Even if condition [23] renders the grammar adequate at the observational level, it does not really provide an explanation of these facts.

But this is not all. Condition [23] is in fact too strong. As it stands, it would exclude, for example, [25b], which is obtained by embedding [25a] in a factitive construction which is then clefted, and which is acceptable:

[25] *a:* Jean a porté ce colis à la prison
      John took this parcel to the prison
      b: c'est à la prison que j'ai fait porter ce colis à Jean
      it was to the prison that I got John to take this parcel

So it would be necessary to complicate [23], by specifying that the two NPs of the *à NP* phrases mentioned are both marked [+HUMAN]. I shall not, however, pursue this question further, as I now propose to consider these facts from a completely different viewpoint, that suggested by Klima (1970) to account for facts of English which are rather similar to those presented here.

We shall leave aside for the moment the traditional problem of generative grammar, that of deriving well-formed surface structures from deep structures, by means of transformations which are ordered and subject to certain constraints. We shall turn to another question, which has until now been considered quite distinct from the first: whereas the first has to do with 'competence', this has to do with 'performance'. It concerns the model of recognition or comprehension, the model of the hearer. How does a native speaker come to understand the meaning of a sentence he hears? More specifically, how does a native speaker, from the surface structure that he hears, recover the deep structure grammatical relations which determine the semantic interpretation of the sentence?

A natural way of answering this question would be the hypothesis that native speakers make use of certain heuristic techniques, 'a set of well-organized strategies' (Klima), which enable them to recover the deep structure relations from indications given in the surface structure. Such strategies, which would enable the speaker to recognize the main clause of a sentence, the subject of a clause, the object, etc, have been proposed and studied in recent work by Bever, Fodor, Mehler, etc. The results of these studies are set out in Bever (1970).

Let us suppose that there are one or more strategies for recognizing the deep structure subject, direct object and indirect object underlying the various surface structures. These strategies will rely on various data, such as the position of a phrase in relation to the verb in surface structure, certain morphological marks (cases, prepositions,) the lexical content of the different elements, etc. Let us now look again at the examples under discussion, [18–20]. We can see that [20] is straightforward from the point of view of comprehension strategies: each of the three deep structure functions, subject (S), direct object (DO), and indirect object (IO), is marked in surface structure in an unequivocal way that distinguishes it from the other two, DO by its place immediately after the verb with no intervening preposition, IO by the form *à NP*, and S by the form *par NP*.[4] Again, in [15*b*], we may suppose that the relative order of the two *à NP* phrases, before and after DO, serves to differentiate them as being respectively S and IO. In each case, as well as the lexical-semantic and contextual information which may be given, the surface structure provides structural indications, either syntactic or morphological or both, which make it possible to recover the deep structure. But this is not the case for [18] and [19]. Given that, in [26], *à Paul* can be interpreted equally well as subject or as indirect object:

[26] j'ai fait porter ce message à Paul
    I got Paul to take this message/I had this message taken to Paul

we see that, in [18*c*] or [19*c*], for example, the structural difference between S and IO has disappeared from the surface structure. This is a case of what Klima calls *absolute structural ambiguity* (or *functional ambiguity*). Klima's thesis is that language cannot tolerate this type of ambiguity,[5] though it tolerates lexical ambiguity (lexical homonymy, *cf: Pierre a déjà volé* (Peter has already stolen/Peter has already flown)), or structural ambiguity due to the fact that two or more constructions have different surface phrase structures represented by the same sequence of morphemes (structural homonymy, *cf: Pierre a tué l'homme à la carabine* (Peter killed the man with the rifle), *j'ai reçu le livre du garçon* (I received the book from the boy/I received the boy's book), *flying planes can be dangerous*). The crucial point is that there are many reasons for attributing two different *surface* structures to a sentence such as *Pierre a tué l'homme à la carabine*, say [NP Pierre] [V a tué] [NP l'homme à la carabine] and [NP Pierre] [V a tué] [NP l'homme] [PP à la carabine] (here I am simplifying), whereas there is no positive reason to differentiate sentences such as [18] and [19] in the same way.

Klima proposes the following hypothesis:

When there are multiple occurrences of the same category in one construction, without lexical or morphological differentiation, then a

simple algorithm exists for distinguishing their function, and no transformation will have such an effect on a string as to interfere with the
effectiveness of the algorithm.

There is a way here of accounting for the facts while dispensing with
condition [23]. Provisionally, we might suggest replacing condition [23]
by the following strategy (or heuristic), which is a first approximation to
Klima's type of algorithm:

[27] STRATEGY I: All else being equal, and in the absence of particular
morphological marks or lexical-semantic distinctions, if two prepositional phrases of the form *à NP* are present in a sentence
containing a factitive construction, the position *faire V (NP)* ——
is that of the indirect object of *V*.

This strategy would operate like a filter. There would be no constraint on
transformations like [21], and [19] would be generated on the same footing as [18] and [20]; [19] would then be grammatical in the technical sense
of the term. But subsequently the surface structures would be subject to
[27], which would exclude [19], while allowing [18] and [20]; so [19]
would be unacceptable. The same strategy would also predict that [15c]
would be unacceptable, and would help to account for the fact that [15d] is
relatively more acceptable than [15c].

R. Kayne (personal communication) has pointed out to me two difficulties that are apparently attendant on the use of this strategy. In the
first place, insofar as [15b] is relatively acceptable, how can the strategy
predict that it is *à Jean* which is interpreted as subject and *à Pierre* which
is interpreted as indirect object? It seems to me that, when a direct object
(*ce message* in [15b]) is present, it is the position to the right of the direct
object – which will itself have been indicated by an appropriate strategy –
which is crucial. Furthermore, it must be asked whether [15b] is acceptable apart from the special intonational features which in a way put *à Jean*,
the subject, 'outside' the sentence, and clearly there are special strategies
which take intonational factors into account. In the case of sentences with
no direct object present, such as ?*j'ai fait répondre à Pierre à Jean*, it
seems to me that, insofar as they are interpretable, which is doubtful
(*cf* the above-mentioned constraint on sequences of two animate *à NP*s),
it is the first *à NP* which is interpreted as indirect object, in accordance
with [27].

In the second place, how can [27] differentiate between a sentence like
[18c] and a sentence like [28]?

[28] j'ai dit à Jean que je ferai porter ce message à Pierre
I have told John that I will have this message taken to Peter/
I have told John that I will get Peter to take this message

(in which *à Jean* is the indirect object of the main verb *dire*, the embedded sentence being ambiguous).

The crucial point is this: the hearer, when he applies perceptual strategies, processes the string from left to right. In the case of [28], *à Jean* is immediately recognized as the indirect object of *dire* (which is marked in the lexicon with the feature [+ —— *à* NP S]); and this element will play no role when the hearer comes to deal with *à Pierre*. On the other hand, with [18c], when the hearer comes to *à Jean*, he cannot yet disambiguate it between a subject interpretation and an indirect object interpretation. He will have to keep this twofold possibility in view until he reaches *à Pierre*, when strategy [27] will intervene to decide, interpreting *à Jean*, retrospectively, as subject.

The essential innovation in the use of a strategy like [27] consists in attributing to perceptual strategies – that is, to mechanisms traditionally considered as belonging to performance – a function traditionally given either to conditions on specific rules (*cf* [23]), (applying to the grammar of a specific language), or to universal constraints (part of the general theory, involving innate language universals). This alteration obviously raises the question whether we should reconsider the traditional distinction between competence and performance. I shall return briefly to this question at the end of the chapter.

Quite apart from the difficulties encountered in formulating non-*ad hoc* constraints on transformations in order to account for the facts, there are other arguments in favour of choosing a perceptual strategy rather than a constraint on transformations. Transformations, and constraints on transformations, have an all-or-nothing character. If the structure index of a transformation is satisfied by a given sequence, then the transformation can apply – or must apply, if it is obligatory – and if the conditions in which constraints apply are fulfilled, the transformation is blocked. With a perceptual strategy, on the other hand, we are prepared for a good deal of variation and some fluidity of intuition, as other factors (other strategies) may come into play, to counterbalance the effect of the strategy.

Indeed, if the examples are examined more closely than I have done so far, it will be seen that they are not quite so clear-cut as they appear in my presentation of them, in which, for example, [19] is entirely excluded and [25*b*] is entirely acceptable. I have in fact simplified. In the first place, though speakers of French decidedly prefer [18] to [19], they do not generally accept [18] unreservedly; in any case, they decidedly prefer, for example, [29] to [18c], in that in [29] the subject is unequivocally marked by the preposition *par:*

[29] c'est par Jean que j'ai fait porter ce message à Pierre
   it was by John that I had this message taken to Peter

Also, some speakers find [18] and [19] ambiguous; for them there is simply a distinct hierarchy of possible interpretations: the interpretation of an *à NP* phrase in the context /V NP —— as an IO is quite natural, whereas its interpretation as S is difficult for them. Again, sentences such as [25b] do not seem to be altogether acceptable. There are also inter-mediate cases, such as [30], which are about halfway between [25b] and [19] in acceptability:[6]

[30] c'est à la bibliothèque de Harvard que j'ai fait emprunter ce livre à
   Pierre
   it was from Harvard library that I got Peter to borrow this book/
   it was Harvard library that I got to borrow this book from Peter

I do not see how the classic type of conditions on transformations can account for facts of this sort, but they can be dealt wtih quite naturally by allowing *several* different (perceptual) strategies to operate as filters. Some of these strategies, like [27], would use structural information, others morphological aspects, others semantic or selectional features. Of course, the exact way in which these various strategies would interact is still to be decided: do they operate simultaneously, is there a hierarchy in them, etc? For example, in [25b], *Jean* is fairly easy to interpret as subject because of the acceptability of [25a] as opposed to the anomaly of [31]:

[31] *la prison a porté ce colis à Jean
   *the prison took this parcel to John

A semantic strategy, which would take into account the fact that *la prison* cannot normally be the subject of *porter NP à NP*, would therefore operate here as well as [27]. If [30] is less natural than [25b], but more natural than [19], this is probably because [32b], though less natural than [32a], is perfectly possible nonetheless, and in this case a semantic stra-tegy cannot by itself completely differentiate the subject from the in-direct object:

[32] *a:* Pierre a emprunté ce livre à la bibliothèque de Harvard
   Peter borrowed this book from Harvard library

    b: la bibliothèque de Harvard a emprunté ce livre à Pierre
    Harvard library borrowed this book from Peter

And lastly, if [19] is almost impossible, it is because both [33*a* and *b*] are equally natural and therefore a semantic strategy is useless; so the whole onus of the interpretation rests on [27]:

[33] *a:* Jean a porté ce message à Pierre
      John took this message to Peter
   b: Pierre a porté ce message à Jean
      Peter took this message to John

    This being said, the fact remains that the use of strategy [27], although it provides a way to avoid constraining movement transformations in a non-*ad hoc* manner and is more in accordance with the character of the data, is itself rather an *ad hoc* procedure. There is something arbitrary in the formulation of [27] which was also present in [23]: why is it the indirect object which is preferred in the position /V NP —— ? We cannot yet claim that this dissymmetry between the treatment of subject and indirect object has been explained.
    Fortunately, it is not difficult to subsume strategy [27] under a more general hypothesis; but before formulating this, I should first like to consider some other facts which appear to be of quite a different kind, but which, as we shall see, raise problems very like those set by factitive constructions. We shall then be able to propose with more conviction a general hypothesis on the nature of certain strategies which use structural information, and of which [27] is only one particular case.

1.1 Appendix

I have completely left out of the discussion a type of sentence to which at first sight the same considerations seem to apply. I mean factitive sentences in which either the subject or the indirect object of the embedded sentence has undergone the CLITIC-PLACING transformation. Superficially, the facts seem to be parallel to those of [18–19], *cf*:

[34] *a:* je lui ferai porter ce message à Pierre (in which *lui = à Jean* in [18])
      I will get him to take this message to Peter
   b: *je lui ferai porter ce message à Jean (in which *lui = à Pierre*)
   c: je lui ferai porter ce message par Jean (*id*)
      I will have this message taken to him by John

However, there are differences between sentences of type [34] and those of [18–19]. In the first place, whereas we saw that the difference between [18–19] is one of relative acceptability, it is clear that [34b], with *lui* the indirect object and *à Jean* subject, is completely excluded. Secondly, if we consider [35]:

[35] *a:* c'est à Pierre que je lui ai fait porter ce message
          it was to Peter that I got him to take this message
      b: à qui lui as-tu fait porter ce message?
          to whom did you get him to take this message?

we see that, as in [34], *lui* must be interpreted as subject and *à Pierre* or *à qui* as indirect object of *porter*. In other words, strategy [27] is not relevant here, and the significant generalization is that, when a 'dative' clitic pronoun and an *à NP* phrase are present together in a sentence containing a factitive construction, the 'dative' pronoun is always interpreted as subject and the *à qui* phrase as indirect object.

Thirdly – and this point is crucial – we also have the following facts:

[36] *a:* c'est à Marie que je ferai répondre Jean
          it's Mary that I shall get John to reply to
      b: voilà la fille à qui j'ai fait répondre Jean
          there's the girl whom I got John to reply to

[37] *a:* ?je lui ferai répondre Jean
          I'll get John to reply to him/her
      b: *je me ferai répondre Jean

Sentences [36–37] differ from the preceding ones by the absence of a direct object. Of the three rules (*cf* [12–14]) which operate in the derivation of factitive constructions, they have undergone only rule T_1. The result is that they do not constitute a case of absolute structural ambiguity and, as expected, the examples of [36] are acceptable. But [37] raises a problem, which strategy [27] cannot settle (it should be noted that *je lui ferai répondre par Jean* is grammatical, whereas *?je me ferai répondre par Jean* is slightly dubious). R. S. Kayne (1969, forthcoming) has studied these facts very closely, but apparently he has not yet succeeded in finding a satisfactory explanation for them. In view of the complexity of the phenomena, I think it is preferable deliberately to leave aside these constructions involving clitic pronouns; the problems they raise are still awaiting a solution.

I must refer briefly to another type of fact for which I have no explanation at present, but which may have some connection with these matters.

Whereas [38] is quite normal (with the interpretation that *Pierre* is subject and *Marie* indirect object), I find [39*a*] difficult to accept, and [39*b*] is quite impossible:

[38] c'est à Pierre que je ferai présenter Paul à Marie
      it's Peter that I shall get to introduce Paul to Mary

[39] *a*: ?c'est à Pierre que je le ferai présenter à Marie
        it's Peter that I shall get to introduce him to Mary
      b: *c'est à Pierre que je me ferai présenter à Marie
        it's Peter that I shall get to introduce me to Mary

(these sentences become acceptable if *à Pierre* is replaced by *par Pierre*).

As we see, the only difference between [38] and [39] is that a noun phrase – functioning as direct object in this case – has been replaced by a clitic pronoun, non-reflexive in [39*a*] and reflexive in [39*b*].

2 Noun phrase complements

It is known that there is a general correspondence between 'possessive adjectives' and noun phrase complements in *de NP*, whatever the range of semantic relation may be between these elements and the head noun of the NP to which they belong:

[40] *a*: le livre *de Jean*
       John's book
      b: *son* livre
       his book

[41] *a*: l'arrivée *de Jean*
       John's arrival
      b: *son* arrivée
       his arrival

[42] *a*: l'histoire *de la France*
       the history of France
      b: *son* histoire
       her history

It is also known that the relationship between the noun phrase complement and the head noun is often ambiguous, and that this ambiguity is also found in the relationship between the 'possessive adjective' and the head noun. Thus, in [43*a*], *Jean* can be either the painter of the portrait, the person represented in the portrait, or the owner of the portrait, and these distinctions are also present in [43*b*]:

[43] *a:* le portrait de Jean
      John's portrait
   b: son portrait

From now on, I shall use the following symbols to indicate the nature of the relation between the *de NP* or the possessive adjective, and the head noun: S to indicate a relation comparable to that between subject and verb, O to indicate a relation comparable to that between object and verb, and POSS to indicate that *the N of NP* can be paraphrased by *the N that NP has;* this does not, of course, preclude other interpretations.

It has been generally agreed by transformationalists that 'possessive adjectives' are not present as such in deep structure, and that phrases such as [40*b*–43*b*] should be derived from structures similar to those of [40*a*–43*a*], in which the NP of the noun phrase complement is a pronoun; therefore in the derivation of phrases [40*b*–43*b*] there occurs a movement transformation, formally similar to those subsumed under [21]. For the sake of clarity, I shall represent this transformation by [44]:[7]

[44] POSSESSIVE-FORMATION

$$X - \begin{bmatrix} \text{Art} \\ +\text{DEF} \end{bmatrix} - Y - N - Z - de - \begin{bmatrix} \text{NP} \\ +\text{PRO} \end{bmatrix} - W$$

1	2	3	4	5	6	7	8
$\Rightarrow$ 1	$2\frown7$	3	4	5	$\emptyset$	$\emptyset$	8

(Condition: 1–8 is dominated by NP, and 4 is the head noun of 1–8.)

Further, noun phrase complements in *de NP* can undergo the normal movement transformations, in the same way as the *à NP* phrases in factitive constructions; *cf* [3] above.

I shall be concerned here with noun phrases presenting multiple occurrences of the sequence *de NP*, on which these various movement transformations, in particular [44], may operate. We saw that [43] was ambiguous, as *Jean* could be interpreted either as S, or as O, or as POSS, in relation to *portrait*. There are constructions in which for example S and O are both present. Often, S and O are differentiated morphologically, by the presence of different prepositions: thus, in [45*a*] and [46*a*], O is marked by *de* and S by *par*, and in [47*a*] O is marked by *pour* and S by *de*. On the other hand, in [45*b*–47*b*], S and O are both marked by *de*:[8]

[45] *a:* le portrait d'Aristote par Rembrandt
      the portrait of Aristotle by Rembrandt
   b: le portrait d'Aristote de Rembrandt
      Rembrandt's portrait of Aristotle

[46] *a:* la critique de Harris par Chomsky
        the criticism of Harris by Chomsky
    b: la critique de Harris de Chomsky
        Chomsky's criticism of Harris

[47] *a:* la haine des Nazis pour les Juifs
        the hatred of the Nazis for the Jews
    b: la haine des Juifs des Nazis
        the Nazis' hatred of the Jews

What happens if we subject the *de NP* phrases in constructions like [45–47] to movement transformations, particularly [44]? We get the following picture:

[48] *a:* son portrait par Rembrandt (*son* = of Aristotle)
    b: *son portrait de Rembrandt (*son* = of Aristotle)
    c: son portrait d'Aristote (*son* = Rembrandt's)

[49] *a:* sa critique par Chomsky (*sa* = of Harris)
    b: *sa critique de Chomsky (*sa* = of Harris)
    c: sa critique de Harris (*sa* = Chomsky's)

[50] *a:* leur haine pour les Juifs (*leur* = the Nazis')
    b: *leur haine des Nazis (*leur* = of the Jews)
    c: leur haine des Juifs (*leur* = the Nazis')

We observe the following facts: *de NP* phrases can be moved by rule [44] and converted into 'possessive adjectives' in all cases, except where the *de NP* corresponds to an O and is followed by another *de NP* corresponding to an S. For the other movement transformations (question formation, relative formation, clefting), the facts are more complicated because of the action of further restrictions (see section 2.1), but the restriction under discussion is also found, *cf* for example:

[51] *a:* de qui as-tu vu le portrait par Rembrandt?
        whose portrait by Rembrandt did you see?
    b: *de qui as-tu vu le portrait de Rembrandt?
    c: de qui as-tu vu le portrait d'Aristote?
        whose portrait of Aristotle did you see?

[52] *a:* Aristote, dont j'ai vu le portrait par Rembrandt
        Aristotle, whose portrait by Rembrandt I saw
    b: *Aristote, dont j'ai vu le portrait de Rembrandt
    c: Rembrandt, dont j'ai vu le portrait d'Aristote
        Rembrandt, whose portrait of Aristotle I saw

So the situation is very similar to the one we found in the case of the factitive constructions. In the absence of a universal constraint, such as the A-over-A principle or Ross's constraints (1967), classic transformational theory would permit us to exclude [48b–52b] only by imposing a rather bizarre *ad hoc* constraint on each of the movement transformations. In other words, we shall have to add yet another condition on [21], in addition to [23]:

[53] *Condition*: [21] is blocked (i) : if term 3 of the structure index = *de NP*, and (ii): if term 4 of the structure index = *de NP U*, both sequences *de NP* being dominated by the same NP. (A similar condition will have to be formulated for [44].)

Besides the fact that the formulation of this condition is still inadequate,[9] it is obviously entirely *ad hoc* and unilluminating, providing no more than a reformulation of the observed facts, without giving any explanation of them. Without spending any more time on the formulation of [53], therefore, let us put the problem the other way, and ask in what way a model of comprehension could recover the base relations (S and O) from the surface facts. We may think that in this case, too, native speakers can call on partial heuristic strategies, getting information from data such as word-order and morphological distinctions, etc. We see that, in [45a] and [46a], the subject is unequivocally marked (as in factitive constructions) by the preposition *par;* in [47a], on the other hand, it is the object which is marked by the preposition *pour*. But in [45b–47b], this morphological information is not present, and both S and O have the form *de NP*; so it seems that here it is the order (i) O, (ii) S, which allows us to differentiate them – from this point of view it is noteworthy that whereas in [47a], the order S–O is the opposite of that in [45a], in [47b] we have the same order as in [45b]. Now whereas in [48a–52a], the morphological information provided by the prepositions makes it always possible to determine unequivocally whether an S or an O is involved (depending on the preposition), this information has disappeared in cases (*b*) and (*c*), and so they are cases of absolute structural ambiguity in Klima's sense. I propose therefore to cancel condition [53] on [21] (and the corresponding condition on [44]), and to replace them by the following strategy:

[54] STRATEGY II: All else being equal, and in the absence of particular morphological marks, if a sentence contains two *de NP* phrases, or one *de NP* phrase and an equivalent pronoun (*son, dont, en,*

etc), which can be understood as complements of the same noun, one the subject and the other the direct object of the noun, the position /N —— is that of the direct object.[10]

This strategy accounts for all the facts of [45–52], in particular both for the non-acceptability of examples [48b–52b] and for the order inversion of the S and O phrases in [47b] in comparison with [47a].

In the case of factitive constructions, an important argument in favour of strategy [27] was that movement of the IO was in fact possible even if an S of the same form *à NP* was present, provided that certain semantic conditions were met (*cf* [25b] and [30]), and this seemed to indicate that the unacceptable constructions were not excluded for strictly grammatical reasons. It might be possible to find similar arguments for noun phrase complements.

Notice firstly the contrast in acceptability between the following examples (in which *Rembrandt, Aristote, les Juifs, les Nazis* keep the same functions as above):

[55] ?le portrait de Rembrandt d'Aristote

[56] ?*la haine des Nazis des Juifs

Whereas [55] is more or less acceptable, I find it very difficult to understand [56] otherwise than with the interpretation that it is the Jews who hate the Nazis. There is a quite natural explanation for this, but it is not based on grammatical considerations (or even on semantic considerations, for it has to do with the native speaker's knowledge of the world): almost everyone knows that Rembrandt, not Aristotle, was a great painter, and everyone knows also that the Jews had (at least) as much reason for hating the Nazis as the Nazis did for hating the Jews. When information of this sort is not present, I think every speaker would unfailingly interpret *Pierre* as being the object and *Paul* as being the subject in [57–58] (leaving aside the cases of POSS):

[57] le portrait de Pierre de Paul
     Paul's portrait of Peter

[58] la haine de Pierre de Paul
     Paul's hatred of Peter

Secondly, consider the case in which S and O are differentiated in terms of the feature [± HUMAN], as in [59]:

[59] *a:* j'ai lu la description du cataclysme par Pline
     I have read the description of the disaster by Pliny

   b: j'ai lu la description du cataclysme de Pline
   I have read Pliny's description of the disaster

Clearly there exist here, independently of the structural information, lexical-semantic indications for locating the deep subject and object in the surface structure. So not only does the permutation of the two *de* NPs become possible, as in [55], *cf:*

[60] ?j'ai lu la description de Pline du cataclysme

but certain movement transformations can apparently apply to the *de NP* functioning as O, *cf:*

[61] *a:* ?(ce cataclysme) j'*en* ai lu la description de Pline
      b: ?le cataclysme *dont* j'ai lu la description de Pline

   As in the case of factitive constructions, it is difficult to see how it would be possible to account for these differences in terms of constraints on transformations, whereas they are comprehensible in terms of the combined action of different strategies which would apply to different aspects of the surface structure (taking into account also the semantic information supplied by the lexical items). Admittedly, the problem of the exact way in which these different strategies would interact remains to be solved, in particular whether they are in any hierarchy. For example the fact that there is no difference in acceptability between [48b] and [50b] (compared with [55–56]) would seem to indicate that the strategy using purely structural considerations [54] to some extent prevails over lexical-semantic strategies.

2.1 Appendix

I pointed out earlier that movement transformations raise special problems when they apply to noun complement prepositional phrases. Hence for some speakers [51a], though undoubtedly better than [51b], is not altogether acceptable. Similarly, some speakers seem to make a distinction between [62a and b]:

[62] *a:* ?c'est d'Aristote que j'ai vu le portrait par Rembrandt
          ?it was of Aristotle that I saw the portrait by Rembrandt
      b: c'est Aristote dont j'ai vu le portrait par Rembrandt
          it was Aristotle whose portrait by Rembrandt I saw

Moreover, the following sentences, corresponding to [45] and to [47], are unacceptable:

[63] *a:* *par qui as-tu vu le (un) portrait d'Aristote?
      b: *c'est par Rembrandt que j'ai vu le (un) portrait d'Aristote
      c: *Rembrandt, par qui j'ai vu le (un) portrait d'Aristote, . . .

[64] *a:* *pour qui méprises-tu la haine des Nazis?
      b: *c'est pour les Juifs que je méprise la haine des Nazis
      c: *les Juifs, pour qui je méprise la haine des Nazis, . . .

In view also of the impossibility of deriving [65a] from the underlying structure [65b]:

[65] *a:* *c'est aux ennemis que César a décrit la reddition de la ville
           *it was to the enemy that Caesar described the surrender of the town
      b: César a décrit [$_{NP}$ la reddition de la ville aux ennemis]
           Caesar described [$_{NP}$ the surrender of the town to the enemy]

we can formulate a constraint of very general application, which prevents a prepositional phrase embedded in an NP from being moved to the left, if the preposition is other than *de* (and even with *de* there would be some restrictions). This new constraint will not be examined in detail here, though there is reason to suppose that here again perceptual strategies, other than those considered in this chapter, are concerned.

In the first place, the distinction that this constraint makes between *de* and other prepositions calls for notice. The ordinary constraints on transformations do not usually take cognizance of this sort of difference. Secondly, example [65] is very instructive. [65a] is in fact quite acceptable if it corresponds, not to [65b], but to [66]:

[66] César a décrit aux ennemis la reddition de la ville
      Caesar described to the enemy the surrender of the town

Similarly, [64b], for example, becomes acceptable if we take it as an approximate paraphrase of [67]:

[67] c'est par égard pour les Juifs que je méprise la haine des Nazis
      it is on behalf of the Jews that I despise the Nazis' hatred

In other words, when *à NP* or *pour NP* are verb complements or sentence complements, they can be moved perfectly well. This suggests that there is a hierarchy in the functions of prepositional phrases, according to whether they are verb (or sentence) complements, or noun complements. The main function of a phrase of the form *à NP, pour NP,*

par NP, etc, is to be a verb (or sentence) complement; these phrases are
noun complements only secondarily. When a phrase of this type appears,
for example, in the context *c'est* —— *que* . . . , a recognition strategy would
give priority to its interpretation as a verb or sentence complement. In
contrast the function of *de NP* phrases as noun complements is at least as
important as their function as verb or sentence complements (*de* is the
'unmarked' preposition in NPs). This would explain why these phrases
behave differently in relation to movement transformations. However,
it must be admitted that this would not really explain why sentences such
as those in [63–64] are entirely unacceptable. A closer examination of the
facts is called for.

3 Interrogative sentences

The syntax of French interrogative sentences involves very complex
problems, which I do not claim to resolve here (see Kayne, 1972, for a
study of some aspects of the problem). However, I should like to point
out that at least some of these problems are of the same type as those we
have just been looking at, and should be treated in the same way.

As we know, the derivation of interrogative sentences involves the
WH-FRONTING rule, a special case of [21], which moves the interrogative phrase to the front of a sentence (or an embedded sentence). It is this
rule that accounts for the position of *où* in [68*b*]:

[68] *a:* Pierre travaille à Vincennes
　　　　Peter works at Vincennes
　　b: je voudrais savoir *où* Pierre travaille
　　　　I should like to know *where* Peter works

This rule applies vacuously for the case where the interrogative phrase is
the subject of the (embedded) sentence, *cf:*

[69] je voudrais savoir *qui* travaille à Vincennes
　　I should like to know *who* works at Vincennes

[70] *qui* est venu hier?
　　who came yesterday?

After WH-FRONTING has applied, a rule permuting the subject and the
verb may operate, which I shall call STYLISTIC INVERSION,[11] following
Kayne (1969, 1972); I shall formulate it, still following Kayne, but
simplifying, in this way:

[71] STYLISTIC INVERSION : X　*wh*　NP V Y
　　　　　　　　　　　　　　1　2　　3　4 5 ⇒ 1 2 4 3 5
　　(where *wh* represents an interrogative phrase)

Still simplifying considerably, the derivation of sentence [72] can be represented as in [73]:

[72] où travaille Pierre?

[73] BASE: Pierre travaille où → (WH-FRONTING) →
où Pierre travaille → (STYLISTIC INVERSION) →
où travaille Pierre

Rule [71] is of wide application.[12] In particular it can apply if the interrogative word fronted by WH-FRONTING is a direct object. Take the case of a simple transitive sentence like [74a]: [74b], the corresponding question in which the questioned word is the subject, is obtained by vacuous application of WH-FRONTING, and [74c], in which the questioned word is the object, is obtained by WH-FRONTING and STYLISTIC INVERSION:

[74] *a:* Pierre a mangé une pomme
Peter ate an apple
b: *qui* a mangé une pomme?
who ate an apple?
c: *qu'*a mangé Pierre?
what did Peter eat?

The problem which interests us here is illustrated by the following sentences, [75], which are apparently strictly parallel to [74], the only difference being that, in [74], the object is [−HUMAN], whereas it is [+HUMAN] in [75]:

[75] *a:* Pierre a rencontré Paul
Peter met Paul
b: *qui* a rencontré Paul?
who met Paul?
c: **qui* a rencontré Pierre?

It is immediately obvious that the reasons why [75c] is unacceptable are not connected with any impossibility of having *qui* as a fronted direct object (*cf* [76], which is the result of a further transformation permuting the subject clitic pronoun and the auxiliary; see note 11), nor with any restriction on STYLISTIC INVERSION if the object is marked [+HUMAN] *cf* [77]:

[76] qui Pierre a-t-il rencontré?
whom did Peter meet?

[77] l'homme qu'a rencontré Pierre
the man whom Peter met

Intuitively, it is clear enough that the impossibility of having [75c] is linked with the impossibility of finding in the surface structure any indication at all, whether structural, morphological or anything else, which would enable us to distinguish the subject from the object. In other words, [75c] is a case of absolute structural ambiguity. So we are once more forced either to attach an *ad hoc* condition, similar to [23] and [53], to rule [71], or to turn to a perceptual strategy similar to [27] or [54]. I shall not pause to formulate a condition on [71] (for it will soon be clear that this is in fact impossible), but shall at once propose the following strategy:

[78] STRATEGY III: In a sentence of the form X *qui* V NP Y, where *qui* is an interrogative, in the absence of any morphological or semantic criterion differentiating the subject from the object, the position /V ⎯ is that of the object.[13]

In the case of interrogative sentences, the indications that it is preferable to resort to strategy [78] rather than use a condition on transformation [71] are much more clear-cut than they were in the case of noun complements or even in the case of factitive constructions. At the moment I have no explanation to offer for these differences.

The first thing to be noticed is that traditional grammarians are unanimous in ascribing the unacceptability of sentences like [75c] to the ambiguity inherent in them (see Martinon, 242, n 2, Grevisse, 130, Wagner-Pinchon, 535, Chevalier *et al*, 93). In fact, as in the case of the factitive constructions, sentences [75b–c] do seem to be recognized as being ambiguous by many French speakers, though with a strong preference for the interpretation in which *qui* is subject. Secondly, sentences which in other respects have exactly the same derivation as [75c] become more acceptable because of morphological differences, *cf* [80] compared with [79], and [82] compared with [81]:

[79] *a:* cet imbécile critiquer*a* Pierre
this idiot will criticize Paul
b: *qui critiquer*a* cet imbécile?

[80] *a:* ces imbéciles critiquer*ont* Pierre
these idiots will criticize Peter
b: qui critiquer*ont* ces imbéciles?
who will these idiots criticize?

[81] *a:* ce conférencier ci*te* cet auteur
        that lecturer quotes this author
      b: *quel auteur ci*te* ce conférencier?

[82] *a:* ce conférencier *a* cité divers auteurs
        that lecturer quoted various authors
      b: quels auteurs *a* cités ce conférencier?
        which authors did that lecturer quote?

It is probable, too, that differences of acceptability arise between the
written and the spoken language, due to the presence in the written
language of morphological distinctions which are not phonetically marked
in the spoken language; the following sentences, which seem to me quite
natural in their written form, would be very doubtful if spoken:

[83] *a:* que*ls* auteurs ci*te* ce conférencier?
        which authors does this lecturer quote?
      b: que*l* anima*l* mang*ent* ces poisso*ns*?
        what animal do these fish eat?
      c: qui frapp*ent* ces policier*s*?
        who are those policemen hitting?

Thirdly, the interrogative sentences under review can be made more
acceptable by the effect of selectional restrictions or semantic information which resolve the ambiguity of the construction. Thus, the verb
concerner requires an abstract subject and can have a human object, *cf*
[84*a–b*]; hence there is no ambiguity in [84*c*] and it is acceptable for many
French speakers:[14]

[84] *a:* cette décision concerne Pierre
        this decision concerns Peter

      b: *Pierre concerne $\begin{cases} \text{Paul} \\ \text{cette décision} \end{cases}$

      c: qui concerne cette décision?
        who does this decision concern?

Similarly, *réunir* requires an object specified [−SEMANTICALLY
SINGULAR] (see Chapter 3); *cf* [85*a–b*]. Hence [85*c*] is acceptable:

[85] *a:* l'entraîneur a réuni l'équipe de rugby
        the trainer assembled the Rugby team
      b: *l'équipe de rugby a réuni l'entraîneur
      c: quelle équipe a réuni l'entraîneur?
        which team did the trainer assemble?

The factors that remove the ambiguity of an interrogative sentence of this type, and which at the same time make it more acceptable, may, in the last resort, relate to the native speaker's knowledge of the world. For example, take the verb *commander;* in a 'normal' world where 'order' prevails, sentence [86a] is quite natural, and [86b] is bizarre to say the least:

[86] *a:* ces officiers commandent ces soldats
these officers command these soldiers

    b: ces soldats commandent ces officiers
these soldiers command these officers

    c: quels soldats commandent ces officiers?
what soldiers do these officers command?/what soldiers command these officers?

[86c] is theoretically ambiguous: it is a question corresponding either to [86a] or to [86b]; nevertheless, in this 'normal' world, it certainly seems to me that the most natural interpretation is that in which [86c] corresponds to [86a] – in other words, the order of preference for readings is the opposite of what we had for [75c], for example. But it is not difficult to imagine a situation – the Russian Revolution of 1917, for instance – in which [86b] would have become normal; it would be in no way surprising if the conditions for interpreting [86c] were modified under such circumstances. Similarly a sentence like [81b] seems fairly acceptable to me personally, no doubt because it seems more natural to me that a lecturer should quote an author, rather than the other way round. And so on.

4

At the end of section 1, I remarked on the *ad hoc* aspect which strategy [27] still had. It should now be clear that strategies [27], [54] and [78] have distinct similarities; we should be able to generalize so that they can be presented as special cases of one general strategy.

Each of these strategies has the function of determining from a structurally absolutely ambiguous surface form, which element corresponds to the deep subject and which element corresponds to the deep object (direct or indirect as the case may be). Let us recapitulate the gist of each strategy:

[27] . . . the position /V (NP) —— is that of IO

[54] . . . the position /N —— is that of O

[78] . . . the position /V —— is that of O

The following observation can be made: each strategy interprets as an object the phrase which in surface structure occupies the position corresponding to that in which an object is generated in deep structure. This fact implies that strategies [27], [54] and [78], which apply to particular cases, might be replaced by a more general strategy (I shall restrict myself here to instances of structural ambiguity caused by two occurrences of the same category):

[87] STRATEGY IV: All else being equal, in the absence of particular morphological marks or lexical-semantic information, whenever a sentence has absolute structural ambiguity in surface structure because the same category occurs twice, it is acceptable only in the reading (it is acceptable with the preferred reading) in which at least one of these two occurrences keeps the position that it had in deep structure.

Notice that this strategy also predicts that sentences in which both occurrences of identical categories have been moved from their deep structure position are less acceptable for both their possible readings; and this does seem to be the case, cf:[15]

[88] *a:* l'homme à qui c'est $\left\{\begin{array}{l}?*\text{à}\\ \text{chez}\end{array}\right\}$ Pierre que j'ai fait porter ce

message...

the man whom it was to Peter's (house) that I got to take this message ...

b: Rembrandt, dont c'est $\left\{\begin{array}{l}*\text{Aristote dont}\\ *\text{d'Aristote que}\end{array}\right\}$ j'ai vu le portrait, ...

c: la femme dont j'ai vu $\left\{\begin{array}{l}?*\text{son}\\ \text{ce}\end{array}\right\}$ portrait est très belle

(where *son* = *de Rembrandt*)

the woman of whom I saw this portrait is very beautiful

It would obviously be necessary to try to apply this strategy to other cases, to see if it has real generality. I cannot embark on an exhaustive study of that question within the framework of this chapter, but I shall mention just one more case in which the strategy seems to me to be applicable. This concerns sentences like [89*a*–90*a*], to which a transformation permuting the object and its predicative complement can be applied in certain circumstances, *cf* [89*b*–90*b*]:

[89] *a:* on a nommé ce pauvre type président
          they appointed this poor fellow President
      b: on a nommé président ce pauvre type

[90] *a:* je trouve tous ces bonshommes ridicules
          I find all these little men ridiculous
      b: je trouve ridicules tous ces bonshommes

In these sentences, the object and its predicative complement are differentiated either because they belong to different categories (NP and adjective in [90]), or by their internal structures (absence of determiner in the predicative noun in [89]). But this is not always the case, *cf:*

[91] *a:* ils ont surnommé le barbu le vieux sourd
          they nicknamed the bearded man the old deaf man
      b: ils ont surnommé le vieux sourd le barbu
          they nicknamed the old deaf man the bearded man

In fact it is extremely difficult to accept [91*b*] as being synonymous with [91*a*]; whereas the natural interpretation of [91*a*] is that in which a bearded man has the nickname '*le vieux sourd*', the natural interpretation of [91*b*] is that in which an old deaf man has the nickname '*le barbu*'; these facts follow directly from [87] if we posit the deep structure *verb — object — predicative complement.*

However, although the examples of [91] offer confirmation of the hypothesis set out in [87], other sentences which are related to these provide what seem at first sight to be counter-examples, *cf:*

[92] *a:* ils l'ont surnommé le barbu
          they nicknamed him the bearded man
      b: c'est le vieux sourd qu'ils ont surnommé le barbu
          it was the old deaf man that they nicknamed the bearded man

One of the two NPs which follow the verb in the deep structure has been moved by CLITIC-PLACING or by CLEFTING. At first sight, [87] would predict that the NP remaining to the right of the verb, *le barbu*, corresponds to the deep object – in other words, these sentences should have an interpretation akin to that of [91*a*]. But the opposite is true; both examples of [92] mean that an old deaf man was nicknamed '*le barbu*'.

In fact, these apparent counter-examples can be explained by the existence of independent constraints on the movement of predicative complements in this construction. Thus, although [93*b*] is grammatical, [94*b*] (corresponding to [89]) is not grammatical:

[93] *a:* ce pauvre type est président
       this poor fellow is President
     b: ce pauvre type l'est (président)
       this poor fellow is (it) (President)

[94] *a:* on l'a nommé président
       they appointed him President
     b: *on l'a nommé ce pauvre type

The facts are less clear for cleft sentences than they are for clitic pronouns. However, I consider that, firstly, [95] is rather unnatural and is only possible with an extra contrastive accent on *président;* secondly, [92*b*], provided there is a contrastive accent on *le vieux sourd*, can also be interpreted in the sense of [91*a*]:

[95] ?c'est président qu'on a élu ce pauvre type
       ?it was President that they elected this poor fellow

In other words, independent reasons can be given for saying that, in normal cases of sentences like [89–91], only the direct object can be moved to the left; so the problem of avoiding absolute structural ambiguity does not arise in sentences like [92].

5.

I shall not here explore the theoretical implications of the approach that I have adopted. The essential point to grasp is that what we have witnessed is, so to speak, a redistribution of the roles played by the theory of competence and the theory of performance: classes of facts which up to now have been described in (grammatical) terms of transformations or of constraints on transformations (or on derivations, as in Lakoff, 1969, 1971), are now described in terms of behavioural constraints. For a full theoretical discussion of this new approach, the reader is referred to Klima (1970) and Bever (1970). I shall, however, deal here with one or two points which call for special notice.

Firstly, if strategy [87] proves to be effective, this would tend to give a degree of psychological reality to a concept of deep structure which is similar to that of Chomsky (1965), in being not too remote from the surface structure and not identical with semantic structure; as we have seen, ideas like that of deep subject, and deep direct or indirect object, are crucial to the present formulation. At the same time, this analysis serves to cast doubt on the validity of other proposals which have been made about the order (or absence of order) of the elements in the underlying structure of sentences: see for instance, Fillmore (1968) and McCawley (1970).

Günther Brettschneider (personal communication) has pointed out to me that it would perhaps be possible to reformulate perceptual strategies without reference to deep structure and the syntactic functions that it defines. Strategies would be defined directly in terms of semantic functions such as agent, theme, beneficiary, etc (cf the conception of thematic functions in Gruber, 1965, and Jackendoff, 1969; see Chapter 5 of this book). But this reformulation soon meets with many difficulties, cf:

[96] *a:* Jean a loué cette maison à Pierre
    John rented this house to Peter/John rented this house from
      Peter
  b: c'est à Jean que j'ai fait louer cette maison à Pierre
    it was John that I got to rent this house to/from Peter
  c: *c'est à Pierre que j'ai fait louer cette maison à Jean

[97] *a:* Jean a acheté ce livre à Pierre
    John bought this book from Peter/John bought this book for
      Peter
  b: c'est à Jean que j'ai fait acheter ce livre à Pierre
    it was John that I got to buy this book from/for Peter
  c: *c'est à Pierre que j'ai fait acheter ce livre à Jean

[96a] and [97a] are ambiguous, but for different reasons; in one case, it is because of the lexical ambiguity of *louer* (to rent); in the other case, it is because of the fact that the indirect object of *acheter* (to buy) can be the source of the purchase or its destined recipient. In both cases, the semantic functions of the indirect object are quite different, depending on which reading is chosen. But whatever the interpretation is, sentences [96b–c] and [97b–c] behave exactly as predicted by strategy [87].

The following facts are even more remarkable:

[98] *a:* Pierre méprise Paul
    Peter despises Paul
  b: qui méprise Paul?
    who despises Paul?
  c: *qui méprise Pierre?

[99] *a:* Pierre dégoûte Paul
          Peter disgusts Paul
      b: qui dégoûte Paul?
          who disgusts Paul?
      c: *qui dégoûte Pierre?

The semantic relation between the subject and the object in [98] is almost exactly the reverse of what it is in [99] (*cf* Chapter 5). Now, sentences [98*b–c*] and [99*b–c*] behave in exactly the same way, as strategy [87] predicts, if we define *Pierre* and *Paul* as being, respectively, the deep subject and object of [98*a*] and [99*a*]. So it is clear that perceptual strategies cannot avoid recourse to these relatively abstract notions of deep syntactic functions (subject, direct or indirect object, etc), which do not directly coincide with semantic functions.

It is undoubtedly also important to show in what sense the strategies proposed differ from the transderivational constraints suggested by Lakoff (1970b). In effect, Lakoff proposed enriching the grammatical theory with mechanisms which, in certain conditions, block a derivation if, at a certain stage, it 'encounters' another derivation. At first sight, we might in fact think that perceptual strategies are simply notational variants of transderivational constraints. But this is not so, for two reasons. First, transderivational constraints, besides their enormous power, have no explanatory character: if we consider the examples that Lakoff gives, we see that these constraints merely provide a means of giving a precise formulation of the facts, no more. Perceptual strategies, on the other hand, represent the application to the particular case of language of psychological mechanisms which are both specific and have a field of application extending beyond language. We may therefore hope that a linguistic theory drawing partly on grammatical mechanisms whose power remains limited, partly on perceptual mechanisms which are also specific, may delimit the characteristics of human language much more clearly than would a theory allowing mechanisms as powerful as derivational and transderivational constraints.

Second, and this is more important, transderivational constraints, like transformations and constraints on transformations, characteristically allow all or nothing: they can block, or not block, a derivation at a certain stage, in comparison with another derivation, and that is all. But as we saw in the case of factitive constructions and even more clearly in the case of interrogative sentences, the facts considered are not of this kind; it was not merely a question of blocking certain constructions (with a particular interpretation), because these constructions were structurally ambiguous: this blocking of a transformation really only arises as the extreme case. Even if a transderivational constraint is capable of blocking the derivation of [75c] (*qui a rencontré Pierre?*) from *Pierre a rencontré wh + PRO* by reference to the possible derivation of the same sentence from *wh + PRO a rencontré Pierre*, not only does it explain nothing, but it is not capable of accounting for the fact that the difference between the two possible readings of [75c] is not that one is grammatical and the other ungrammatical, but rather that there is a hierarchy as between the two readings. Furthermore, it is not capable of accounting for the fact that, for many speakers, sentences like [84c]: *qui concerne cette décision?*, or (*cf* note 14) *qui amuse cette histoire?*, though better than [75c], are nevertheless rather doubtful. It is clear that all these facts are connected, and that to resort to different strategies, operating on the different aspects of syntax, morphology and semantics, seems the only way of accounting both for what they have in common and for how they differ.

This brings me to a concluding observation. One of the things that struck me most, and it is something which this chapter does not explain, was the considerable variation between the intuitions of different speakers, particularly in the case of interrogative sentences. For some of my informants, for example, as soon as the ambiguity could be resolved in one way or another, all interrogative sentences showing STYLISTIC INVERSION became acceptable – only sentences of the type of [75c] were rejected (or rather, considered to be less good); for other informants, all sentences of the type of [79–86] tend to be unacceptable, and various intermediate dialects are also found (there are even some speakers for whom all sentences of the form *qui V NP?* are relatively doubtful, even if *qui* is interpreted as subject). I cannot offer any explanation of these differences here, but I feel that an analysis which did no more than distinguish different dialects and describe each of them in terms of different grammatical rules and constraints would only be superficial. On the other hand, we can now begin to see how an analysis in terms of the interaction of grammatical rules and various strategies might throw light on these facts. Klima and Bever have emphasized the fact that the various systems (systems of grammatical rules, perceptual strategies, etc) which determine the way adult language functions, are all learned at the same time and that they act upon each other; in particular, 'the way we use a language as we learn it can determine the manifest structure of language once we know it' (Bever, 1970). It is quite possible that the interaction between these systems during the learning period affords a certain degree of latitude, in that it can come about in different ways, and this would account for differences in linguistic intuition between speakers of a language, without our having to postulate mechanisms, still less grammars, differing fundamentally from one speaker to another. Obviously, this is speculative, and long and varied psycholinguistic research will certainly be necessary before we can progress beyond the realm of conjecture.

Notes

1 For French, see Marie-Louise Moreau's thesis (1970).
2 Here I am simplifying. First, to account for [7b], term 2 of the structure index of transformations [12–14] should mention not only *faire* but a small class of verbs including *faire, laisser, regarder*, etc., and it should be specified that [12] is obligatory for *faire* and optional for the other verbs. Furthermore, R. S. Kayne (personal communication) has pointed out to me that to account for other facts, it is probably necessary to reformulate [12–14]. These matters do not affect the problems which concern us here.
3 For an analysis of constructions of this type, see Kayne (1969, forthcoming), who proposes deriving them from underlying structures in which the sentence embedded under *faire* has undergone the passive transformation (more precisely, the AGENT POSTPOSING transformation; *cf* Chomsky, 1970).
4 As well as structural and morphological indications, there are, of course, lexical considerations which enable us to distinguish, for example, [20d] from *à Jean, j'ai fait porter ce message par pneumatique* (to John, I got this message sent by express letter), or *j'ai fait porter ce message à Pierre par Jean* (I got this message taken to Peter by John) from *j'ai fait partir cet homme à Bruxelles par le train* (I got this man to leave for Brussels by train).
5 In fact, [26] is also a case of absolute structural ambiguity; yet [26] is acceptable in both its readings (see also [43] below). As the quotation that is to follow indicates, Klima makes a distinction between multiple occurrences of a category and cases where the category occurs only once; in the latter case, apparently, absolute structural ambiguity is permissible.
6 It should be noted that [30] has an additional reading, in which *à la bibliothèque de Harvard* is a locative (*cf: Pierre s'est promené à la bibliothèque de Harvard* (Peter walked to Harvard library)) and not a subject or an indirect object.
7 The sign ⌒ is used here to indicate that 7 is incorporated in 2. In fact rule [44] is a simplification. In the first place, it should really be broken down into several successive stages. Secondly, there are good reasons (*cf* Kayne, 1969) for thinking that underlying at least some 'possessive adjectives' we do not have *de NP* but rather *à NP* (*cf: un ami à moi* (a friend of mine) beside *mon ami*, or *sa bague, à Jeanne* (that ring of Joan's), etc). Phrases like [40–43] would therefore be represented at a certain level by *le livre à Jean, le livre à lui*, etc, and in [44] term 6 would be *à* and not *de* (a further transformation would then convert *à* into *de* under certain conditions in the context N — NP). In fact this is not important for the point which concerns us here. If the restrictions that I am about to discuss are to be dealt with in terms of constraints on transformations, these constraints (condition [53]) would have to

apply to whatever transformations move the pronoun (term 7 of [44]) over the head noun of the phrase, and [53] would need only slight modification. If on the other hand these restrictions are to be treated in terms of perceptual strategies, the details of the transformational derivation are not important, the correspondence between the surface structures (*a*) and (*b*) of examples [40–43] being what matters.

8 I shall not go into the question here of what exactly is the deep structure of phrases [45–47]. In my opinion (but see note 7) this deep structure would not be much different from the surface structure, especially if we accept Chomsky's theory of nominalizations (1970; see also Chapter 1, section 3.3 of this book). The essential point is that everyone would agree that in [45] and [46] (*d'*) *Aristote* and (*de*) *Harris* are generated in the base immediately to the right of *portrait* or *critique*, whether the latter terms are nouns (as for Chomsky, 1970) or verbs (as for Lakoff, 1970c) in deep structure; *Aristote* in [45] and *Harris* in [46] are therefore in any case defined as the deep objects of *portrait* and *critique* respectively.

9 As the second *de NP* is not explicitly mentioned in the transformation, it is inadequate to the extent that the last part of the condition ('both sequences *de NP* being dominated by the same NP') is impossible to state. One would have to introduce quite a number of further complications, and perhaps even the functional notions of subject and object, for the formulation to be correct.

10 I have not included cases where one of the phrases in *de NP* can be interpreted as possessive, and cases where the three functions O, S and POSS are present, as in *le portrait d'Aristote de Rembrandt de ce collectionneur célèbre* (Rembrandt's portrait of Aristotle owned by this famous collector). In this case, only the *de NP* corresponding to POSS can be moved, *cf: son portrait d'Aristote de Rembrandt*, as opposed to **son portrait (d'Aristote) de ce collectionneur célèbre*, or **son portrait (de Rembrandt) de ce collectionneur célèbre*. So there is a hierarchy among POSS, S and O. Notice that if, instead of a human POSS, we have a non-human locative, as in *le portrait d'Aristote de Rembrandt du Louvre* (Rembrandt's portrait of Aristotle in the Louvre), movement of the subject is possible, *cf: son portrait d'Aristote du Louvre*. These facts confirm the part played by strategies using semantic information.

11 As Kayne (1972) has pointed out, this rule is quite different from the SUB-JECT-CLITIC INVERSION rule, as Kayne has named it, which applies in the derivation of (*Pierre*) *est-il venu?* I shall not be concerned here with this type of interrogative sentence.

12 It applies elsewhere than in interrogative sentences, *cf: l'homme qu'a rencontré Pierre* (the man that Peter met). It is also subject to certain further restrictions which do not concern me here (see Kayne, 1972).

13 The variable X in [78] is necessary, as we have exactly the same type of facts in indirect interrogative sentences, *cf: je voudrais savoir qui a rencontré Pierre* (I should like to know who met Peter).

14 Although other French speakers find it very difficult to accept. I shall say something at the end of this chapter about the variations of intuition between one speaker and another. The same problems arise with a sentence like *qui amuse cette histoire?* (who does this story amuse?), which, although unambiguous, is rejected by some speakers and accepted by others. I must say, too, that the following sentences:

[1] qui a réuni l'entraîneur? – (Il a réuni Pierre, Paul et Jacques)
who did the trainer gather together? – (He gathered together Peter, Paul and James)

[11] qui commandent ces officiers? – (Ils commandent ces fantassins)
who do these officers command? – (They command these infantrymen)

are, for me, more difficult to accept than [85c] or [86c]. This is no doubt because in the latter, where only the determiner (*quel*) is questioned, the presence of a lexically full noun immediately defines the semantic relation with the verb, which is not the case with [I] and [II]. For example, *réunir* requires a [−SEMANTICALLY SINGULAR] object, and *quelle équipe* is explicitly marked with this feature, whereas *qui* is unspecified for it. (Note that *qui a-t-il réuni?* is fully acceptable.)

15 If *le garçon à qui je lui ai fait porter ce message* (the boy to whom I got him to take this message) is acceptable, it is because the clitic pronoun *lui* can only be interpreted here as subject (*cf* section 1.1).

Bibliography

AKMAJIAN, ADRIAN, 1970, 'On deriving cleft sentences from pseudo-cleft sentences', *Linguistic Inquiry* 1.2, 149–168

ANDERSON, STEPHEN, 1970, 'On the linguistic status of the performative/constative distinction', *NSF Report*, no 26, The Computation Laboratory of Harvard University, 1, 1–36

1971, 'On the role of deep structure in semantic interpretation', *Foundations of Language* 7.3, 387–396

BACH, EMMON, 1968, 'Nouns and noun phrases' in Bach and Harms, eds, 91–122

BACH, EMMON, and HARMS, R. T., eds, 1968, *Universals in Linguistic Theory*, New York, Holt, Rinehart and Winston

BAR-HILLEL, YEHOSHUA, 1971, 'Out of the pragmatic wastebasket', *Linguistic Inquiry*, 2.3, 401–407

BEVER, T. G., 1970, 'The cognitive basis for linguistic structures' in J. Hayes, ed, *Cognition and the Development of Language*, New York, Wiley, 279–362

BEVER, T. G., and LANGENDOEN, D. T., 1971, 'A dynamic model of the evolution of language', *Linguistic Inquiry*, 2.4, 433–463

BIERWISCH, MANFRED, 1968, 'Two critical problems in accent rules', *Journal of Linguistics* 4.2, 173–178

1970, 'On classifying semantic features', in Bierwisch and Heidolph, eds, 27–50

BIERWISCH, MANFRED, and HEIDOLPH, K. E., eds, 1970, *Progress in Linguistics*, The Hague, Mouton

BLINKENBERG, ANDREAS, 1960, *Le problème de la transitivité en français moderne*, Copenhagen, Munksgaard

BRESNAN, JOAN, 1968, 'On instrumental adverbs and the concept of deep structure', *Quarterly Progress Report*, no 92, Research Laboratory of Electronics, MIT, 365–375

1970, 'On complementizers: towards a syntactic theory of complement types', *Foundations of Language* 6.3, 297–321

1971, 'Sentence stress and syntactic transformations', *Language*, 47, 257–281

1972, *The Theory of Complementation in English Syntax*, PhD Dissertation, MIT (unpublished)

CHAPIN, PAUL, 1967, *On the Syntax of Word-Derivation in English*, The MITRE Corporation, Bedford, Mass

CHEVALIER, JEAN-CLAUDE *et al*, 1964, *Grammaire Larousse du Français contemporain*, Paris, Larousse

CHOMSKY, NOAM, 1957, *Syntactic Structures*, The Hague, Mouton
  1964, *Current Issues in Linguistic Theory*, The Hague, Mouton
  1965, *Aspects of the Theory of Syntax*, Cambridge, Mass, MIT Press
  1968, *Language and Mind*, New York, Harcourt and Brace
  1969, 'Form and Meaning in natural languages' in J. D. Roslansky, ed, *Communication*, Amsterdam, North Holland, 64–85
  1970, 'Remarks on Nominalization' in Jacobs and Rosenbaum, eds, 184–221
  1971, 'Deep structure, surface structure, and semantic interpretation' in Steinberg and Jakobovits, eds, 183–216
  1972, 'Some empirical issues in the theory of transformational grammar', in Peters, ed, 63–130
  1973, 'Conditions on transformations', in S. Anderson and P. Kiparsky, eds, *A Festschrift for Morris Halle*, New York, Holt, Rinehart and Winston, 232–286

CHOMSKY, NOAM, and HALLE, MORRIS, 1968, *The Sound Pattern of English*, New York, Harper and Row.

CLÉDAT, L., 1900, '*De* et *par* après les verbes passifs', *Revue de Philologie française*, 14, 218–233

DELL, FRANÇOIS, 1970, *Les Règles phonologiques tardives et la morphologie dérivationnelle du français*, PhD Dissertation, MIT, unpublished

DOUGHERTY, RAY C., 1969, 'An interpretive theory of pronominal reference', *Foundations of Language*, 5.4, 488–519
  1970a, 'Recent studies on language universals', *Foundations of Language*, 6.4, 505–561
  1970b, 'A grammar of coordinate conjoined structures', I: *Language*, 46.4 (1970), 850–898, II: *Language* 47.2 (1971), 298–339

DUBOIS, JEAN, 1967, *Grammaire structurale du français*, II: *Le verbe*, Paris, Larousse
  1969, *Grammaire structurale du français*, III: *La phrase et les transformations*, Paris, Larousse.

DUBOIS, JEAN *et al*, 1966, *Dictionnaire du français contemporain*, Paris, Larousse

DUCROT, OSWALD, 1972, *Dire et ne pas dire*, Paris, Hermann

DUCROT, OSWALD, and TODOROV, TZVETAN, 1972, *Dictionnaire encyclopédique des Sciences du langage*, Paris, Seuil

EMONDS, J. E., 1970, *Root and Structure-Preserving Transformations*, PhD Dissertation, MIT, distributed by the Linguistic Club of Indiana University, Bloomington, Indiana. (A revised version (under the same title) is to appear in 1975 from MIT Press).

1972a, 'A Reformulation of certain syntactic transformations', in Peters, ed, 21–62

1972b 'Evidence that indirect object movement is a structure-preserving rule', *Foundations of Language* 8.4, 546–561

FAUCONNIER, GILLES, 1971, *Theoretical Implications of Some Global Phenomena in Syntax*, PhD Dissertation, University of California at San Diego, unpublished

FILLMORE, C. J., 1968, 'The case for case,' in Bach and Harms, eds, 1–88.

1970, 'The grammar of hitting and breaking', in Jacobs and Rosenbaum, eds, 120–133

FILLMORE, C. J., and LANGENDOEN, D. T., eds, 1971, *Studies in Linguistic Semantics*, New York, Holt, Rinehart and Winston

FODOR, J. A., 1970, 'Three reasons for not deriving *kill* from *cause to die*', *Linguistic Inquiry* 1.4, 429–438

GAATONE, DAVID, 1970, 'La transformation impersonnelle en français', *Le Français moderne* 38, 389–411

GARCIA, ERICA, 1967, 'Auxiliaries and the criterion of simplicity', *Language* 43, 853–870

GLEITMAN, LILA, 1969, 'Coordinating conjunctions in English', in Reibel and Schane, eds, 80–112

GOUET, MICHEL, 1971, 'Lexical problems raised by some of the "Foutre" constructions', *Studies out in Left Field*, Chicago, 79–85

GREVISSE, M., 1955, *Le Bon Usage*, Gembloux, Duculot

GRICE, H. P., 1967, *Logic and Conversation*, unpublished, manuscript. (The William James Lectures, Harvard University for 1967)

GRINDER, JOHN, and POSTAL, PAUL M., 1971, 'Missing antecedents', *Linguistic Inquiry* 2.3, 269–312

GROSS, MAURICE, 1967, 'Sur une règle de cacophonie', *Langages* 7, 105–119

1968, *Grammaire transformationnelle du français: Syntaxe du verbe*, Paris, Larousse

1969, *Lexique des constructions complétives*, Paris, Laboratoire d'Automatique documentaire et linguistique du CNRS, mimeographed

GROSS, MAURICE, HALLE, MORRIS, and SCHÜTZENBERGER, M.-P., eds, 1973, *The Formal Analysis of Natural Languages*, The Hague, Mouton

GRUBER, JEFFREY, 1965, *Studies in Lexical Relations*, PhD Dissertation, MIT (distributed by the Linguistic Club of Indiana University)

1967, *Function of the Lexicon in Formal Descriptive Grammar*, Santa Monica, California: Systems Development Corporation, TM-3770/000/00

HAASE, A., 1965, *Syntaxe française du XVIIᵉ siècle*, Paris, Delagrave

HALL, BARBARA, 1965, *Subject and Object in Modern English*, PhD Dissertation, MIT, unpublished

HALL-PARTEE, BARBARA, 1970, 'Negation, conjunction and quantifiers: Syntax versus semantics', *Foundations of Language* 6.2, 153–165

1971, 'On the requirement that transformations preserve meaning', in Fillmore and Langendoen, eds, 1–22

HASEGAWA, KINSUKE, 1970, 'Transformation and semantic interpretation', *NSF Report* no 26, The Computation Laboratory of Harvard
University
HATCHER, A. G., 1944a, 'Il tend les mains versus il tend ses mains', *Studies
in Philology* 41, 457–481
    1944b, 'Il me prend le bras versus il prend mon bras', *Romanic Review*
    35, 156–164
HELKE, MICHAEL, 1970, *The Grammar of English Reflexives*, PhD Dissertation, MIT, unpublished
JACKENDOFF, RAY S., 1969a, 'An interpretive theory of negation', *Founda-
tions of Language*, 5.2, 218–241
    1969b, *Some Rules of Semantic Interpretation for English*, PhD Disser-
    tation, stencilled, MIT
    1971a, 'Modal structure in semantic representation', *Linguistic
    Inquiry* 2.4, 479–514
    1971b, 'On some questionable arguments about quantifiers and nega-
    tion', *Language* 47.2, 282–297
    1972, *Semantic Interpretation in Generative Grammar*, MIT Press,
    Cambridge, Mass, and London. (Revised version of 1969b)
JACKENDOFF, RAY S., and CULICOVER, PETER, 1971, 'A reconsideration
of dative movements', *Foundations of Language* 7.3, 397–412
JACOBS, RODERICK and ROSENBAUM, PETER S., eds, 1970, *Readings in
English Transformational Grammar*, Waltham, Mass, Ginn-Blaisdell
JAKOBSON, ROMAN, 1965, 'A la recherche de l'essence du langage',
Diogène 51, 22–38
KATZ, J. J., 1970, 'Interpretative semantics versus generative semantics',
Foundations of Language 6.2, 220–259
    1971, 'Generative semantics *is* interpretive semantics', *Linguistic
    Inquiry* 2.3, 313–331
    1972, *Semantic Theory*, New York, Harper and Row
KATZ, J. J., and FODOR, J. A., 1963, 'The structure of a semantic theory',
Language 39, 170–210
KATZ, J. J., and POSTAL, P. M., 1964, *An Integrated Theory of Linguistic
Descriptions*, Cambridge, Mass, MIT Press
KAYNE, R. S., 1969, *The Transformational Cycle in French Syntax*, PhD
Dissertation, MIT, unpublished
    1972, 'Subject inversion in French interrogatives', in J. Casagrande
    and B. Saciuk, eds, *Generative Studies in Romance Languages*, Rowley,
    Mass, Newbury House, 70–126
    forthcoming, *French Syntax. The Transformational Cycle*, Cambridge,
    Mass, MIT Press (revised version of Kayne, 1969)
KIEFER, FERENC, and RUWET, NICOLAS, eds, 1973, *Generative Grammar in
Europe*, Dordrecht, D. Reidel Publishing Company (*Foundations of
Language Supplementary Series*)
KIMBALL, JOHN, 1970, '*Remind* remains', *Linguistic Inquiry* 1.4, 511–523
KIPARSKY, PAUL and KIPARSKY, CAROL, 1970, 'Fact', in Bierwisch and
Heidolph, eds, 143–173
KLIMA, E. S., 1964a, 'Negation in English', in Fodor and Katz, eds, *The*

Structure of Language, Englewood Cliffs, NJ, Prentice-Hall, 246–323
1964b, 'Relatedness between grammatical systems', *Language* 40, 1–20; also in Reibel and Schane, eds, 227–246
1970, 'Regulatory devices against functional ambiguity.' (Paper delivered at the Conference on the Formal Analysis of Natural Languages, IRIA, Rocquencourt, in April, 1970, but not submitted for publication in the Proceedings of the Conference (= Gross, Halle and Schützenberger, eds, 1973)).
KURODA, S.-Y., 1969, 'Attachment transformations', in Reibel and Schane, eds, 331–351
1970, 'Some remarks on English manner adverbials', in R. Jakobson and Sh. Kawamoto, eds, *Studies in General and Oriental Linguistics*, Tokyo, TEC Co, 378–396
LAKOFF, GEORGE, 1966, 'Stative adjectives and verbs in English', *NSF Report*, no 17, Harvard Computational Laboratory.
1968a, 'Instrumental adverbs and the concept of deep structure', *Foundations of Language* 4.1, 4–29
1968b, 'On pronouns and reference', stencilled, Harvard University
1969, 'On derivational constraints' *Papers from the 5th Regional Meeting of the Chicago Linguistic Society*, University of Chicago, 117–139
1970a, *Linguistics and Natural Logic*, mimeographed, The University of Michigan
1970b, 'Some thoughts on transderivational constraints', mimeographed, The University of Michigan
1970c, *Irregularity in Syntax*, New York, Holt, Rinehart and Winston; text dating from 1965, which was first circulated in mimeographed form
1970d, 'Repartee', *Foundations of Language* 6, 389–422
1970e, 'Global rules', *Language* 46.3, 627–639
1971, 'On generative semantics', in Steinberg and Jakobovits, eds, 232–296
forthcoming, *Generative Semantics*, New York, Holt, Rinehart and Winston
LAKOFF, GEORGE, and PETERS, P. S., 1969, 'Phrasal conjunction and symmetric predicates', in Reibel and Schane, eds, 113–142
LAKOFF, GEORGE, and ROSS, J. R., 1966, 'Is deep structure necessary?', stencilled, MIT
LEES, ROBERT B., 1960, *The Grammar of English Nominalizations*, Bloomington, Indiana, Indiana University Press
LEES, ROBERT B. and KLIMA, E. S., 1963, 'Rules for English pronominalization', *Language* 39, 17–28; also in Reibel and Schane, eds, 145–159
MARTIN, ROBERT, 1970, 'La Transformation impersonnelle', *Revue de Linguistique Romane*, 135–136; 377–394
MARTINON, PHILIPPE, 1927, *Comment on parle en français*, Paris, Larousse
MCCAWLEY, J. D., 1968a, 'Concerning the base component of a transformational grammar', *Foundations of Language* 4.3, 243–269

1968b, 'The role of semantics in a grammar', in Bach and Harms, eds, 124–169

1968c, 'Lexical insertion in a transformational grammar without deep structure', *Papers from the 4th Regional Meeting of the Chicago Linguistic Society*, University of Chicago, 71–80

1970, 'English as a VSO language', *Language* 46, 286–299

MOREAU, MARIE-LOUISE, 1970, *Trois aspects de la syntaxe de C'EST*, Doctoral Thesis, University of Liège, unpublished

NEWMEYER, F. J., 1969, *English Aspectual Verbs*, University of Washington, Seattle

1970, 'On the alleged boundary between syntax and semantics', *Foundations of Language* 6.2, 178–186

PERLMUTTER, DAVID, 1969, 'Les pronoms objets en espagnol', Paris, Larousse, *Langages* 14, 81–133.

1970, 'The two verbs *begin*', in Jacobs and Rosenbaum, eds, 107–119

1971, *Deep and Surface Structure Constraints in Syntax*, New York, Holt, Rinehart and Winston

PETERS, P. S., ed, 1972, *Goals of Linguistic Theory*, Englewood Cliffs, NJ, Prentice-Hall

PICABIA, LÉLIA, 1970, *Études transformationnelles de constructions adjectivales en français*, Paris, CNRS, LADL

POSTAL, PAUL, M., 1964 ,'Underlying and superficial linguistic structure', *Harvard Educational Review* 34, 246–266

1970a, 'On the surface verb *remind*', *Linguistic Inquiry* 1.1, 37–120

1970b, 'On coreferential complement subject deletion', *Linguistic Inquiry* 1.4, 438–500

1971, *Cross-Over Phenomena*, New York, Holt, Rinehart and Winston

1972, 'A global constraint on pronominalization', *Linguistic Inquiry* 3.1, 35–59

REIBEL, D. A., and SCHANE, S. A., eds, 1969, *Modern Studies in English*, Englewood Cliffs, NJ, Prentice-Hall

ROHRER, CHRISTIAN, 1971, *Funktionelle Sprachwissenschaft und Transformationelle Grammatik*, Munich, Fink Verlag

RONAT, MITSOU, 1972, À propos du verbe *remind* selon Paul M. Postal', *SILTA* (Bologna), 1.2, 233–67

ROSENBAUM, PETER S., 1967, *The Grammar of English Predicate Complement Constructions*, Cambridge, Mass, MIT Press

ROSS, J. R., 1967, *Constraints on Variables in Syntax*, PhD Dissertation, MIT, stencilled; distributed by the Linguistic Club of Indiana University, Bloomington, Indiana

1969a, 'Adjectives as noun phrases', in Reibel and Schane, eds, 352–360

1969b, 'Guess who', *Papers from the 5th Regional Meeting of the Chicago Linguistic Society*, The University of Chicago, 252–286

1970a, 'Auxiliaries as main verbs', in Todd, ed, *Philosophical Linguistics*, Series One, Evanston, Illinois, Great Expectations, 77–102

1970b, 'Gapping and the order of constituents', in Bierwisch and Heidolph, eds, 249–259

1970c, 'On declarative sentences', in Jacobs and Rosenbaum, eds, 222–272

1972, 'Doubl-Ing', *Linguistic Inquiry* 3.1, 61–86

RUWET, NICOLAS, 1967, *Introduction à la Grammaire générative*, Paris, Plon. (English translation by Norval S. H. Smith, 1973, North-Holland Linguistic Series, North-Holland Publishing Company, Amsterdam and London)

1969, ed, *Tendances nouvelles en Syntaxe générative* (= *Langages* 14), Paris, Larousse

in preparation, 'Personnellement'

SANDFELD, KR., 1929, *Syntaxe du Français contemporain: I. Les Pronoms*, Paris, Champion

SELKIRK, LISA, 1970, 'On the determiner system of noun phrase and adjective phrase', stencilled, MIT

STÉFANINI, JEAN, 1962, *La Voïx pronominale en Ancien et en Moyen Français*, Aix-en-Provence, Ophrys

STEINBERG, D. and JAKOBOVITS, L., eds, 1971, *Semantics: an Interdisciplinary Reader in Philosophy, Linguistics and Psychology*, Cambridge, Cambridge University Press

WAGNER, R.-L. and PINCHON, JACQUELINE, 1962, *Grammaire du Français Classique et Moderne*, Paris, Hachette

Index of names

Akmajian, A. 33, 86
Anderson, S. 24, 35 n. 13, 146, 259 n. 37

Bach, E. 15, 20
Bar-Hillel, Y. 24, 257 n. 19
Bever, T. G. 14, 269; 290, 293
Bierwisch, M. 34 n. 2, 171
Blinkenberg, A. 87
Boons, J.-P. 91, 182 n. 17, 259 n. 31
Borel, M. 156
Bresnan, J. 28, 31, 34 n. 2, n. 4, 35 n. 14, 116
Brettschneider, G. 291
Browne, W. 258 n. 30

Carnap, R. 33
Chapin, P. 186, 208
Chevalier, J.-C. 285
Chomsky, N. *passim*
Clédat, L. 191, 215, 257 n. 14
Culand, P. 180 n. 10

Dachelet, R. 180 n. 10
Dell, F. 209

Dougherty, R. C. 15, 23, 33, 34 n. 3, n. 4, 35 n. 14, 83, 107, 126, 135, 147, 214, 259 n. 37
Dubois, J. 167, 172, 173, 174, 175, 177, 244, 259 n. 34, 260 n. 40
Ducrot, O. 95, 176

Emonds, J. E. 4, 7, 8, 9, 10, 11, 14, 34 n. 8, n. 9 n. 11, 96, 182 n. 18, 257 n. 20

Fauconnier, G. 14, 108, 225
Fillmore, C. J. 15, 24, 35 n 13, 107, 146, 147, 149, 190, 247, 248, 249, 260 n. 40, 291
Fodor, J. A. 15, 23, 24, 30, 112, 123 n. 12, 134, 135, 136, 137, 138, 146, 168, 256 n. 5, 269

Gaatone, D. 183 n. 18
Garcia, E. 54
Gleitman, L. 35 n. 13
Gouet, M. 258 n. 28
Grevisse, M. 87, 285
Grice, H. P. 180 n. 9
Grinder, J. 33